WILDLIFE of the British Isles

Introduced by

SIR DAVID ATTENBOROUGH

In support of
the Royal Society
for Nature
Conservation's

WILDLIFE
of the British Isles

Bob Gibbons

COUNTRY LIFE BOOKS

CONTENTS

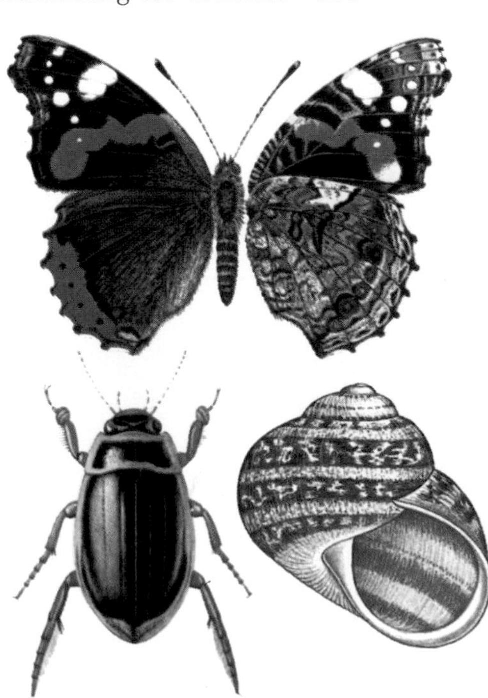

First published in 1987
by The Hamlyn Publishing Group Limited,
a Division of
The Octopus Publishing Group plc,
Michelin House,
81 Fulham Road,
London SW3 6RB.

Second impression 1988

ISBN 0 600 55335 3

Printed by Mandarin Offset in Hong Kong

Introduction by Sir David Attenborough

An Introduction to Fish, Amphibians and Reptiles 156

An Introduction to British Birds 176

An Introduction to British Mammals 224

Introduction by Sir David Attenborough

The countryside of Britain is surely one of the loveliest in the world, an unending source of delight and solace for all of us. It is the product of centuries of man living in harmony with nature. But now, unfortunately, that harmony is breaking down. Technological advances, the demands of motorways, industrialisation, pollution, drainage, modern farming methods and the sheer numbers of people are all taking their toll. In the last 35 years the loss or damage to wild places, and to plants and animals that are dependent on them, has been devastating. Increasingly the countryside of the British Isles which we took for granted in the past is simply no longer there for our children to enjoy.

It is a dismaying fact that since 1949 an area of prime natural habitat equivalent to the size of the Lake District has been destroyed including the destruction or complete disappearance of much of our best loved and most beautiful countryside. Even more disturbing, this destruction is accelerating. Ancient woodlands, flower-rich grasslands, wet meadows, ponds and hedgerows have all declined rapidly. Destruction is occurring at such a rate that if action is not taken now there will be little for future generations to enjoy. That is why The Royal Society for Nature Conservation (RSNC) has launched The British Wildlife Appeal.

The Appeal, which I am privileged to Chair, is being run by the RSNC in conjunction with all 48 associated Local Nature Conservation Trusts which combined make up the largest wildlife conservation organisation in the United Kingdom. Together, the Society and Trusts think nationally and act locally to protect land and endangered wildlife, to provide information, enjoyment and advice, and to make sure the changes to our countryside do the least harm to wild plants and animals. The Trusts gain from being part of the RSNC, drawing strength from the nationwide membership and from the exchange of ideas and practical experience. With the support of over 180,000 members the Trusts care for 1,680 reserves around the country which cover nearly 50,000 hectares.

Over the last 25 years, however, the price of land has risen as much as 50-fold and the existing resources of the Trusts and the RSNC are no longer enough to meet the challenge. The amount of wildlife-rich land now on offer to the Trusts has doubled in the last two years but sadly, through lack of funds, they are unable to take full advantage of the situation. So the Appeal is now an urgent one. It has been mounted at two levels. The RSNC has set itself the target of raising £5 million from a national appeal and the regional Trusts aim to raise £5 million through local appeals. The money will be spent in attaining four major objectives:

- To buy land with endangered species or declining habitats.
- To conserve that land and other sites in their care.
- To promote greater public awareness of the threat to our wildlife.
- To give everyone a chance to get to know and enjoy wildlife whether in town or country.

By pressing for balanced policies for the use of our countryside, the RSNC and the Trusts are determined to halt and reverse the decline of our wildlife. WATCH, the Society's club for young people, involves its members in caring for wildlife and the environment. It is an extremely important and growing part of the RSNC which uses practical projects to involve young people in the problems of their environment as early as possible. Membership is around 25,000 with an additional 900 affiliated schools and clubs.

The organisation has led the way in the field-by-field surveys of important wildlife sites. By the year 2000 a national catalogue of sites will have been

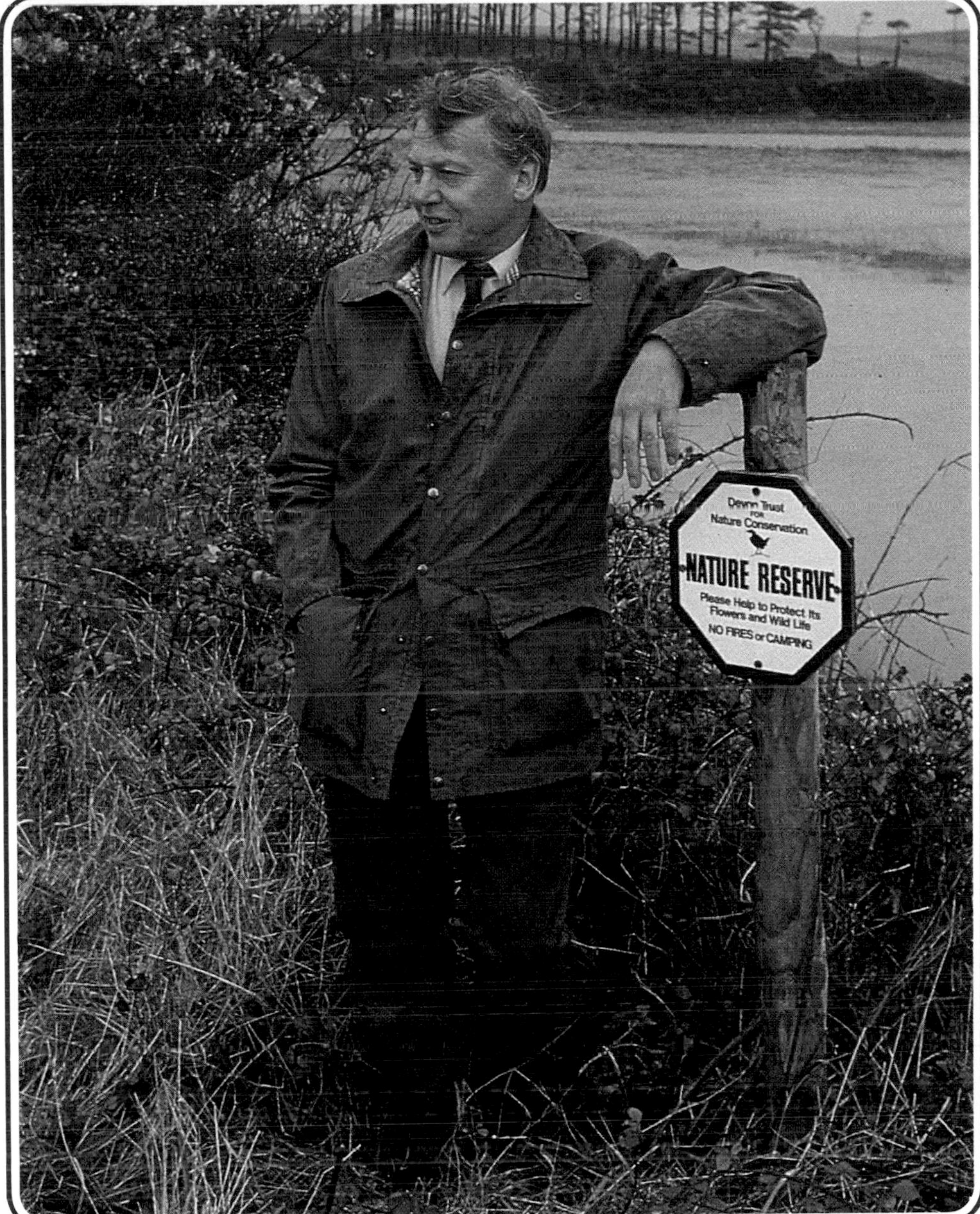

Sir David Attenborough at the Otter Estuary Nature Reserve, Budleigh Salterton, which is under the management of The Devon Trust for Nature Conservation.

In support of the Royal Society for Nature Conservation's

compiled so that we can manage sympathetically the countryside we have left.

With the increasingly good records, and under the members' watchful eyes, the RSNC and the Trusts monitor what is happening to the prime wildlife sites. They alert government and public to damage threatening or being done to nationally important sites, give evidence at planning enquiries and respond to proposals for river improvement by water authorities. From farmers to foresters and from public industry to private individuals, more and more people are asking about conservation.

It is a significant fact that whilst the threats to our natural heritage have been accelerating, the public enjoyment of the countryside and its wildlife has never been greater. This interest has given rise to many excellent books on natural history which in turn have helped promote a greater awareness and knowledge of our environment. The Appeal is therefore particularly pleased to associate itself with *Wildlife of the British Isles*, a book whose colourful pages bear testimony to the richness of the wildlife of these islands.

Our lives would be so much the poorer without the wild flowers, insects, birds and mammals that so superbly decorate these pages, but we must act now. Remember, for our wildlife . . .

. . .TOMORROW IS TOO LATE.

David Attenborough

An Introduction to the

British Countryside

The countryside of Britain is one of the most varied and attractive in the world. Amongst the 400 or more islands that make up the British 'archipelago', there is a huge variation in scenery, weather, geology and even day-length, all overlain by the varied changes that man has wrought through the centuries depending on the use he has made of each area of land.

There is no simple reason for this great diversity, though at the heart of much of the variety lies the complicated geology of Britain, which is the most geologically varied area, for its size, in the world. The geology of a country is the key to almost everything. In a direct way, it affects the fertility and quality of the soil which in turn produces the particular wild fauna and flora. The same

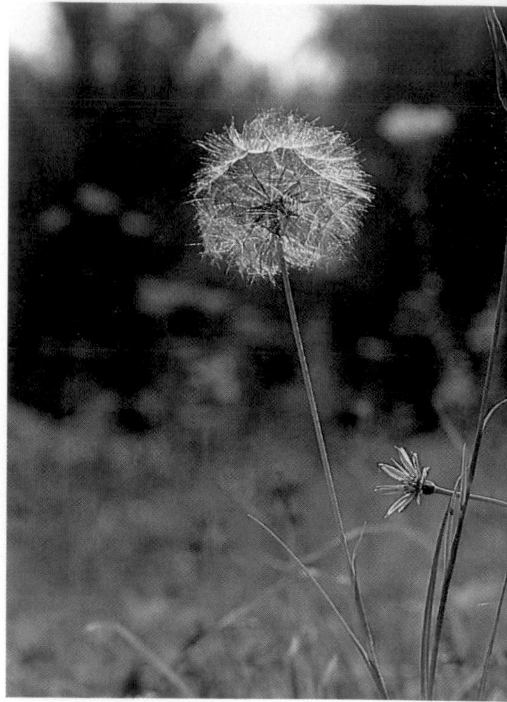

Below The beautiful Sussex Weald, etched with a patchwork of fields, woodlands and hedgerows, a product of the influence of man on the natural geological variation of the land

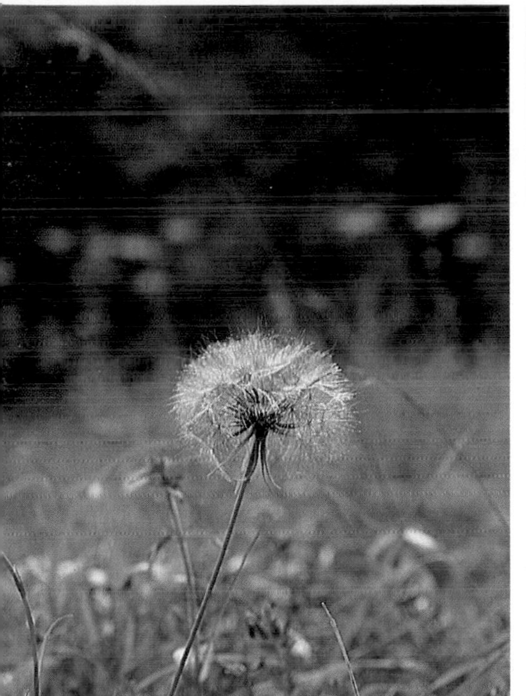

Above The British Countryside is rich in many beautiful wildflowers. This goatsbeard sometimes called jack-go-to-bed-at-noon closes its flowers at midday

characteristics also influenced where man settled and what type of agriculture he practised.

The geology works in other ways, too. The older rocks are usually harder, and often more folded and convoluted, so they tend to protrude as hills and mountains, whereas the softer younger rocks erode easily into gentle hills, valleys and plains. This affects climate, as well as the settlement and agriculture patterns. Even on a very small scale, the geology contributes to our varied landscape and wildlife. There are many parishes that cross several geological strata, each giving rise to different soils, and this directly affects the habitats and land-uses of the area with, for example, heathland on a sandy area, woodland left undisturbed on stiff clay-with-flints soil, open downland on steep limestone hills, and wet meadows on the alluvium of the valley floor. There are very few parts of the countryside where this delightful small-scale mosaic cannot be seen, and the more you know of geology, the more you can appreciate its significance.

The climate of Britain is also varied. The surrounding seas generally serve to make the climate milder and wetter, but the Gulf Stream which warms the western parts of Britain is especially important. Most of Britain's weather systems come from the west bringing warm, or at least mild, rain to the western coasts and hills. As the rain passes eastwards across the country, it steadily loses its strength and diminishes. By the time it reaches the eastern counties it may have disappeared altogether. At the same time, the eastern counties are more affected by the presence of the huge landmass of Europe and Asia, and they tend to get the overspill from their continental systems – bitterly cold in winter, and clear and sunny in summer. The situation is further complicated, by the fact that Britain is a very long and thin island, about 1,100 kilometres from top to bottom, so that the north of Scotland and the Shetland Isles have a totally different climate from Cornwall or the Isle of Wight at the southern extremity of the country. This difference in latitude also greatly affects day length patterns, with the most northerly area having very long summer days, but extremely short ones in winter; while southern parts have a more moderate variation. This has a direct effect on our wildlife through factors such as differences in length of daylight feeding hours.

The influence of man overlies all this natural variation. There have been men living in Britain for tens of thousands of years. The earliest people, in the old Stone Age, are believed to have been wholly nomadic and they left few traces on the land. Signs of any previous colonisations were virtually wiped out by the last great Ice Age, which only began to ameliorate some 15,000 years ago. The receding ice, which came as far south as the Scilly Isles, South Wales and the Midlands, left a bare surface, ripe for colonisation by plants. In those days, and up to 8,000 or 9,000 years ago, Britain was not a group of islands, but part of the European mainland attached by a broad area of land between Kent and Norfolk stretching across to France, Holland and Germany. Therefore the plants and animals forced into south Europe by the ice could recolonise Britain, and the post Ice Age tundra landscape was soon replaced by successive waves of pioneer trees such as birch, pine and juniper, followed by the more stable woodland trees like oak and lime.

About 7,000 to 8,000 years ago, Britain was almost wholly covered by a huge natural forest. But, from Neolithic times onwards, some 5,000 years ago, man has steadily cleared the woodland, at first just to herd game into clearings, then later to cultivate areas around settlements. By the Iron Age or Roman times, much of the countryside was already under cultivation, including many areas no longer used for agriculture today, and the mosaic of intimate features was already established. Through Saxon times and the medieval period this pattern was consolidated, though the area of cleared land gradually increased. Each part of the countryside was intensively used in addition to the crop-growing areas: heathlands were grazed and woodlands yielded both timber and smaller wood products; downlands, commons and water meadows all provided grazing for a variety of different animals, while hay meadows produced the stored winter fodder for the ploughing oxen. It was an efficient and effective regime and it lasted for so long that almost all our native wildlife, at least in the lowlands, is adapted to this system. Sadly, there have been dramatic changes in the last 40 years, not only because of the greatly increased population and its enlarged food and space requirements, but also because of the demise in traditional countryside management which favoured so much of our native wildlife. Nevertheless, the British Isles are still rich in natural life, as we shall see in succeeding pages.

The Brecon Beacons

HABITATS

INCLUDING: Woodlands - Deciduous and Coniferous • Eroding Coasts • Depositional Coasts • The Open Sea • Farmland • Heathlands • Grassland and Downland • Towns and Gardens • The Uplands • Wetlands • Open Waters • •

OLD WOODLANDS

Woodlands hold a special place in our collective memory, as places of shelter and refuge, and even as places to be feared. There have always been woodlands around us, throughout history, and they probably mean more to us than any other part of the countryside.

Old woodlands are one of our countryside's most nostalgic and evocative natural habitats; they are also one of the most complex and varied. The recent history of British woodlands stretches back for 10,000 years or more, and there are some woods which have been present on the same site for the whole of this time. Other woods have not been in existence for quite so long having perhaps grown up on abandoned Roman or medieval farmland, but they still have all the characteristics of the original woods. These ancient woods are amongst the most fascinating because of their unchanged structure and the special plants and animals associated with them.

The Deciduous Woodland Ecosystem

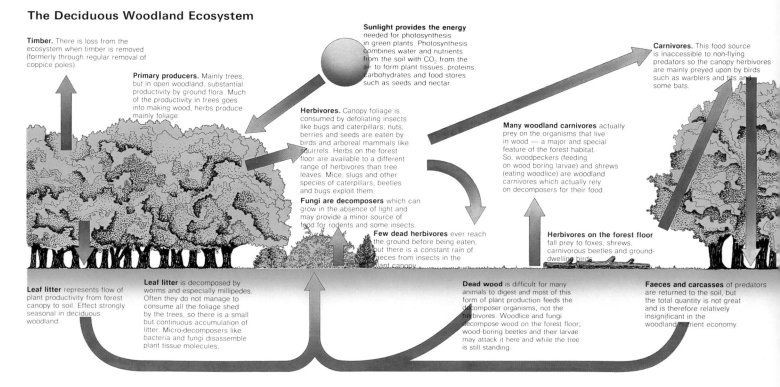

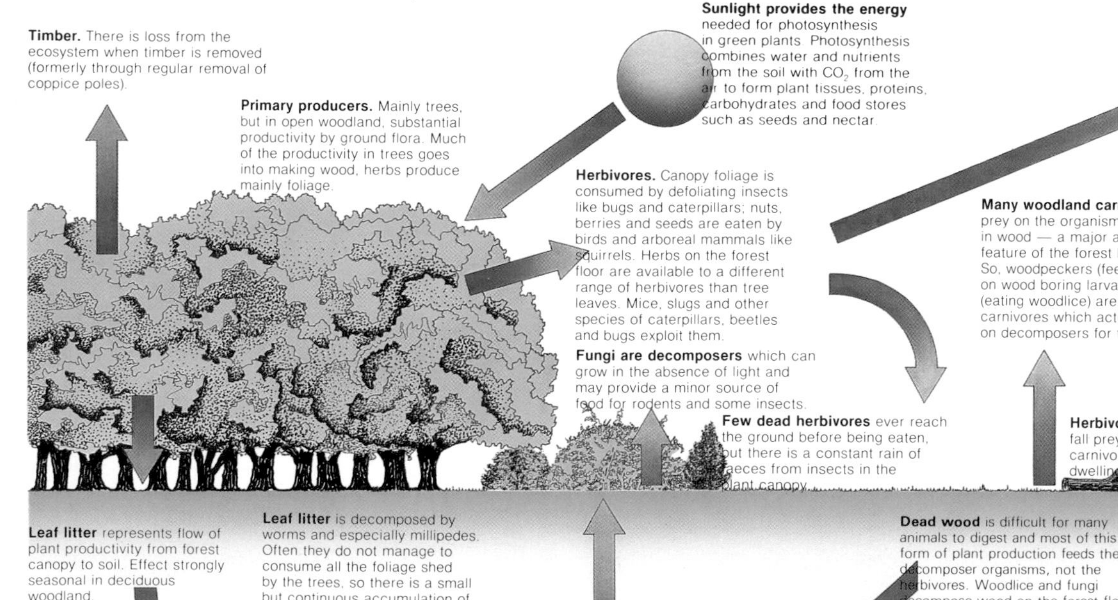

Timber. There is loss from the ecosystem when timber is removed (formerly through regular removal of coppice poles).
Primary producers. Mainly trees, but in open woodland, substantial productivity by ground flora. Much of the productivity in trees goes into making wood, herbs produce mainly foliage.
Sunlight provides the energy needed for photosynthesis in green plants. Photosynthesis combines water and nutrients from the soil with CO_2 from the air to form plant tissues, proteins, carbohydrates and food stores such as seeds and nectar.
Herbivores. Canopy foliage is consumed by defoliating insects like bugs and caterpillars; nuts, berries and seeds are eaten by birds and arboreal mammals like squirrels. Herbs on the forest floor are available to a different range of herbivores than tree leaves. Mice, slugs and other species of caterpillars, beetles and bugs exploit them.
Fungi are decomposers which can grow in the absence of light and may provide a minor source of food for rodents and some insects.
Few dead herbivores ever reach the ground before being eaten, but there is a constant rain of faeces from insects in the plant canopy.
Carnivores. This food source is inaccessible to non-flying predators so the canopy herbivores are mainly preyed upon by birds such as warblers and tits and some bats.
Many woodland carnivores actually prey on the organisms that live in wood — a major and special feature of the forest habitat. So, woodpeckers (feeding on wood boring larvae) and shrews (eating woodlice) are woodland carnivores which actually rely on decomposers for their food.
Herbivores on the forest floor fall prey to foxes, shrews, carnivorous beetles and ground-dwelling birds.
Leaf litter represents flow of plant productivity from forest canopy to soil. Effect strongly seasonal in deciduous woodland.
Leaf litter is decomposed by worms and especially millipedes. Often they do not manage to consume all the foliage shed by the trees, so there is a small but continuous accumulation of litter. Micro-decomposers like bacteria and fungi disassemble plant tissue molecules.
Dead wood is difficult for many animals to digest and most of this form of plant production feeds the decomposer organisms, not the herbivores. Woodlice and fungi decompose wood on the forest floor; wood-boring beetles and their larvae may attack it here and while the tree is still standing.
Faeces and carcasses of predators are returned to the soil, but the total quantity is not great and is therefore relatively insignificant in the woodland nutrient economy.

Woodlands have a special relationship with man. Almost since the beginnings of settlement, they have been used for fuel, timber, forage and other products. The time span of a woodland is so much longer than for other habitats, with individual trees living for hundreds of years, that woods have a continuity and stability which often outlives surrounding changes. Because of the height of trees woodlands are more markedly three-dimensional than other habitats and often extend over large areas. Thus the interior is protected from the wind, frost, and even rain and sun that are constantly changing on the outside of the wood, and even the difference between day and night is less significant than in the open countryside. Organisms living in the wood can therefore rely on a stable, humid atmosphere, devoid of extremes, allowing a vast range of species to flourish, each using a different aspect of the wood whether it be on the woodland floor, up in the canopy or somewhere in between.

It was once assumed that almost all woods would become dominated by oaks if nature were left to take its course. It is now clear that the situation is much more complex; man has favoured one species or another over the centuries masking the great natural variation of woods. In a wood where no planting or consistent removal of trees has taken place, the natural canopy tends to be a mixture of several species with one species – such as ash or lime – becoming dominant where circumstances particularly favour its growth. For example, ashwoods are a particular feature of many limestone areas, especially in the north and west, where other trees are able to do less well.

Over the centuries, woods have been managed by man in different ways. For old woodland it is almost certain to have been in one of two ways, either as coppice-with-standards (see top of page 13, left) or as wood pasture. The great majority of medieval woods were managed as

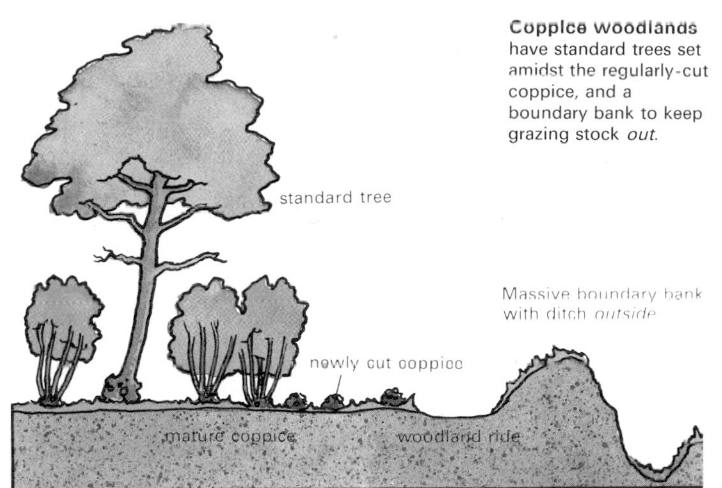

Coppice woodlands have standard trees set amidst the regularly-cut coppice, and a boundary bank to keep grazing stock *out*.

A typical ancient wood pasture system, with pollarded trees set amidst rough grazing land, and a huge boundary bank designed to keep domestic stock *in*.

coppice-with-standards which not only produced a range of woodland products but also provided ideal conditions for a wonderful display of flowers and a vast array of animals. In other circumstances, where timber was needed but grazing was equally important, a system called wood pasture developed, allowing animals to graze around and between the trees. However grazing animals would tend to prevent the regeneration of young trees and if the timber supply was to be maintained animals had to be periodically excluded from parts of the wood to allow the new trees to establish. If wood products, like those from coppice, were required then individual trees could be pollarded; this involves cutting them off at about head height and allowing the new branches to grow out of reach of grazing animals. Ancient pollarded beeches and oaks are a feature of many of these wood pastures.

Most old woods, whatever their origins and position, are excellent places for wildlife. The range of trees and shrubs encourages more birds, insects and other animals to breed and feed. Ancient trees are full of nooks, cracks and crannies giving homes to hole-nesting birds, bats and other mammals, and numerous insects and spiders. Dead or dying wood is a wonderful feeding-ground for woodpeckers, treecreepers and other birds because a surprisingly large number of insects (especially beetles and flies) spend their growing larval stages eating dead wood and they, in turn, provide food for birds and even for other insects. An old woodland is a wonderful place, vibrating with all manner life at every level, alive with colour and sound every spring and summer.

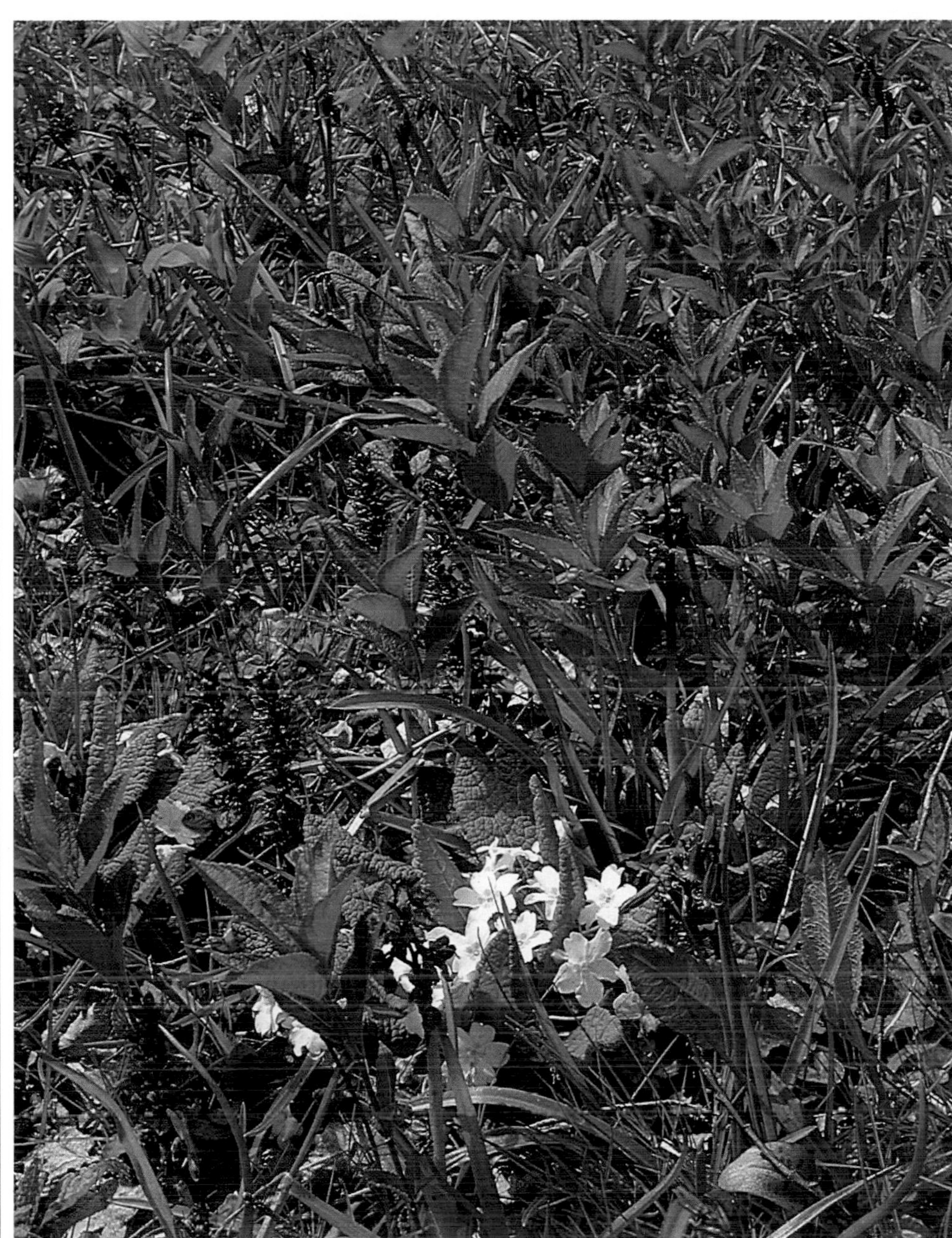

A mass of spring flowers in old coppiced woodland, including early purple orchids, yellow primroses bluebells, and bugle spikes. The cropping of the coppice poles once every seven years or so – depending upon what they are intended for – opens up the canopy and allows these flowers to bloom

PLANTATIONS

Although woodlands are our most ancient natural habitat, there are also many woods that have only come into existence in more recent times, either by natural colonisation of abandoned farmland, or by deliberate planting. These, though different, have their special value, too.

Not all our woodlands are ancient; many are of recent origin either by natural means or, more frequently nowadays, by the efforts of man. Any piece of cleared land, except on the highest hills and mountains or other exceptionally inhospitable places, will revert naturally to woodland if it is allowed to do so. Over the centuries, many areas of farmland have been abandoned through changing circumstances, and their cultivation or grazing has ceased. Such areas are soon invaded by pioneer trees like birch, followed by longer-lived species such as oak; within a century or so they will become mature woodland. To the trained eye, however, such woods are usually quite different to ancient woodlands for they lack the ancient coppice or pollard stools, the dead wood that naturally forms on aged trees and the myriad plants and animals that survive only in old woodland, unable to colonise the newer woods. In other respects they are similar to the ancient woods, for they have a natural range of trees and shrubs, with a developing shrub and ground layer below the canopy, and many of the more mobile woodland birds and mammals will move in as conditions become right.

In marked contrast to natural woodland are the plantation woods. Man has been planting trees for hundreds of years, in small quantities at first and usually using trees that were native locally. Since the 1900s, though, and more especially in this century since the two world wars devastated our natural timber stock, there has been a steadily accelerating rate of planting of coniferous trees; and all except the Scots pine are alien to Britain. Conifers are favoured over broadleaved trees because generally they grow much faster, and therefore produce a quicker economic return. Consequently, a plantation is usually quite different to a natural wood in the species of tree that it contains, consisting of only one or two species in contrast to the great range of trees and shrubs that make up a natural ancient woodland. The structure of plantations is also quite different to that of a natural woodland. In any one block, all the trees are likely to be of the same age; there is virtually no shrub layer and most conifers shade out any ground-living flowers; much of the natural variation in slope, soil and drainage will also have been lost during the planting phase. So those man-made woods are much more uniform and simple than natural woods and, as a result, support many less plants and animals. However, there are a number of species that specialise in plantations, and are more readily

The Coniferous Woodland Ecosystem

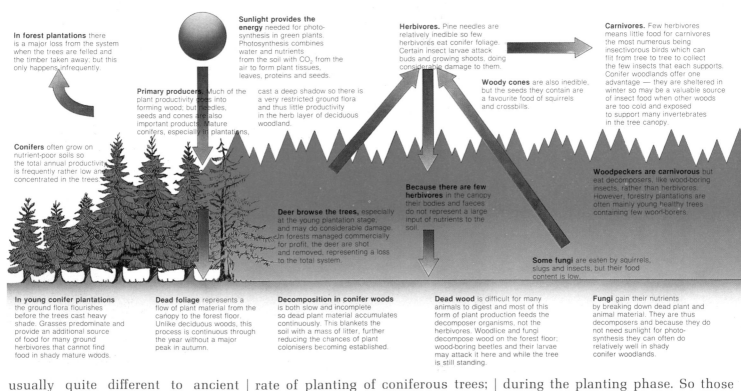

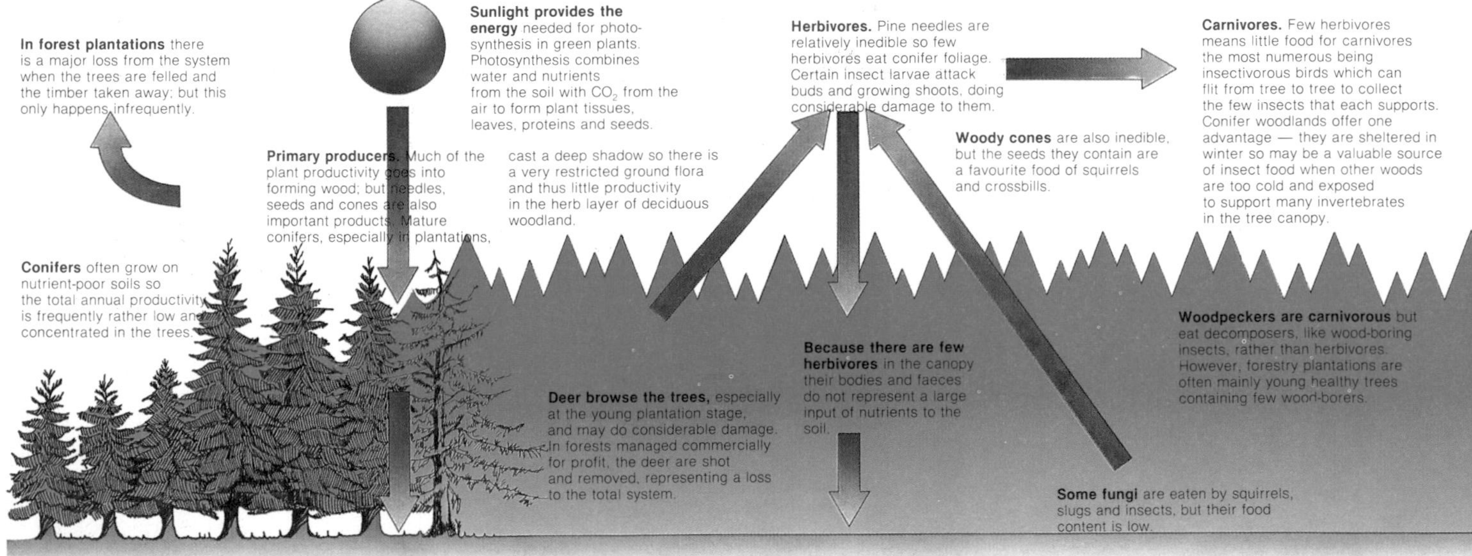

In forest plantations there is a major loss from the system when the trees are felled and the timber taken away; but this only happens infrequently.

Herbivores. Pine needles are relatively inedible so few herbivores eat conifer foliage. Certain insect larvae attack buds and growing shoots, doing considerable damage to them.
Carnivores. Few herbivores means little food for carnivores the most numerous being insectivorous birds which can flit from tree to tree to collect the few insects that each supports. Conifer woodlands offer one advantage — they are sheltered in winter so may be a valuable source of insect food when other woods are too cold and exposed to support many invertebrates in the tree canopy.

Woody cones are also inedible, but the seeds they contain are a favourite food of squirrels and crossbills.
Conifers often grow on nutrient-poor soils so the total annual productivity is frequently rather low and concentrated in the trees.
Woodpeckers are carnivorous but eat decomposers, like wood-boring insects, rather than herbivores. However, forestry plantations are often mainly young healthy trees containing few wood-borers.
Because there are few herbivores in the canopy their bodies and faeces do not represent a large input of nutrients to the soil.
Deer browse the trees, especially at the young plantation stage, and may do considerable damage. In forests managed commercially for profit, the deer are shot and removed, representing a loss to the total system.
Some fungi are eaten by squirrels, slugs and insects, but their food content is low.

Dead foliage represents a flow of plant material from the canopy to the forest floor. Unlike deciduous woods, this process is continuous through the year without a major peak in autumn.
Decomposition in conifer woods is both slow and incomplete so dead plant material accumulates continuously. This blankets the soil with a mass of litter, further reducing the chances of plant colonisers becoming established.

Fungi gain their nutrients by breaking down dead plant and animal material. They are thus decomposers and because they do not need sunlight for photosynthesis they can often do relatively well in shady conifer woodlands.

found in this habitat than in our native woods.

The best way to see wildlife in any plantation is by following the rides which allow access for maintenance, fire-fighting and felling. Several species of deer particularly favour plantations, while a number of birds use conifers for nesting, roosting and feeding or all three. Goldcrests are commoner in conifer plantations than elsewhere, while crossbills and siskins have steadily increased their range in Britain by making use of the additional food and nest-sites provided by this habitat. Other birds, like the secretive long-eared owl, regularly chose these areas to roost and breed emerging at night to hunt over the surrounding countryside. Some insects, such as the pine beauty moth, the pine weevil or the large yellow underwing are especially associated with conifer forests, and some quickly become pests as the uniform stands of trees allow them to spread rapidly through the plantation. Below the tree canopy there may be virtually no flowers or shrubs but, after a few years, the rapidly-accumulating needle litter soon begins to support an interesting range of mushrooms and toadstools, and some older conifer plantations are a mass of such fungi each autumn.

Today, about 70 per cent of our woodland cover is plantation of one sort or another and, though they can never replace our beautiful ancient woods, they do have a wildlife all of their own and should not be ignored by the naturalist wanting to see the range of Britain's wildlife.

A wide mown ride provides a welcome open flowery area in a dense plantation of conifer trees, where you may watch wildlife

THE ERODING COASTLINE

As befits an island nation, the coastline of Britain is one of our greatest glories, not only for its beauty and variety but also for its immensely rich wildlife. Although it might appear unchanging, the coast is a particularly dynamic situation, and many areas are rapidly eroding.

The British Isles have one of the longest and most varied coastlines in Europe with at least 7,000 miles of mixed rocky cliffs, sand-dunes, estuaries, saltmarshes, mudflats and beaches. Although it may look stable, on a calm day at least, the coast is actually an immensely dynamic, ever-changing system constantly being rearranged by tidal currents and winter gales. Even within the last 200 or 300 years, since accurate maps became readily available, there is plenty of evidence to indicate a wealth of changes in the coastline; but before that, stretching back several thousand years, the changes have been enormous.

During the last Ice Age, which only ended 12,000 to 15,000 years ago, a large amount of the world's store of water was locked away in the huge ice sheets which stretched as far south as the Midlands and south-west of England. As a result, the sea levels were at least 100 metres lower than they are today, and an immense amount of land which was exposed is now submerged beneath the sea. Britain was part of Europe, joined by a broad area of land stretching across the North Sea from Norfolk and the Dover Straits to the south and east, while Ireland was part of the same landmass. As the ice melted, two changes occurred: the sea level gradually rose, flooding and submerging huge area of land as it went; and the land surface itself changed its height above sea level. As the heavy burden of ice was removed from the north of Britain the land rose like a cork, and is still rising slowly; while the southern parts, from about The Wash southwards, gradually tilted downwards like the other half of a see-saw.

Naturally, the changes in levels meant that new stretches of rock were constantly being exposed to the power of the sea. Wherever a coast is open to the full force of the waves, and especially along the western coasts where currents are strongest and the wind power is greatest, erosion takes place as rock, soil or any other material is removed by the waves and carried out to sea. Different types of rock or sediment vary in their resistance to the power of the sea. Where older, harder rocks occur, they stand out as headlands or lines of rocky cliffs. Moderately soft rocks, like chalk, erode quite rapidly into a characteristic coastline which is a mixture of unstable cliffs, arches where the sea has cut right through underneath a headland, and stacks where the arches have collapsed. The softest, most recent rocks, such as those making up much of the south and east coats of England, erode rapidly producing a slumped cliff that rarely becomes vertical, as new material constantly slips down to form a pile at the base. In parts of the country where soft rocks are exposed to strong winds and wave action, such as on parts of the Dorset or Suffolk coasts, the coastline can recede quite rapidly and roads, fields and even houses fall into the sea.

For obvious reasons, eroding coasts are hostile to many forms of wildlife, especially where exposure to wind and waves is at its greatest, as animals and plants are constantly dislodged. Hard rock areas tend to have the richest flora and fauna, partly because the substrate tends to last long enough to allow both plants and animals to gain, and maintain, a foothold, especially in areas sheltered from the full force of the sea. Such areas, for example around the coasts of Cornwall or South-west Wales, also tend to have the clearest waters (with less sediment being moved around), and this extra light allows a luxuriant growth of the life on the regularly-submerged rocks. The softer rocks tend to erode more rapid-

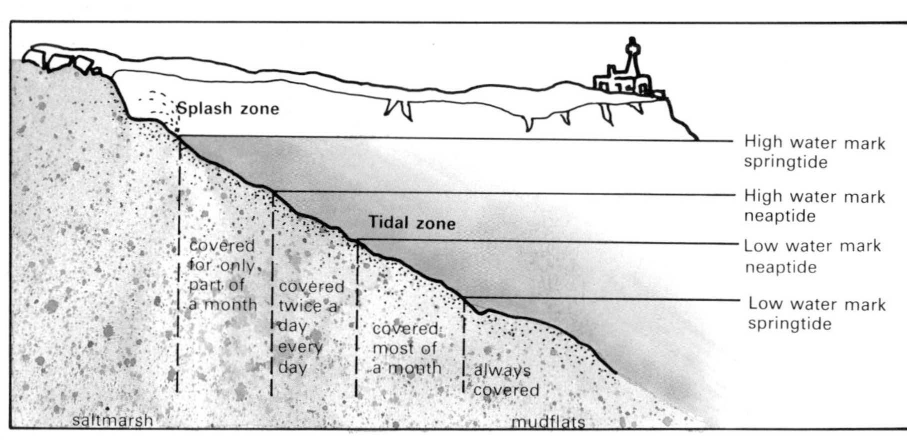

The Tides

The tides are the result of gravitational pull from the sun and moon on the water of the world's oceans. There are two high and two low tides each day, but their height varies according to the position of the moon. 'Spring' tides are the highest, while neap tides are the least high, as the diagram shows. The ever changing state of the tides means that at any time the water will be covering more or less of the land Plants and animals in this tidal zone have adapted to various areas up the beach depending upon the amount of exposure they can stand.

ly, allowing insufficient time for most plants or animals to establish themselves, so the flora and fauna are poorer, though much depends on the exposure of the rocks. Even the slightest amount of shelter from the prevailing winds and currents can rocks. Some chalk cliffs are an exception, such as those at Bempton in Yorkshire which support wonderful seabird colonies. In contrast, the hardest cliffs tend to be rather poor for flowers, since few species can penetrate the rock adequately, and it is the slightly softer – but not too rapidly-eroding – rocks that support the widest range of plants. The very softest cliffs have quite a different range of species including a few that only occur in such situations. In some ways the conditions offered are ideal,

Precipitous cliffs on the Glamorgan coast pounded by the waves. It is the force of these crashing breakers that has shaped our coastline over the centuries

offer a haven to a much greater variety of life.

Above the tide-lines, cliffs offer a home to a variety of plants and animals and these, too, vary according to the nature of the rock. Britain has some of the finest seabird colonies in the world, with many of them occurring on the hard, high cliffs of north and west Britain. For breeding birds, the most important factor is usually the presence of suitable stable ledges on which they can nest and these tend to be found readily in the harder

with a constant supply of nutrients from the slumping rock, a warm, usually frost-free environment and little competition from other plants, but any flower which establishes a foothold has to be able to move and recolonise readily as areas of cliff constantly fall or become buried. There is even a butterfly species – the Glanville fritillary – which only survives in such situations as the combination of circumstances ideally suits its lifestyle, and is restricted to the south coast of the Isle of Wight.

DEPOSITIONAL COASTS

Not all of our coastline is eroding away, and the resulting material from eroding coasts tends to come back to the sheltered parts of the coast. These softer coasts, with their sand-dunes, mudflats and shingle bars, offer a quite different range of wildlife, but fascinating nonetheless.

We have seen (previous page) how the sea acts as a constant eroding force wherever a coast is exposed to wind and waves, and vast quantities of material have been removed from the shores of Britain in the last few thousand years. Initially, all this material is picked up by the sea, for example it is estimated that the erosion of the cliffs in Christchurch Bay, on the Hampshire-Dorset border, by about one metre per year adds at least 100,000 tonnes per year to the sediment load of the Solent. But the amount of material the sea can carry is dependent on its energy, and this in turn varies from place to place and according to the season. All the silt and rocks picked up has to be deposited somewhere. Some of it forms marine sediments but, due to the complicated nature of the tides and currents around the British Isles, much finds its way back to the coast and wherever conditions are sheltered it will be deposited.

Different sizes of materials gather in different places. In very exposed situations, virtually nothing is left behind by the sea, except for very big boulders. In rather more sheltered places, the larger gravels and pebbles are released to form features such as shingle banks or spits, and even within these there is a noticeable gradation, with the larger stones being flung to the top by storm waves and never removed and successively smaller pebbles being found down the beach. Where the sediment is moved along the coast by longshore drift, a characteristic set of coastal features is formed, in which a sand or shingle beach can be extended for several kilometres along the coast, often blocking estuaries and forming bars, such as at Chesil Beach, Dorset or Orfordness, Suffolk. Within this sheltering outer bar, mudflats and saltmarshes are able to form, as the sea has virtually lost all its energy and even very fine particles can drop out of suspension and remain.

Depositing coasts, therefore, have a characteristic range of habitats, depending upon the balance of exposure and shelter, and upon the type of material available to form the coastal features. Each such habitat supports a particular range of plants and animals, dependent on its characteristics and varying according to latitude or additional factors such as disturbances.

Wherever large quantities of sand are deposited, sand-dunes are likely to appear as the mobile sand is reworked by the wind and carried above high water-mark to form low hills. The dunes closest to the sea are usually bare and mobile, whilst older dunes further inland become successively more established and vegetated (see panel).

The Estuary and Saltmarsh Ecosystem

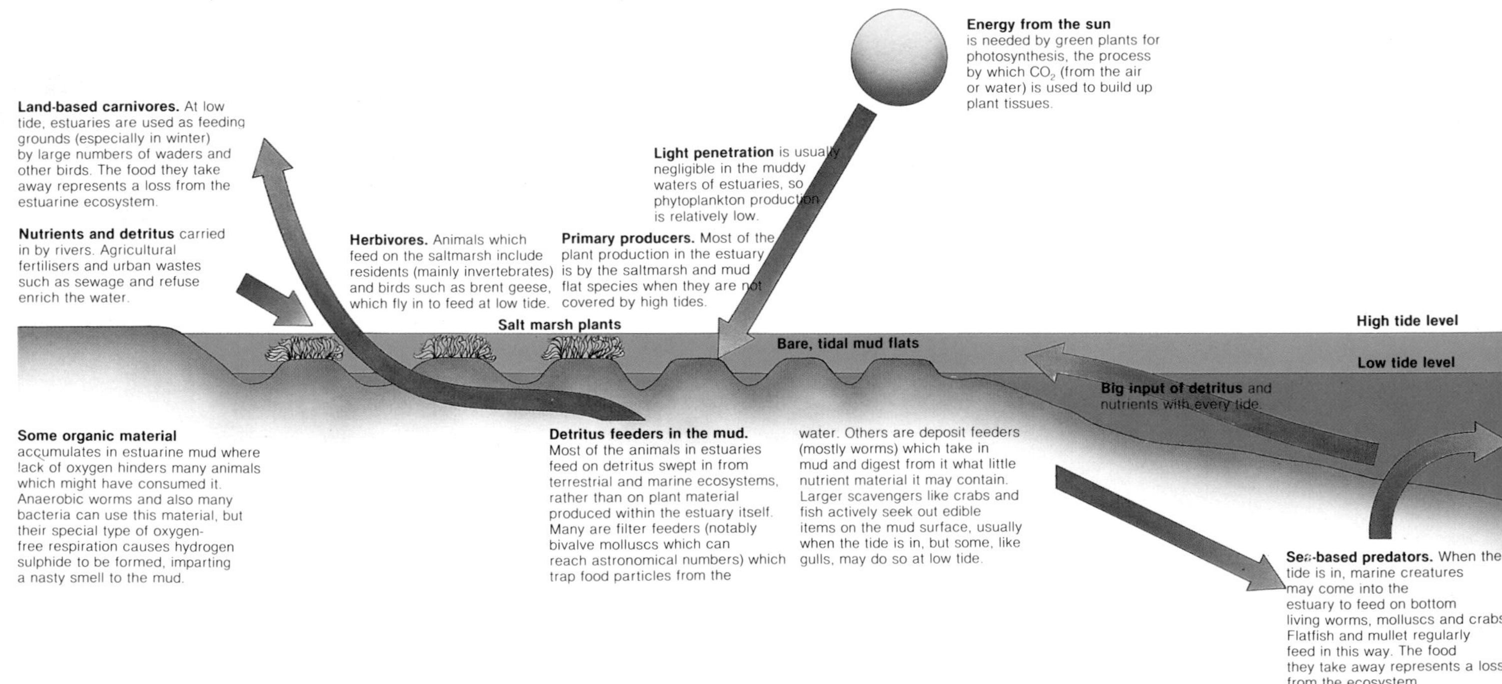

Energy from the sun is needed by green plants for photosynthesis, the process by which CO_2 (from the air or water) is used to build up plant tissues.
Land-based carnivores. At low tide, estuaries are used as feeding grounds (especially in winter) by large numbers of waders and other birds. The food they take away represents a loss from the estuarine ecosystem.
Light penetration is usually negligible in the muddy waters of estuaries, so phytoplankton production is relatively low.
Nutrients and detritus carried in by rivers. Agricultural fertilisers and urban wastes such as sewage and refuse enrich the water.
Herbivores. Animals which feed on the saltmarsh include residents (mainly invertebrates) and birds such as brent geese, which fly in to feed at low tide.
Primary producers. Most of the plant production in the estuary is by the saltmarsh and mud flat species when they are not covered by high tides.
Salt marsh plants
Bare, tidal mud flats
High tide level
Low tide level
Big input of detritus and nutrients with every tide.
Some organic material accumulates in estuarine mud where lack of oxygen hinders many animals which might have consumed it. Anaerobic worms and also many bacteria can use this material, but their special type of oxygen-free respiration causes hydrogen sulphide to be formed, imparting a nasty smell to the mud.
Detritus feeders in the mud. Most of the animals in estuaries feed on detritus swept in from terrestrial and marine ecosystems, rather than on plant material produced within the estuary itself. Many are filter feeders (notably bivalve molluscs which can reach astronomical numbers) which trap food particles from the water. Others are deposit feeders (mostly worms) which take in mud and digest from it what little nutrient material it may contain. Larger scavengers like crabs and fish actively seek out edible items on the mud surface, usually when the tide is in, but some, like gulls, may do so at low tide.
Sea-based predators. When the tide is in, marine creatures may come into the estuary to feed on bottom living worms, molluscs and crabs. Flatfish and mullet regularly feed in this way. The food they take away represents a loss from the ecosystem.

Gravelly shingle would appear an inhospitable habitat but, wherever it is stable and no longer moved by the sea, sufficient soil becomes trapped in the spaces to allow early plant colonisers to come in; and it is not long before trees such as oak, albeit in a rather stunted form, can establish themselves. Britain has some of the finest shingle systems in Europe, such as the extraordinarily 27 kilometre long shingle bar of Chesil beach, Dorset or the huge triangular shingle point at Dungeness in Kent, which has been gradually extending outwards since pre-Roman times, but did not exist at all 3,000 years ago!

A view of Cuckmere Haven, East Sussex, where the river Cuckmere breaches the chalk downs and flows down to the sea, passing through a broad shingle bar

In very sheltered areas, especially in estuaries or behind spits and bars, saltmarshes and mudflats form on the finest deposited sediments. In shallow, very slow-moving water, saltmarshes form as various salt- and immersion-tolerant plants become established, whilst lower down the shore the mud remains as bare mudflats. Both areas are noted for their abundance of invertebrates and they are vital feeding-grounds for huge numbers of wintering birds.

The Sand-dune Ecosystem

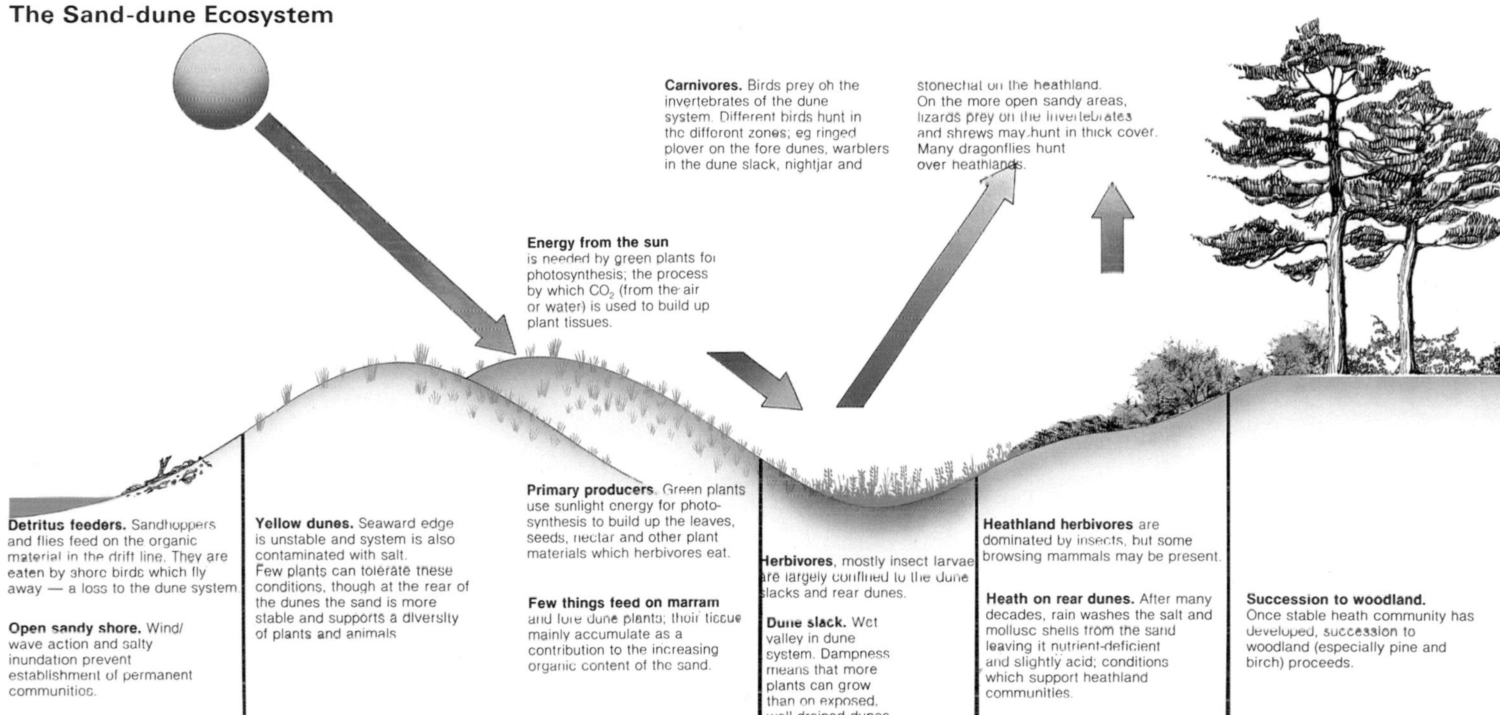

Carnivores. Birds prey on the invertebrates of the dune system. Different birds hunt in the different zones; eg ringed plover on the fore dunes, warblers in the dune slack, nightjar and stonechat on the heathland. On the more open sandy areas, lizards prey on the invertebrates and shrews may hunt in thick cover. Many dragonflies hunt over heathlands.
Energy from the sun is needed by green plants for photosynthesis; the process by which CO_2 (from the air or water) is used to build up plant tissues.
Detritus feeders. Sandhoppers and flies feed on the organic material in the drift line. They are eaten by shore birds which fly away — a loss to the dune system.
Open sandy shore. Wind/wave action and salty inundation prevent establishment of permanent communities.
Yellow dunes. Seaward edge is unstable and system is also contaminated with salt. Few plants can tolerate these conditions, though at the rear of the dunes the sand is more stable and supports a diversity of plants and animals
Primary producers. Green plants use sunlight energy for photosynthesis to build up the leaves, seeds, nectar and other plant materials which herbivores eat.
Few things feed on marram and fore dune plants; their tissue mainly accumulate as a contribution to the increasing organic content of the sand.
Herbivores, mostly insect larvae are largely confined to the dune slacks and rear dunes.
Dune slack. Wet valley in dune system. Dampness means that more plants can grow than on exposed, well drained dunes.
Heathland herbivores are dominated by insects, but some browsing mammals may be present.
Heath on rear dunes. After many decades, rain washes the salt and mollusc shells from the sand leaving it nutrient-deficient and slightly acid; conditions which support heathland communities.
Succession to woodland. Once stable heath community has developed, succession to woodland (especially pine and birch) proceeds.

THE OPEN SEA

As a group of islands, the British Isles – and indeed the British themselves – have always been dominated by the effects of the sea. Nowhere in Britain is more than about 100 kilometres from the coast, and a very large area of the country is directly affected by the sea.

The British Isles, like most land-masses, lie surrounded by an area of shallow seas known as the Continental shelf, where the depth of the sea shelves gently to about 200 to 300 metres. Beyond this, the floor drops away steeply, eventually reaching depths of many thousands of metres, and this area is usually known as the open ocean. The nearest points of this deeper water are some 50 kilometres west of the west coast of Ireland, or about 130 kilometres north off the mainland of Scotland, the seas surrounding Britain are composed entirely of the shallower, Continental shelf variety.

Although the position of Britain is fairly northerly, the temperature of the seas around the country are variable and generally warmer than you might expect; this has a considerable effect on the marine flora and fauna. The main dominating influence on the sea temperature, and on much of our climate, is the current known as the North Atlantic Drift or, more popularly, as the Gulf Stream. This current originates in the Gulf of Mexi-

The sea contains a soup of tiny planktonic creatures which move with the tides. There are two types of plankton – zooplankton, mainly the larvae of larger marine animals, and phyto-plankton or marine algae

co, derived from the forces produced by the rotation of the earth, and it sweeps warm water across the Atlantic onto the west coast of Britain. The whole west coast is bathed with warm water, contributing to the milder, wetter weather experienced by these areas. The current carries on northwards, round the top of Scotland, to be diverted southwards into the North Sea, cooling steadily as it goes. Eventually it meets the flow of water coming northwards from the English Channel area. Thus the west coast of Britain supports many Atlantic marine species, some of which extend into north-east Scotland, while the south-west coasts are just warm enough for a few south-west European (or Lusitanian) species. The North Sea is generally cooler and, being cut off from the Atlantic influence, has a different, and generally poorer, flora and fauna. The English Channel is a place of graduated change, with Atlantic and Lusitanian species extending eastwards as far as their tolerance of changing salinity and temperature allows; a marked change occurs around the Isle of Wight area.

The plant and animal life of the sea falls roughly into two groups; the pelagic species which float or swim freely in the water, and the benthic group – the members of which live attached or very close to the sea-bed. The pelagic creatures are further divided into plankton which are wholly dependent on currents for their movements, and nekton which are strong enough swimmers to move where they want, resisting current movements if necessary. The latter include the pelagic fishes, such as herring or mackerel. The most important primary producers of food in the sea are the tiny free-floating plants known as phytoplankton which are mainly small forms of algae. In the relatively shallow, well-lit, nutrient-rich waters of the Continental shelf, these grow and reproduce rapidly utilising energy from sunlight and converting it into organic materials. Increased production of phytoplankton in the spring is soon followed by an eruption of herbivorous zooplankton (small, floating, plant-eating animals) which feed on the plant matter. Both the phytoplankton and the developing zooplankton (many of which are the tiny larvae of much larger marine creatures) are fed upon by larger herbivorous or carnivorous sea creatures, which may themselves be prey to larger carnivores, as food chains in the sea tend to be particularly long (below).

Most people only see the few marine organisms washed up on the shore, most have never seen the marine life that occurs below the low-tide mark around our shores, and it is often assumed that the teeming life seen in pictures is only associated with tropical waters. In reality, the clearer waters around our coasts support a tremendous density of life, in many different forms, as exotic and colourful as anything to be seen elsewhere. Particularly favourable areas, such as the seas around Lundy in the Bristol Channel, or the Isles of Scilly south-west of Land's End, are of exceptional interest, and the former has become our first Marine Nature Reserve.

The Marine Ecosystem

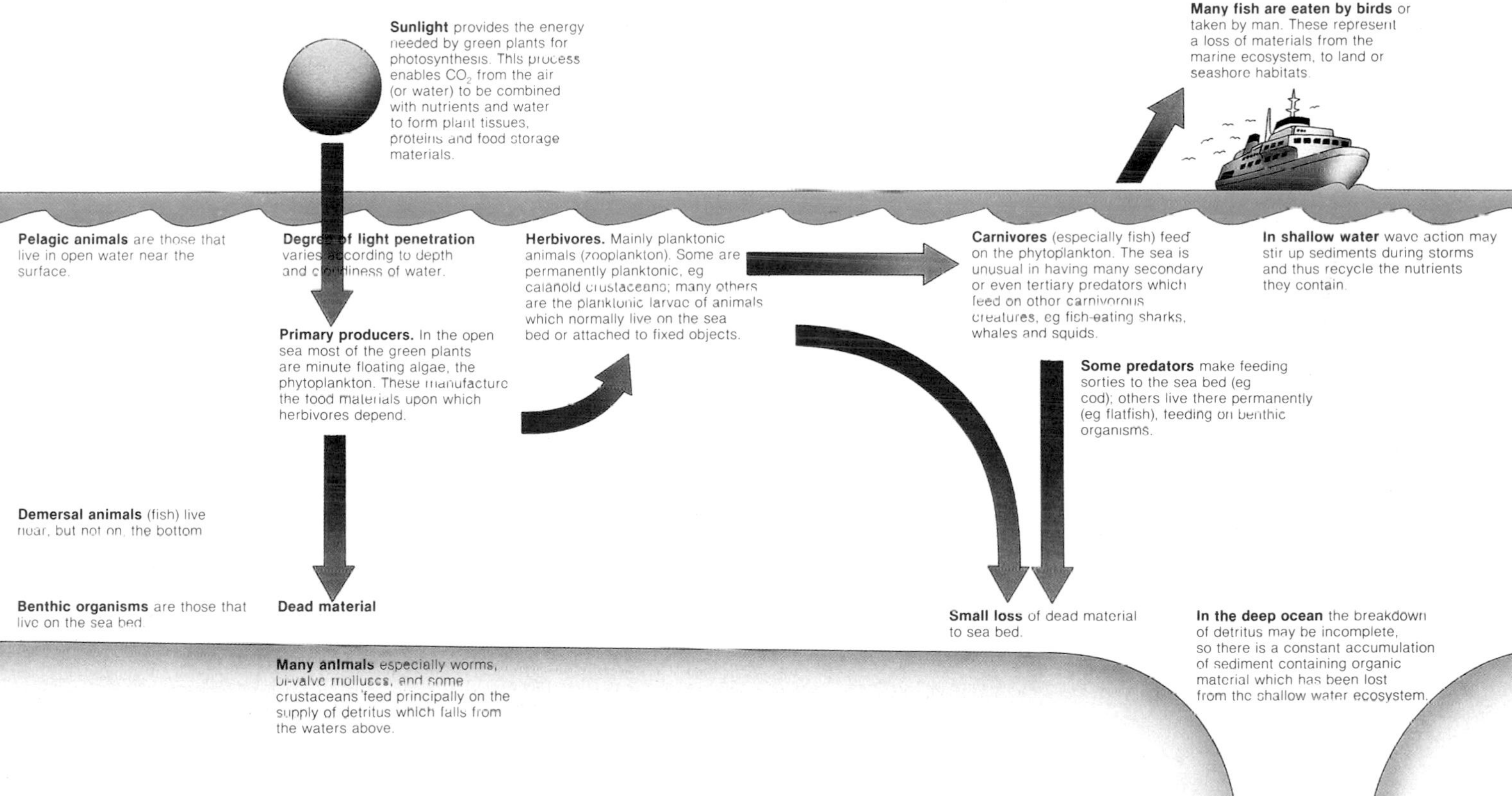

Sunlight provides the energy needed by green plants for photosynthesis. This process enables CO_2 from the air (or water) to be combined with nutrients and water to form plant tissues, proteins and food storage materials.
Many fish are eaten by birds or taken by man. These represent a loss of materials from the marine ecosystem, to land or seashore habitats.
Pelagic animals are those that live in open water near the surface.
Degre f light penetration varies ccording to depth and c iness of water.
Herbivores. Mainly planktonic animals (zooplankton). Some are permanently planktonic, eg calanoid crustaceans; many others are the planktonic larvae of animals which normally live on the sea bed or attached to fixed objects.
Carnivores (especially fish) feed on the phytoplankton. The sea is unusual in having many secondary or even tertiary predators which feed on other carnivorous creatures, eg fish-eating sharks, whales and squids.
In shallow water wave action may stir up sediments during storms and thus recycle the nutrients they contain.
Primary producers. In the open sea most of the green plants are minute floating algae, the phytoplankton. These manufacture the food materials upon which herbivores depend.
Some predators make feeding sorties to the sea bed (eg cod); others live there permanently (eg flatfish), teeding on benthic organisms.
Demersal animals (fish) live near, but not on, the bottom
Benthic organisms are those that live on the sea bed
Dead material
Small loss of dead material to sea bed.
In the deep ocean the breakdown of detritus may be incomplete, so there is a constant accumulation of sediment containing organic material which has been lost from the shallow water ecosystem.
Many animals especially worms, bi-valve molluscs, and some crustaceans feed principally on the supply of detritus which falls from the waters above.

The ecosystem of the sea, shown here in a simplified diagram, is a complex and fragile network of interdependence. The slightest interference, from pollution for example, can lead to its total break down

FARMLAND

About four-fifths of the British countryside could be classed as farmland, so this type of land plays an important role in maintaining our wildlife heritage. However, this figure is somewhat misleading it includes many areas of land which are not really farmed.

The farmed countryside of Britain is an historic patchwork, reflecting the piecemeal clearances from the ancient 'Wildwood' which have been going on for thousands of years. It is a mosaic of arable fields, leys, pastures, orchards, copses and waste land, linked together into an interconnecting system by virtue of endless kilometres of hedgerows, lanes and roadside verges. Apart from the areas of distinct natural habitat, like the woodlands, it is the hedgerows that are the most vital part of the farmland system for wildlife. They allow animals, and even plants, to move freely from place to place, as well as supporting many resident species.

The most obviously farmed area is the arable land, which makes up about one-third of the countryside. This is the land that is regularly ploughed and seeded for growing annual crops or short-lived grass leys. It is very intensively used, often producing more than one crop per year, and most such areas receive liberal doses of fertilisers and pesticides throughout the year. Almost all plants and animals are viewed as competition to the main crop, so the management of such areas is designed to reduce their numbers. It is inevitable, therefore, that arable land is the poorest area of the countryside for wildlife, though at times – when the spraying programme is mis-timed for example – they can become a riot of colour as the amazingly resilient poppy appears in vast numbers. Not so long ago, these crop fields supported a wonderful display of arable weeds – all perfectly adapted to regular disturbance – and it would be no surprise to find 40 or 50 different species in a field. Nowadays, the combination of better seed-cleaning and programmes of herbicide use, has reduced their numbers drastically and many have become great rarities. Few insects survive in arable land because there is little or no food-plants bar the crop, and those that feed on this are the target of regular sprays of powerful insecticides to prevent their numbers multiplying. Likewise, the intensity of use of the land prevents all but a few birds from breeding in arable fields, though some, like the rooks and woodpigeons, will feed on almost any type of crop whenever they can.

Rather more hospitable are the pasturelands, areas of 'permanent' grassland that may have never been ploughed, but which nowadays are usually reseeded every few years. They were once the home of a wide range of plants and animals, including many of our most attractive flowers, but most are now treated with regular doses of fertiliser which improves the grass growth and wipes out the more attractive species. In less intensively farmed areas, such as on

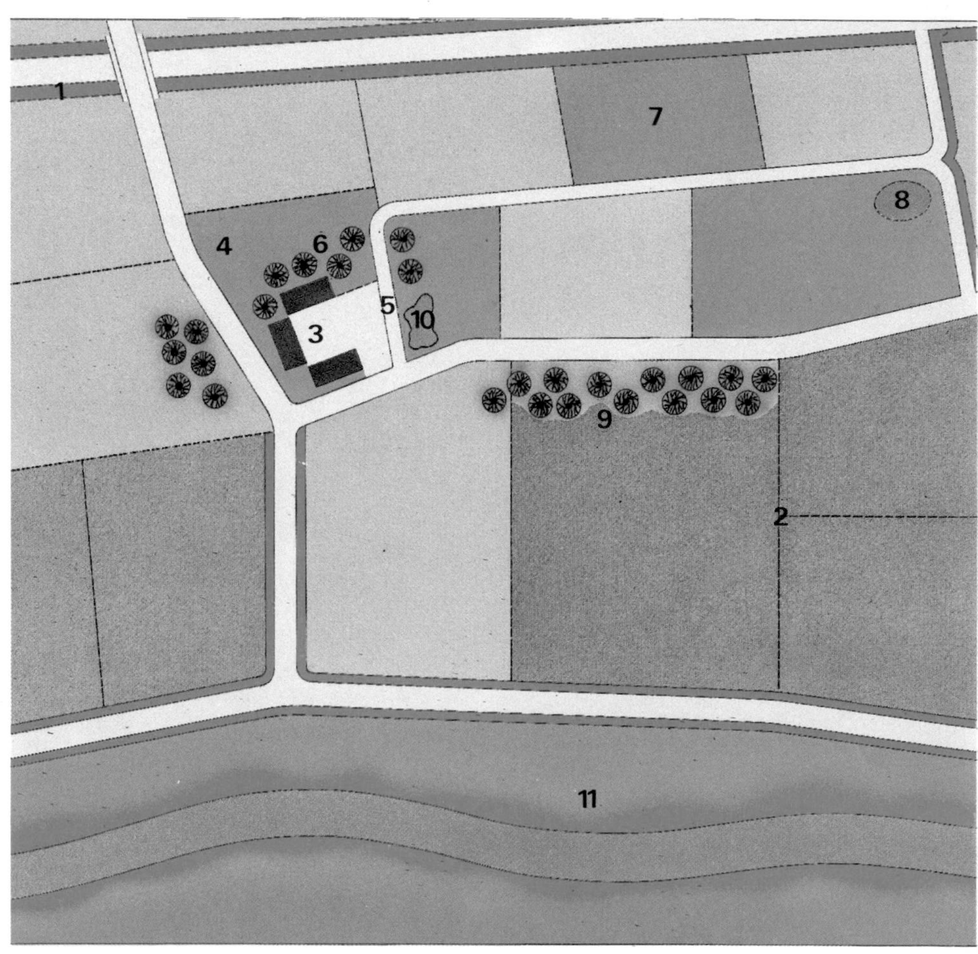

Above are the habitats and ecology of a generalised farm.
1. Hedges on the farm perimeter
2. Internal hedges or fences
3. The farm buildings
4. Grassland paddocks next to the farm
5. Tracks and tracksides, good for weeds
6. Trees near farm, good for rooks
7. Permanent grassland, better for flowers and birds
8. Dew pond, good for wildlife
9. Copses, often rich in birds and mammals
10. Main farm pond
11. Flood meadows by river, too wet to plough

steep hillsides or on very wet soil, the grassland may never be improved, and it is here that the most varied wildlife is to be found. Hay meadows, too, were once filled with flowers, but their area has declined, and those that are left tend to be more frequently ploughed and fertilised, greatly reducing the flora and fauna that once depended on them. Here and there, though, it is still possible to find a contaminated with fertiliser and pesticide run-off to offer a very rich habitat. Even the farmyard itself can be a good place for wildlife, with characteristic birds including collared doves and house sparrows, particular plants like pineapple weed and common mallow.

The make-up of farmland, and its value for wildlife, varies enormously throughout the country, depending on largely of arable land with few hedges or copses. As a result, its value for wildlife is low. In contrast, in areas where the topography makes ploughing difficult or the climate is unsuitable for arable farming, there tends to be a more intimate mixture of small fields with hedges and hedgerow trees, lanes, copses and unfarmed land, and these areas may have a rich and varied fauna and flora.

colourful, traditional hay meadow.

Other strands in the farmland web include farm ponds and dew ponds, which may be a haven for many birds, mammals, insects, flowers and amphibians; ditches and streams may support similar wildlife, though in most arable areas they become too soil, topography and climate. For example, much of East Anglia is low-lying and fertile, offering ideal conditions for cultivation, so it consists

Harvest time on the chalk of southern England. Nowadays, increasingly intensive agriculture means less and less wildlife in the fields themselves with more species depending on the hedges, woods and odd rough corners between the fields. Mechanisation of most operations has led to larger and larger fields

HEATHLANDS

Heaths are the lowland equivalent of upland moors – wide open areas of rough uncultivated land, dominated by heathers and gorse. They are amongst the wildest of our lowland habitats, familiar walking territory to most city-dwelling southerners, yet strangely they have all been created, by the activities of man, within the last few thousand years.

There is abundant evidence to show that the whole of lowland Britain including the present heathland areas, was well-wooded 7,000 or 8,000 years ago. Yet by Neolithic times, about 5,000 years ago, man was beginning to clear the woodland as grazing grounds and, later, for cultivation; and many of our heaths date from these early Neolithic and Bronze Age times. By late medieval times, there were vast areas of heathland over much of lowland Britain, though only relatively small areas remain today, mainly in Dorset, Hampshire, Surrey and East Anglia.

The main factor affecting the development of heathland was the soil. In areas where the underlying rock was acid, especially on free-draining rocks such as sands and gravels, the fertile ground that lay below the original woodland soon became infertile and acid once the protective covering of trees was removed. The most successful colonisers of these poor soils are the heathers, especially bell-heather and ling, which quickly dominate large areas, especially if the land is grazed or lightly burnt regularly. Once these heaths developed, they were well-used in historical times especially for grazing stock, as a source of bracken as bedding, or gorse as fuel and fodder (surprisingly many domestic stock can eat gorse, particularly when the spines are young).

More recently, heaths have been neglected as a resource, and grazing has ceased on virtually all of them except the New Forst in Hampshire which is large enough for the traditional system to have been maintained. When heaths are not grazed, on all except those on very poor soils such as in the Poole Basin in Dorset, birches and other trees soon begin to invade, followed, in due course, by oaks and other trees. An abandoned heath soon becomes a woodland, and this can be readily observed on most of the former Surrey heaths which are now birch or oak woodland. Today, most of the remaining heaths are publicly-owned as some form of nature reserve or public open space, and are carefully managed to keep their open character, retaining as many of the characteristic heathland plants and animals as possible.

Despite the fact that they are not natural, heathlands have their own special plants and animals, many of which occur nowhere else in Britain. Their open, unshaded nature and dry light soils means that they are very warm areas in spring and summer, and they are particularly favoured by species that mainly occur further south in Europe. Many insects, especially bees and wasps, favour warm sandy south-facing slopes on heaths, revelling in the warmth and using the light soil to make their nest-burrows.

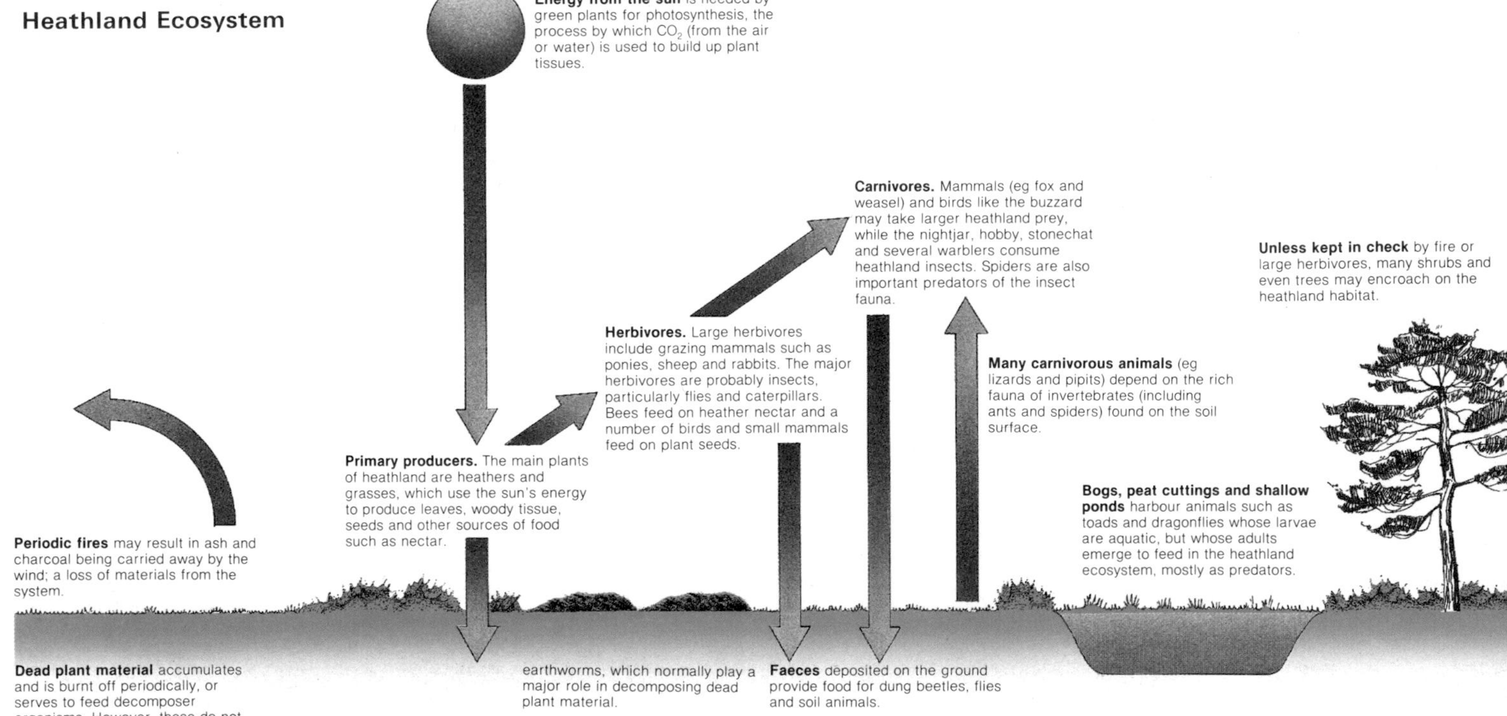

Heathland Ecosystem
Energy from the sun is needed by green plants for photosynthesis, the process by which CO_2 (from the air or water) is used to build up plant tissues.
Carnivores. Mammals (eg fox and weasel) and birds like the buzzard may take larger heathland prey, while the nightjar, hobby, stonechat and several warblers consume heathland insects. Spiders are also important predators of the insect fauna.
Unless kept in check by fire or large herbivores, many shrubs and even trees may encroach on the heathland habitat.
Herbivores. Large herbivores include grazing mammals such as ponies, sheep and rabbits. The major herbivores are probably insects, particularly flies and caterpillars. Bees feed on heather nectar and a number of birds and small mammals feed on plant seeds.
Many carnivorous animals (eg lizards and pipits) depend on the rich fauna of invertebrates (including ants and spiders) found on the soil surface.
Primary producers. The main plants of heathland are heathers and grasses, which use the sun's energy to produce leaves, woody tissue, seeds and other sources of food such as nectar.
Bogs, peat cuttings and shallow ponds harbour animals such as toads and dragonflies whose larvae are aquatic, but whose adults emerge to feed in the heathland ecosystem, mostly as predators.
Periodic fires may result in ash and charcoal being carried away by the wind; a loss of materials from the system.
Dead plant material accumulates and is burnt off periodically, or serves to feed decomposer organisms. However, these do not
earthworms, which normally play a major role in decomposing dead plant material.
Faeces deposited on the ground provide food for dung beetles, flies and soil animals.

The heathland ecosystem, shown here in a simplified diagram, has been created by man over the last few thousand years through the clearance of woodland for grazing. Only small areas of lowland heathland now survive in southern England

A view of heathland on the sandy soils of the Isle of Purbeck, Dorset. The soils in this area are highly infertile and very acid, and plants other than heathers have difficulty in colonising, though pines are often planted in such soils. In the foreground there is a group of self-sown pines

All our native reptiles occur on heaths – they are particularly famous for adders, for example – and two rarities, the sand lizard and the elusive smooth snake, are virtually confined to heaths in Britain. Several birds, including some very rare species, particularly favour heathland among them the Dartford warbler, the stonechat, the red-backed shrike (now almost extinct in Britain), the nocturnal nightjar and that dashing falcon, the hobby. There are even a few plants that are particularly characteristic of heaths. Ling and bell-heather are found on almost every heath but, in a few places, there are much rarer heathers such as the Dorset heath and the Cornish heath. Other special plants include the beautiful wild gladiolus found in the New Forest, marsh gentian in wetter areas and the strange pink flowers and stems of the totally parasitic plant, dodder which twines its way over gorse and heather bushes, extracting its food from them as it goes.

Heaths are something of an oddity amongst Britain's natural habitats in that their value is as much in their uniformity as their diversity. To find large areas just dominated by one or two species of plant is a rarity in Britain, and though heathland may not be as varied or as rich in species as a wood or a lake, its value lies in the number of especially adapted species which only occur here. Because heaths were marked on early maps, including the first Ordnance Survey maps at the beginning of the 19th century, we can easily work out how much heathland there used to be and how it has declined over the last two centuries. Sadly, the conclusions are that it has declined dramatically, and we have only a fraction of our once-extensive heaths left. This, in turn, has put great pressure on those species that depend upon these areas for their survival, and many have become rare or even extinct as a result.

GRASSLAND AND DOWNLAND

The word grassland usually conjures up images of uniformly green swards in farmland or on playing fields. Many grasslands, though, have a particularly varied flora and fauna, and it is not unusual to find over 100 different flowers in one field or down.

Grass grows exceptionally well in the moist, mild climate of the British Isles, and wherever land is grazed or mown, the vegetation is almost certain to be dominated by grasses. Unlike most plants, grasses have the special quality of being able to grow continuously both from the base and along the length of the leaves, so that whenever they are cut or bitten off, they are able to regrow, except in the coldest or driest of weathers. This means that grasses can out-compete most other plants in such situations, and therefore large areas become dominated by grasses forming lawns, meadows, pastures or downland. Oddly, grassland is not a natural habitat in Britain, and it only occurs where the tree-cover has been removed and is kept clear by mowing or grazing, yet fields of lush green grass make up one of the most familiar scenes in the countryside.

Despite their apparent uniformity, grasslands are immensely variable and they contain within them a complex community. Agriculturally (and almost all our grasslands are used agriculturally), grasslands can be classified into pastures which are grazed by stock; meadows which are cut for hay, though they may then be grazed; and leys which are more like arable land as they are ploughed and reseeded very frequently and most often used for silage. From the natural history point of view, although the type of mowing or grazing has some effect, the natural communitites are equally affected by soil characteristics, slope, drainage and other factors. Unfortunately, though, the most dominant factor nowadays in grassland composition is the amount of fertiliser or herbicide which is applied and the intensity of management. A semi-natural grassland that has developed over hundreds of years of grazing or mowing, without addition of artificial chemicals, is a complex community of many different plants – often over 100 in a single field with many associated insects and other invertebrates. However, the addition of fertiliser promotes the growth of a few species of palatable grass, and kills off all the attractive broad-leaved herbs – the flowers – leaving a monotonous green sward devoid of flowers and insects. Herbicides have the same effect, because they either kill off

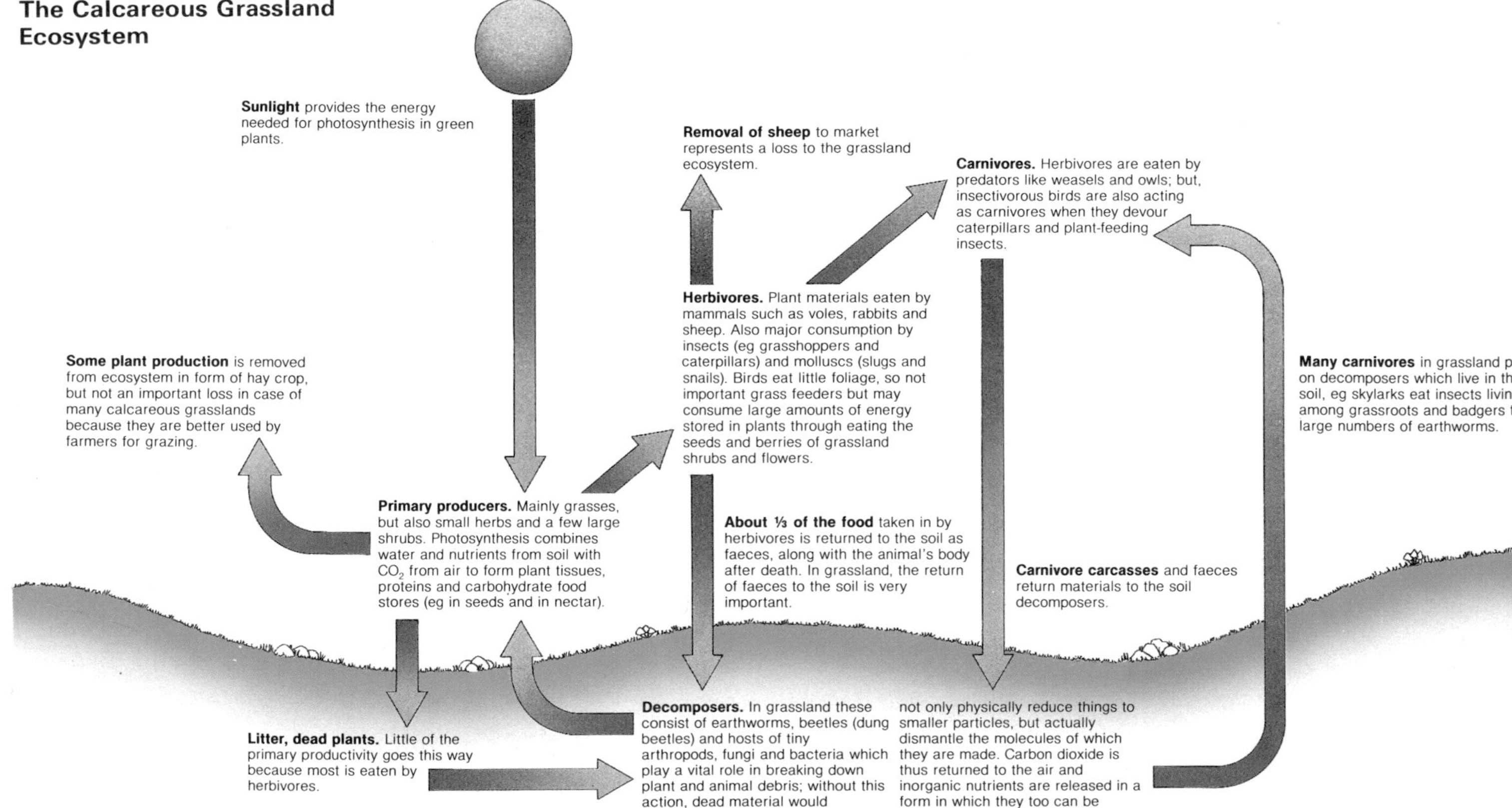

The Calcareous Grassland Ecosystem
Sunlight provides the energy needed for photosynthesis in green plants.
Removal of sheep to market represents a loss to the grassland ecosystem.
Carnivores. Herbivores are eaten by predators like weasels and owls; but, insectivorous birds are also acting as carnivores when they devour caterpillars and plant-feeding insects.
Herbivores. Plant materials eaten by mammals such as voles, rabbits and sheep. Also major consumption by insects (eg grasshoppers and caterpillars) and molluscs (slugs and snails). Birds eat little foliage, so not important grass feeders but may consume large amounts of energy stored in plants through eating the seeds and berries of grassland shrubs and flowers.
Some plant production is removed from ecosystem in form of hay crop, but not an important loss in case of many calcareous grasslands because they are better used by farmers for grazing.
Many carnivores in grassland pre on decomposers which live in the soil, eg skylarks eat insects living among grassroots and badgers ta large numbers of earthworms.
Primary producers. Mainly grasses, but also small herbs and a few large shrubs. Photosynthesis combines water and nutrients from soil with CO_2 from air to form plant tissues, proteins and carbohydrate food stores (eg in seeds and in nectar).
About ⅓ of the food taken in by herbivores is returned to the soil as faeces, along with the animal's body after death. In grassland, the return of faeces to the soil is very important.
Carnivore carcasses and faeces return materials to the soil decomposers.
Litter, dead plants. Little of the primary productivity goes this way because most is eaten by herbivores.
Decomposers. In grassland these consist of earthworms, beetles (dung beetles) and hosts of tiny arthropods, fungi and bacteria which play a vital role in breaking down plant and animal debris; without this action, dead material would accumulate steadily. Decomposers not only physically reduce things to smaller particles, but actually dismantle the molecules of which they are made. Carbon dioxide is thus returned to the air and inorganic nutrients are released in a form in which they too can be reabsorbed by living plants.

A simplified diagram illustrating the way in which grazing animals, such as rabbits and sheep, maintain the grassland ecosystem

everything prior to reseeding with grasses only or selectively kill off the broad-leaved herbs leaving just the grasses.

Where near-natural grasslands do occur, away from intensive agricultural improvements, they are wonderful places full of colour and life. Old undisturbed hay meadows are probably the most beautiful; the peak of flowering occurs just before the hay is cut in midsummer with ox-eye daisies, clovers, dandelions, orchids, bugle, selfheal and many others vie with each other for light.

Pastures can be of many different types. They are usually found on soil that is unsuitable for ploughing as arable or mowing for hay, so are rich assemblage of butterflies – especially the blue species – which feed on various downland plants such as horseshoe or kidney vetch. Other pastures include small damp fields, often enclosed by old stock-proof hedges, which come alive in spring and summer with colourful wetland flowers like kingcups, yellow iris, ragged-robin and marsh orchids. Other interesting grasslands occur on common land, where ancient rights allow local people to graze their animals and social circumstances have prevented them from being agriculturally improved. There are even a few common lands that are cut annually for hay, with the produce being shared amongst the commoners, and these are exceptional for their rare flowers.

If a grassland is not mown or grazed regularly, it very quickly becomes rough and tussocky and is soon invaded by shrubs and trees, especially if there is a wood nearby as a source of seed. There are many areas of old chalk or limestone downland that are now either a dense scrub of dogwood, spindle, buckthorn and other bushes, or a mixture of rough grassland and scrub. Such places have lost many of their original downland plants and butterflies which only thrive where the turf is very short, but have usually gained small mammals and birds which make use of the food and cover; they also support a different range of in-

The beautiful rolling downland of southern England is a totally artificial habitat maintained by grazing.

If the sheep and rabbits are removed it soon becomes 'scrubbed-up' shading out the low growing flowers

generally in damp places or on the steeper, less accessible slopes. Downlands, which are a type of pasture, are the wide open grasslands that occur on dry chalk or limestone hills usually grazed by sheep. They are notable for their wonderful range of flowers, particularly orchids, and a

sects which prefer the taller grasses and the shelter provided by the bushes. Eventually, such areas turn into secondary woodland with the loss of all the grassland species. This often happens when an area of downland sits in the middle of an arable farm without stock to graze it.

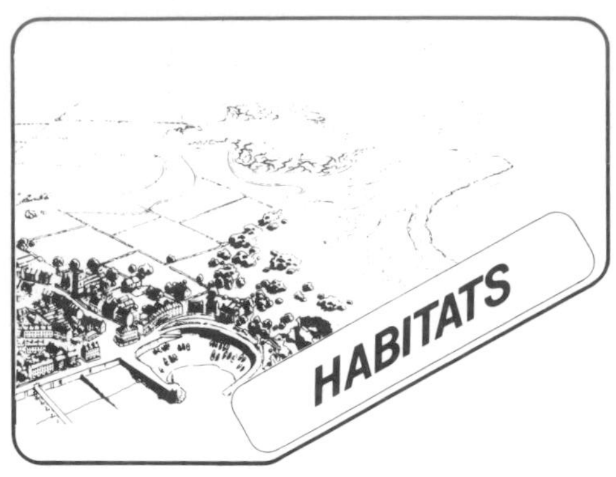

THE UPLANDS

In contrast to the gentle low-lying lands of south and east Britain, most of the north and west of the British Isles consists of a dramatic landscape of rugged hills and mountains. Virtually all of our National Parks are in the uplands, an indication both of the value we put on upland scenery and its relatively unspoilt nature.

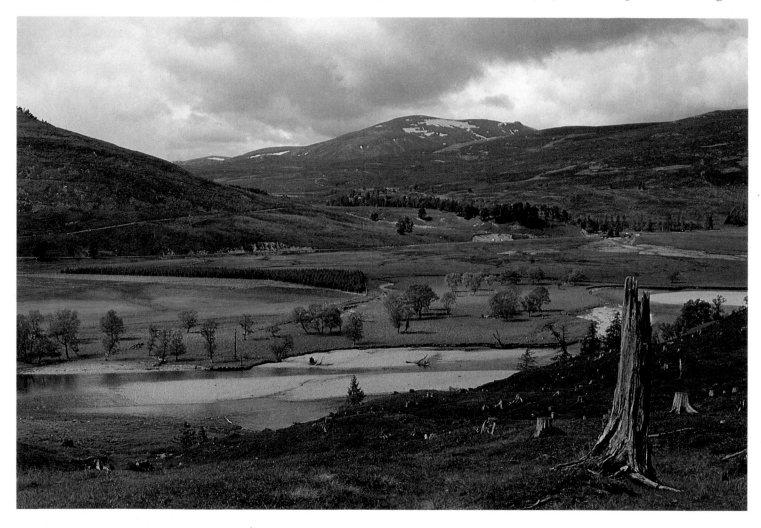

The word uplands does not have a strict definition. Roughly speaking we could consider it to be land lying above 500 metres, but this rule cannot be followed too precisely because land well below this level in the north of Scotland may be more upland in character than much higher land in the south-west of England. The most significant point is that the uplands are characterised by a cold, frequently wet climate with regular winter snow cover, an open treeless aspect and an uncultivated nature. We call the highest and steepest parts of the uplands 'mountains', though none of our hills reach any great height, and the few which exceed 1200 metres are mere pimples when compared to the Alps or Himalayas. Nevertheless, they have a character all their own, and the plants and animals that occur there have to be adapted to a severe winter climate and a very short summer growing season. There are many special species that are found only in the uplands.

Despite their remarkably natural appearance, the uplands of Britain are, in a sense, man-made. Six thousand years ago, all the uplands as high as the natural tree line (which was at least as high as 700 metres in places) were wooded, thinning out at the higher levels to an open, stunted forest of dwarfed birches, pines or junipers and then dwarf shrubs such as willows or wild azaleas. From mesolithic times onwards, and especially by the Iron Age, man had begun to clear these woodlands. It appears that early man was particularly attracted to these upper wooded areas, probably because they were less dense and easier to clear by fire in the absence of axes, and the resultant clearings proved to be good for gath-

The upper reaches of the Dee Valley, above Braemar, with the Cairngorms behind still with snow on the high peaks in mid-June

ering concentrations of game animals. Later other areas were cleared for cultivation or as pasture, to drive out wolves or for timber. Unlike most British trees, the pines which covered most of Scotland do not regrow from cut stems, so the woodland cover did not reappear. The woods could have recovered by a combination of regeneration from seed and coppice regrowth for those species that were able to do so, but most of the uplands were kept clear of trees by a combination of heavy grazing of sheep and cattle, coupled with deer, and by burning; the worsening climate also tended to make tree growth less likely and encouraged peat formation.

Nowadays, our uplands consist primarily of vast areas of moorland and bog, with cliffs and screes where harder rocks protrude and lakes wherever the climate is wet enough.

Because the uplands have changed so much in historical times and have been so intensively grazed and burnt, we have lost much of our native mountain wildlife over the millennia. Both our flora and fauna in these areas are much poorer than in equivalent areas elsewhere in Europe as the changes have forced the original species out, and there has been little chance for new species to colonise. Nevertheless, there are still specialised mountain species, mostly survivors from just after the Ice Age, or new colonisers from the lowlands that have adapted to the harsh conditions in the hills. As far as mammals and birds are concerned, one of the dominating features of the upland countryside is the amount of space and the lack of disturbance. It is the only place left where birds with huge territories – like golden eagles – or very shy mammals such as the native wildcat can occur. The density of animals in the uplands is usually low, but they include some of our most attractive species, as well as some of our rarest.

The flowers of the mountains do not, on the whole, compare with the famous floral displays in mountain ranges of the Pyrenees or Alps. Most mountain plants tend to favour open, lime-rich conditions and not too much grazing, so the extensive peaty moors and heavy grazing do not suit them. Here and there, however, where conditions are just right, there are real natural rock gardens such as on the Ben Lawers range in central Scotland where a lime-rich mica-schist rock produces a series of soft cliffs covered with masses of alpine flowers. Such outcrops of rock occur elsewhere, but they are rare, colourful gems in a rather impoverished landscape.

The Upland Ecosystem

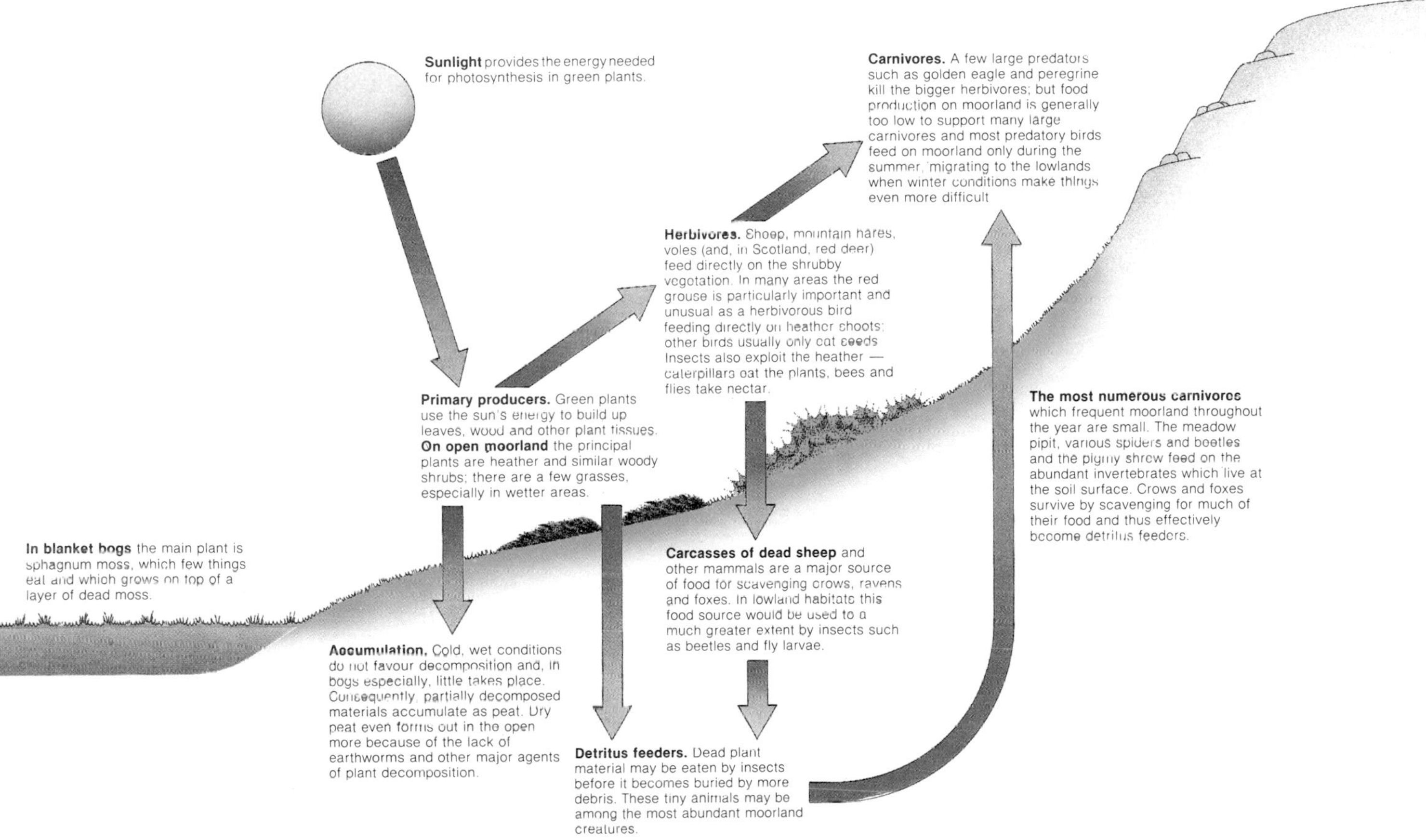

Sunlight provides the energy needed for photosynthesis in green plants.
Carnivores. A few large predators such as golden eagle and peregrine kill the bigger herbivores; but food production on moorland is generally too low to support many large carnivores and most predatory birds feed on moorland only during the summer, migrating to the lowlands when winter conditions make things even more difficult
Herbivores. Sheep, mountain hares, voles (and, in Scotland, red deer) feed directly on the shrubby vegetation. In many areas the red grouse is particularly important and unusual as a herbivorous bird feeding directly on heather shoots; other birds usually only eat seeds. Insects also exploit the heather — caterpillars eat the plants, bees and flies take nectar.
Primary producers. Green plants use the sun's energy to build up leaves, wood and other plant tissues. **On open moorland** the principal plants are heather and similar woody shrubs; there are a few grasses, especially in wetter areas.
The most numerous carnivores which frequent moorland throughout the year are small. The meadow pipit, various spiders and beetles and the pigmy shrew feed on the abundant invertebrates which live at the soil surface. Crows and foxes survive by scavenging for much of their food and thus effectively become detritus feeders.
In blanket bogs the main plant is sphagnum moss, which few things eat and which grows on top of a layer of dead moss.
Carcasses of dead sheep and other mammals are a major source of food for scavenging crows, ravens and foxes. In lowland habitats this food source would be used to a much greater extent by insects such as beetles and fly larvae.
Accumulation. Cold, wet conditions do not favour decomposition and, in bogs especially, little takes place. Consequently partially decomposed materials accumulate as peat. Dry peat even forms out in the open more because of the lack of earthworms and other major agents of plant decomposition.
Detritus feeders. Dead plant material may be eaten by insects before it becomes buried by more debris. These tiny animals may be among the most abundant moorland creatures.

Natural woodlands are very few, though some do still remain. Most upland woods are planted because the moorlands have been seen as prime land for reafforestation, and now many of our largest conifer forests lie over former moorland.

A simplified diagram which gives just a hint of how the cold, and very unproductive upland ecosystem works

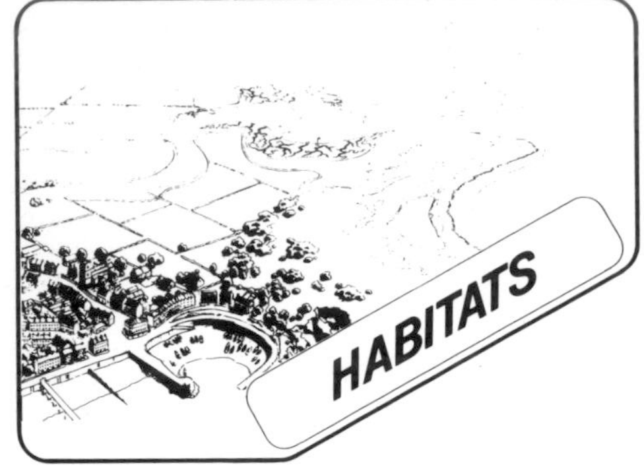

LAKES, PONDS AND RIVERS

Britain is by no means a dry country, and you are never far from open water of one sort or another be it lakes, ponds, rivers, canals, reservoirs or streams. These varying open water systems may support very different assemblages of wildlife according to their size, rate of flow, chemical nature of the water, depth and many other factors.

A lake or pond in southern Britain is one of the most favourable enviroments that we have for the existence of natural life. Water, of course, is constantly available, unlike most terrestrial habitats where it often becomes deficient in high summer just when it could be best used; nutrients are usually readily on offer, if the water is of the right chemical composition; and the temperature excesses of the outside air are smoothed out, as water warms and cools more slowly than air, so that aquatic organisms are spared the greatest heat of summer or the coldest weather of winter. Consequently, many of our freshwater bodies are teeming with life, and even a cubic centimetre of pond-water contains huge numbers of minute, but visible, aquatic organisms.

Still water bodies, however, are more complicated than they seem. One of the main reasons that so many organisms can survive our cold winters, and not be frozen solid, is due to an unusual property of water. Unlike most other substances, it becomes densest at 4° Centigrade, and is lighter either if it is warmer than this or if it is colder. Consequently, freezing water and ice both float to the top of water, and this ice forms from the top downwards rather than throughout the water. Thus a protective layer is formed which maintains the lower levels at about 4° Centigrade, except in prolonged, very cold weather when lower levels may begin to freeze. This property of water also accounts for another feature of still water bodies; in summer, the upper layers of a water body become warmer than those not reached by the sun, so they float on the colder water below. The warmer the upper layers, the more isloated they become from the colder layers below, as mixing is prevented and, in effect, two separate systems are formed with little interchange between them. For example, oxygen may become used up in the lower layers by the decomposers, but it will not be replaced from the oxygen-rich upper layers, so decomposition will cease, and similarly nutrients may be used up in the upper layers during periods of rapid growth of plants, yet will not be replaced from the nutrient-rich lower layers. This feature affects considerably the way in which the still water ecosystem works. In winter, the separation is broken, as the surface

The Ecosystem of Ponds and Lakes

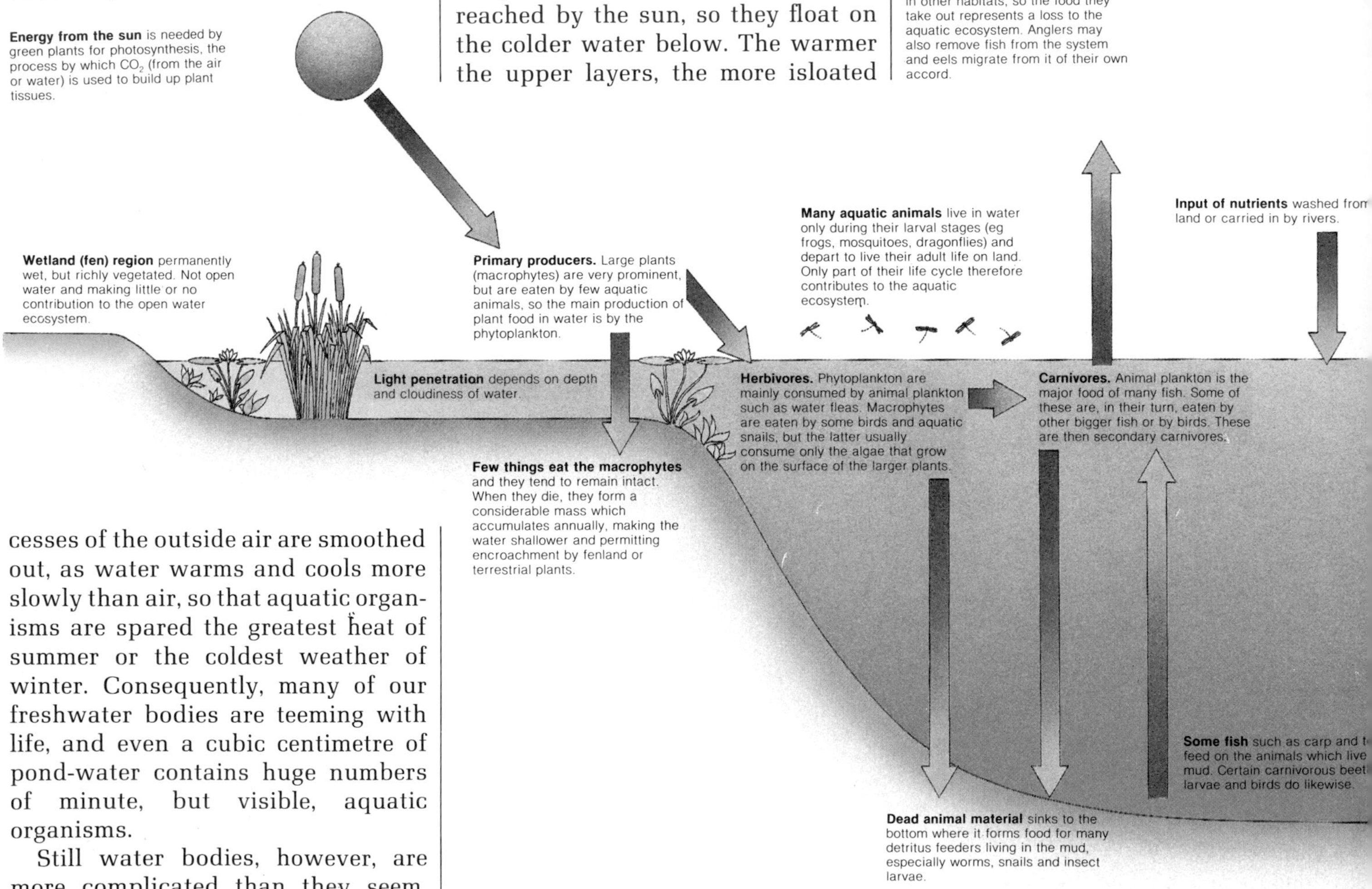

Energy from the sun is needed by green plants for photosynthesis, the process by which CO_2 (from the air or water) is used to build up plant tissues.

Wetland (fen) region permanently wet, but richly vegetated. Not open water and making little or no contribution to the open water ecosystem.

Primary producers. Large plants (macrophytes) are very prominent, but are eaten by few aquatic animals, so the main production of plant food in water is by the phytoplankton.

Light penetration depends on depth and cloudiness of water.

Few things eat the macrophytes and they tend to remain intact. When they die, they form a considerable mass which accumulates annually, making the water shallower and permitting encroachment by fenland or terrestrial plants.

Many aquatic animals live in water only during their larval stages (eg frogs, mosquitoes, dragonflies) and depart to live their adult life on land. Only part of their life cycle therefore contributes to the aquatic ecosystem.

Many fish are eaten by birds like the heron and osprey, or by otters and mink. These animals live and die in other habitats, so the food they take out represents a loss to the aquatic ecosystem. Anglers may also remove fish from the system and eels migrate from it of their own accord.

Input of nutrients washed from land or carried in by rivers.

Herbivores. Phytoplankton are mainly consumed by animal plankton such as water fleas. Macrophytes are eaten by some birds and aquatic snails, but the latter usually consume only the algae that grow on the surface of the larger plants.

Carnivores. Animal plankton is the major food of many fish. Some of these are, in their turn, eaten by other bigger fish or by birds. These are then secondary carnivores.

Some fish such as carp and t feed on the animals which live mud. Certain carnivorous beet larvae and birds do likewise.

Dead animal material sinks to the bottom where it forms food for many detritus feeders living in the mud, especially worms, snails and insect larvae.

A simplified diagram showing the way in which ponds and lakes cycle nutrients. Still waters can be productive habitats which supports many aquatic plants and animals

layers cool down rapidly, and winter storms cause mixing of the two levels to start the cycle again.

Although there are lakes and ponds everywhere in Britain, as a general rule, those in the south are largely of artificial origin such as reservoirs, gravel pits, farm ponds, industrial lakes and so on, whilst those in the north are largely natural. There are two reasons for this. Firstly, the whole of northern Britain has suffered more recent glaciation than the south, and this has tended to move surface material around causing depressions or blocking of valleys leaving an ideal surface for the formation of water bodies. Secondly, the climate of northern and western areas is such that the amount of rainfull exceeds the amount of water being evaporated (as it is both cooler and wetter), so water bodies do not gradually disappear. In contrast, in the south, the natural fate of any water body is to disappear as it dries out and becomes colonised by aquatic and later wetland plants.

Rivers are rather different and there are many species that only occur in these water forms, though they do share a large number of plants and animals with still freshwaters. The dominant feature is the rate of flow, which is usually faster in the uplands and slower in the lowlands, but life in rivers is also influenced by the chemical nature of the water (for example, whether it is acid or lime-rich), the type of rock over which it flows, the temperature of the water, in addition to man-induced features such as pollution, fish-farming and flood-control management. Rivers tend naturally to flood, and they carve very varied courses with deep areas, shallows, beaches, riffles and broad flood-plains; these are inclined to be richest in natural life because of the range of niches available. Many rivers, however, have been straightened, deepened and controlled to prevent flooding, and these usually have a much poorer flora and fauna. Canals tend to have a natural history rather similar to that of a slow-moving lowland river, with a rather low diversity of wildlife if it is well-used by boats, higher if it is infrequently used.

A lovely unpolluted river in the English Midlands, showing all the features that a good wildlife river should have, such as rich vegetation on the bankside

WETLANDS

In contrast to open waters (see pages 30–31), wetlands are areas of habitat that are decidedly wet but are mainly vegetated. They include marshes, bogs, fens and river-banks, but may also include habitats such as lake-fringing reedbeds which are midway between the two types.

Over much of the country, open water naturally gives way to wetland, as vegetation gradually colonises the water, and many wetlands are just stages in this natural procession of succession. Like many transitional habitats, they are very rich in species and notable for their displays of flowers, their breeding birds and their abundance of insects, especially the large attractive dragonflies and damselflies. There are many different types of wetland each with their own characteristic species.

Bogs are one of the most distinctive types of wetland. Wherever the ground water is very acid or the wetland is fed mainly by rainwater a bog develops. The acid conditions favour the growth of a limited range of plants, especially species like the bog mosses and cotton grass, but their dying remains do not decompose in this environment. Consequently, peat builds up consisting of layer after layer of slightly decomposed plant material, and the active, growing surface of the bog goes on moving upwards, often pulling the ground-water layer with it, so forming a sort of domed, raised bog. Although bogs tend to be rather poor in species, as few plants or animals can survive under such acid conditions, they do have a number of features of special interest. For example, most of the British species of insect-eating (insectivorous) plants occur in bogs – the sundews, butterworts and bladderworts – and this is almost certainly because this habit allows them to supplement their diet sufficiently to survive under these difficult conditions. Oddly enough, the acid water of bogs is the preferred habitat for many of our native dragonfly species, which choose to lay their eggs here rather than in seemingly more productive neutral, nutrient-rich waters.

Bogs are also interesting from an historical point of view. As the layers of peat build up over the centuries in a regular sequence, they trap debris from each age and this includes vast quantities of pollen and plant spores. These grains can later be identified and from the information it is possible to reconstruct the history of the vegetation in the area around the bog. This can reveal, for instance, when the nearby forests were first cleared or when cereal cultivation started, and in most cases quite accurate dates can be given for each event.

Fens are rather similar to bogs, but they occur where the ground-water is much richer in nutrients. They, too, develop on a peat formed from their own remains, but more decomposition takes place in the less acid conditions and the peat is less obviously made up of plant remains. These conditions favour plant growth more than bogs, and fens are noted for their range of colourful, and often rare, plants, with many associated insects. Fens are frequently found on water-logged river floor-plains, around the margins of infilling lakes and at springheads and seepages. Marshes are similar to fens and share much of the same wildlife; however, they lie directly on soil rather than peat and do not usually contain quite so many interesting species. River-banks are often similar in character to fens or marshes as the water from the river seeps outwards through the soil producing water-logged conditions.

Fens, bogs and marshes all provide suitable nesting habitat for several species of wading birds, especially redshanks, curlew and snipe; they are often good areas for water voles, otters and other wetland mammals.

Reedbeds are a particular type of wet habitat that can be midway between water and wetland. Many lakes, ponds and even estuaries become colonised by plants of the common or Norfolk reed, with its characteristic tall stems and feathery flower heads. Where conditions are suitable, it tends to dominate to the exclusion of virtually all other plants and for a period forms pure reedbeds. In saline conditions or where the reeds are harvested regularly for thatching, such as parts of the Norfolk

The Water's Edge

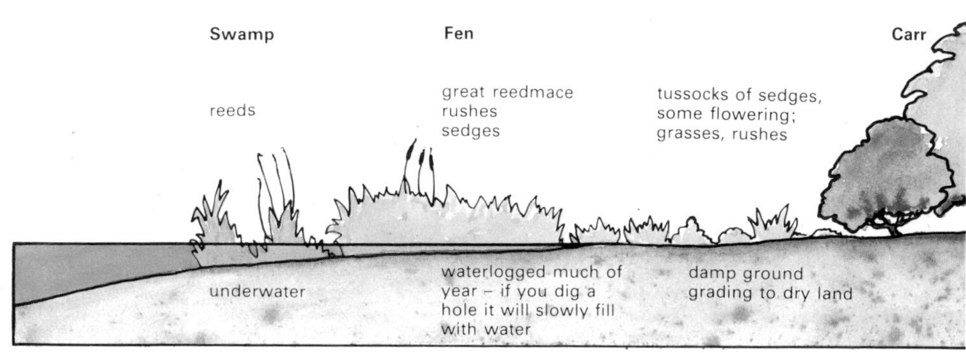

A diagram showing the way in which water bodies are gradually colonised by different plants. From open water a swamp forms where reeds grow with their lower half submerged. Further up the sedges, rushes and reedmace flourish forming a fen. Moving away from the open water the ground becomes dryer where sedges and some flowers grow. Eventually a 'carr' forms with scrub and trees being the dominant vegetation

Broads, these beds may last unchanged for ages. They are notable as breeding grounds for many birds like bearded reedlings, reed warblers, sedge warblers, bitterns and others. The insects that live on the leaves, especially aphids, provide an exceptional pre-migration food supply in autumn for numerous birds – wagtails, swallows, warblers – and many others frequently congregate in reeds to feed and roost, stoking up their fat reserved before the long journey south. Swallows may travel thousands of miles on migration to their breeding grounds in South Africa returning to the same area in this country every year.

Cranberry
Vaccinium oxycoccus

Bog rosemary
Andromeda polifolia

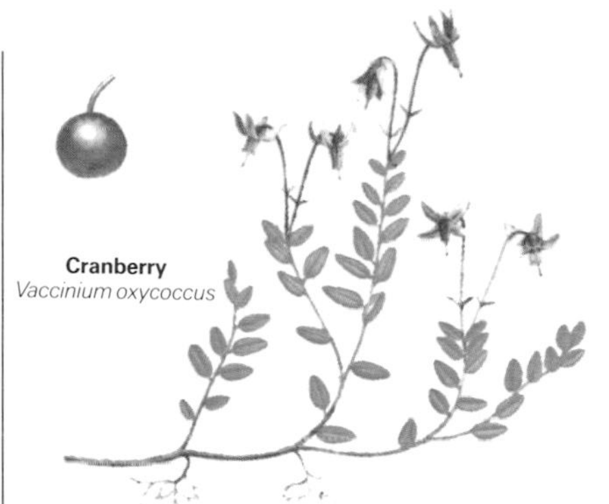

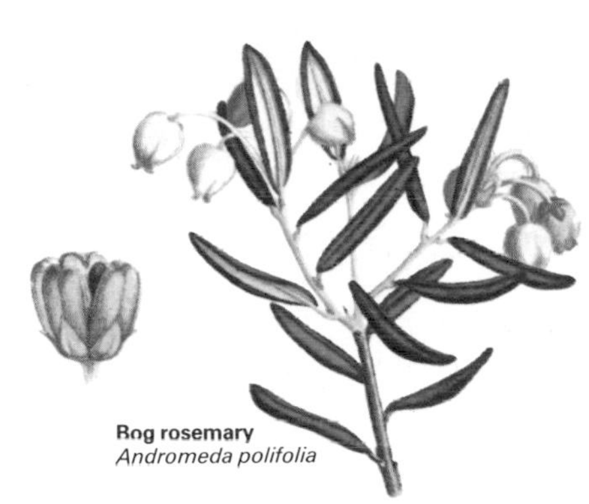

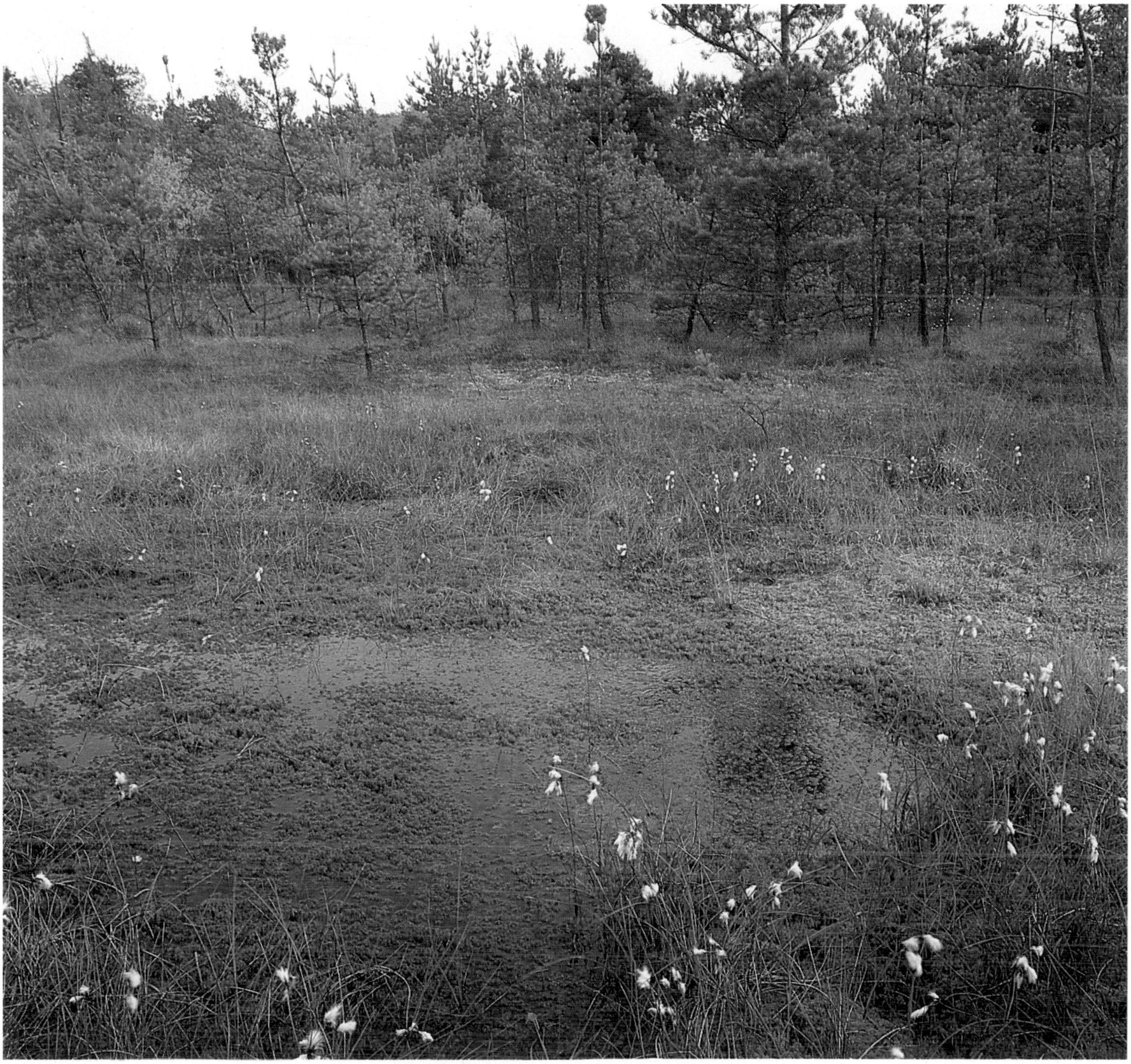

A bog surrounded by conifers and cotton grass. Sphagnum moss soaks up water like a sponge and can be seen here almost completely covering the surface like a blanket

TOWNS AND GARDENS

Although towns and gardens might seem, at first sight, to be one of the less attractive habitats for wildlife, on closer examination they turn out to be rich in species, with many common animals and birds at high densities, and even a few specialities of their own.

The urban habitat is, in reality, a very varied one. Only about half, or less, of the available area is built on, and the remainder is a fascinating mosaic of gardens, verges, parks, cemeteries, building sites, waste ground, dockyards and canals, whilst even the hard surfaces of buildings and pavements have some attractions for a few species. Many animals, such as foxes, occur at higher concentrations in towns and cities than they do in the countryside; while a survey of trees in Edinburgh revealed over one million trees at a much higher density than in the area around the city.

All gardens can support some wildlife, but specially designed, they can be particularly interesting habitats

Urban areas can never be suitable for those wild creatures that require wide open, undisturbed, spaces such as golden eagles or hen harriers, but a vast range of other animals and plants find the diversity, warmth and extra food much to their liking. There are even beekeepers who prefer to keep their bees in urban areas because there is much less risk of pollution or deaths from insecticides than in many parts of the countryside.

Perhaps the most important part of the built environment is the private garden. There are estimated to be at least one million gardens in Britain, a much bigger area than that managed as nature reserves, and many of these are havens for wildlife. The concentrated diversity of a garden and the deliberate attempts to keep plants in flower, together with the shelter and extra food provided, make for an exceptionally rich habitat, mimicking some of the richest natural areas, like the woodland edge, and in some ways better. Gardens vary enormously, of course, but they do not have to be large and rural to be interesting. For example one medium-sized suburban garden in Leicester that has been closely studied over the years revealed some remarkable statistics. Over a ten-year period, some 30,000 hoverflies of 91 different species were recorded; over 500 species of ichneumons (a sort of parasitic wasp) were noted in three years, while over 11,000 individuals of 21 different species of butterfly were caught and marked in a nine-year period. Even in this well-studied garden much probably escaped notice, and the possibilities for all the gardens in a large town or city are extraordinary.

Parks and other urban open spaces have some similarities with gardens, though they are usually more open and less sheltered, and have fewer flowers but more trees. Many parks have lakes of some sort, too, and these are often oases for wildlife, with wintering and breeding birds, flowers, amphibians and insects such as dragonflies. Even more highly managed boating lakes with concrete sides can prove interesting, and one such lake in Southampton, Hampshire, proved to be one of the richest sites for amphibians in the country, with all the British newts plus frogs and toads in large numbers. Larger parks, such as Richmond Park on the outskirts of London, or Sutton Park in the West Midlands (which are more like protected areas of countryside), tend to support many old trees which are something of a rarity now in the countryside. These may be homes to hole-nesting birds, roosting or breeding bats, wood-boring insects, fungi and many other interesting species. The main disappointment about parks, from the wildlife point of view, is that the grass is mown so closely and is sometimes even fertilised. This not only prevents new and different plants from coming into the turf, but also prevents butterflies from breeding, goldfinches from feeding on the seed-heads and other wildlife delights. If just a proportion of the grass could be left rougher, our parks would be even better.

An important feature of an interesting urban area is that the green areas should link up in some way. This allows species to gradually colonise new areas and extend their range, to move if conditions become unfavourable (as they often do, when derelict sites are built on, for example) and for the less committed urban-dwellers like badgers to move in temporarily to feed. Gardens make their own network, but this is greatly extended by linear featues such as railway lines, old canals and even motorways as all have rough margins and unobstructed routeways.

Finally, the buildings and hard surfaces themselves may add to the rich tapestry. Many birds, from kestrels and seabirds to swifts and house martins, will use buildings for nest-sites, often in large numbers. Bats roost more frequently in buildings than in natural sites, while starlings, pigeons and other birds make use of buildings as roosts. Less well-maintained buildings can also support an abundance of plants, from the pioneer lichens through to the pretty yellow Oxford ragwort.

An almost-aerial view of Lewes, East Sussex showing the high proportion of green, even behind terraced houses

AN INTRODUCTION TO

PLANT LIFE

Our British flora may not be the richest in the world, but it is, nevertheless, a diverse and fascinating blend of Arctic, Continental, Mediterranean and other species, together with a few that are specialities of the British Isles.

Islands often develop their own unique range of plants, but in Britain we have suffered a complete eradication of our flora during the Ice Ages, and there has not been time since for new species to evolve. Thus our flora consists mainly of those species that colonised while we were still attached to the mainland of Europe, up to 7,000 years ago, plus those that have come in after we became an island and a tiny proportion that have evolved enough to be considered new species. There are also flowers that do occur elsewhere but are at their best in Britain because the climate suits them so well; the bluebell, for example, is one of the glories of our woods and cliffs in late spring, but this would be an exceptional sight for anyone living outside Britain.

The British flora is constantly changing. The gradual fluctuation of climate has caused plants to come and go, and increasingly man's activities have led to the loss of habitat for a number of demanding species which as a result have become extinct in Britain. At the same time, though, new species are colonising. A few of these, such as some European orchids with their very light seeds, have recolonised naturally, but the great majority of new plants has come in with man for one reason or another. The Romans introduced many species deliberately, though many others came in accidentally, and the same process has been going on ever since – as food and garden plants, weeds, seeds in wool or on car tyres – and some have found conditions sufficiently to their liking for them to reproduce and spread. The Oxford ragwort, for example, originally introduced to Oxford Botanic Gardens from Sicily, has been able to find a completely new niche on walls, pavements and railway banks, and has spread throughout the country. This sort of naturalisation makes it difficult to say which plants are native and which are not. Most books on flowers include at least some of the obviously non-native species so long as they are well-established and able to spread naturally. Overall, our current flora stands at about 2,000 species of flowering plants (which includes grasses, sedges, trees and others that are often thought of as not having flowers), though it could be a lot higher if all the aliens and all the species in 'difficult' large groups like the dandelions are included. In any event, there is a wealth of interest for anyone venturing out to look at flowers, both in the countryside and in the town.

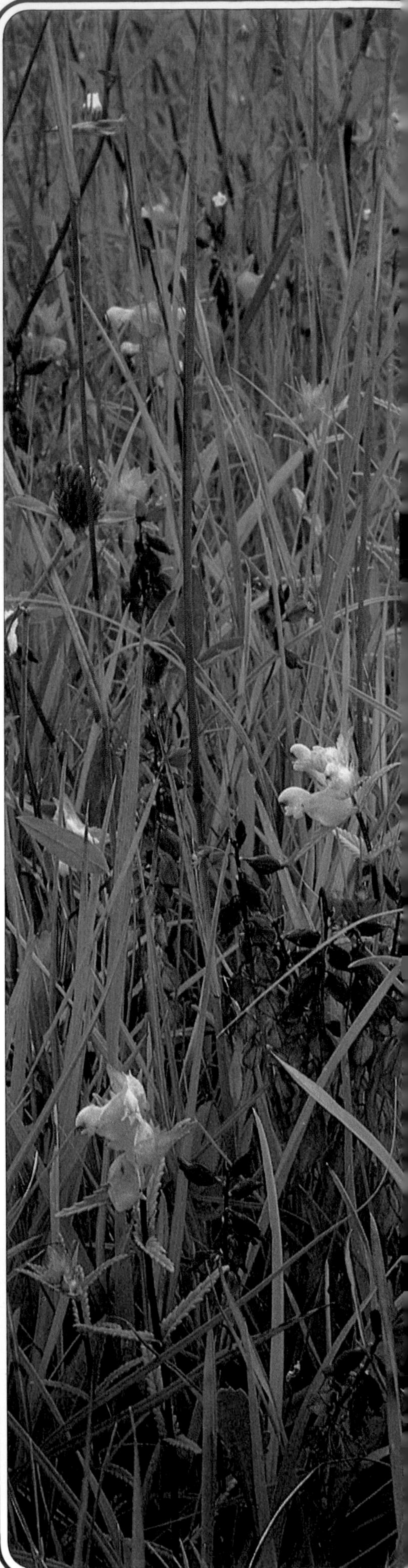

A dense mass of flowers in an ancient hay meadow in Oxfordshire

PLANTS

INCLUDING: Woodland • Grasses • Downland and Meadow •
Plants in, and Around Water • Heathland • Hedges •
Bog Plants • Mountain • Plants of Native •
Pinewoods • Seaweeds • Coastal
Flowers • Fungi • Shrubs
Mosses • Trees
Ferns

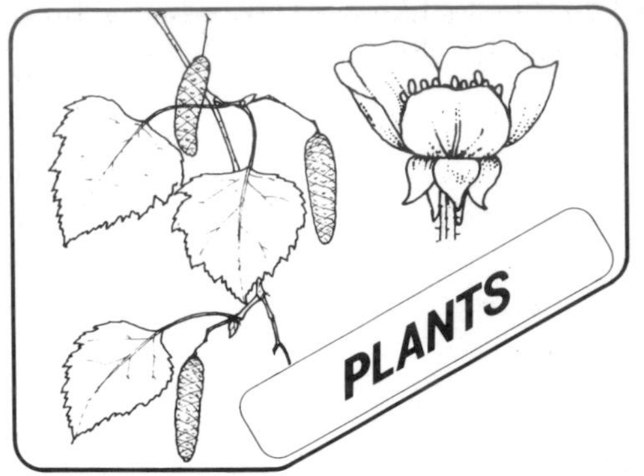

Earliest Woodland Flowers

Long before the short dark days of winter have given way to the light and warmth of spring, the first woodland flowers are beginning to bloom, apparently undeterred by frost, low light levels and even an occasional blanket of snow.

The first primroses or snowdrops are eagerly awaited each year as a sign that spring must be on the way at last – but why should some flowers bloom so early under these apparently harsh conditions, and with so few insect pollinators about? Collectively, these earliest spring woodland flowers are known as the pre-vernal or 'before spring' phase, and the main reason for their early-flowering behaviour lies in the seasonal patterns of the woodland habitat.

In summer, woods can be very dark places. Away from edges and glades, the amount of light reaching the woodland floor when the tree and shrub canopy is in full leaf is extremely low, even on sunny days at midday. You only have to try taking photographs in deep shade under these circumstances to discover just how dark it is! There are also very few insects about in the depths of the woodland at this time – most of the day-fliers are to be found along the rides, edges and glades where there is more sunshine. The majority of forest trees come into leaf in May, depending upon the species, with the commonest dominant tree – oak – being one of the latest; even after their leaves have begun to open, most trees do not develop their densest canopy for a few weeks. The advantages to flowering before this period are obvious therefore – there is much more light available to ground-dwelling plants in the weeks and months before tree leaves appear than there is afterwards. It might seem questionable why some species should flower as early as February, or even January, when the trees do not leaf out until April or May. The probable answer is that they avoid the intense competition for light and nutrients that occurs when the majority of woodland flowers are growing strongly in late April and May. By this time, woodland floors are usually covered with greenery, all growing and flowering strongly, whereas in late winter there

A selection of the earliest woodland flowers. Look out for the snowdrops before the snow is off the ground. Not much later you will see primroses and lesser celandine, followed by violets and the others shown here

is much less going on. Pollination at this early stage is not the problem it might appear to be. Although relatively few insects fly this early, any warm sunny day will bring out a few bumblebees, hibernating butterflies, bee-flies, winter gnats and others and, because there are so few plants in flower, they will soon be drawn to those that are, thus greatly increasing the chances of successful cross-pollination.

Amongst the earliest flowers each year are the snowdrops. These are reckoned to be native only in a few localities in south-west England, where they occur naturally in woods well away from houses. Elsewhere, they have usually been planted initially – though they will frequently spread vigorously on their own accord afterwards – and these may be of the native species or varieties brought in from elsewhere. Their hardiness, and the magnificent displays they species of violet, especially the scented sweet violet, in both blue and white forms, the common dog violet and the wood violet, all flower very early too. Violets have an interesting fail-safe mechanism by which they can produce seeds later in the year without producing normal flowers first; this ensures that the population is not hit too hard by an unusually cold spring. Primroses are amongst the earliest and most popular of woodland flowers, flowering well before the trees come into leaf. In south-west England, where the winters are milder, they are often in bloom in February, though elsewhere they appear in March or April. They are frequently accompanied by the white flowers of wood anemone, or windflowers as they are evocatively known, and by several rather less conspicuous flowers such as the green spikes of dog's mercury. At about the same time, there is a flower that looks like wild strawberry, but is actually the barren strawberry, a Potentilla rather than a true strawberry, with more silvery low-growing leaves and little gaps between the petals. Other familiar early flowers include the pussy willow, male catkins of the sallows, which often grow along the edges of woodlands.

Not all woods have the same range of flowers, by any means. There is a natural variation in the plants that occur in different parts of the country, depending on climate, but there is much more variation locally according to soils. These affect the flora both by influencing the trees that can form the wood, and by directly affecting the flowers on the woodland floor. For example ash, which is most likely to occur on calcareous soils, has a more open canopy which allows more flowers to succeed under it than beech which has a very dense canopy. Also, older woods are more likely to have a

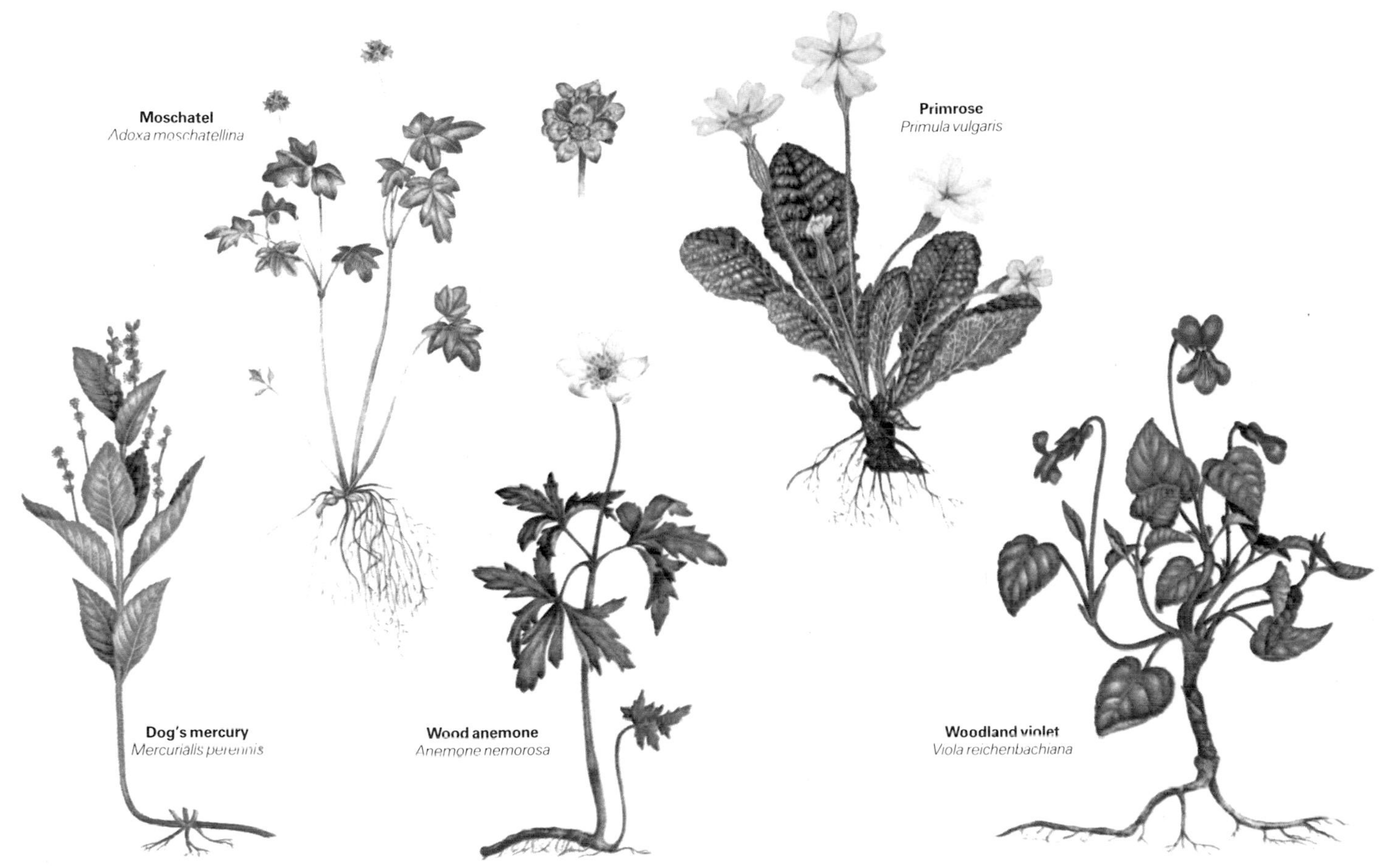

More early woodland flowers. The types of plants seen will vary across the country depending on the climate, soil type and the trees that form the wood

present so early in the year, often in January, account for their enormous popularity. They are followed soon afterwards by lesser celandines, close relatives of the buttercup, which are frequent in woods though by no means confined to them. Several

full range of these flowers than more recent woods or plantations. Many of these species are in fact indicators of old woodland particularly when they are seen growing in profusion. It may take centuries for these plants to become established in this way.

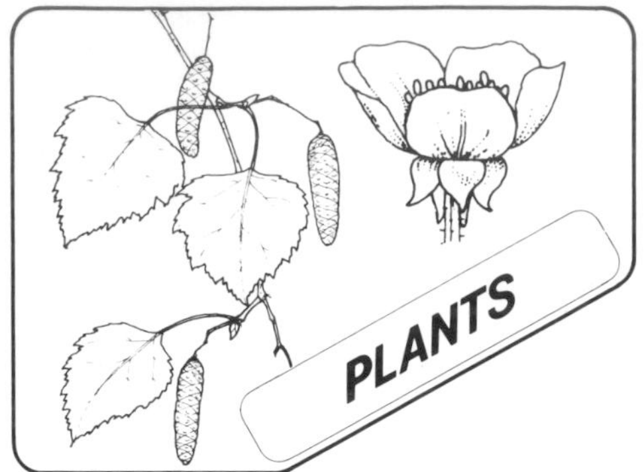

Spring Woodland Flowers

Spring is the perfect time for woodland flowers and it is during April and May that the blaze of colour is at its height. The blue haze of a mass of bluebells or the sheets of white made by ramsons are just two aspects of this exciting season.

By spring time, the great majority of woodland plants have come into flower reaching their peak in May in southern England, a little later further north. It is at this time that our woodlands look their best with colourful masses of bluebells, orchids, ramsons , yellow archangel and many other flowers in full bloom, together with the last remnants of the early spring flowers. This is the best time for woodland plants to flower, utilising the longest possible days and the most warmth, just before the light is blotted out by the dense summer leaf canopy. It is a time of tremendous activity in the wood, everything pulses with life, and insects are everywhere feeding on the flowers whenever the sun is shining.

Perhaps the most characteristic of all woodland flowers is the bluebell, growing in magnificent carpets of blue spreading throughout a whole woodland. It epitomises spring woodlands, but is also a special feature of the British Isles. The mild British climate, particularly towards the west, is ideal for the bluebell; its leaves are able to develop sufficiently in late winter before flowering to build up enough food reserves for the plant to flower and fruit so successfully. Over most of continental Europe it is a rarity, either because the winters are too cold or the summers are too hot and dry. Its below-ground bulbs allow it so survive from year to year, though it fails to spread into new woods, even when they are planted close to an existing old wood, and like certain other flowers (see below) it can be regarded as a good indicator of ancient woodland.

A dense carpet of bluebells under a canopy of beech and oak, making a glorious display of colour in May. Surprisingly, such a sight is virtually confined to Britain, as bluebells grow better here than almost anywhere else in the world

The mixture of plants that can occur in any woodland varies widely depending on the area, the soil and the age of the woodland. Most people will have noticed that some woods seem to be rich in flowers, whilst others are rather dull, and one of the most significant factors in determining this is the history of the woodland itself. Older woods, that have been in the same place for hundreds of years, have many more species of plants, in particular the characteristic woodland plants, than do newer woods. In our present climate, many plants are unable to spread from one wood to another, so any new wood that has arisen within the last few hundred years, whether naturally or by planting, fails to acquire many of the typical flowers. Looking at this the other way round, you find that you can also use certain plants as indicators of which woods are particularly ancient. If there is a range of such plants, for example yellow archangel, wood sorrel, Solomon's seal, bellflower and even the familiar bluebell, then you can be fairly certain that you are in an ancient wood, with a history stretching back many hundreds of years. More recent woods may have a few such flowers, but never more than a handful of species, or just confined to one area that might be more ancient than the remainder.

Some spring woodland flowers are particularly characteristic of certain soils. For example the beautiful lily-of-the-valley, with its nodding spikes of delicate white bells, is especially typical of woods on limestone, though it occurs on other soils less frequently. It is abundant in hard limestone areas in north-west England but rather rare elsewhere. Similarly, the strange flowers of herb Paris, with their striking-looking cross of four leaves below

the flower, are a feature of calcareous woods on chalk or limestone throughout the country. Other species, in contrast, prefer acid soils such as the little wood sorrel, with its delicate pinkish-white flowers and clover-like leaves, or the aromatic wood sage. Others, like the beautiful oxlip (a relative of cowslips and primroses) are confined to one area of the country, either for climatic reasons or because their preferred soil-type only occurs in one place. The true oxlips are restricted to East Anglia, centred on Suffolk, because it is only here that the chalky boulder clay, a legacy of a previous Ice Age, occurs. The false oxlip, which looks rather similar but is actually a hybrid between primroses and cowslips, occurs more widely wherever the two parents are found closeby.

Woodland plants in spring. A dazzling selection of the beautiful flowers you are likely to see in April and May. The variety of species found in any particular wood may be different as may their relative abundance

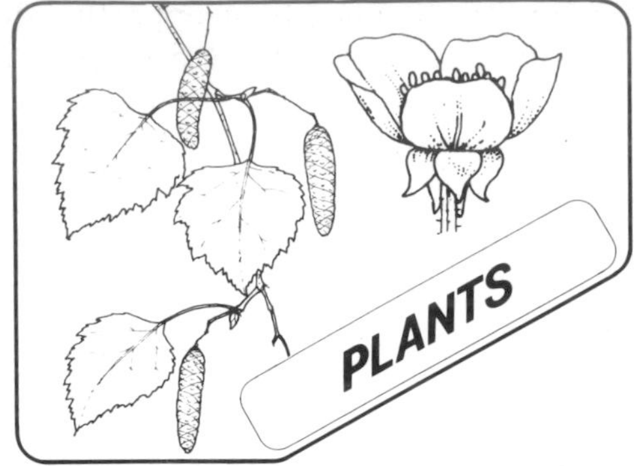

Summer Woodland Flowers

Summer is a quieter time for flowers in woods, and we have to look more carefully for the deep-shade specialists, like the bird's-nest orchid, or watch out for sunny glades where foxgloves or St John's-wort occur, but there are some surprising finds to be made.

By the time summer arrives, woodlands take on quite a different aspect. The dense leaf canopy of the tree-cover cuts out most of the sunshine, leaving just a dull greenish light to filter through to the woodland floor. Here and there, there may be pools of light where a tree has fallen, or a ride cuts through the wood, or perhaps larger bright areas where the understory of hazel has recently been coppiced (see pages 12–13) and there are fewer standard trees. Plants that flower at this time of year have to adopt a rather different strategy to those that flower in spring, and there are generally rather less of them. Some have special adaptations to survive in low light conditions, such as the yellow bird's-nest or some of the orchids, others grow mainly in glades and clearings or have a particular ability to survive long periods of shade whilst waiting for a brief period of sunshine in which to flower.

Today, many woods are intensively managed, or have been in the recent past, so they tend to lack a natural structure of young trees, older trees and glades where aged trees have fallen. Consequently, the best places to look for summer woodland flowers in most woods are along rides, around the edges of woods – especially the southern edges – and along paths. Rides can be particularly good, as they are often wide enough to let in plenty of light, and they frequently have swathes that are cut regularly, giving suitable conditions for a range of plants to survive and flower. They are often better for flowers than the woodland edges as these are usually adjacent to fields that are sprayed or grazed, neither of which is beneficial to flowers.

The traditional management of woods by coppicing also gives the opportunity for many summer woodland plants to flower. Every seven to ten years an area of hazel, or other coppice, is cut back to the base to harvest the supply of poles produced by the bushes. The canopy of trees over the coppice is usually kept very thin to encourage the growth of hazel (this is the system known as coppice-with-standards), so when the hazel is cut sunlight floods into the area for several years until it regrows and shades the light out again. Besides

The beautiful blue flowers of bugle are characteristic of wood margins and open glades after the trees have been cut down. You may also see them in hedgerows

the normal spring flowers, which do well here, these are excellent places for summer flowerers such as the dark red betony, the rose-coloured flowers of orpine, a relative of the beautiful pink 'gloves' in the following season. It needs light, so it is most often to be found in glades and clearings, but its short-lived nature (it dies after flowering, like all biennials) means that it has to be an opportunist, moving into newly-created clearings as they arise. Long-established clearings are too difficult to colonise, so it is most often found where there

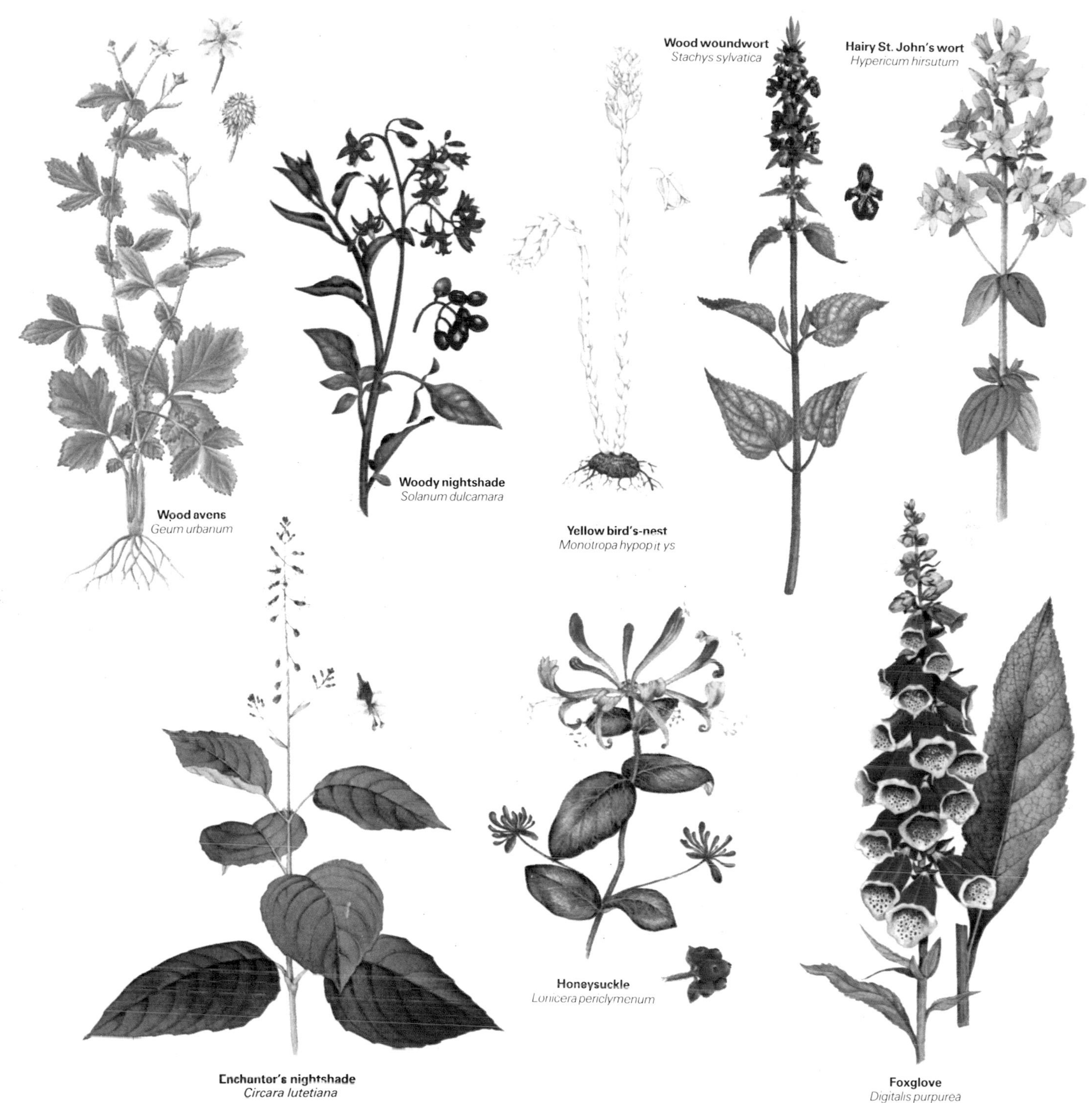

stonecrops, and for several of the attractive yellow St John's-worts amongst others. Sadly, though, woodlands that are managed as coppice are now rare, so such chances for the summer flowers are greatly reduced.

A typical glade flower of woodlands in the summer is the foxglove. This is a biennial plant, growing a rosette and tap-root system in its first year, and sending up its tall spikes of

Summer woodland flowers. Here is a selection of the sorts of flowers you are likely to find growing in woodlands in summer. Look especially for them along paths, the edges of woods, rides and open glades

has been a fire, or where a tree has recently fallen exposing ground that has been kept bare of plants by the deep shade. It tends to grow in great masses wherever it does occur, producing a beautiful splash of colour (and a fine source of nectar for insects) followed by literally millions of dust like seeds which will waft their way into another clearing to flower two years later.

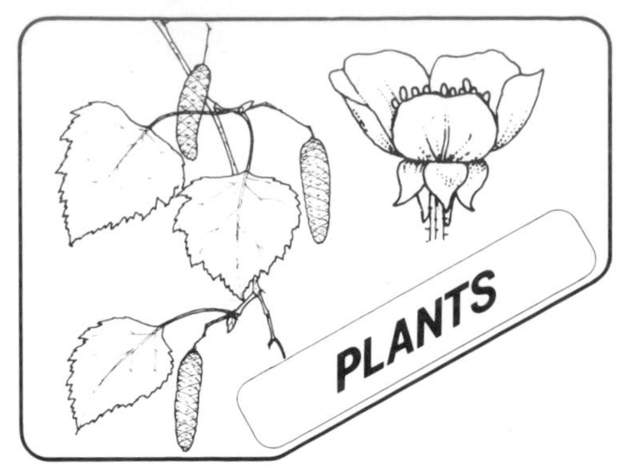

WOODLAND ORCHIDS

Some of the most exciting and unusual of our plants, whether in woodlands or elsewhere, are our native orchids. It comes as a surprise to many people that we have any native orchids at all, though in fact there are over 50 species. Of these, a number occur frequently in woodland and several are totally adapted to the deep shade of old woods.

Perhaps the most unusual orchids are the species that have no green colouring (chlorophyll) to trap the sun's energy, and are wholly reliant on using the breakdown products of leaf mould and other rotting material. To achieve this, they rely on an association with soil-living fungi around their roots. This particular arrangement, known as a mycorrhizal association, allows these orchids not only to grow in dense shade where nothing else can grow, but it also appears to make it possible for them to survive below the ground, without any visible sign of their presence for many years. They are almost unique amongst British flowers in having this way of life, which is more akin to that of toadstools and other fungi than to normal flowering plants.

The commonest of the three orchids sharing this lifestyle is the bird's-nest orchid, so-called because its root system is a tangled ball looking something like a bird's nest. It occurs in dark woodlands throughout the country, except in the far north, and is usually found on chalky soils. Its favoured habitat is dark beech woods on chalk and in some beech plantations it can become abundant, perhaps because its associated fungus does well here. These saprophytic plants (as plants relying on rotting material are called) cannot compete well with green plants which grow more vigorously, so they tend to be found in the darkest parts of woods. Much rarer is the coralroot, a rather dull pinkish or brownish flower, found in damp northern woods, and so-called because its roots look rather like a lump of coral. Rarest of them all is the spurred coralroot, or ghost orchid, which aptly sums up both its appearance and habits. This plant has only ever been known from a few sites in Britain, in the Chilterns and on the Welsh borders, but it has only been seen in recent years in the Chilterns. It flowers very sporadical-

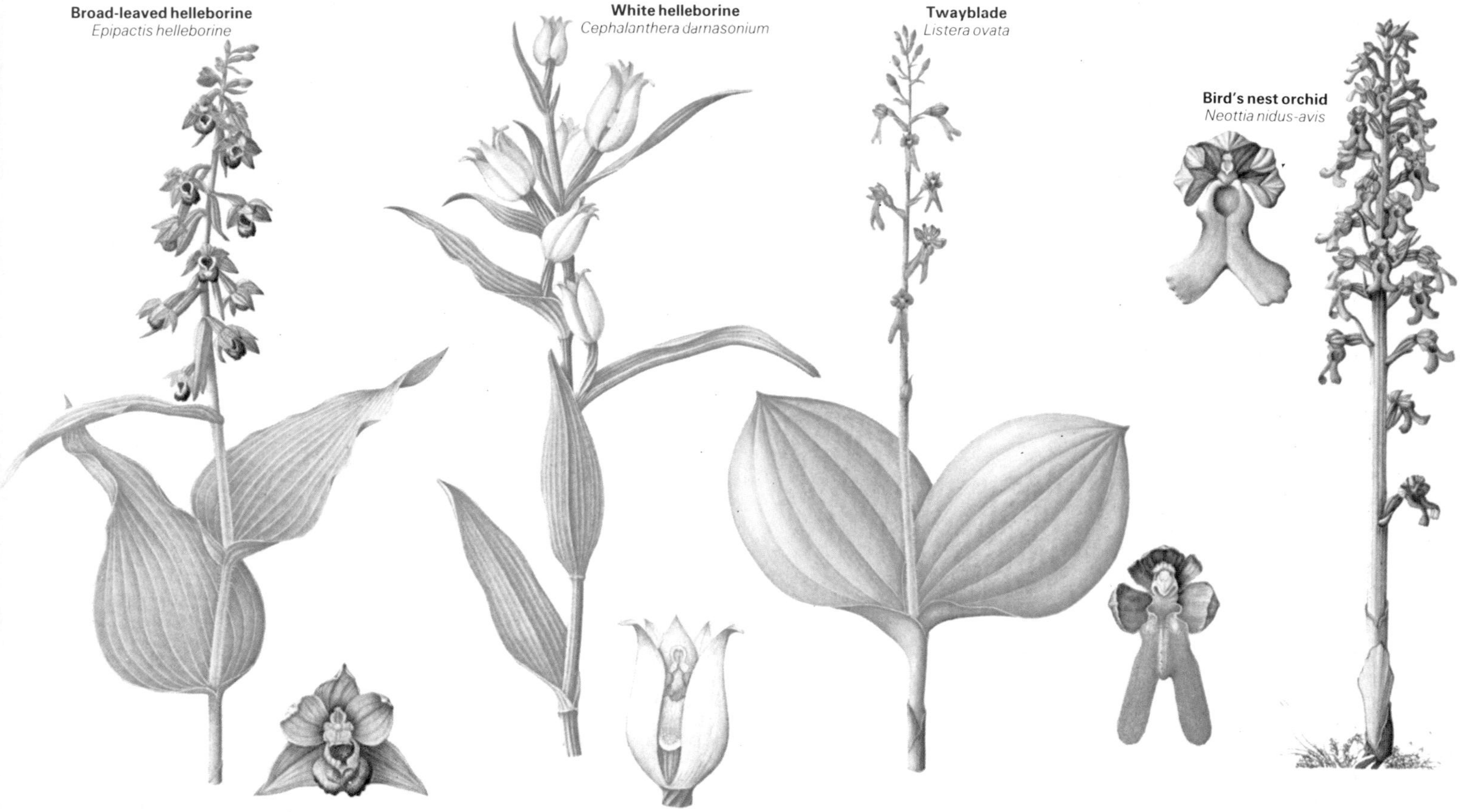

Broad-leaved helleborine
Epipactis helleborine

White helleborine
Cephalanthera damasonium

Twayblade
Listera ovata

Bird's nest orchid
Neottia nidus-avis

A selection of commoner woodland orchids that you might expect to find. The curious bird's nest orchid is a colourless saprophyte that usually grows in deep shade – as it does not need sunlight – flowering May-July, living off rotting leaf mould

ly, often with no reported flowerings for several years, and when it does so it can be at any time during the summer. It seems most likely to flower after a damp spring, perhaps because its fungus grows strongly then, but it is by no means predictable.

Other woodland orchids are not quite so strange in their habits and contain chlorophyll, but all of them share a degree of reliance on the association with fungi; those that live in deeper shade are probably partly using sunlight and partly relying on their fungal partner. The lady orchid, which is virtually confined to woodlands in Kent, is one of the most beautiful of our native plants, producing tall stately spikes with masses of pink and white flowers, each resembling the figure of a lady in a smock. The early purple orchid is much commoner and, as its name suggests, is deep reddish-purple; it flowers early in the year, usually in April and May. Like a number of other orchids, it also occurs on chalk downland looking slightly different there. One of the commonest of our woodland orchids is the twayblade, so-called because of its distinctive pair of oval leaves at the base of the flowering stem. Its greenish spike of flowers is not much to look at from a distance, but the individual man-shaped flowers are fascinating on closer scrutiny. Like many orchids (see page 49), they have a specialised pollination mechanism, and the twayblade's is one of the more bizarre. Running down the 'body' of the flower is a channel which produces nectar; this attracts small insects such as flies which crawl up the channel drinking as they go. When they reach the 'head' of the flower, where the reproductive parts are, and touch the male parts a minor 'explosion' occurs and, at the same time, a drop of glue is extruded which serves the joint purpose of frightening the insect and sticking the male parts (the pollinia) to the insect's head. It then flies off with the pollinia attached and will eventually visit another flower, preferably on another plant, which it will pollinate.

The other main groups of woodland orchids are the butterfly orchids and the helleborines. There are two butterfly orchids, the greater and the lesser, both with etherally beautiful creamy flowers, strongly scented, especially at night. They are pollinated mainly by night insects such as moths. The helleborines include the white and the more attractive sword-leaved helleborines, both of which occur most frequently in beech woods on chalk, and several other species related to the broad-leaved helleborine, such as the violet helleborines and the narrow-lipped helleborines which are rather difficult to identify individually.

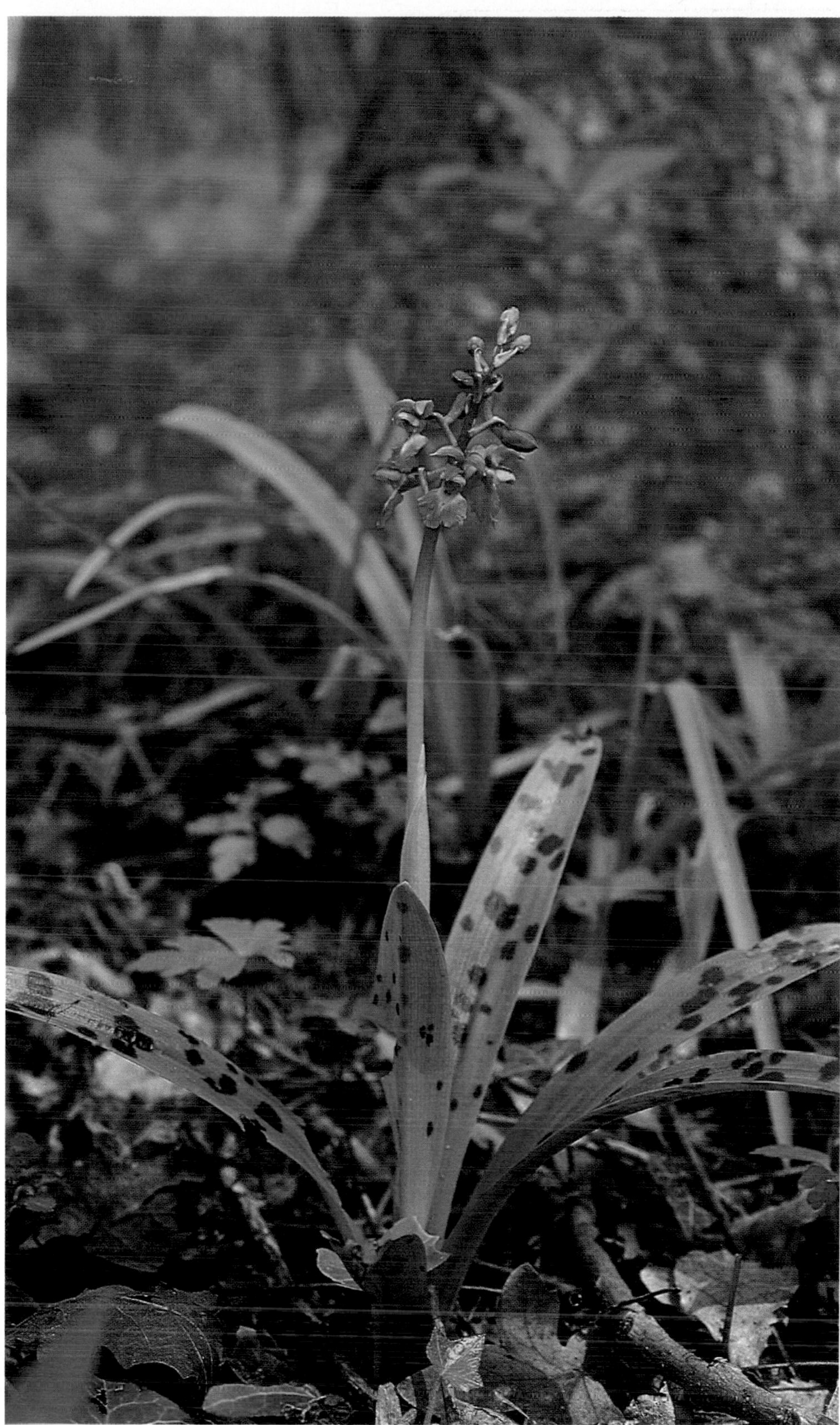

The beau iul early p chid growing in dense coppiced woodland. This is one of our earliest orchids to flower, usually appearing in late April or May, and its glossy purple-blotched leaves are easily identified even when the flowers are not open

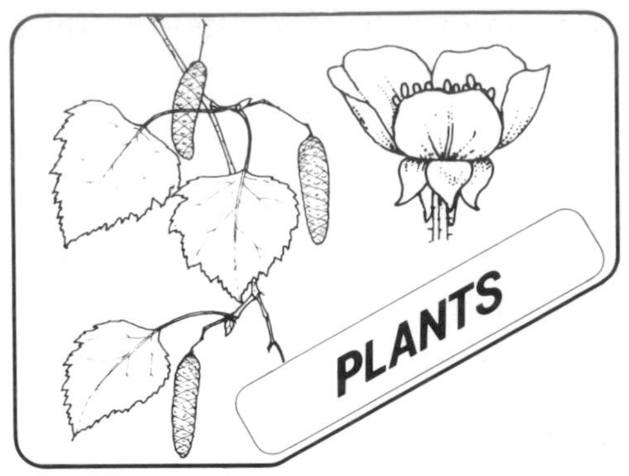

GRASSES

Grasses are flowers, too! For some reason, it is often thought that grasses are different from other plants and that they are not flowers at all. In fact, although they form a distinctive and easily recognised group, they are as much flowering plants as any others, and they have much of interest to the naturalist.

There are a number of distinctive features shared by all the British grasses. Their flowering heads are rather different from ordinary flowers in that they have been greatly modified to achieve cross-pollination with the aid of the wind rather than insects. Since the main function of colourful petals and strong scents in other flowers is to attract insects, those flowers that are not dependent on them have no need of these distinctive features. Consequently grasses (and, incidentally, most trees which are also wind-pollinated) have very small flowers aggregated into loose groups with the stamens (the pollen-producing male parts of the flower) dangling loosely in the breeze, and the stigmas (the female parts which are designed to recieve the pollen) greatly branched and very sticky to increase the chances of collecting pollen. Wind-pollination is clearly a chancey business, with the pollen blowing off in all directions, and only the tiniest proportion finding its way to the stigmas of the right plant. Nonetheless, it clearly works, as grasses are very successful and fertile. Pollen is produced in such huge quantities by wind-pollinated plants that it is even found, in quite large proportions, in the air over the mid-Atlantic, so it is little wonder that some grains find their way to their target. It is also, of course, the pollen grains of grasses that are primarily responsible for

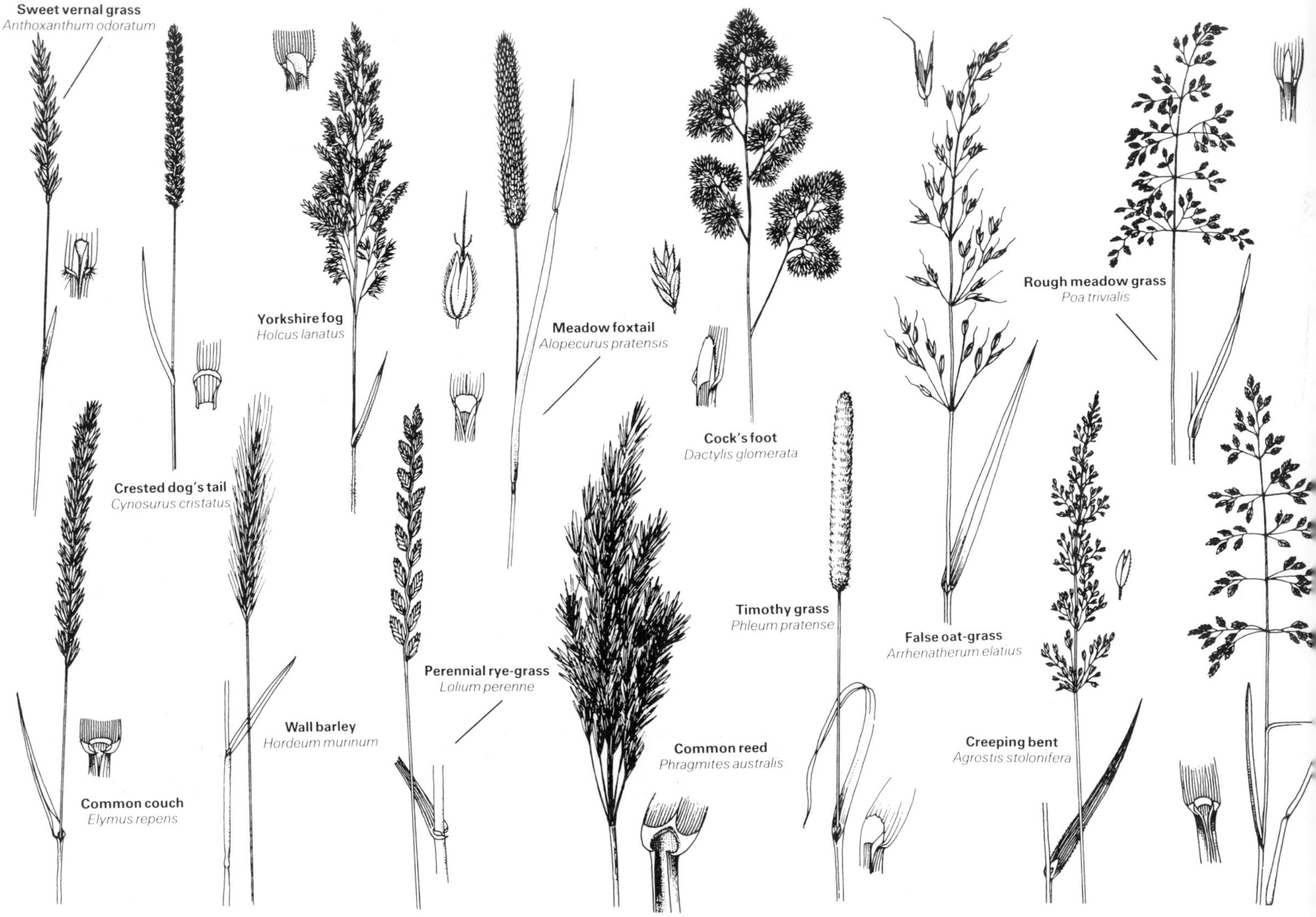

Sweet vernal grass *Anthoxanthum odoratum*
Yorkshire fog *Holcus lanatus*
Meadow foxtail *Alopecurus pratensis*
Cock's foot *Dactylis glomerata*
Rough meadow grass *Poa trivialis*
Crested dog's tail *Cynosurus cristatus*
Timothy grass *Phleum pratense*
False oat-grass *Arrhenatherum elatius*
Perennial rye-grass *Lolium perenne*
Wall barley *Hordeum murinum*
Common reed *Phragmites australis*
Creeping bent *Agrostis stolonifera*
Common couch *Elymus repens*

A selection of commoner grasses. Look carefully at the flowers and the bases of the leaves when trying to identify them

causing hayfever in so many people!

Another feature of grasses that gives them such ecological significance is their ability to grow at any point along the stem or leaf; this means that they can be cut or grazed continuously and still grow rapidly, whereas many other plants cannot stand regular mowing or grazing. It is for this reason that grasses soon come to dominate cut and grazed areas, forming grasslands such as lawns, meadows and pastures. Most such grasses are also able to spread vegetatively, without producing flowers, by means of runners or stolons, so that they can survive indefinitely even when continuously prevented from flowering.

But grasses do not only grow in grasslands. There are species of grass that are adapted to woodland, sand-dunes, mountains and even saltmarshes, lakes and rivers. The water flote-grasses, for example, look like normal upright grasses when growing in damp places, but they are also able to produce floating strap-shaped leaves when inundated by standing water. The cord-grasses, or Spartina grasses, are unusual in that they can live in sea water and stand being totally immersed. These grasses, are able to colonise coastal mudflats, trapping silt and raising the level as they go to form saltmarshes, and they have been used as a means of reclaiming coastal mudflats from the sea, to stablilise coasts and eventually to produce new farmland. There are other species of grass that are the basis of sand-dune formation; the marram grass, in particular, has the ability to grow upwards through sand to a height of many metres above its starting point, so it can continue to survive and help stabilise blowing sand even when the sand is piling over it. In most circumstances, the sand ultimately becomes established as dunes by the presence of marram and other grasses.

The other feature that grasses have in common is that they are generally considered to be rather difficult to identify! There are over 150 species of grass in Britain, and since they all have greenish flowers, it does mean that they need to be looked at closely to see the differences between species. The distinctions depend particularly upon the structure of the flower spike, the shape of the flower parts and the shape of two structures – the ligules and the auricles – that occur where the leaves meet the stem. (The ligule is the outgrowth at the junction of the sheath and blade; auricle the 'ear-like' growths at the junction of sheath and blade.) In practice, though, relatively few grasses occur commonly in any one area, and you can soon learn to identify the common species.

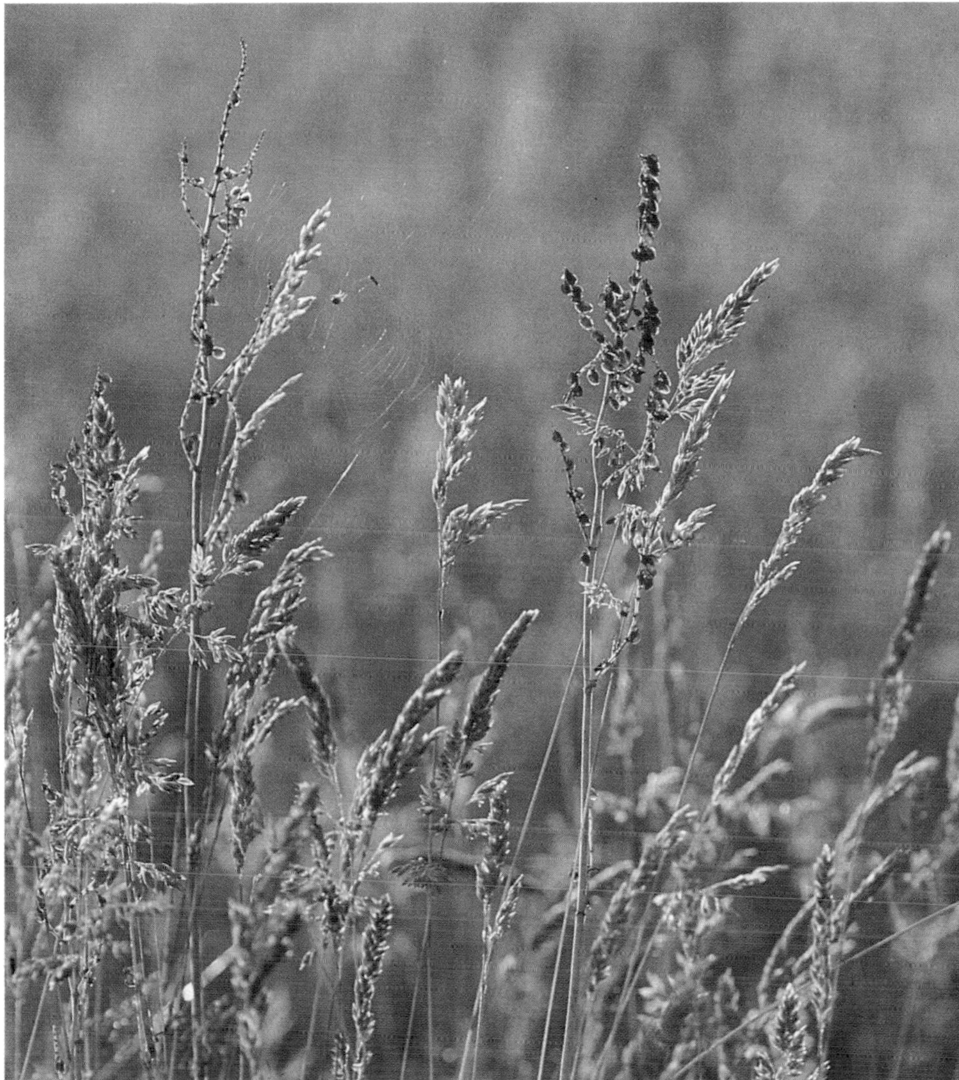

A mass of beautiful meadowland grasses, including bents and Yorkshire fog, resplendent in the evening sun. It is worth spending a little time learning to identify them

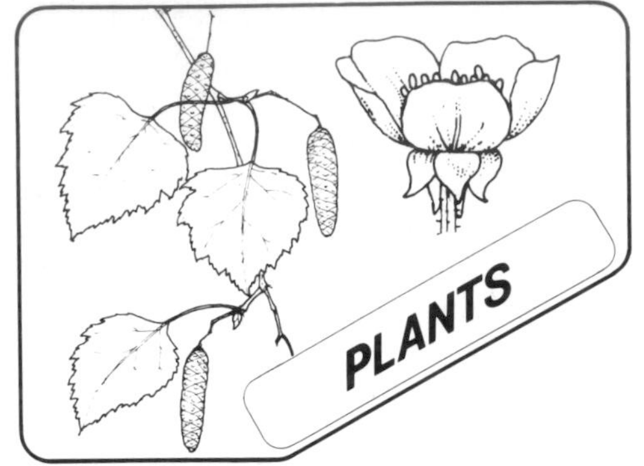

ORCHIDS OF DOWNLAND

To see wild orchids at their best, a visit to some of our limestone or chalk downlands in high summer is essential. A really good piece of downland could easily have six or more species in flower at once, giving a wonderful opportunity to see these flowers in their native habitat.

The wide open turf of downland on chalk and limestone hills is the orchid habitat *par excellence* in Britain. The steep scarps of hills in the Chilterns, on the North and South Downs, in the Cotswolds, on Salisbury Plain and elsewhere are famous for their displays of orchids of many different colours. It is quite possible for ten, or even more, different species to occur in one site, though half a dozen different species is a more likely total.

The predominant colour of the downland orchids is red or pink which can make identification rather more difficult. First to flower is usually the early purple orchid (the same species that occurs in woodlands) which has wine-red flowers and shiny leaves blotched with black. A similar species, the green-winged orchid, flowers at about the same time, but it is usually smaller, has unspotted leaves and the side petals are striped with green. A little later, in June, come the common spotted orchids, which are more lilac-coloured and have less shiny leaves with smaller spots than the early purple, while the flowers are distinctively marked with darker dashes and dots on the lower petal. By high summer, two other pink-flowered species have appeared; these are the fragrant orchid, of which some forms are fragrant, and the pyramidal orchid – similar, but with a distinctly triangular rather than cylindrical flower spike. The attractive little dwarf or burnt orchid has flowers that are very pale pink dotted with red below but dark red above. They are rather rare and tend

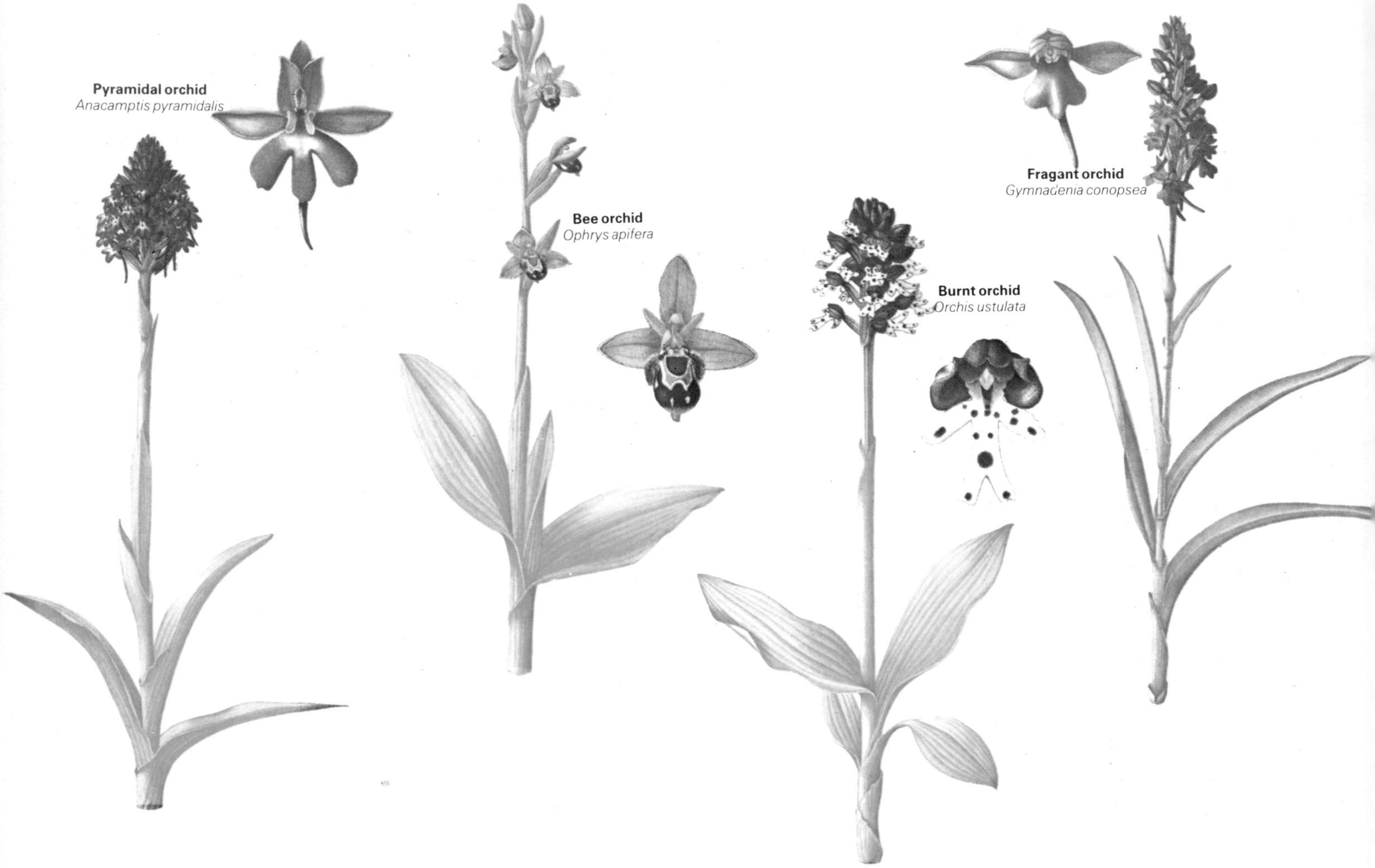

Pyramidal orchid
Anacamptis pyramidalis

Bee orchid
Ophrys apifera

Burnt orchid
Orchis ustulata

Fragant orchid
Gymnadenia conopsea

A selection of downland orchids that you may find, if you are lucky. The upper illustrations show an enlargement of each flower, revealing how strange some of the shapes are, and how attractive the individual flowers are on close inspection

A close-up of the bee orchid, one of the most beautiful and intriguing of our downland orchids. It can be seen in June-July

to grow mainly on prehistoric earthworks, where the turf is very ancient.

There are also other colours. Several species have greenish flowers, particularly the striking-looking man orchid with a spike of flowers each shaped just like a little man; the diminutive greenish-yellow musk orchid, usually rather rare, but occasionally occurring in thousands where conditions are suitable; the tiny greenish-red frog orchid; and the twayblade, the same species as in woodlands, though usually looking a little yellower out here in the open. The greater butterfly orchid, with its beautiful spikes of almost luminous creamy-white flowers each said to look, rather fancifully, like a delicate butterfly, is frequent, while the last to flower each year is the white-flowered autumn lady's-tresses, sending up little spikes with tiny spiralling flowers each autumn.

Besides their obvious beauty, the orchids are fascinating plants for many reasons. They have developed some intriguing pollination mechanisms, amongst which the most bizarre must be those of the bee orchids and their close relatives. The bee, fly and two species of spider orchid are all closely-related representatives of a group of species that occur mainly in south Europe. They share the particular feature of having flowers that look strikingly like insects, with the lower lip developed as the furry body, the side petals looking like wings and two of the upper petals reduced in width to look like antennae! The flowers attract the males of particular species of insect, which believe they have found a mate! Some species even produce a scent that resembles that of the appropriate female insect. Often, the males of an insect emerge before the female and they are strongly attracted to the orchid flowers with which they will attempt to mate, fail – not surprisingly – and move onto another flower, but in doing so they take with them an abundance of orchid pollen with which they will pollinate the next suitable flower. This is therefore a very precise mechanism for ensuring cross-pollination, since the appropriate male insects will only be attracted to the one species of orchid so, for a while, they will just keep moving from plant to plant pollinating as they go. In Britain though, the delicately-balanced equilibrium seems to have largely broken down, and the bee orchid and the two spider orchids are normally self-pollinated, either because the right insects

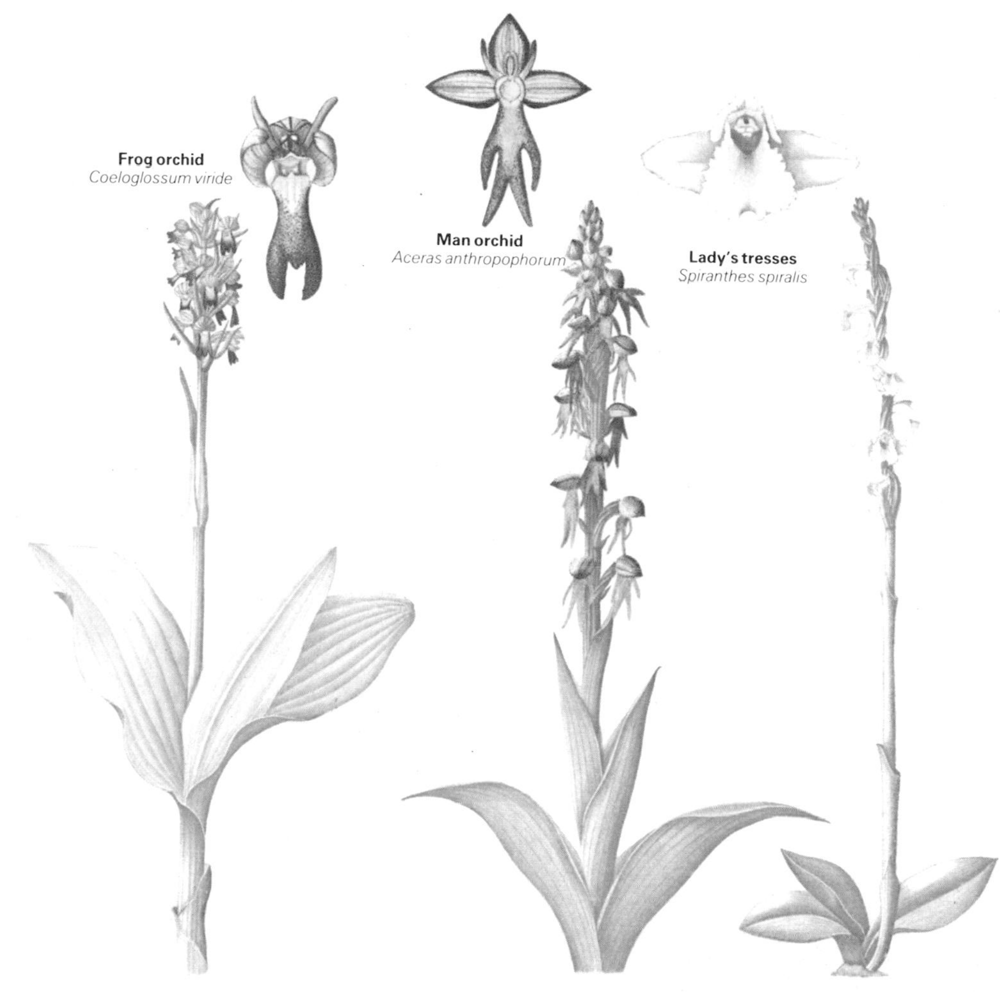

The frog orchid, which is now rare in Britain, just on the northern edge of its European range, has one of the strangest flowers. It grows on any soil type on rock ledges and on dune slacks

no longer exist or the timing has gone awry. The fly orchid is still pollinated in this way by the males of a little wasp, but it has been shown that only a small percentage of flowers are successfully pollinated; the reason being that the wasp is not common enough and the timing is not quite right – the males are led astray by the real females before they have done much pollinating!

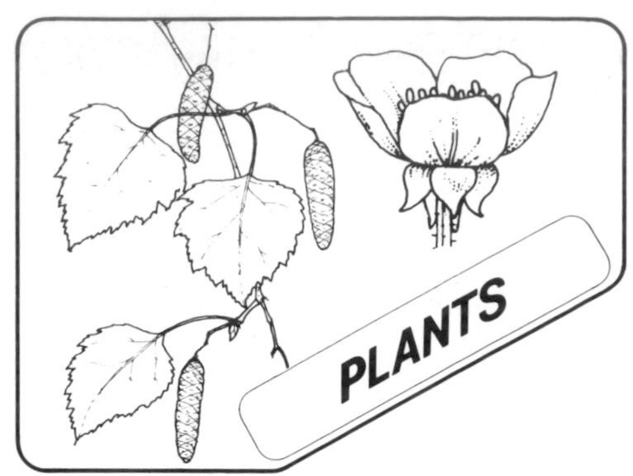

DOWNLAND FLOWERS

From early summer onwards, the springy turf of a sheep-grazed downland is a mass of colourful aromatic flowers vying with each other for space. This is one of the richest of all our habitats for wild flowers with as many as 40 different species in a square metre.

The chalk grassland habitat is rather a strange one. It is favourable enough to allow a very wide range of plants to grow there, but it is not sufficiently fertile for any of them to become aggressively dominant, which accounts for the very high density of species. In fact, the least fertile downlands, with a long history of sheep-grazing (which tends to gradually remove nutrients, especially as the sheep used to be removed at night to deposit their dung on the arable fields) are usually the richest in flowers, and the addition of fertilisers rapidly reduces the number of species by allowing just a few grasses and others to swamp the herbs.

The most interesting downlands tend to be the oldest established, partly for the reasons mentioned above, and some of the grassland has been in existence since Roman or even prehistoric times. There are a number of plants that are confined to the chalk downs, and many of these show a definite preference for older downland. For example, the oddly-named bastard-toadflax (which is the only British member of the tropical sandalwood family) with its tiny greenish-white flowers, the pretty yellow flowers of horseshoe vetch (which is one of the finest of all butterfly food-plants, supporting Adonis and chalkhill blues) and the deep blue-purple flowers of clustered bellflower are all highly unlikely to occur in downland that has been ploughed in this century. The powers of dispersal of such plants seem to be very limited so that they cannot easily recolonise more recent grassland, but also the increased nutrient levels which ploughing and cultivation brings about do not suit them. None of them actually indicate, for instance, Roman of Bronze Age turf – they are just very unlikely to occur in recently ploughed downland. Neverthless, some downland flowers do seem to prefer

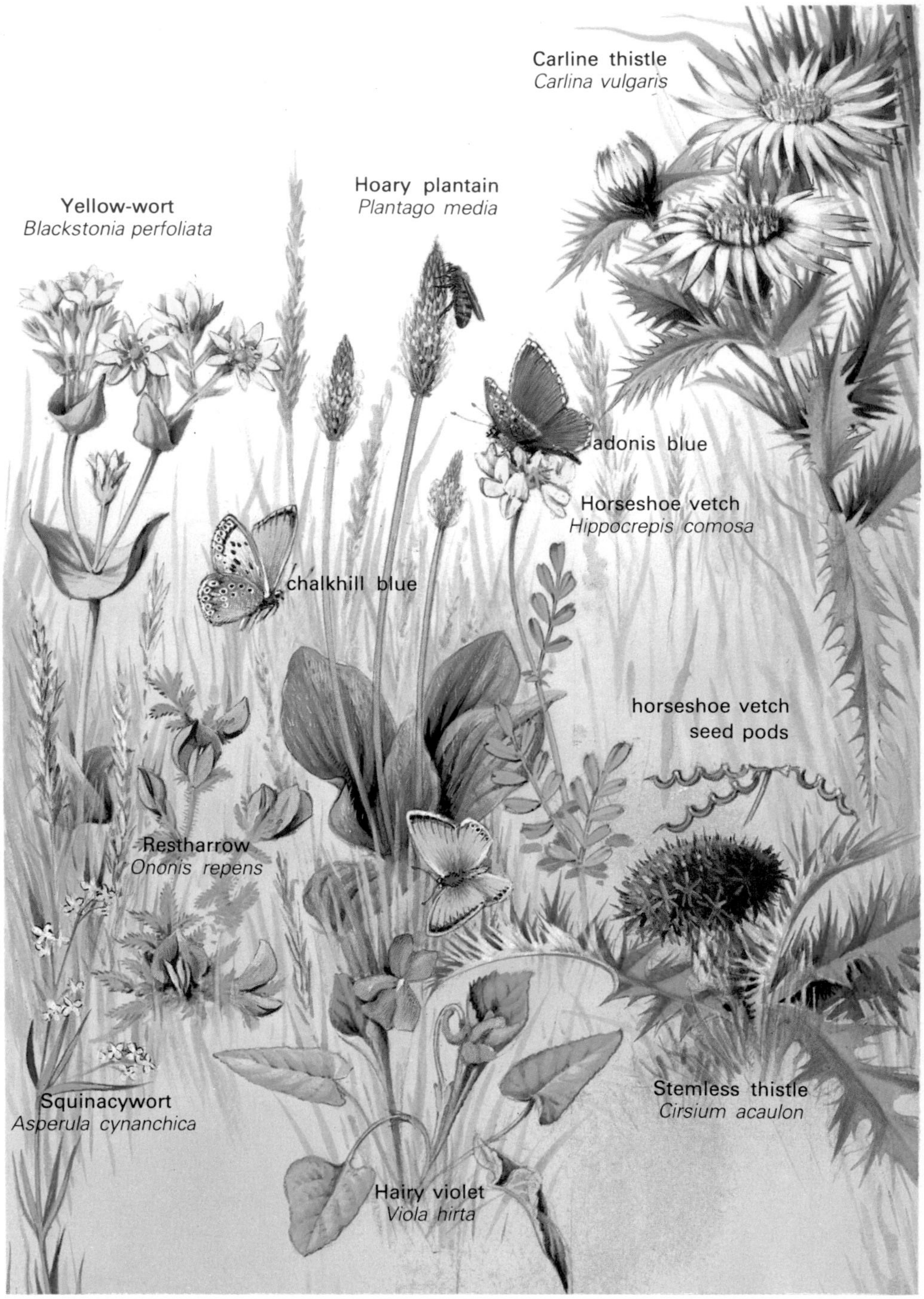

Carline thistle *Carlina vulgaris*
Yellow-wort *Blackstonia perfoliata*
Hoary plantain *Plantago media*
adonis blue
Horseshoe vetch *Hippocrepis comosa*
chalkhill blue
horseshoe vetch seed pods
Restharrow *Ononis repens*
Squinacywort *Asperula cynanchica*
Stemless thistle *Cirsium acaulon*
Hairy violet *Viola hirta*

An in-habitat selection of some of our commoner and more colourful wild downland flowers, showing some of the butterflies that use them as food-plants for their caterpillars. The horseshoe vetch is the food-plant of the Adonis blue butterfly. Sites which are favoured by these beautiful butterflies are steep south-facing downs where the grass is grazed short by rabbits and sheep. The best places to see this species are Dorset, Surrey, Kent and Wiltshire, during May and June, and during August and September

ancient earthworks which are often the very oldest downland turf. The very beautiful blue pasque flower (which is a type of anemone that flowers around Easter – hence the name) only occurs in a few places in Britain, always on chalk or limestone grassland, and in many of its sites it is found on some form of ancient earthworks or on very ancient common land. The attractive orange-yellow flowered field fleawort, which is actually a type of ragwort though more delicate than most, also tends to grow most often on old earthworks, as does the dwarf orchid (see page 48).

The colour and form, not to mention the scents and sounds, of a downland tend to vary through the summer season. The brown turf of winter

Ox-eye daisy *Leucanthemum vulgare*
Ribwort plantain *Plantago lanceolata*
Meadow vetchling *Lathyrus pratensis*
Daisy *Bellis perennis*
Giant puffball *Calvatia gigantea*
Lady's bedstraw *Galium verum*
Yarrow *Achillea millefolium*
Fairy ring *Marasmius oreades*
Black knapweed *Centaurea nigra*
Yellow rattle *Rhinanthus minor*
Parrot toadstools *Hygrophorus psittacinus*
Self-heal *Prunella vulgaris*
Common mouse-ear *Cerastium fontanum*
Rough hawkbit *Leontodon hispidus*
Field mushrooms *Agaricus campestris*

More downland flowers, and a few mushrooms and toadstools. This selection is more likely to be found on the richer soil near the foot of the downland slopes, where there is a little more water and nutrients. Field mushrooms are a great delicacy; they taste nothing like their domesticated cousins. They grow vigorously and in the right warm damp weather can grow from a 'button' to the open mushroom in a few hours. Be very careful that you are in fact picking mushrooms

Kidney vetch, one of our best butterfly flowers, growing in ungrazed chalk downland

begins to go a little greener, at first just flecked with the reds of the early orchids, or the blues of violets and chalk milkwort. Many of the early summer downland flowers are yellow, such as the delicate yellow of the cowslips, the golden yellow of bulbous buttercups and the yellow flowers of horseshoe vetch and bird's-foot-trefoil. High summer brings blues and white in the form of other milkworts, wild thyme, basil, squinancywort (once used to help cure tonsilitis), dropwort and bellflowers. Late summer seems to be a time of mauves and purples, as small scabious, devil's-bit scabious, betony, knapweed and the autumn gentian or felwort all flower profusely. From April right through to early November, there is always something of interest on a downland, and at their peak in June and July, the abundance of scented, beautiful flowers is positively stunning.

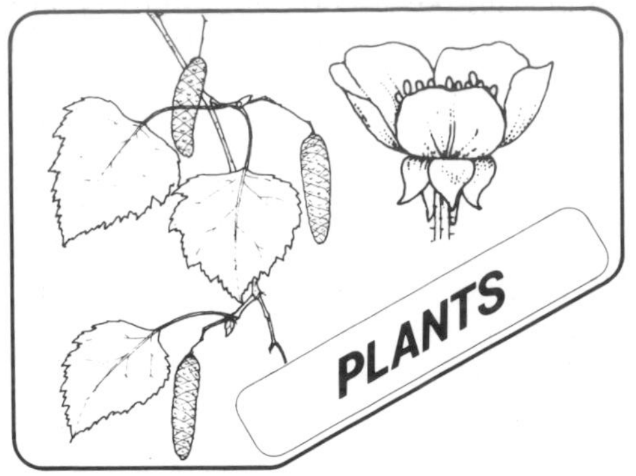

FLOWERS OF THE MEADOW

Meadows are amongst the most evocative of all habitats, conjuring up visions of a mass of tall colourful summer flowers, with hazy swarms of butterflies above. Sadly, such places are now rare, but where they do still occur, the reality can be very similar to this ideal.

Meadows, as distinct from downlands, are enclosed grasslands often on damp or clayey soil, most often used to produce a hay crop. Although they share a few flowers with the dry calcareous grasslands of the downs, many of the species are different. The soil is damper and more fertile (though if it is very fertile, relatively few flowers will be found growing there) and the management for hay suits different species compared to the grazing regime of most downlands.

One of our most exciting and exotic plants is the snake's-head fritillary. It is a relative of the lilies and, though once quite common, nowadays it is confined to a few alluvial river valley meadows, especially along the Thames and in Suffolk. In early May, it produces beautiful hanging purple bell-shaped flowers, with usually two or three on each plant, and these are covered by a regular chequered pattern of small dark squares. The resemblance of the flowers to old-fashioned dice boxes is said to have given rise to the name from *fritillus*, a dice-box. Every population of fritillaries also has a proportion of pure white flowers, often as much as a third of the population, which add an attractive

A mass of the beautiful snake's-head fritillary, growing wild in a damp meadow near the Thames. Such sights are now rare, but where they do occur, the fritillaries often grow in dense masses with both white and purple flowers together

variety of colour to a fritillary meadow. The fritillary is now so rare that about 90 per cent of the British population is said to occur in just one meadow, not far from Swindon in Wiltshire. This beautiful plant has suffered considerably from ploughing and fertilising of its preferred habitats, but it is also a naturally fussy plant, doing best in damp alluvial meadows that are fertile but not artificially fertilised and which are cut for hay late each summer. The Wiltshire meadow, which is now a National Nature Reserve, is a very ancient common, where the hay crop is sold off each year in lots according to an ancient custom; such areas are known as 'lammas lands'.

The fritillary is one of the earliest meadow plants to flower, though a few others flower at the same time. The cuckooflower, also called milkmaids or ladies smock, produces lovely pale pink flowers in damp meadows during April and May, proving an irresistible attraction for spring butterflies, some of which lay their eggs on its stems and leaves. One orchid is particularly characteristic of hay meadows that are not too wet; the green-winged, or green-veined orchid, flowers in May and June, often colouring parts of the meadow deep purple with the density of its spikes, though it, too, often produces a few white and pale forms amongst the others. These are followed by masses of flowers in June, such as the white and yellow oxeye daisies (or moon daisies, as they are sometimes known), the yellow flowers of hay rattle so-called because its dry brown seed-heads rattle in the hay when it is gathered, yarrow, buttercups, red, white and strawberry clovers, plantains and hawkbits.

Some meadow plants have a curious habit that must give them a competitive edge over their immediate neighbours in the cut-throat world that makes up a dense grass sward. Hay rattle and several other members of the same family, such as lousewort, red rattle and the eyebrights, have all developed an ablility to attach their roots to those of other plants and siphon off some of the nutrients. They do not totally rely on the other plants, only removing water and mineral salts, so they are known as semi-parasites. But this habit clearly helps them along as the surrounding vegetation is often rather stunted where such plants are abundant. Other grassland plants succeed because they can spread by means of underground stems and roots, allowing them to extend their range and density without having to flower, produce seeds and establish the seedlings in the closed turf. A good example is the curious little adder's-tongue fern, which looks quite unlike a fern, and hardly behaves like one. In late winter, it sends up single tongue-shaped fronds, which later bear a short spore-producing spikelet from their bases. The spores are a rather unsuccessful way of establishing new plants in the sward (though they probably help the fern to establish itself occasionally in new sites), but the creeping underground stems continually grow outwards and push up new fronds, so that the fern often creates large and beautiful expanses which may be densely dotted with fronds. Many of the grasses, and some of the sedges, share this very particular type of habit – the mark of a well-adapted meadow plant.

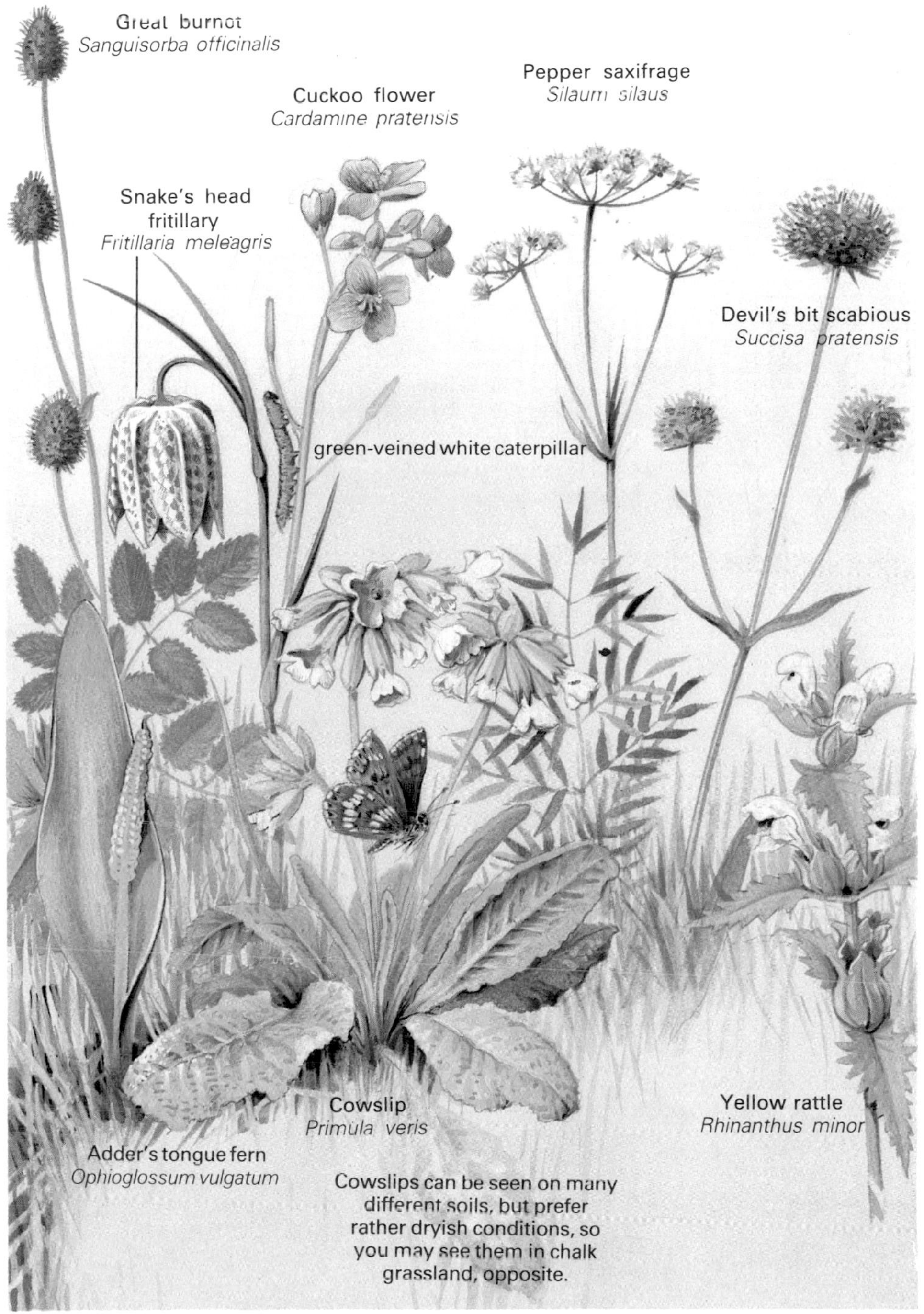

A selection of flowers to be found in unimproved meadows, where these still exist. Several of these, such as the snake's-head fritillary or the tiny adder's-tongue fern, are usually good indicators of very old meadows

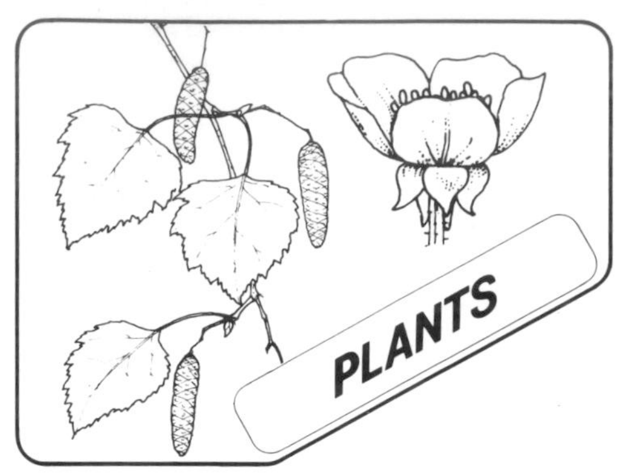

PLANT-LIFE IN WATER

The sight of a lake covered with white water-lilies or the mass of summer flowers that appear in slow-moving rivers is one of the most attractive and evocative to be found. A whole range of plants have taken to life in the water, making use of the constant supply of nutrients and protection from the excesses of the British climate.

For any plant that has the necessary adaptations, life in water is particularly attractive. Aquatic plants are spared the perennial problem of droughts or shortages of nutrients, and the blanket of water protects them from extremes of heat and cold in summer and winter. Most plants, though, cannot survive long periods of immersion, and only specialised plants are successful in this environment.

Plants have evolved two mechanisms to cope with living in more or less permanent water. One group needs to be rooted in the bottom mud, these are more limited to shallow water, while the other group are free-floating and can grow in any depth of water. All aquatic plants need light from the sun, like other green plants, and, since the intensity and quality of light decreases with depth, plants need to have some leaves at or near the surface. This naturally limits the spread of rooted plants, as they cannot produce indefinitely long stems to their leaves at the surface.

The floating aquatic species, though they are able to live in deep water, are limited to reasonably still waters as they are swept away by strong currents. Consequently, they are absent from most rivers, except those that are very slow-moving and

Plants that grow in water may be either floating or rooted in the shallows. The free-floating species can be found in any depth of water where the surface is still. The rooted aquatics are a much more varied group

Reedmace
Typha latifolia

Branched Bur-reed
Sparganium erectum

Water lobelia
Lobelia dortmanna

Bog bean
Menyanthes trifoliata

Water plantain
Alisma plantago-aquatica

Mare's tail
Hippuris vulgaris

Frog-bit
Hydrocharis morsus-ranae

have plenty of still stretches. Because they are not rooted, it also means that they have to depend completely on obtaining their nutrient supply directly from the water, through their roots (if they have any) and their leaves and stems. They tend, therefore, to be more limited to nutrient-rich waters. The commonest free-floating types are the duckweeds, which are tiny round-leaved plants that can cover the surface of a pond or canal making it look completely green like a lawn. There are several species, in different shapes and sizes, and they include the extraordinarily tiny rootless duckweed which, with a diameter of less than one millimetre, is easily Britain's smallest flowering plant (though actually it never flowers in Britain). Most of the species produce leaves that float on the surface, but the leaves of the ivy duckweed are just submerged. Other floating species are more conspicuous and attractive; the frogbit, for example, has kidney-shaped floating leaves and produces pretty white three-petalled flowers in summer. The rather strange and exotic water-soldier has rosettes of spiky, almost cactus-like leaves that sink to the bottom each winter and rise to the surface in spring. It has separate male and female plants and for some reason virtually all the British plants are female. One other intriguing group of floating aquatics are the bladderworts; these are insectivorous plants, catching insects as part of their diet, and they do this by means of little bladder-traps amongst their foliage which open when a trigger is touched pulling in water plus the prey. Enzymes then digest the unfortunate creature and this helps the plant to survive in difficult circumstances where nutrient levels are low.

Rooted aquatics are a more varied group, including such attractive plants as arrowhead, yellow flag, the white and yellow water-lilies, the beautiful bogbean, all the water-crowfoots (white-flowered relatives of the buttercups) and many others (see illustrations opposite). All share the necessary ability to transport oxygen down through the plant from the leaves above the surface, and most have spongy buoyant tissues.

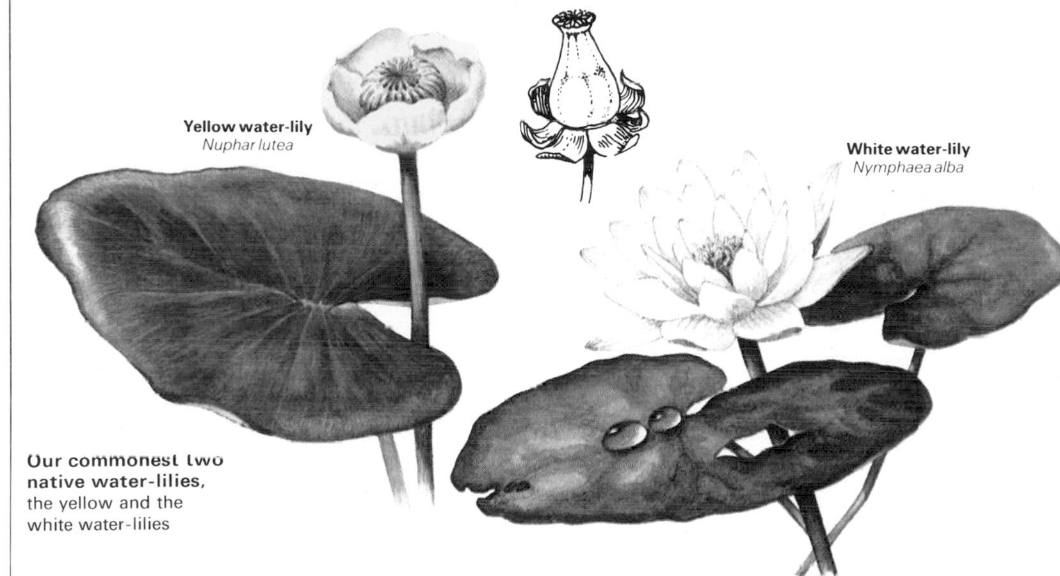

Our commonest two native water-lilies, the yellow and the white water-lilies

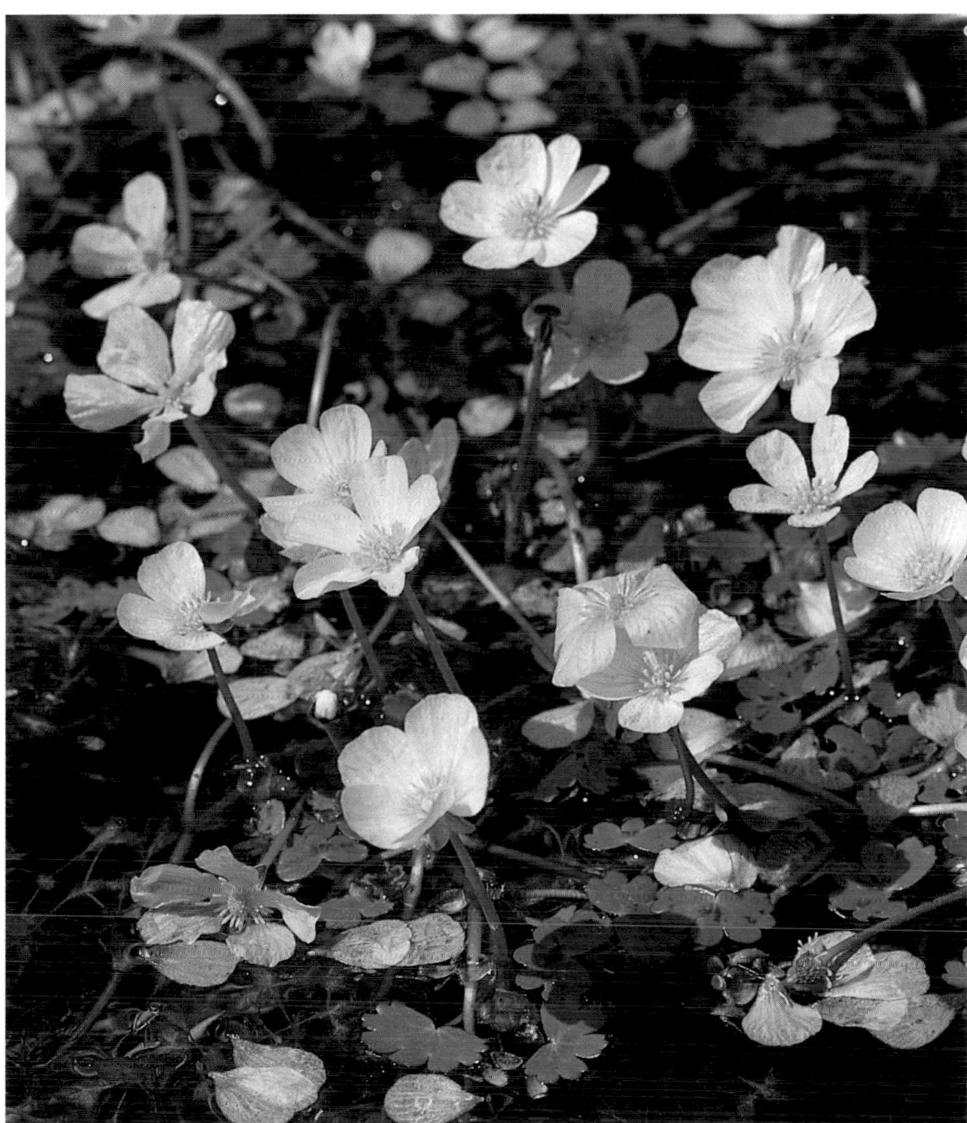

One of the water crowfoots, aquatic cousins of the buttercup, growing in a clear unpolluted river. It flowers May-September

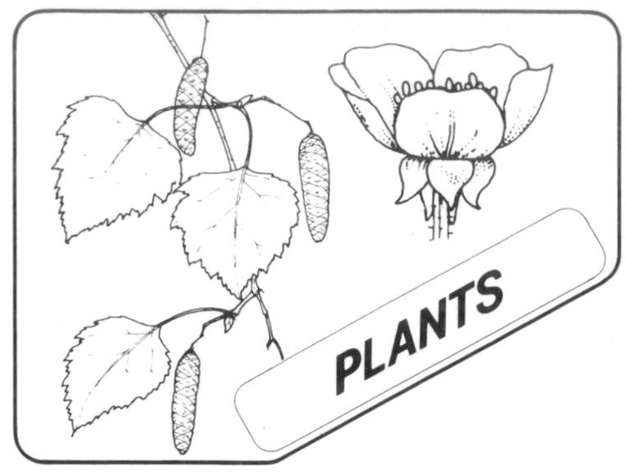

PLANTS AROUND WATER

Beside water, on river-banks and along the edges of lakes and ponds, there is an enormous variety of colourful flowers, such as purple loosestrife, yellow flag or marsh marigolds. Such plants can tolerate being submerged occasionally, but spend most of the time living in ideal conditions with their feet in the water and their heads in the air.

There are a surprising number of plants that have as their preferred habitat the junction between water and land – the water's edge. It is a rather special place, giving the best of both worlds to its inhabitants, and there are several plants that grow nowhere else. One noticeable feature of these plants is that they frequently flower in high summer or later rather than in the spring, whereas plants of drier habitats, such as sand-dunes, tend to flower early. There are two reasons for this: firstly, watery habitats warm up less quickly than dry ones because water itself is slow to heat up and cool; and secondly, plants in drier habitats flower early to avoid the summer drought, while wetland plants have no such problem to contend with. This means that by late June or July, the water's edge is often a riot of colour with purple loosestrife, angelica, great willowherb, hemp agrimony, pink balsam all flowering together, often lasting well on into the autumn. To colonise new habitats and spread, waterside plants often have some interesting dispersal mechanisms. The pink-flowered Himalayan balsam, for example, produces capsules that literally explode when fully

The male catkins and female cones of the common alder, one of the most familiar of our waterside trees, in spring

The beautiful blue flowers of the water forget-me-not

ripe, shooting their seeds up to several metres away, some onto the damp ground nearby and others into the water; whilst the willowherbs and hemp agrimony have light feathery seeds that blow readily in the wind. Many waterside plants also possess seeds that float; for example the seeds of alder (a waterside tree), yellow flag and great willowherb are very bouyant, failing to become waterlogged even after weeks of immersion. This means that the dispersal mechanism can throw a proportion of the seeds into the water, where they will gradually drift with the wind or current until washed up somewhere else; because they will inevitably come to rest on a waterside bank somewhere, the chances are that they will find themselves in a favourable place for germination and growth. A plant such as the Himalayan balsam (or policeman's helmet as it is also called because of the shape of its flowers), which was introduced into this country from the Himalayas, has been able to spread rapidly along rivers and around lakes by this very means.

Some plants, like the amphibious bistort, are – as its name suggests – able to grow both around and in water. The bistort is particularly unusual in that it has two quite distinct looking forms, which are often thought to be different plants, according to whether it is growing in water or on dry land. On land, it produces upright slightly hairy plants with leaves with rounded bases and roots only growing from the base. When in water it is completely hairless and floats on the surface by means of different-shaped leaves; it has roots at the base of each leaf stalk. Other plants such as water flotegrass or yellow flag grow well in or out of water but do not produce two forms.

There are even a few trees that are particularly adapted to life around the water. Alder is, perhaps, the most characteristic as it is often found close to the water, and is well adapted to this life. As well as having floating seeds, alders also have special nodules on their roots, containing bacteria, which help the tree to make nitrogen compounds from the air (something that most plants are unable to do). In the same way that the insectivorous habit helps plants of bogs and acid lakes to supplement their diet, so this nitrogen-fixing helps the alder. Most willows also grow around or close to water, especially the white and crack willow and the sallow. The related black poplar is usually found close to ponds and it is quite a characteristic sight by village ponds in a few areas, though generally it is a rather rare tree nowadays. Its arching boughs and bosses on the stem make a distinctive shape.

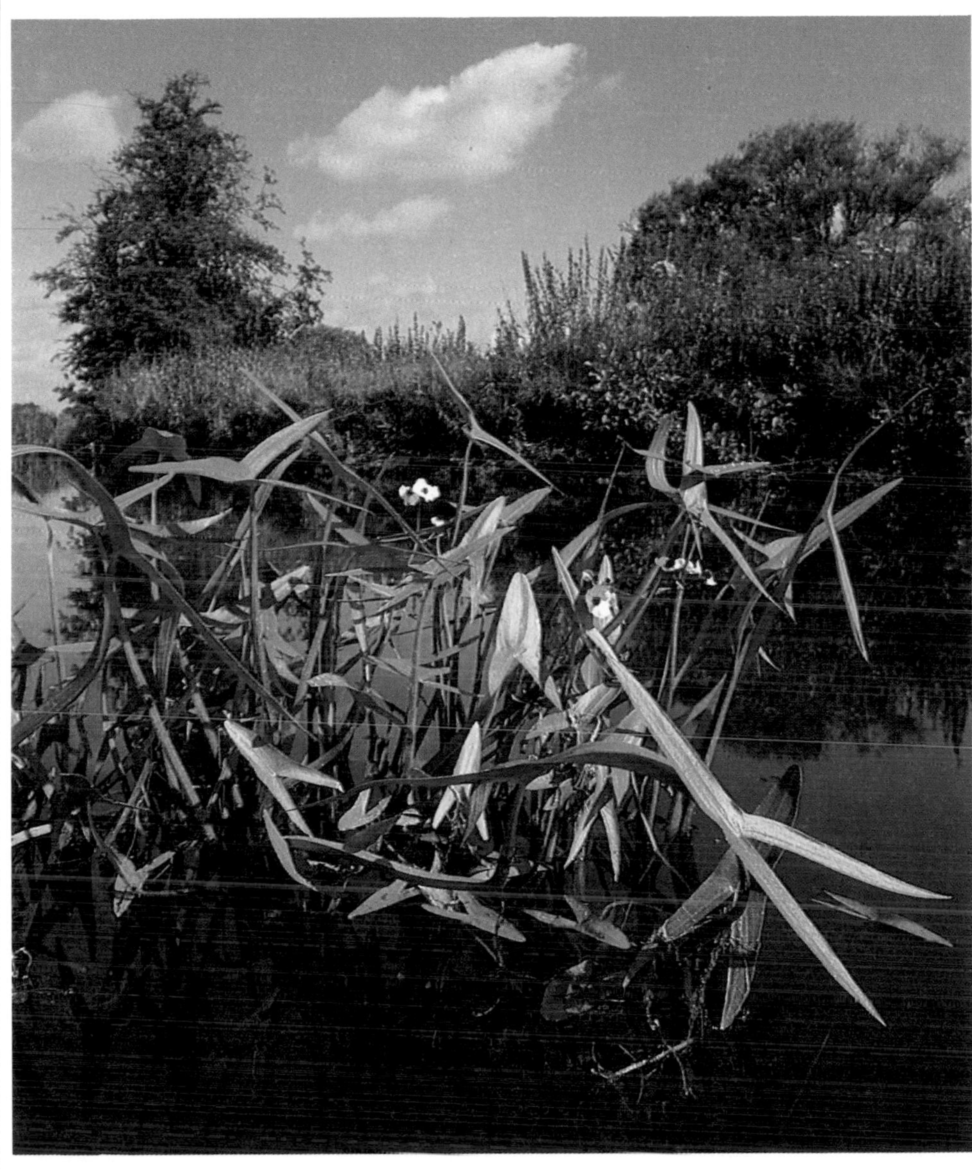

A low-level view of the flowers and arrow-shaped leaves of the curious arrowhead, seen here growing in a slow-flowing lowland river

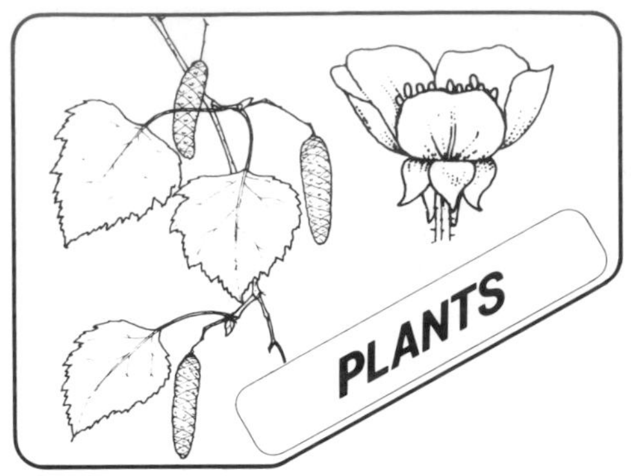

FLOWERS ON CLIFFS AND ROCKS

The cliffs and rocks of our coasts may seem to be inhospitable places for flowers, with hardly any soil, exposure to the winds and constant salty spray, yet they support a wealth of attractive plants which are a magnificent sight in spring and early summer.

A visit to the western coasts of Britain, such as Dorset, Cornwall or south-west Wales, in May will reveal a wonderful display of coastal flowers covering the cliffs and rocks, and it is a pity that most high summer holiday visitors miss this wonderful sight. In milder areas, especially in the south-west, the first cliff flowers begin in March, with early blooms of sea campion, or the attractive white clumps of Danish scurvygrass (so-called because of its high vitamin C content which used to help to prevent the incidence of scurvy amongst sailors) amongst the rocks. By April, the pink tussocks of thrift, the pale blue flowers of spring squill, looking like tiny little lilies, and the darker blue of bluebells (which often occur as a cliff plant in western areas, where it is humid enough) are in bloom. In some areas, especially Dorset and Devon, the yellow flowers of the wild cabbage appear in spring, growing strongly from amongst the fleshy grey-green leaves. This is the ancestor, not only of cabbages, but of several other brassica-type vegetables, such as sprouts or cauliflower; the wild plant is edible, but lacks the softness of the cultivated forms. Quite a few of the ancestors of our vegetables occur on the coast; for example the wild sea beet is the ancestor of sugar beet and beetroots, whilst wild carrot and wild parsnip both frequently occur here.

On limestone cliffs, such as in several parts of Wales and in Devon, there are some special cliff plants that only grow in these areas. The rare yellow goldilocks (different to, and not related to, the woodland one), is found in Devon and elsewhere, and the tiny yellow whitlowgrass in south Wales.

By the end of May, the great majority of cliff plants have come into flower, providing a magnificent display of colour. The sea campion, thrift and others have carried on flowering, whilst they are joined by the lively yellow flowers of golden samphire, the paler yellow-green of the unrelated sea samphire (which is actually in the carrot family), the pink flowers of wild thyme, rock-sea-spurrey, stonecrop and mallow.

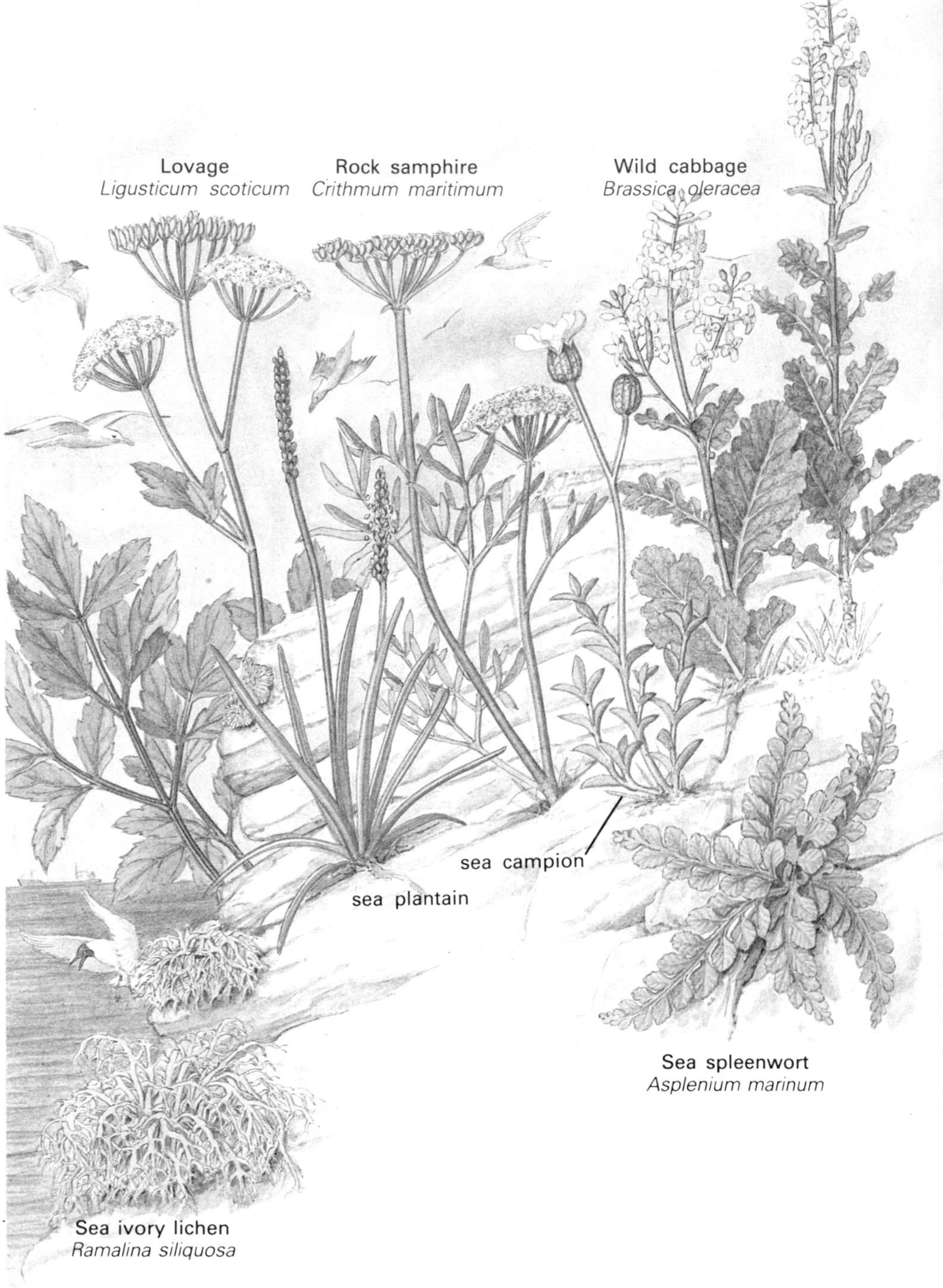

Lovage *Ligusticum scoticum*
Rock samphire *Crithmum maritimum*
Wild cabbage *Brassica oleracea*
sea campion
sea plantain
Sea spleenwort *Asplenium marinum*
Sea ivory lichen *Ramalina siliquosa*

A selection of coastal cliff and rock plants that occur in various parts of the country. As well as the flowering plants, the picture also shows two widespread non-flowering plants – the sea spleenwort and the lichen, sea ivory

In many places around our coasts, these have been joined by several introduced species that have found a suitable niche on our cliffs and now add to the display. In the south-west, the beautiful pink, magenta or yellow flowers of the Hottentot fig (a native of South Africa) spread freely over many of the rocky cliffs, looking completely at home. On many cliffs round much of the country, though especially in the south-west, the red, white or pink flowers of red valerian flourish right through the summer, and in some places the attractive flowers of white stonecrop occur in abundance. The mild climate of the coast, especially in the south-west, allows these exotic species to survive and spread even if their original home is somewhere much warmer. In the Isles of Scilly, which have the mildest climate in the country, a very high proportion of the flora consists of exotic species that have gone wild giving the islands a strangely foreign look to botanists accustomed to the rest of Britain.

Plants that grow on cliffs anywhere near the sea must be able to stand the effects of salt spray which can be highly damaging. Many are particularly fleshy and swollen, and this is an adaptation to the drying effect of the salt winds. Despite this difficulty, there are actually a whole range of plants that only grow on cliffs near the sea, partly due to the milder climate, but also because they have a particular requirement for the salt, or some other chemical which is provided by sea spray.

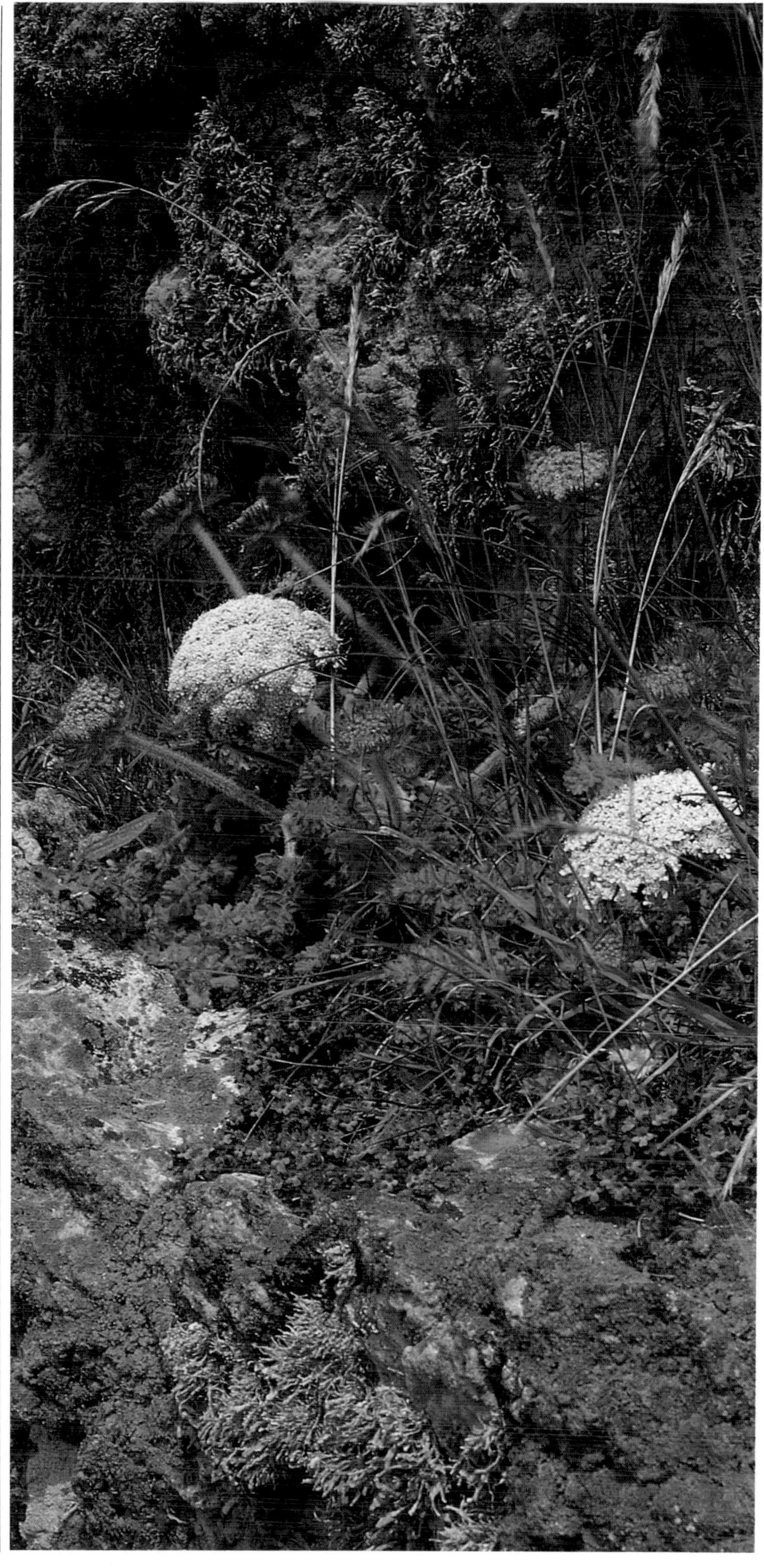

A dense mass of flowers growing on a sandstone cliff on the Isle of Wight including the white heads of wild carrot and wild thyme

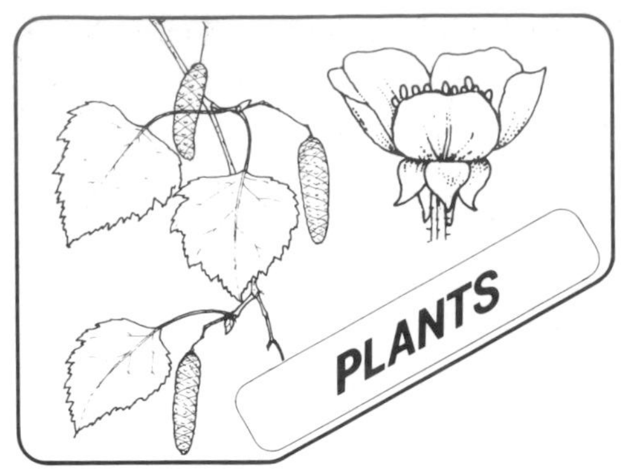

FLOWERS OF SAND & SHINGLE

All around the coasts, there are many areas of sand and shingle, including sandy beaches, dunes and shingle spits. Such places have their own special flowers, many of them very beautiful, which have adapted to life in an unstable environment and thrive in these unlikely areas.

Sand is hardly the most congenial environment for plant growth; there is little true soil between the grains, and water and nutrients drain out rapidly leaving the surface dry and infertile. Add to this the problems of surviving salt spray and the instability of sandy areas moved by the sea or blown by the wind, and you have an exceptionally harsh enrivonment. Below high water-mark, conditions are just too difficult for any flowering plant to survive (though there is a little group of flowering plants, the eelgrasses, that normally grow submerged by the sea and occasionally occur in very sandy conditions) but, just above high water-mark, there is quite a range of specialised species that not only survive but do well.

On some beaches, there is often a zone of plants just above the drift-line with scentless mayweed prominently displaying its large daisy-like flowers, the pretty pink flowers of the sea rocket together with the less distinguished sea beet, various goosefoot species and the oraches, close relatives of spinach. Like some of the cliff plants growing within reach of the spray zone, these plants are often particularly fleshy, a response to the

The beautiful flowers of sea bindweed, which is closely related to the garden weed and a frequent plant of both sand-dunes and coastal shingle. It has succulent kidney-shaped leaves

drying power of salt and the inherently dry nature of sand as a substrate. In other areas, especially where the sand is finer and more mobile, the first colonisers are all grasses, typically marram grass, lyme grass and the various couch grasses, in particular sea couch which is very tolerant of salt. These plants are all able to survive being buried by moving sand and, in very mobile conditions, they are often the first plants to begin to stabilise the dunes at the top of the beach. They are frequently joined by some highly attractive beach plants especially the yellow horned-poppy which has large golden yellow flowers and extremely long seed pods, and the glaucous leaves of sea-holly with its electric-blue flowers. In some places, the less attractive, but interesting, straggly cushions of the prickly saltwort occur on the upper parts of sandy beaches, and the fleshy little stems of the sea sandwort (sometimes known as sea purslane) push up through even quite mobile sand and tolerate periods of immersion in salt water.

More stable dunes, that have been in existence for longer and acquired more soil and vegetation cover, have additional special flowers such as the beautiful pink-flowered sea bindweed which is a close relative of our familiar garden weeds but is more delicate and attractive.

Shingle beaches and bars, where the stones are much larger, tend to have a rather different range of flowers, though a few species are shared between the two habitats. Some flowers only occur on coastal shingle, with no other habitat being right for them, perhaps either because they cannot tolerate very much competition (and there is virtually none on shingle banks) or because they need particular nutrients from the sea spray. The sea pea is an attractive reddish-purple flowered relative of the garden sweet pea which grows abundantly on some shingle banks, especially in the east; sea kale is a large fleshy plant, related to the cabbage, which produces sprays of attractive white flowers in early summer – it used to be eaten as a vegetable and shingle was heaped around the stems to blanch them. Herb Robert, which is common in other habitats, occurs on shingle beaches in a prostrate coastal form and is readily confused with a much rarer plant, the little robin. Both are pink-flowered members of the Geranium family but the little robin is confined to just a few coastal shingle banks. Both sea-holly and the yellow horned-poppy occur frequently on shingle beaches as well as sand, while curled dock is another common feature of shingle. The upper parts of shingle beaches, where more soil has begun to accumulate between the stones and the influence of salt spray is rather less, can support a surprising array of plants including gorse, holly and even oak trees usually growing as flattened rounded clumps rather than the more familiar trees!

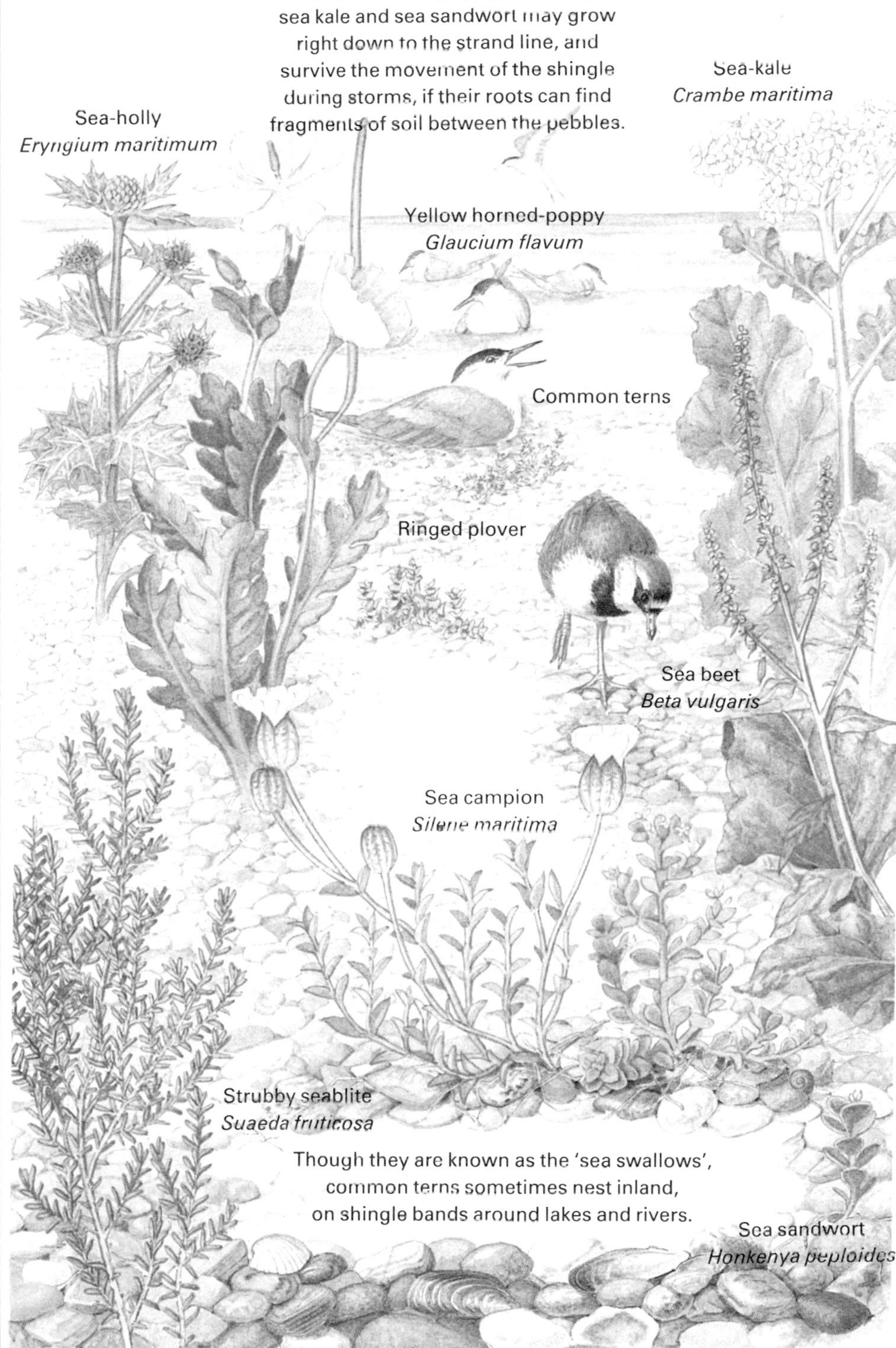
Yellow horned-poppy, sea holly, sea kale and sea sandwort may grow right down to the strand line, and survive the movement of the shingle during storms, if their roots can find fragments of soil between the pebbles.
Sea-holly
Eryngium maritimum
Sea-kale
Crambe maritima
Yellow horned-poppy
Glaucium flavum
Common terns
Ringed plover
Sea beet
Beta vulgaris
Sea campion
Silene maritima
Strubby seablite
Suaeda fruticosa
Though they are known as the 'sea swallows', common terns sometimes nest inland, on shingle bands around lakes and rivers.
Sea sandwort
Honkenya peploides

An in-habitat picture showing a selection of shingle-loving plants, together with two typical birds of the habitat

Quite often, these older, drier shingle areas develop an acid heathland vegetation, dominated by bell heather or ling. This is just part of the natural process of coastal stabilisation.

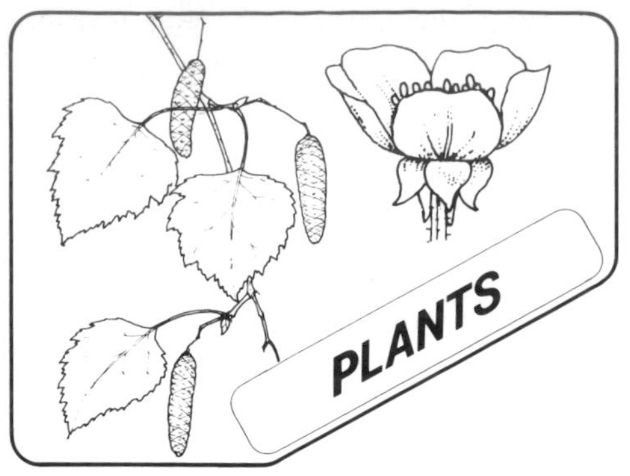

SEAWEEDS

From the upper shore down to well below low tide-mark, all our rockier coasts are covered with seaweeds. They may be best known to most people for their habit of making rocks slippery and bathing difficult, but in fact this area is a fascinating and varied community full of life and interest.

The term seaweeds is a very general one, embracing all the plants that grow in the sea. Virtually all of our seaweeds are members of a group of plants known as algae, related to the green slime that grows on ponds in summer; unlike flowering plants, they do not reproduce by means of flowers and fruit. The only higher plants that have been able to colonise the sea below low tide mark are the eel-grasses, or Zosteras, of which there are three species around our coasts. Their green strap-shaped leaves are often confused with the greener seaweeds.

Algae produce food in the same way as green flowering plants – by using the sun's energy to convert carbon dioxide into carbohydrates – and also possess the green pigment, chlorophyll, which is essential for this process. However, because filtration of sunlight through different depths of seawater produces light of different composition, they have developed different pigments to utilise the light to best advantage. In many cases, these additional pigments mask the green chlorophyll and most seaweeds appear to be brown, red or even purple, though a few are green. Normally the green species are those that occur higher up the shore, where they are exposed most often to the full composition of sunlight, but some, such as the green sea lettuce, are also found to a depth of about 20 metres.

The brown seaweeds are probably the commonest and certainly the best known; they are also usually the largest plants. Most brown seaweeds are attached to rock or other stable substrate, and they usually show a clear zonation up the shore. This is basically controlled by two factors – how much drying out each species can stand when the tide goes out and how quickly they can grow. Those that are most resistant to drying out, such as the spiral wrack and the channelled wrack, grow near the top of the shore though both are slow-growing. The channelled wrack, as its name suggests, has channels along the underside of the fronds, formed by inrolling of the margins and this helps to retain water. For the upper species on a rocky shore, this ability to withstand drying is vitally important, since the difference between total immersion in seawater (when the tissues have to be permeable to water to allow the plant to grow) and many hours on bare rock in hot sunny weather is extreme, and some of the upper rocky shore species are particularly oily to help conserve liquids.

The middle zone of the shore supports more species, growing rapidly and competitively together; the exact

Seaweeds

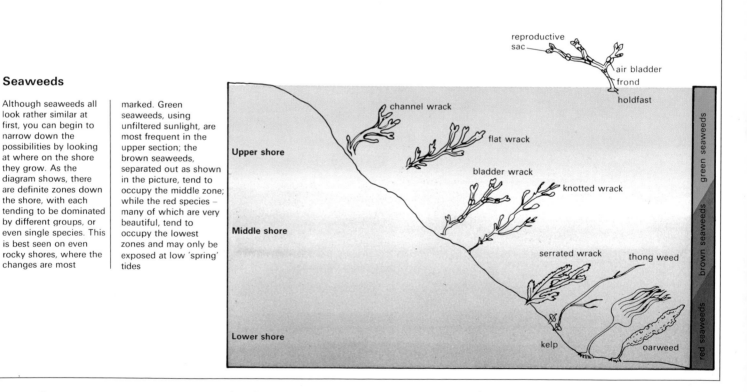

Although seaweeds all look rather similar at first, you can begin to narrow down the possibilities by looking at where on the shore they grow. As the diagram shows, there are definite zones down the shore, with each tending to be dominated by different groups, or even single species. This is best seen on even rocky shores, where the changes are most marked. Green seaweeds, using unfiltered sunlight, are most frequent in the upper section; the brown seaweeds, separated out as shown in the picture, tend to occupy the middle zone; while the red species – many of which are very beautiful, tend to occupy the lowest zones and may only be exposed at low 'spring' tides

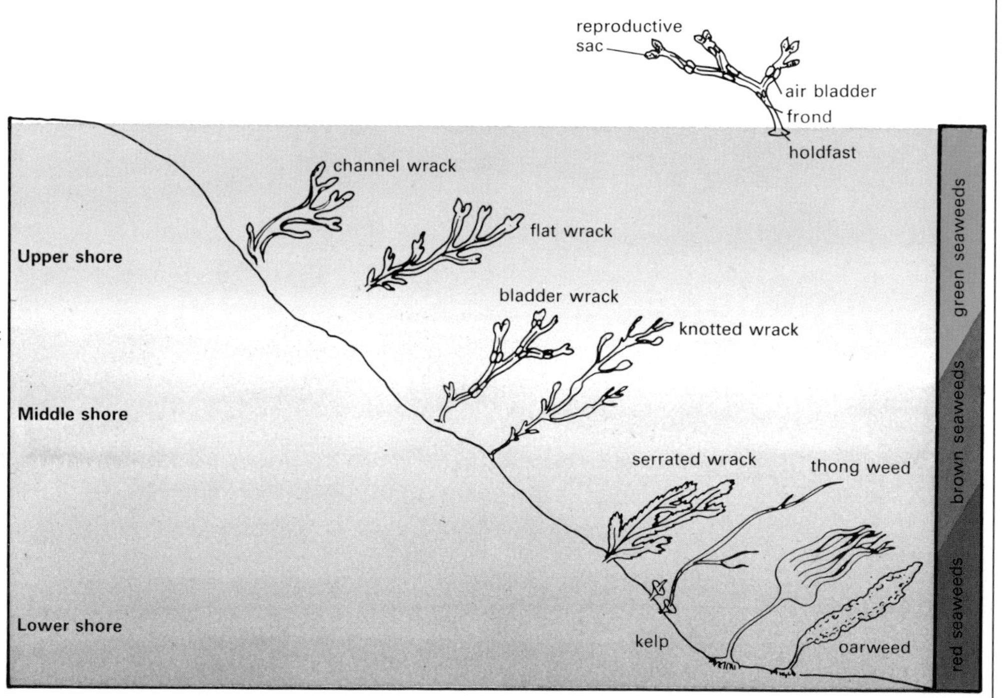

mixture of species depends on how exposed the shore is and how rocky. Some species, often with long fronds, can readily withstand regular up and down and swirling movements, but it takes shorter tougher species to survive more direct action from waves. As an example, the knotted wrack is commonest on sheltered rocky shores where its long elastic fronds do best, because direct action from waves is less here, and they include species which grow up to four-and-a-half metres long and three metres across.

The red seaweeds are generally more delicate and smaller than the brown seaweeds. They are far less clearly zoned than the browns, but tend to favour more sheltered sites including rock pools. Several of them grow as epiphytes on other stronger species, especially on the brown seaweeds.

For centuries, seaweeds have been used as food, and in some parts of the world they still are; in Japan for example some seaweeds are regarded as a delicacy. In northern and western parts of Britain, and especially in western Ireland, species such as laver

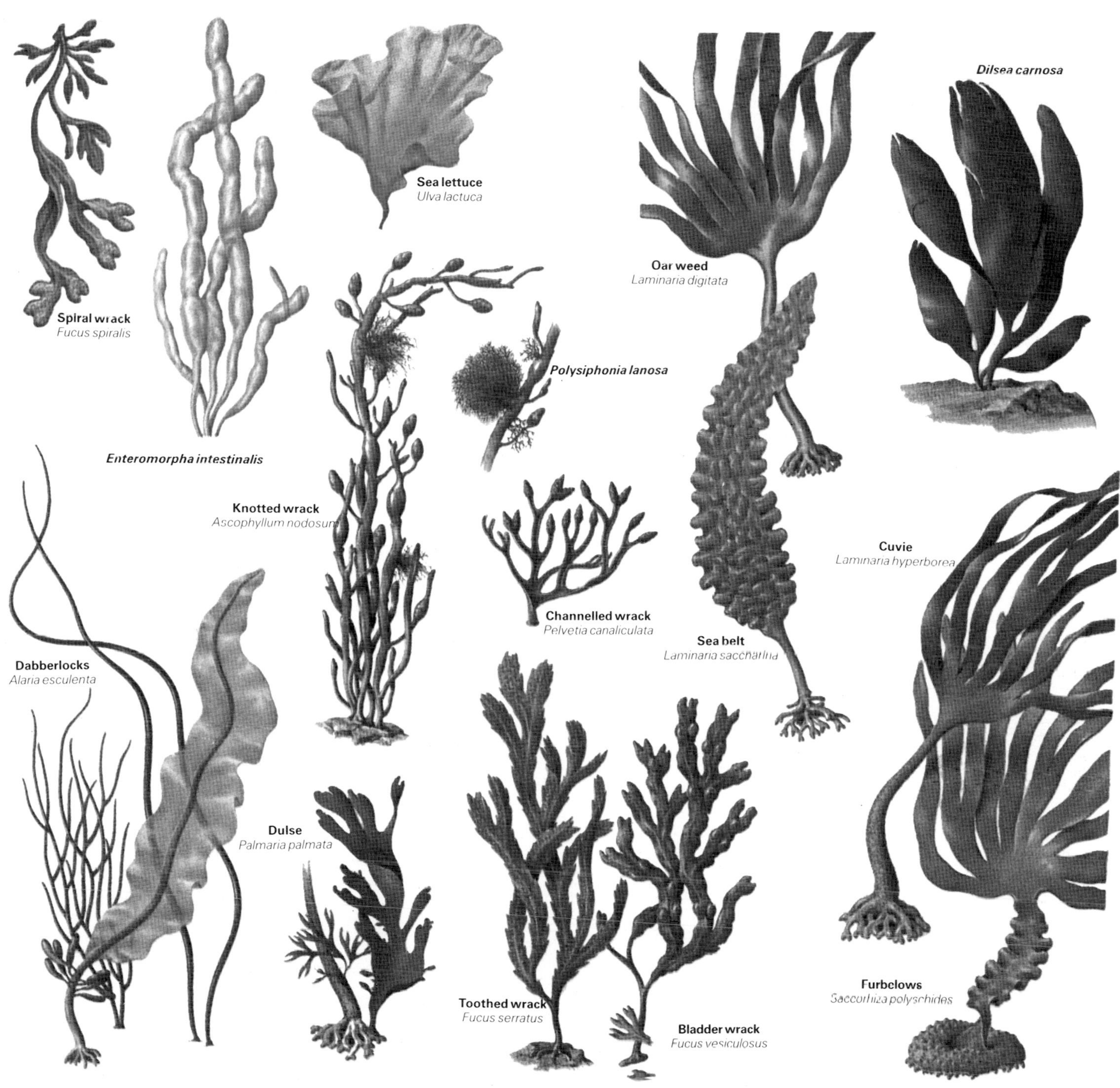

A selection of some of the many attractive species of seaweeds which can be found at different levels on our shores

whilst bladder wrack is commoner on more exposed shore by virtue of its shorter, stronger stems.

Lower down the shore and on below low tide mark to depths of 20 or 30 metres, the kelps replace the wracks. They often have very long fronds, are still collected; it is made into laver bread in South Wales. They are not rich in proteins, so make a poor food on their own; however, they have an abundance of mineral salts and can provide a valuable supplement to the diet.

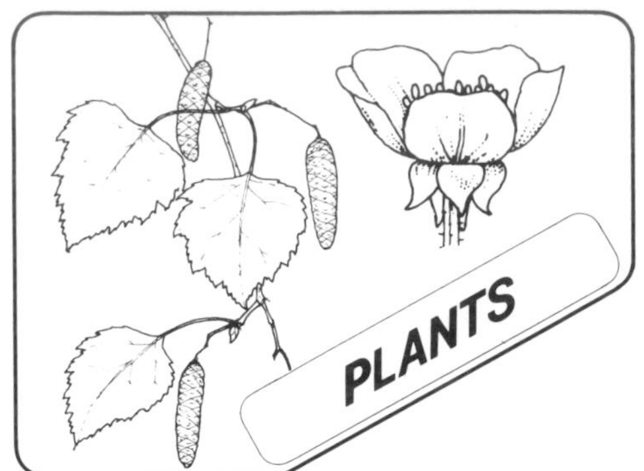

Bog Plants

Bogs may just seem like places where your boots disappear into wet black peaty mud, but they are also home to a delicately-balanced community of plants, many with extraordinarily beautiful flowers and foliage especially when looked at closely.

Bogs are wet peaty acid places with very low nutrient levels. They are hardly the most favourable medium for plant growth and specialised bog plants have to be well-adapted to survive there; some interesting mechanisms have evolved to cope with the conditions. Like many unfavourable places, the competition from strong growing plants is minimal so those that can tolerate the situation can grow freely, and many a bog is enlivened by carpets of beautiful pink cranberry flowers in June, the delicate bells of bog rosemary or sheets of the lovely yellow bog asphodel or the white flowers of cotton grass.

In Britain, we have a number of plants that are able to catch and digest insects as a means of supplementing their diet, and these are known as insectivorous plants. All the British species, with the exception of one or two of the bladderworts which are more nutrient-demanding, occur in bogs. This is a reflection of just how poor bogs are in nutrients, especially nitrates, and the insectivorous habit allows these plants to acquire a little extra food to help them survive even in these very difficult conditions. Interestingly the situation also works in reverse, as there are some specialised insects, such as a plume moth, with larvae which feed on the insectivorous plants!

The commonest of our insect-eating plants in bogs are the sundews. Their leaves, covered with sticky, glistening red hairs, are readily picked out, though they are never more than a few centimetres high, and they are often abundant on bare peat or in shallow water. The most frequent of the three species is the round-leaved sundew which grows almost anywhere in bogs, rapidly spreading if new areas become available. Almost as common is the long-leaved or intermediate sundew, with longer spatula-shaped leaves, growing mainly in damp rather than very wet parts. The one most rarely seen is the great sundew which is also the largest and most impressive species. It favours very wet carpets of floating bog moss and is commoner in the north, where the rainfall is higher, than the south. There are also hybrids between the species, just to confuse the issue.

There are two species of the insect-eating butterworts in mainland Britain, with a third species occurring only in western Ireland. These have distinctive flat rosettes of leaves which are sticky on the upper surface, and readily trap any small insect that lands on them. The pale, or western, butterwort is commoner in the south and west, whilst the larger purple common butterwort is more frequent in the north. They all secrete enzymes from the leaf surface to digest the hapless insects, before reabsorbing the resulting 'insect soup'; it is these enzymes that have given the plants their name for an extract of the leaves can help to curdle milk. The commonest of the bladderworts to occur is the pale-flowered lesser bladderwort, and their extraordinary method of catching insects underwater has already been described (see page 55).

The basis of most bogs are the bog mosses or Sphagnum species. There are about 30 different types in Britain, and every bog in the country has at least a few species. They are able to survive, even if only fed on rainwater, by a remarkable ability to extract minerals from water long after the concentration of nutrients in their

The tiny pink bell-like flowers of cranberry, seen here growing on the surface of a bog. The flowers produce an edible red berry

cells is greater than that in the water. It is the bog mosses that build up in a partially-decomposed form to make peat which underlies every bog. Most of the bog mosses are green, though there are also a few striking red-leaved species.

Other plants of bogs include the tiny trailing stems of cranberry, which produces beautiful little pink flowers in June followed by the deep red edible berries in autumn. Bog rosemary, a dwarf shrub with attractive little pink bell-flowers, is related to the heathers rather than rosemary – its leaves, however, look rather like those of rosemary. The bog asphodel is a relative of the lilies which throws up spikes of golden flowers followed by distinctive reddish fruiting spikes and, in the right conditions, it forms great sheets of colour. One of the most distinctive of bog plants is the cotton grass, though it is only noticed by most people when it produces its fluffy white cotton-like fruits. There are several species, but the commonest over most of the country is the narrow-leaved cotton grass. There is also a heather – the cross-leaved heath – a clubmoss, the beautiful marsh gentian, a special bog orchid and several species of sedges, rushes and grasses that occur in bogs. Together, they make up a community that may lack the variety of some habitats but which compensates for it in colour and interest.

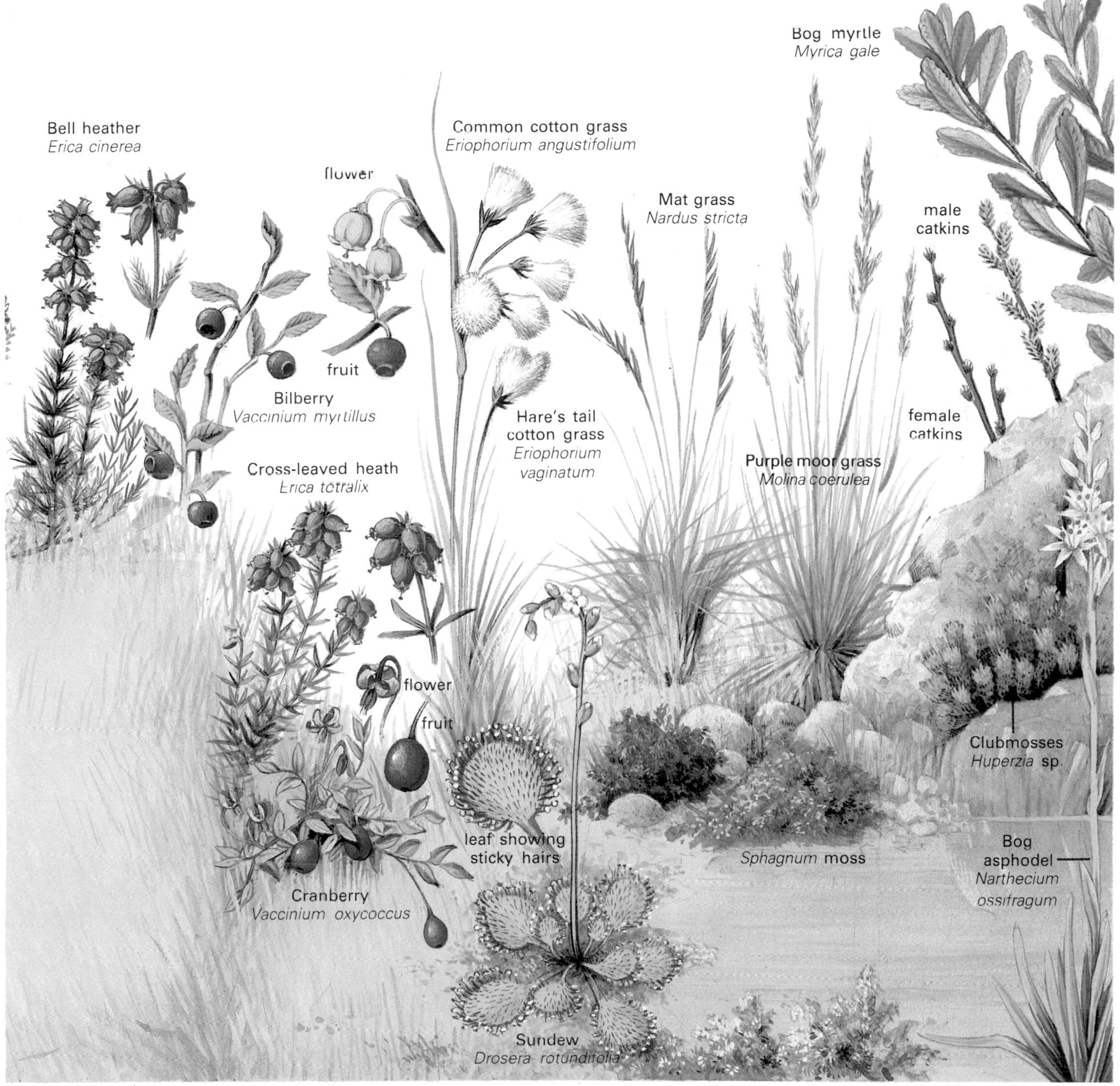

A small selection from the surprisingly wide range of flowers, and other plants, that can make up the thriving bog community

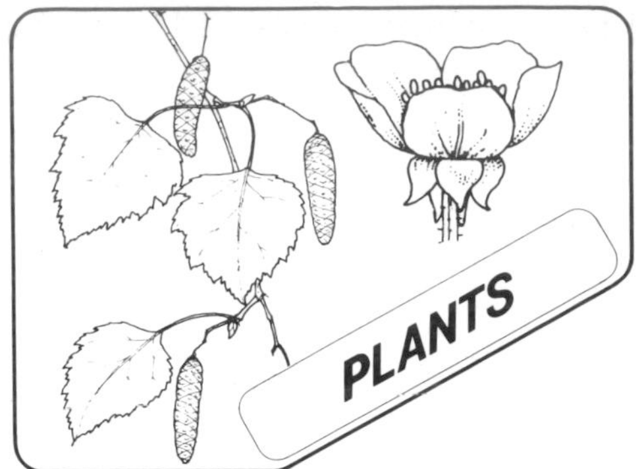

MOUNTAIN FLOWERS

High up in the mist and cloud of some of the mountains of northern and western Britain, the winter snow clears to reveal 'rock gardens' of flowers of dazzling blues, yellows and reds. For those prepared to walk, a marvellous sight awaits them.

Although none of our mountains are very high, with few over 1200 metres, there is a great range of specialised mountain flowers to be found scattered about the uplands. When the last great Ice Age began to retreat from our northern hills leaving the ground ready for colonisation, the first plants to move back were the cold-resistant Arctic species, together with a few that were most at home in the mountains of Europe. As the climate warmed and trees began to colonise the lower areas, these smaller varieties were pushed towards higher, colder ground. Most such species that followed in the wake of the ice need open, uncompetitive conditions in which to survive; they could not stand the shade of the forests so moved into the mountains.

At first, most of our mountains probably had a reasonably rich flora with a wide range of species. Unfortunately, though, most of these colonisers needed lime-rich soil such as was formed in the early post-glacial times, but the inherently acid rocks of most of the uplands and the high rainfall which leaches lime out of the soil have, between them, gradually reduced the amount of suitable habitat for most mountain plants. In more recent centuries, man has put large numbers of domestic stock out onto the hills and reduced the number of flowers in all but the more inaccessible places. We are therefore left with only rather poor remnants of our former mountain flora.

There in no doubt that the best

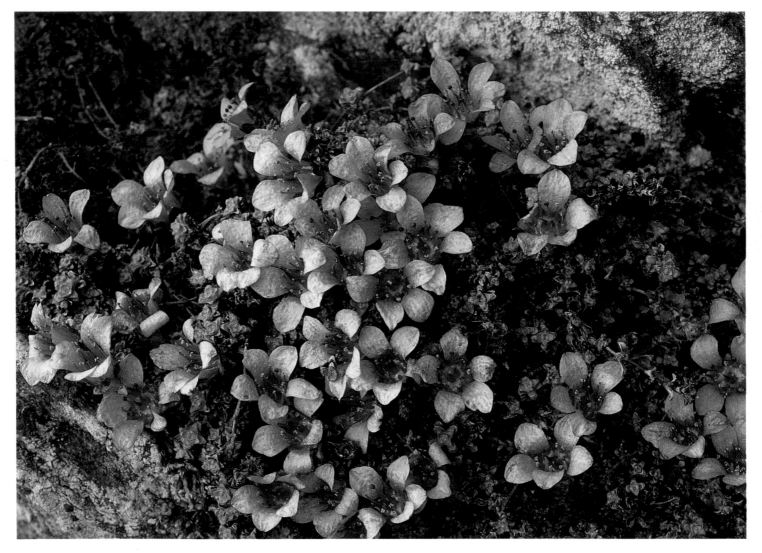

A dense cushion of purple saxifrage growing high on Ben Lawers in Tayside, flowering just as the snow melts

places to find mountain plants in Britain are on uplands where limestone, or other lime-rich rocks, outcrop. In fact, further north, areas of limestone at sea-level have fine displays of mountain flowers. The best areas of all are on the mica-schist rocks of Perthshire which weather readily to give a series of cliffs, ledges and lime rich grassland that are ideal for alpine flowers. Over 60 per cent of our mountin flowers occur on one mountain in this region, and its cliffs and gullies above about 500 metres are a wonderful display of colourful flowers. The intense blue of the alpine gentian, the pink or red of moss campion and purple saxifrage, together with mountain avens, roseroot, other saxifrages, lady's-mantle, globeflowers and a myriad of usually over, before the bulk of the flowers have appeared, for the mountain summer is a short one, and most plants confine their growth and flowering to just a few months, with best displays to be seen in July and August.

To survive in these short summers and harsh winters, the higher mountain plants have evolved many adaptations. Most of those that grow in exposed situations have a dwarf cushion-like habit, frequently with densely hairy leaves. These modifications help to prevent freezing, but also conserve water, since drought is a problem when all available water is frozen for long periods. Most alpines are perennial plants, since the uncertainties of flowering, being pollinated, having time to ripen seed before winter comes and ensuring that enough seeds germinate in the following spring to start the cycle again are too much for most plants. One notable exception to the rule is the snow gentian which is an annual, but it is confined to just one small mountain range so can hardly be classed as successful. Its close relative, the spring gentian – also an upland plant – is a perennial able to reproduce by underground shoots as well as seed.

A familiar feature of many alpine plants is their dazzlingly colourful flowers, and at least one reason for this is their need to attract the few insects which are around to pollinate them. By no means all alpine plants are insect-pollinated, but those that are have to be very attractive and

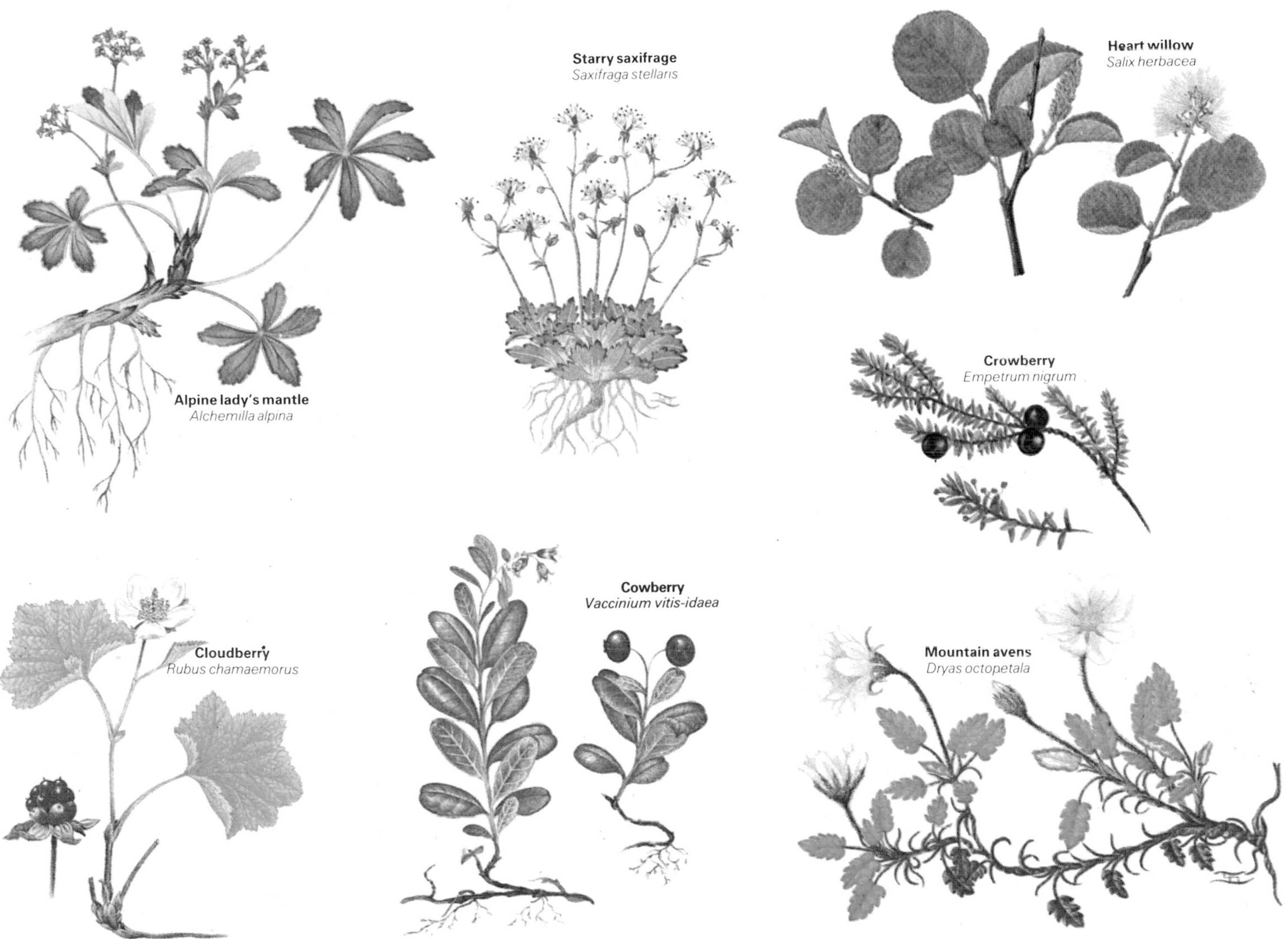

A selection of mountain flowers, from a variety of situations, to show some of the species you might expect to see

other flowers are a marvellous sight. The purple saxifrage is extraordinarily hardy appearing once the snow melts, even as early as March in freezing conditions, and it makes a welcome splash of colour in an otherwise wintry landscape. By June, it is

conspicuous to the few insects which are about. By chance, this often makes them look attractive to us, and perhaps this beauty is added to by the sheer exertion which is needed to see them, in addition to the clean air and attractive scenery.

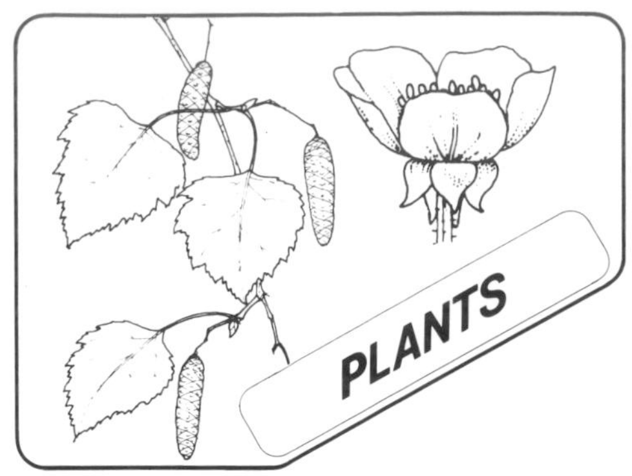

FLOWERS OF TOWNS

A surprising number of flowers have come to terms with urban life and, for those that have, it provides an attractive living environment being warmer than the surrounding countryside. There are plants that have adapted to almost every aspect of town life, living on walls or pavements, as weeds in gardens and even on building sites.

Although towns and cities seem, at first sight, to be rather hostile places for wild flowers, they actually offer a tremendous range of micro-habitats for plants that can cope with disturbance and often poor soils.

Amongst the less natural habitats, walls and pavements may seem the least likely places to find plants. Certainly, new concrete or paving is devoid of obvious life, but it does not take long before mosses and lichens appear on the surfaces. On older walls, with softer lime mortar, there is often a wonderful display of flowers and ferns, though on modern walls plants have to find a home in the less hospitable cement mortar. The more neglected, the better such places become for plants, as little cracks and crannies open up allowing soil to collect and seeds to enter. A few plants specialise in this sort of habitat; the wall or ivy-leaved toadflax, for example, has flowers that grow normally towards the light, but the seed capsules as they ripen grow towards the dark depositing the seeds in cracks. There are also examples of wall bedstraws, wall lettuce, wall speedwell, wall barley and, of course, the wallflower. For many plants, the

A clump of Oxford ragwort growing on an old wall. Although Sicilian in origin, it has naturalised completely through urban Britain

colonisation of walls has been an extension of their ability to grow naturally on cliffs, though some of the species which have adapted to the dry shallow soil that collects on the top of the walls were originally sand-dune plants.

Many plants of urban situations are of foreign origin, coming into the country by accident or design, and finding conditions to their liking. This is partly due to the more intensive activities of man which have brought in a larger number of species but also because there is more bare ground available for new colonisers than in the closed vegetation of natural habitats. A fascinating and well-documented example is provided by the Oxford ragwort; its history in Britain is described in the panel.

Plants that occur where they are not wanted are known as weeds, and this applies in full measure to many plants that have colonised our gardens. Some, such as couch grass, the bindweeds, ground-elder, the yellow Oxalis species, groundsel and others are particularly unpopular because of their abilities to spread and out-compete our favoured garden flowers. Others such as daisies or speedwells in the lawns, or celandines and selfheal under the apples tree are rather more welcome, and certainly do no harm; every garden should have at least a few native plants.

Towns and cities even include a few areas that are more like natural habitats. There are often small areas of woodland and ponds, and the man-made canals and railway banks provide a useful environment for species unable to survive in the more urban parts of towns. Many species have been able to colonise towns and cities by moving in along these corridors, dispersing into new suitable habitats as they arise. Altogether, the total list of flowers for any sizeable conurbation is likely to be very high running into many hundreds of species, and even a medium-sized garden, if searched hard, can turn up 70 or 80 different sorts of wild flowers. As the pressures on the countryside grow our 300,000 or so hectares of gardens have become major wild flower sanctuaries.

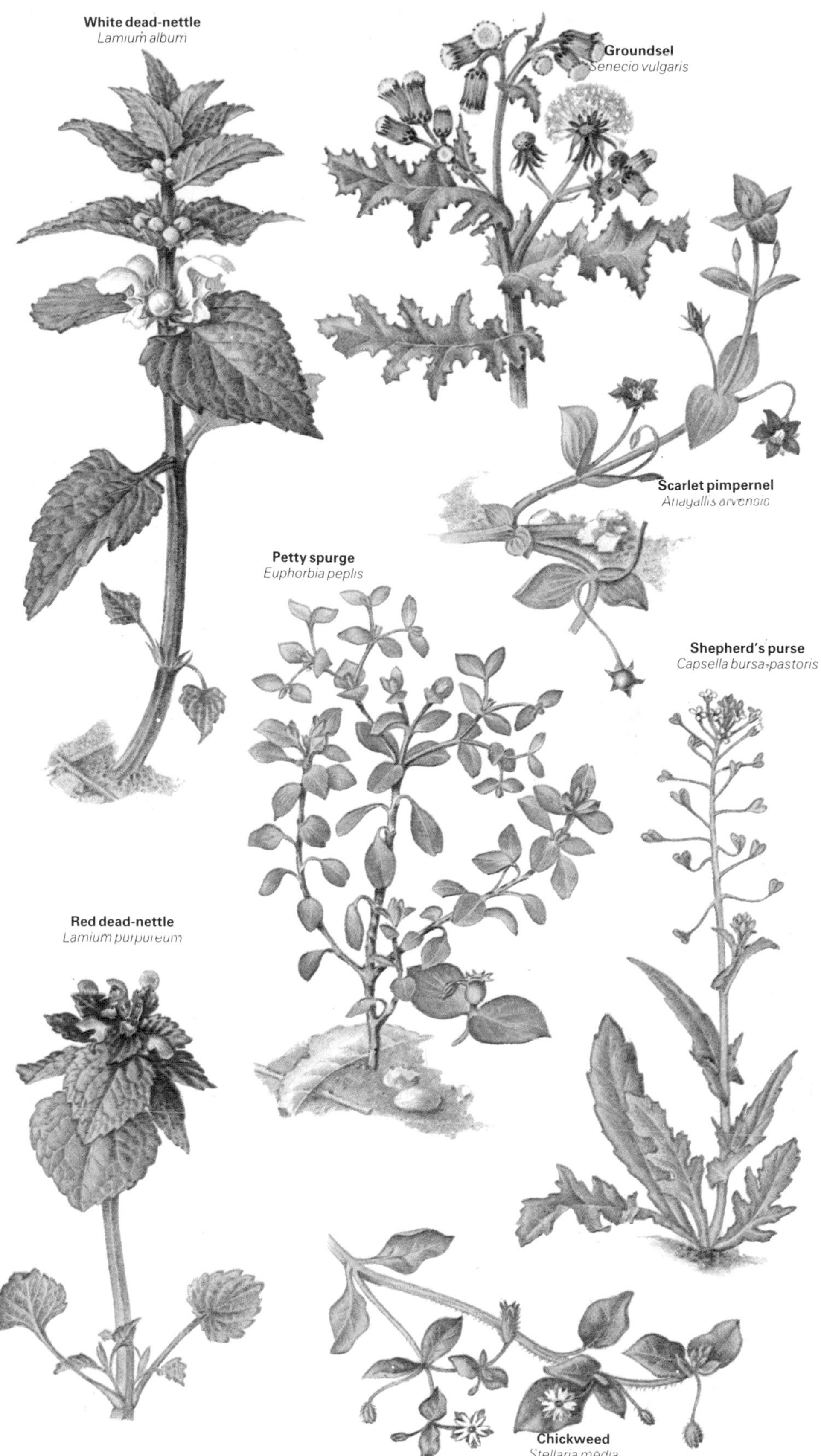

Weeds sometimes described as 'plants out of place' can be very attractive. Look out for the scarlet pimpernel, sometimes known as the poor man's weatherglass, because the flowers remain closed on overcast days

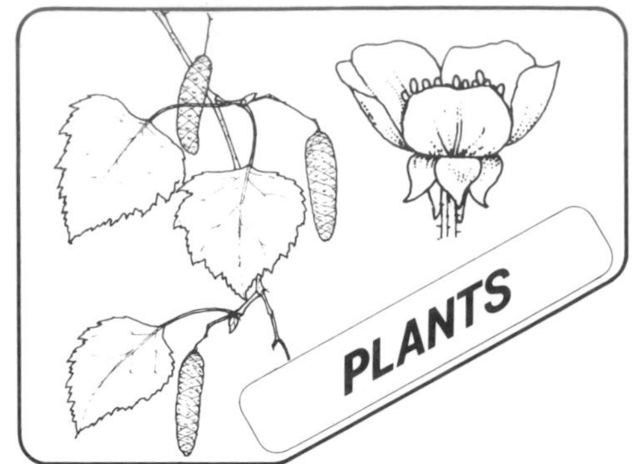

Plants of Native Pinewoods

Once there were extensive pinewoods over much of northern Britain. Now there are only a few remnants scattered through the Scottish highlands, but these still retain a special array of plants and animals, many of which occur nowhere else in the country.

As the ice retreated from Britain thousands of years ago, one of the earliest colonising trees was the Scots pine growing in extensive open forests over most of the country. As the climate warmed, it was ousted from the lowlands by more competitive trees, such as oak and lime, that were able to do better in these conditions. In most of Scotland, though, it remained as the native tree and, until about the 17th century, there were extensive pine forests across the whole country. Then, for various reasons, man began to exploit these forests and, even in the more inaccessible areas, trees were felled and floated down the rivers to the ports. The forests disappeared rapidly and hardly any area was left untouched; all that remains now is a series of remnants, or relics, of this once-extensive great forest. The best known areas are Rothiemurchus and Abernethy in the Spey Valley, the Black Wood of Rannock, Beinn Eighe and Glen Affric; and there are many other smaller areas. Because of their history and origins, these woods have had many thousands of years to develop – perhaps 10,000 for the oldest – and consequently, they have their own specialised flora and fauna many of which are themselves relics of the Ice Age. The trees themselves may be 200 or 300 years old, but the situation itself is of a much greater age. The woods that are left tend to be very

The ancient native pinewoods of Scotland, seen here in the Spey valley, are very different from pine plantations. They tend to be much more open, with areas of heather, and they have a much richer flora. The ranks of purpose planted conifers now being planted in some of the more northerly parts of Scotland create a very different habitat

open in character, with many gaps in the canopy, so there is a mixture of light areas and shadier parts (in contrast to a pine plantation which is deeply shaded throughout, supporting the appropriate light-demanding or shade-demanding flowers. The needle litter has built up over centuries and is deep and stable enough to allow an extensive carpet of mosses to develop; many fungi appear in the autumn.

The flora is not so rich as that of lowland ancient woods but there are many special plants that rarely occur anywhere else. Creeping amongst the mossy carpet are the rosettes and shoots of the creeping lady's-tresses, a rare orchid that sends up spikes of spiralling white flowers in the late summer, often in carpets. The chickweed wintergreen is a lovely flower, white but delicately suffused with pink which is neither a wintergreen nor a chickweed but a relative of the primrose! It is common and widespread in pinewoods and has been able to spread into plantations as well as surviving in other habitats too. There are also true wintergreens and the pinewoods are one of the best places to see them. The most characteristic species of these woods are the intermediate wintergreen, the serrated wintergreen with noticeably one-sided spikes of flowers and the rare, but very beautiful, one-flowered wintergreen. This last species is confined to native pinewoods and even there it seems to be decreasing.

One of the commonest of the pinewood flowers, though not the most conspicuous, is the cowberry which produces little sprays of pink flowers from amongst its dark green leaves followed in autumn by red berries. The pinewoods are good places for 'berry' plants with bilberry, bearberry and crowberry as well as the cowberry – all relatives of the heathers and rhododendrons, except for the crowberry which is in a closely-related family of its own. There are also species which are not confined to pinewoods, such as ling and bell-heather, bracken, wood sorrel and plants like sundew and common butterwort in the wetter areas.

Most native pinewoods have a characteristic under-layer of juniper bushes. Juniper was also one of the earliest colonisers of the post-glacial landscape, coming in even before pine and forming an open tundra-type community. Most of this has been ousted as the climate has warmed, but it still survives as quite a common shrub, occasionally forming its own forests, in the north of Britain, with an outlying population on the chalk and limestone of southern England. Its attractive purplish berries are used as a flavouring for gin.

Native scottish pinewoods support a range of specialised plants, many of which grow nowhere else. Here are some of those that are more widespread, together with some of the characteristic birds

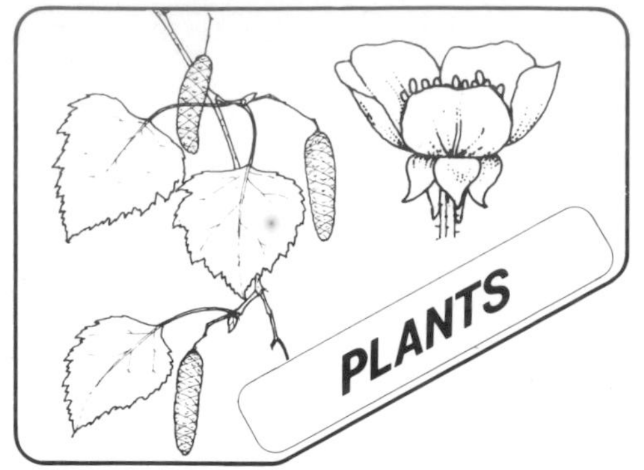

SOME WOODLAND FUNGI

Our woodlands are home to a tremendous variety of fungi – mushrooms and toadstools – which spend most of the year in a dormant state below the soil, but burst forth after the autumn rains to produce a remarkable display of colour, even in the deepest shade.

Fungi are very different from flowering plants, both in the way that they acquire their food and in the method of reproduction. Whereas green plants, which include virtually all the flowering plants, use the energy of sunlight to build up complex chemicals from water and carbon dioxide, fungi do almost the opposite. They are unable to manufacture their own foods directly, so they rely on breaking down the tissues of other animals or plants, dead or alive. If they live on dead material, such as rotting wood, leaf litter and the like, they are known as saprophytes, whereas those that attack living material, sometimes even killing them, are called parasites. The saprophytes, in particular, are an essential part of the woodland ecosystem, allowing nutrients to recycle and preventing the build-up of dead material.

Any old woodland, especially if it has a range of different trees and shrubs, will support many species of fungi, both parasites and saprophytes. If the trees have been allowed to age so that there are dead branches, fallen logs and old stumps, then the number and variety of fungi will be even greater. For most of the year fungi live underground, usually in the form of masses of threads growing through the soil or wood and known as mycelia. A warm, not too dry summer followed by a wet early autumn are ideal conditions for fungi to produce their fruiting bodies. These grow out from the mycelium, often at a considerable rate, and ex-

A bracket fungi – the oyster fungus – growing on the trunk of a dying beech. These are the 'fruiting bodies' of the fungus

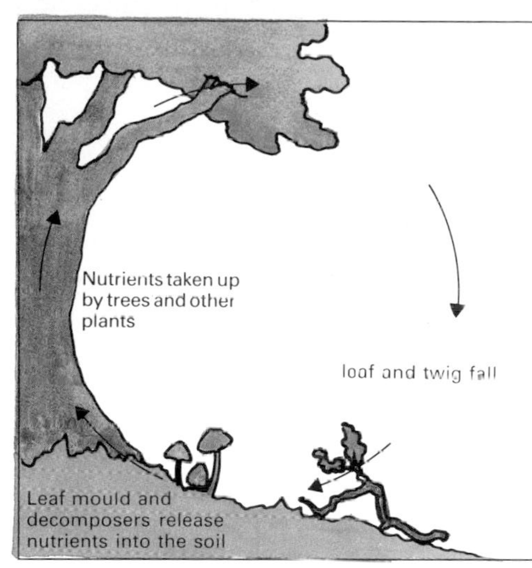

Woodland fungi

In a well-established woodland, there is a continual recycling of nutrients from the soil into plants, and back again, the fungi play a very important role in this cycle. Trees and shrubs absorb nutrients from the soil and incorporate them into their leaves and wood. Leaves fall to the ground annually, and older wood falls to the ground, where both are broken down by fungi, and other decomposers, using them as food, and released into the soil. From here, they can be reabsorbed by the trees

pand to form the typical mushroom or toadstool shape that we know so well. These structures produce vast quantities of spores which blow in the breeze and eventually fall to the ground. A tiny proportion will survive to germinate into new individual fungi.

Some fungi are particularly associated with certain species of tree. For example, the bright red caps of fly agaric, with their white spots, are familiar associates of birch trees. Certain species of Russula are found growing with beech trees, whilst others, such as the sickener (so-called because it is a powerful emetic) are usually seen among pines. Boletus species, too, exhibit particular associations; some grow with hazel, others with Scots pine, and others with oaks and, interestingly, they may change their associations according to the area involved, being found with one species in the north but another in the south. Mostly, this is due to a close relationship between the fungus and the tree – known as a mycorrhizal association – but in other cases they may simply share a common soil preference. Other species may live directly on trees, not necessarily as a parasite, but always preferring standing dead wood of a particular species. The beech-tuft, or porcelain fungus, for example, is a frequent sight growing on dead or dying beech trees, while the Jew's ear fungus almost invariably grows on elder bushes.

Most woodland fungi are seasonal, appearing at the same time of year, though they are heavily dependent on the weather and may not appear at all in some years. The best time is the autumn; but there are spring species such as the strange-looking morel fungus (a well-known delicacy) and even winter ones such as the frost-resistant velvet shank, or the attractive scarlet-coloured red elf-cup, though the latter tends to be confined to warmer areas where the winters are less harsh. Some, such as the unpleasant-smelling stinkhorn, are dependent much more on the weather than on the season and they appear at almost any time, from spring to autumn, after a warm rainy period. Stinkhorns are readily detected by their smell, even from many metres away, and you quickly get to know if any are about in the woods!

Most species last as fruiting bodies for only a few days or weeks, being eaten by slugs or mice, hit by early frosts or even relying on self-digestion to help release the spores. A few species, however, especially the bracket fungi, last for months or even years as tough woody structures on the trunks of trees. The birch bracket fungus used to be collected as a useful tinder for lighting fires and other species are hard and woody enough to act as firewood. Some huge brackets of a metre or more across may be many years old.

Bare-edged russula
Russula vesca

Penny bun
Boletus edulis

Chanterelle
Cantharellus cibarius

Common puff-ball
Lycoperdon perlatum

Death cap
Amanita phalloides

Fungi you are likely to find in a woodland glade. The chanterelle smells faintly of apricots and the bare-edged russula is found especially under oak and beech

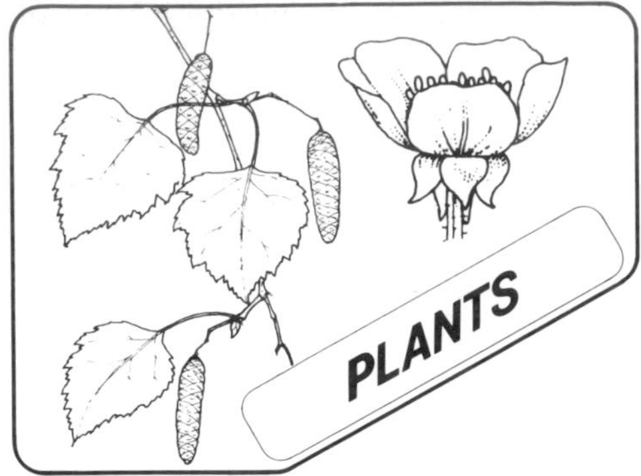

WEEDS OF ARABLE FIELDS

Arable fields have their own special wild plants and, despite modern agricultural methods, the sight of a field red with poppies or filled with other weeds is still not that uncommon for it seems that, whatever method of control the farmer tries, the weeds fight back!

The annual cultivation of crops by ploughing and seeding produces a peculiar type of habitat that is quite unsuitable for the great majority of perennial or slow-growing flowers but, for those which can exploit it, is ideal. After all, the cultivation methods are designed to help the crop plants grow rapidly and successfully without competition, and the very same process suits certain wild plants. These plants, because they are growing amongst the crop and where they are not wanted, are known as arable weeds.

The history of such plants is not always clear, but it is certain that they have a long association with man and farming. Many of them are plants of Middle Eastern or Mediterranean origin, and they followed the early settlers into Britain in prehistoric times. In some cases, their assocation with man is so long-lived and so complete that their natural origins are unknown and there are no truly wild populations in existence. Others, like the cornflower, are known to have been natural colonisers of the bare fertile ground left as the ice retreated from Britain thousands of years ago, and they were naturally adapted to the soil produced by cultivation.

A century ago, arable weeds were abundant, threatening the crop in years when they did particularly well. On the Isle of Wight, in Hampshire, one plant, the field cow-wheat, was known as the 'poverty weed', so completely could it ruin crops. Now, however, it is one of our rarest wild flowers, with only two or three sites left in the country; and this is typical of the story for many species. The fight against arable weeds has intensified due to modern chemicals and better methods of cleaning seeds, so that many of the less adaptable plants or those whose seeds are markedly different from those of the crop plant,

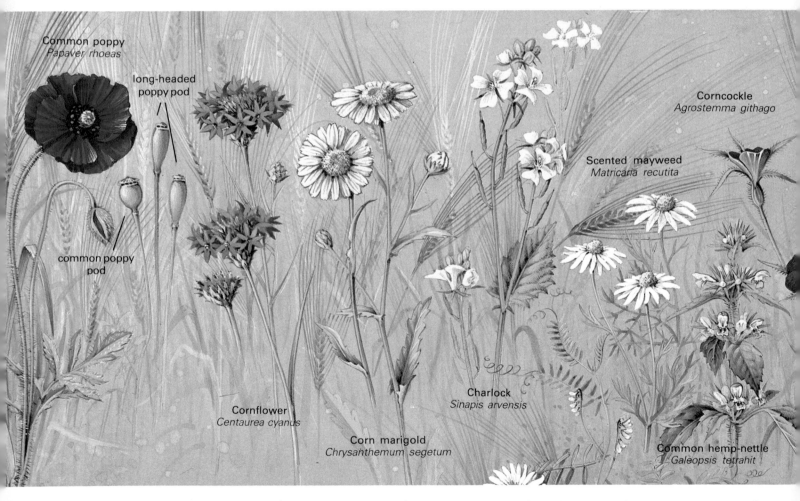

Common poppy *Papaver rhoeas*
long-headed poppy pod
common poppy pod
Cornflower *Centaurea cyanus*
Corn marigold *Chrysanthemum segetum*
Charlock *Sinapis arvensis*
Scented mayweed *Matricaria recutita*
Corncockle *Agrostemma githago*
Common hemp-nettle *Galeopsis tetrahit*

Some beautiful cornfield weeds. Many are now exceptionally rare due to the assiduous use of herbicides by farmers

have been 'weeded out'. Due to these changes in agriculture, the lovely red pheasant's-eye, the beautiful blue cornflower, the purple corncockle and many other highly attractive plants are now virtually extinct, except where areas have been deliberately set aside for them.

By contrast, some weeds have proved exceptionally difficult to often passing through several generations within a year. They also have a rapid and prodigious rate of seed production, with many thousands of seeds ripening, per plant, each year; and an ability to ensure that seed is produced before harvest, so that a new generation is ready in the ground for ploughing time. Alternatively some species have a growth habit that allows them to escape the effects of harvesting, though stubble-burning has reduced the success of this method. The seeds are often similar to those of the crop plant so that they escape the effects of normal seed cleaning and thus are transported to any new field being sown. A further adaption is an ability to survive, as dormant seeds, for decades or even

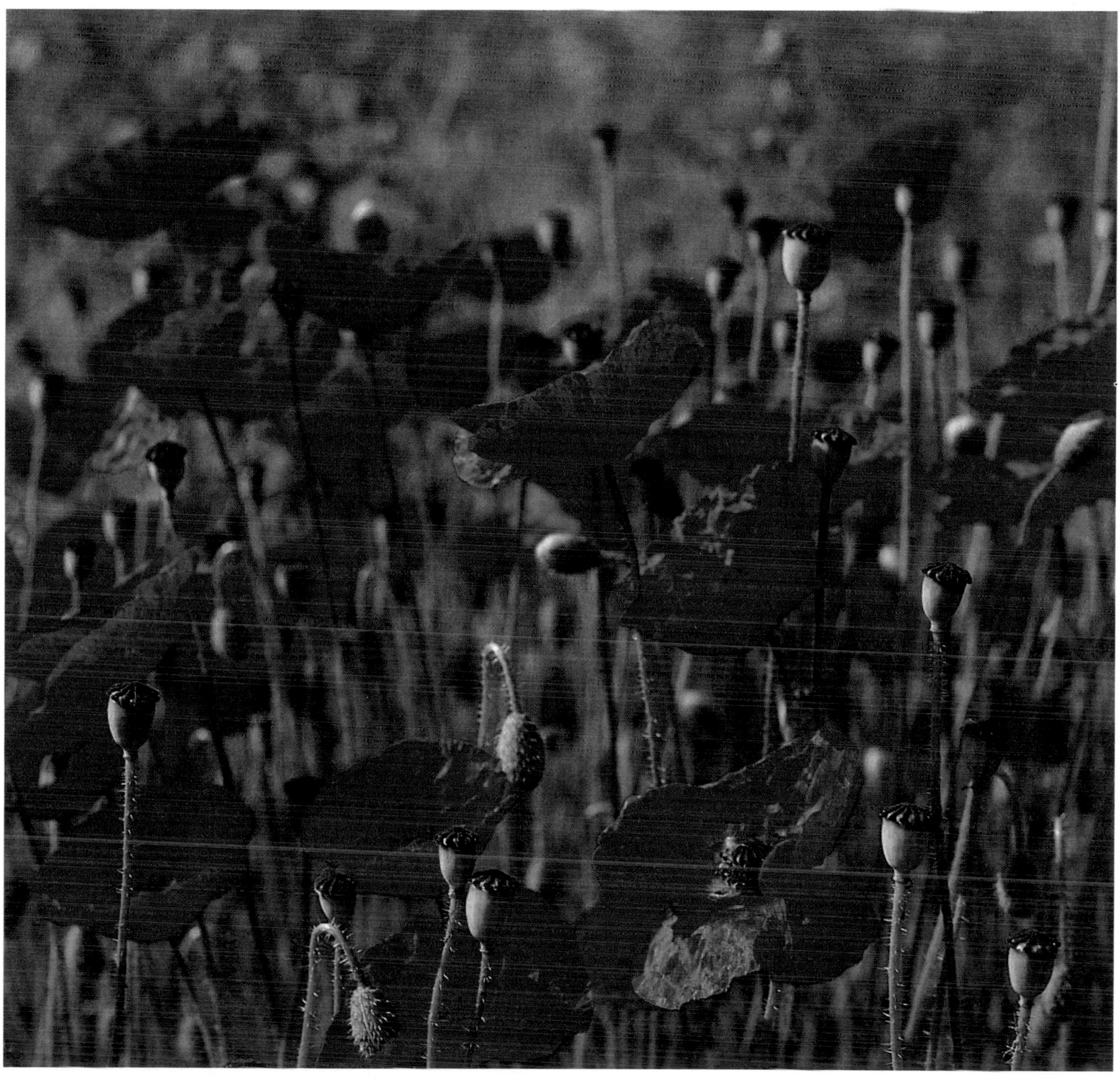

A vivid mass of the wonderful common poppy. Even with modern seed cleaning methods, the poppy may still be seen colouring fields in this way

eradicate or reduce and, though they may decline temporarily, any mistake by the farmer or unusual weather conditions allows them to bounce back as abundantly as ever. Most successful cornfield weeds are characterised by an annual habit, hundreds of years in the soil. It is a familiar sight to see a road cutting or newly-cleared field produce a great mass of poppies or other weeds which, in many cases, can only have arisen from buried seed – the legacy of a previous cultivation.

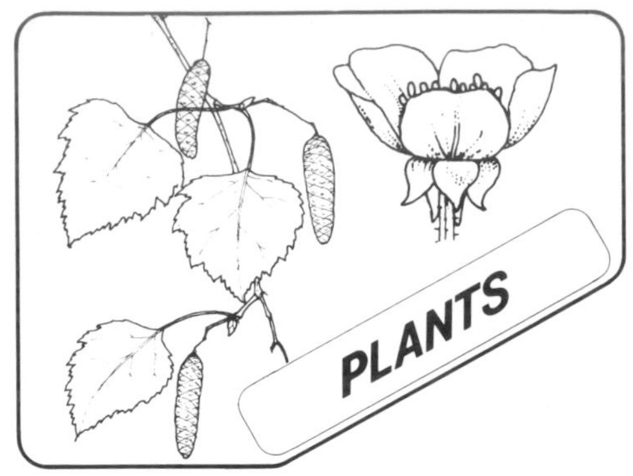

FLOWERS OF LIMESTONE PAVEMENT

Scattered through the hills and dales of northern and western Britain are some strange areas of bright white rock, scraped bare by glaciers that now, despite their barren appearance, support a fascinating mixture of flowers. Most of the plants occur within the deep, almost regular, cracks that give these places their name – limestone pavements.

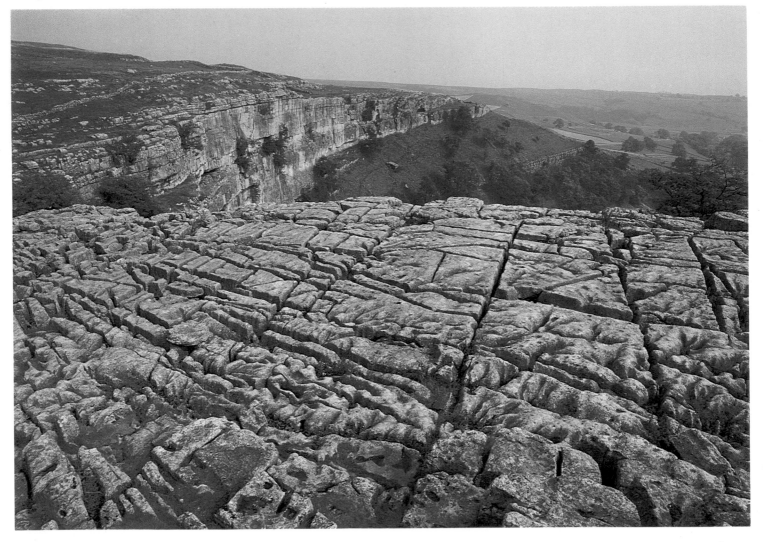

In a few parts of Britain, where hard Carboniferous limestone outcrops, areas of strangely flattened and jointed pale greyish rock occur, often covering large areas. Such places, known from their appearance as limestone pavements, have a strange history. When the ice caps extended southwards over much of Britain, these limestone areas were scraped bare by a huge mass of slowly-moving ice, which ground down the surface to a smooth, nearly-flat layer. After the ice retreated, these flattened surfaces were exposed to the eroding power of rain and frost, and limestone erodes quite quickly as it dissolves in rainwater. Minute cracks in the surfaces were soon enlarged, and gradually the pavement aspect evolved, with broad flat squarish 'paving stones' and deep fissures between them. The slabs are known as clints, while the cracks between them are called grykes.

This combination makes a rather unusual habitat. The surfaces of the clints are bare, infertile places and there is usually little life growing directly on them, except where a little soil has collected in a solution hollow or where small grykes exist. In contrast, though, the grykes are surprising havens for plant life. They may extend downwards for two or three metres or more, and many are up to a metre wide, though others may be smaller. Consequently, they are deep enough to give protection from grazing animals (most limestone pavements are open to stock), shelter from the wind and more humidity than the open limestone surface. In effect, they

A striking view of limestone pavement above Malham Cove in Yorkshire. The deep cracks (the grykes) between the pavement-like blocks (the clints) are clearly visible, though the plants are hidden

have a micro-environment rather like a woodland and, not surprisingly, we find many woodland plants growing here.

Amongst the commoner species which grow in these grykes are dog's mercury, wood anemone, hart's-tongue, lady and male ferns, wood sanicle and various others. The list also includes trees and shrubs, particularly ash, blackthorn, juniper and yew, though the combination of grazing pressure from animals biting the tops off as they emerge from the grykes, and the difficult growing conditions, means that rather few emerge to become trees. In a few places where grazing pressure has been removed, sometimes because the grykes are too deep and dangerous for the stock, open woodland develops, and in some areas, such as upper Ribblesdale, North Yorkshire, there are mature woods developed wholly on limestone pavement.

There are also more specialised plants growing on limestone pavements. Several uncommon or rare ferns occur, especially the green spleenwort, the limestone polypody and the rare rigid buckler fern which is virtually confined to these areas. In the west, the attractive little rusty back fern also occurs, with its rather striking fronds that are dark green above and rusty-brown below. There are many more colourful flowering plants, too. The aptly-named bloody crane's-bill with its lovely red-purple flowers is frequent, while the beautiful spays of white bells of the lily-of-the-valley are often abundant filling shallower grykes with their creeping leaves. The baneberry, or herb-Christopher, is a rare plant of northern limestones that occurs on most of the pavement areas, whilst the rather strange herb-Paris, with its distinctive whorl of four leaves below the flower, is also found. Another very attractive plant that is a special feature of the north-western limestone pavements is the angular Solomon's-seal. It might be confused with the lily-of-the-valley to which it is related, but the flowers are just in ones and twos up the stem and there are leaves all the way up, in contrast to those of the lily-of-the-valley which are basal only.

In other places, perhaps where conditions are rather more sunny, plants that are really at home in limestone grassland occur. These include the beautiful globeflower which produces tall open spikes of butter-yellow flowers like large globe-shaped buttercups, the pretty pink-flowered bird's-eye primrose or the golden yellow flowers of common rock-rose produced in large numbers from creeping mats of leaves and woody stems. Look also for the beautiful lady's mantle with drops of 'magic dew' on the leaves. Altogether they are lovely places, unlike anywhere else in the country, and full of their own special flowers.

The cracks in limestone pavement – the grykes – support all sorts of plants. You may find woodland flowers in the deeper ones, or plants such as this wild strawberry in the shallower more open ones

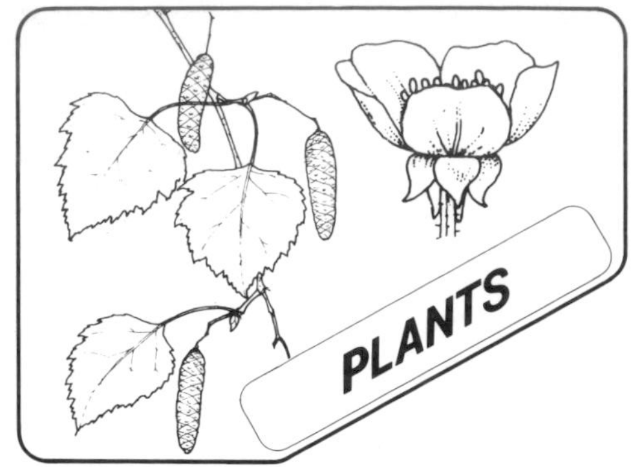

THE FLOWERS OF HEATHLAND

Every August, our heathlands blaze with colour as the ling and heather flower in a glorious profusion of purple. But heathlands are not only a mass of heathers, from spring to autumn there is a succession of different flowers.

Heathlands are infertile with poor acid soils, so the flora is not exceptionally rich. Nevertheless, it is surprising how many different flowers can be found there, especially when you start to look at the habitats around the edges or the wetter areas where heath merges into bog – these contain some of our most beautiful and rare wild flowers.

Of course, the most obvious features of heathland are the heathers or heaths, from which the habitat derives its name. In fact there are quite a few species, with three that occur commonly, and several others that are rare and local. Ling has small pale pink flowers in tight spikes and very reduced drought-resistant leaves, and it is abundant in most types of heath from dry areas through to the higher parts of bogs. Bell-heather has lovely purple bell-shaped flowers and is often dominant on the drier heathlands. The third species is the cross-leaved heath, which is frequent in damp or wet areas, but never in the driest parts. It has a tuft of pale pink bell-shaped flowers at the top of the flowering stem and distinctive cross-shaped whorls of leaves. These are common components of heaths everywhere, but species such as the Dorset heath with its lovely deep red flowers, or Cornish heath, are – as their names

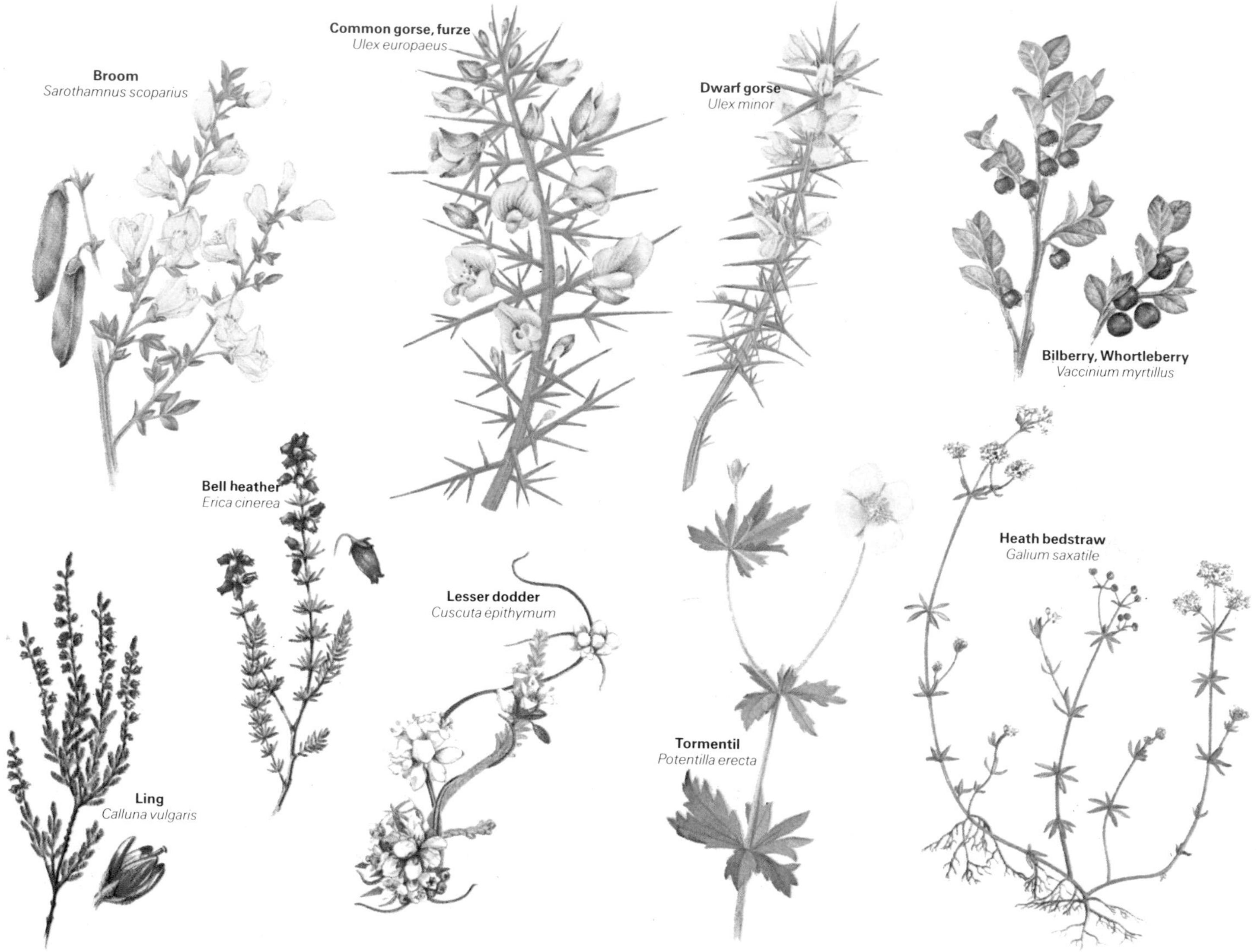

Common gorse, furze *Ulex europaeus*

Broom *Sarothamnus scoparius*

Dwarf gorse *Ulex minor*

Bilberry, Whortleberry *Vaccinium myrtillus*

Bell heather *Erica cinerea*

Heath bedstraw *Galium saxatile*

Lesser dodder *Cuscuta epithymum*

Tormentil *Potentilla erecta*

Ling *Calluna vulgaris*

Some of the most characteristic flowers of heathland These plants are found on almost any type of heathland from lowland areas to those in the north

suggest – much more local.

The other obvious and well-known feature of heaths is gorse and its relatives, but again there are several species involved. Common gorse, or furze, is the most conspicuous growing into bushes that may be two metres high or more. It tends to flower profusely in spring and more sporadically after that; the popping of its seed-pods, as they split to scatter their seeds, is a familiar sound on hot summer days. Dwarf gorse is much shorter, often growing amongst the heather, and it flowers later. Whilst western gorse is similar but tends to replace dwarf gorse in south-western counties; for example, it is abundant on Exmoor and Dartmoor often flowering with the heather. Other gorse-like flowers include broom, with lovely golden flowers and spineless foliage, and the pretty whin which is smaller with fewer flowers and very long sharp spines amongst the leaves.

The strange dodder is worth looking out for; this is a wholly parasitic plant that has to find a host (usually heather or gorse) to which it can attach itself or it cannot survive. When the seedlings germinate, they rotate in wider and wider circles until they find a suitable nearby plant which they then penetrate to remove the nutrients. They then produce tangled masses of pink stems which sprawl over the host bush followed, later in the year, by little clusters of pink flowers. In some years they may be abundant, but in other years you hardly see any. Tormentil is a pretty little plant, related to roses, that produces yellow four-petalled flowers on trailing stems, while heath bedstraw has mats of stems with little whorls of leaves and creamy-white inflorescences. There are also some great rarities to be found on heathland but they are few and far between. For example, the heath lobelia has spikes of beautiful blue-purple flowers but it can only be seen on a few heaths in south-west England, while the wild gladiolus is even more local and its dramatic spikes of red-purple flowers can only be found on New Forest heaths in Hampshire.

Where drainage is poor, but the soil is not wet enough for bogs to form, we find wet heaths, which are often fascinating places for flowers. Besides a number of bog plants, such as sundews, there are some wet heath specialities such as the beautiful blue marsh gentian, the pale pink-flowered lousewort or the rare marsh clubmoss. Wet heaths were the sole home of one of our extinct native plants, the summer lady's-tresses.

A mass of typical heathland flowers including the blue heath speedwell, and the yellow tormentil in the summer sunshine

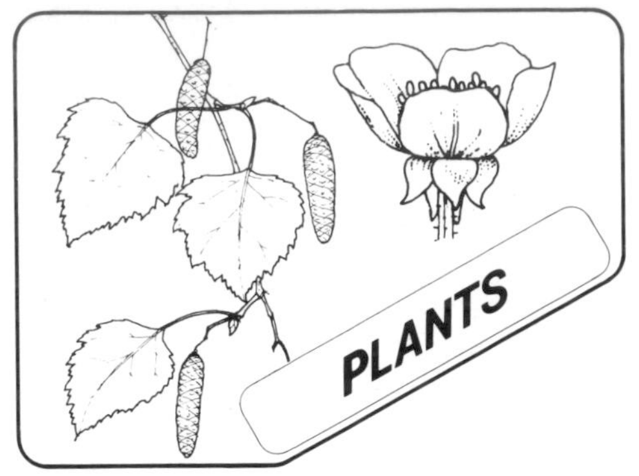

FERNS

Ferns are well known for their graceful fronds which adorn our woodlands, but in fact there are dozens of species in the British Isles in various habitats, all with a life history that is fascinatingly different from that of flowering plants.

Although they look like flowering plants in many respects, ferns are members of a more primitive group of plants that never produce flowers. Instead they have a rather strange life cycle, that has two separate stages, though only one part is normally noticed by the naturalist. The fronds that we see, and think of as ferns, are the spore-producers; at some stage during the year, most often in late summer, some or all of the green fronds begin to develop spore-producing structures on their undersides. These come in various distinctive shapes and sizes, and they are one of the main ways in which different groups of ferns can be distinguished from each other. The male fern, for example, produces tiny groups of spores with a kidney-shaped cap or sori over them; the lady fern has crescent moon-shaped sori; while the hart's-tongue fern has long linear sori that run transversely across the frond like the rungs of a ladder. Bracken, by contrast, produces its spores under the inrolled margins of the fronds, and you have to look more closely to see them, though by autumn it is possible to glimpse the rusty-brown spores appearing from below this fold. Most ferns produce their spores on the mature fronds, but a few have developed special fronds, the sole purpose of which is to bear spores, so that they look more like a flowering plant with a rosette of leaves and some spore-producing structures in the middle; the impressive royal fern does this as does the woodland hard fern and several others. There are also two groups of rather curious ferns, the adder's-tongues and the moonworts, that each produce just one leaf and a little spike of spore-producing bodies coming up from the base of the frond; they hardly look like ferns at all.

When the spores disperse and germinate, they do not grow into new ferns at all, but instead produce a tiny

A small selection of our native ferns, showing some of the variety of frond form to be found. Look also for the variety of spore cases on the underside of the fronds

heart-shaped green plant, rather like a little liverwort. This produces male and female organs for sexual reproduction, and it is the resulting genetic mixture that grows into the other stage of the life-cycle. This tiny gametophyte stage, as it is called, is very dependent upon humid conditions, both to prevent it from drying out and to allow the male and female parts to move through a film of water and fuse together. Consequently, although the main spore-producing plants could live in drier conditions, they tend to be confined to more humid places because that is where the gametophyte generation grows. Thus, the best places to find ferns are in such humid habitats as woodlands, on mountains or in the grykes of limestone pavements (see page 76), and in general the west of Britain, with its milder damper climate, is better for ferns that the east.

In woodland species such as the buckler and shield ferns, male, lady, hart's-tongue and hard fern can be found. Although they may not seem easy to identify, if you look closely at the number of times that the frond is divided (see plates) and the shape of the spore-producing sori, it becomes easier. For example, polypody fern has a main stem with single undivided leaflets coming off from this, and this is known as a pinnate frond; oak fern, in contrast, has a main stem that has side branches, that each produce further side-branches, that themselves produce little leaflets – fronds that divide three times in this way are known as tripinnate. These features are always constant for a given species and you soon learn to notice the degree of branching.

The royal fern is one of Britain's most attractive ferns. Here it is growing by the side of a Lake District river

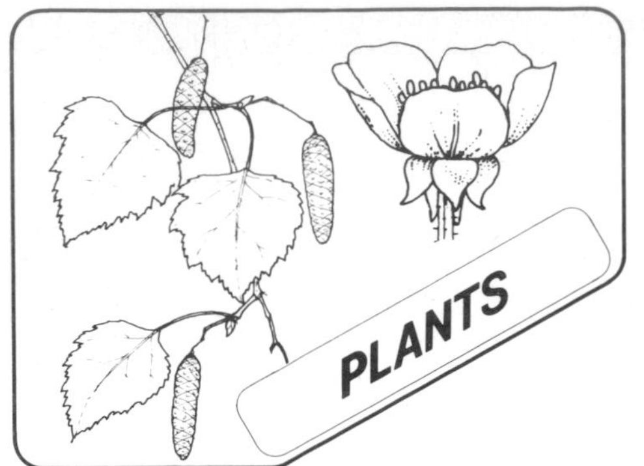

FLOWERS OF HEDGES & VERGES

There are several thousands of kilometres of hedgerows and verges in our patchwork countryside, and many of these provide wonderful habitats for wild flowers, mimicking ancient meadows and woodland edges in a linear form.

Despite the ravages of recent decades, the mosaic that makes up the British countryside is still enormously rich in hedges and roadside verges. Some areas are better than others, since the open intensively-used countryside of eastern England has little use for hedges, whilst the more intimate landscapes elsewhere are full of hedges and verges.

Hedges are very ancient in origin and some date back to pre-Norman times (see page 96); and most are at least 150 years old. Many are actually relics of even older habitats – the edges of former woods, or remaining strips of woodland between two clearances. Consequently, they have direct continuity with very ancient woodland, and such hedges often contain special plants indicating its age. Whatever their origins, hedgerows join up to form a series of continuous mosaics, and the more mobile species can spread along them, even into new hedges; though the oldest ones are always the best for flowers. In many ways, the bases of hedges are most like woodland edges or glades, with a combination of sun and shade, and slightly higher humidity than in open land. Where there are double hedges, such as on either side of an old lane, the conditions are even more like a wood, with shade for most of the day, and shelter from the winds.

As a result, hedges share many flowers with woodland. Typical flowers include red campion, bluebells, primroses, ramsons, hedge parsley, ground ivy, celandines, violets and many others, making a marvellous display in spring and early summer.

Roadside and trackside verges can be even more varied than hedges, though of course the two often go together. They, too, can be a direct link with much more ancient habitats than preceded modern farmland, for the verges have generally escaped the worst of modern agricultural changes. Unfortunately, there was a disastrous phase a few years ago when many verges were regularly sprayed with weedkillers to avoid cutting, and this removed many attractive flowers, leaving little hope of their return. In

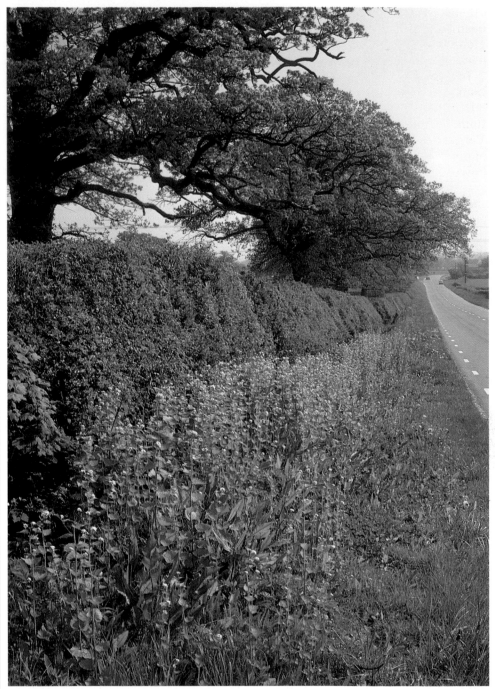

Roadside verges can be teaming with wildlife, a haven next to the roar and rush of the traffic. This hedgerow shows a typical selection of plants that can be found

Autumn in a Cornish hedgerow, with a mass of blackberries, black bryony berries, and ivy flowers. Hedgerows are a massive asset to our countryside – approximately 20% have disappeared over the past forty years

other areas, roadside hedges have been removed, and the field has been ploughed right up to the highway leaving no place for wildlife at all.

In general, though, verges are ribbons of natural grassland, closely mirroring the changing soil conditions of the land over which they lie. Verges on chalk, for example, support many characteristic downland flowers (see page 50) including rarities, and it is by no means unusual for the only records of some flowers in a county to be on a roadside verge. In clay country, the verges are often marvellously broad, reflecting the days when traffic had to constantly make new routes to avoid wet patches in winter; nowadays, the hard-surfaced road avoids the need for this, but the whole corridor comes within the definition of the highway, and the edges provide a rich habitat for flowers. Such areas often mimic traditional hay meadows in their flora; many used to be cut for hay and a few still are. They will probably contain many species of grasses and sedges, together with such choice flowers as meadow crane's-bill, green-winged orchids, lady's mantle, globeflowers and a multitude of others depending on the soil and part of the country where they are found.

Today, most verges are managed by mechanical cutting to keep sight-lines clear for traffic, and to prevent too many trees and shrubs from invading. They tend to be cut less often than they used to be to save money, and this management suits a great variety of plants. If the verge is too frequently cut grass becomes dominated, whilst insufficient cutting leads to a coarse sward from which the more delicate plants will be ousted. The combination of a good hedge with a well-managed verge is an excellent one for cultivating plants, and a surprisingly high proportion of our flora occurs in such situations.

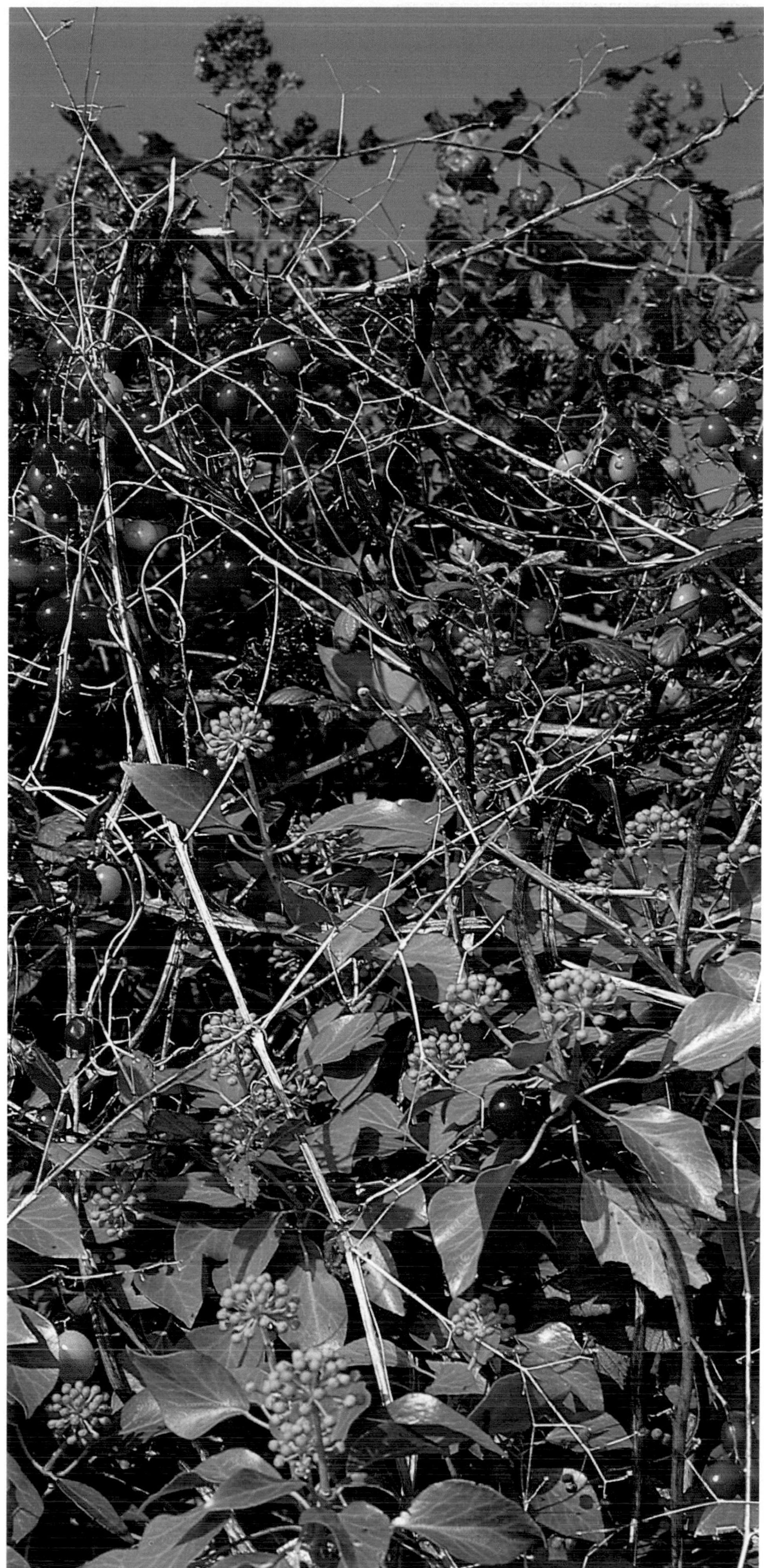

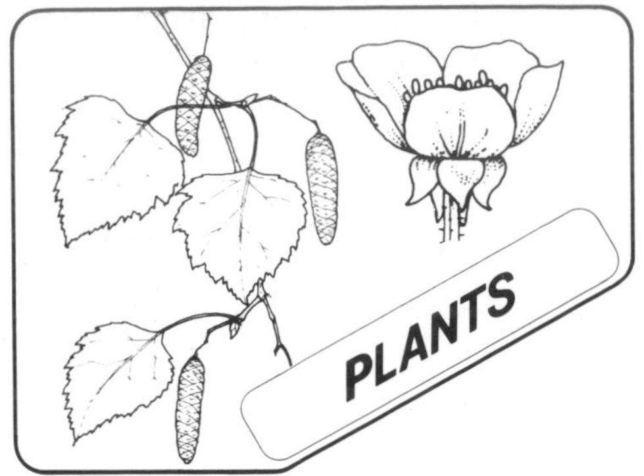

MOSSES, LIVERWORTS & LICHENS

Besides the more obvious flowers of our countryside, there is another community of plants growing pressed close to rocks, trees or the soil, often in damp shady places. These are the mosses, liverworts and lichens, and there are well over a thousand species of them in Britain.

In addition to the 2,000 or so species of flowering plants, the enormous numbers of fungi, and the ferns and horsetails, there are also numerous mosses, liverworts and lichens to be found in the countryside. Collectively, with the fungi, they are often known as the 'lower plants' indicating their more primitive evolutionary position, but is also appropriate to their small size.

The mosses and liverworts are both rather primitive green plants, known together as the bryophytes. Mosses tend to be more upright and leafy, and slightly better at colonising dry places. Liverworts are usually creeping, often comprising just one single heart-shaped or fingered structure, and are more confined to damp sites. However, there are also leafy liverworts that look more like mosses, just to confuse the issue! In general, they all tend to occur in rather shady humid places because part of their reproductive cycle requires a film of surface water. Although a few species, such as the hair mosses, can survive in drier places, most are to be found in woods, on mountains, in gorges and the entrances to caves, and in other damp places. Consequently western and northern Britain has a much richer variety than the east and south-east of the country.

Woodlands have a fine range of species; most of them do not have English names, because only specialists can recognise them but, amongst the more obvious, are the feather mosses, the palm tree moss and the white fork moss which grows in pale green cushions on the bare floor of beech woods in particular. Ancient woods are particularly rich in species and, as with flowering plants, there are some mosses and liverworts that tend to be confined to the oldest woodlands. Bogs and springheads also support many species, including the 30 or so species of the bog-moss Sphagnum and some hair mosses. There are even aquatic species, including the intriguingly-named *Fontinalis antipyretica* which, as its second name suggests, was used to damp down fires.

Lichens are very different plants. They are rarely pure green but more often greyish, yellow or even black, and they come in a variety of forms. The commonest is the encrusting type, which looks like an encrustation on rocks, walls, gravestones, trees and other unlikely situations. A familiar example is the bright orange circular patches of lichen that occur on the roofs of farm buildings, or in similar situations, which is known as *Xanthoria parietina*. There are many

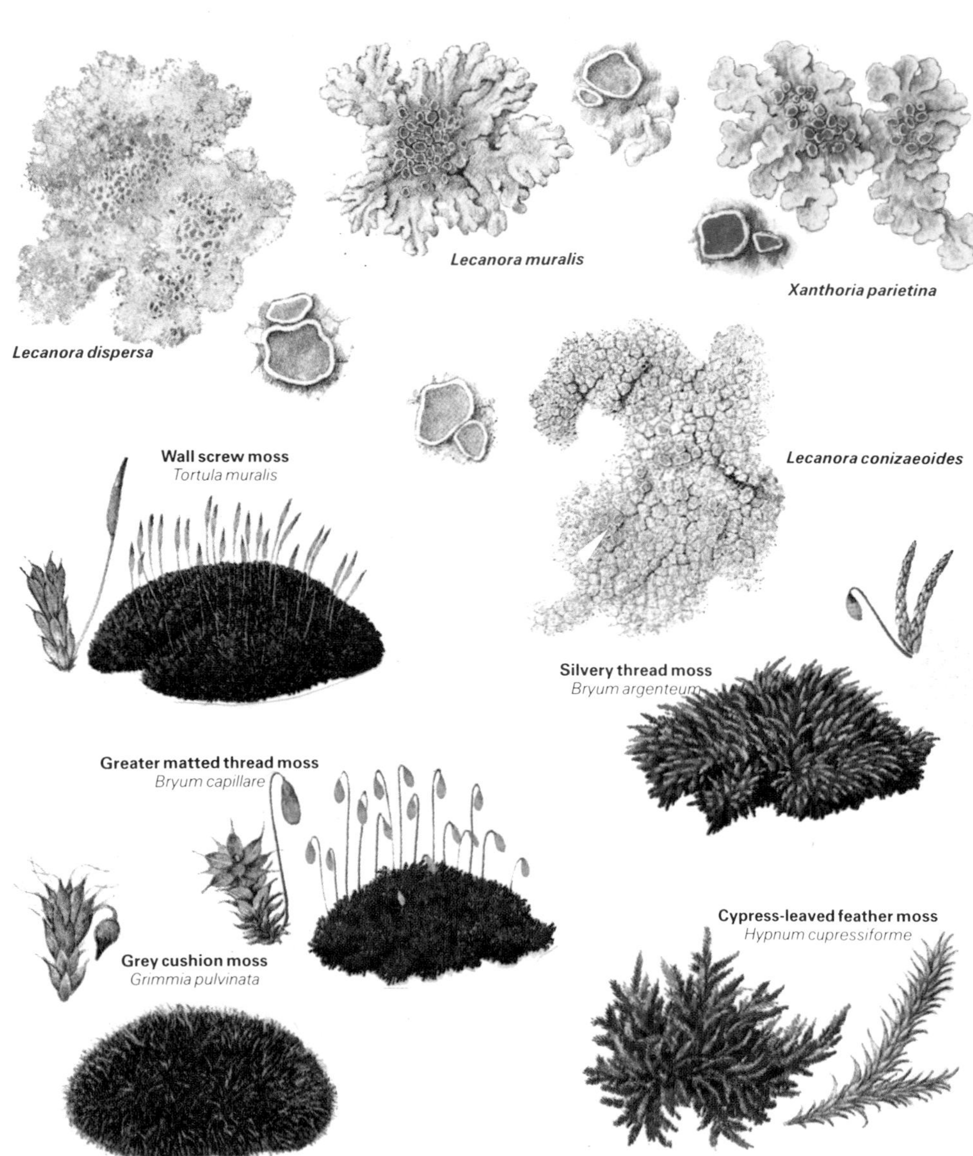

Although they are small, mosses and liverworts show an enormous variety of form and colour. The top four illustrations show a range of encrusting lichens with enlargements of their reproductive organs. Below are five different mosses

hundreds of other species, too, some so ingrained into their substrate that you can barely see them, others looking like just a thin powdery layer, perhaps with tiny jam-tart-like fruiting bodies. It has been said that you can only see the true colour of the bark of trees in polluted areas where lichens fail to grow, because they cover the tree surface so thoroughly elsewhere! There are also stronger-growing lichens, looking rather like greyish liverworts, such as the tree lungworts which predictably grow on the bark of trees and the dog lichen which grows in all sorts of places including sand-dunes. There are also beard-lichens, which look like miniature tangled bushes, and often hang down from branches, rocks or tree trunks.

One of the strangest things about lichens is the fact that they occur at all. They are not a straightforward plant, but are a combination between a fungus and an algae. It is odd enough that two quite different plants should associate in this way, but even more extraordinary that they should form so many stable, repeatable, self-reproducing entities that we can recognise as species. It is also rather strange that, despite being able to separate out and identify the individual algae and fungi from many lichens, it has not been possible to persuade the appropriate two organisms to combine together to form a lichen.

This unusual association forming their structure accounts for some of the features of lichens that differ from those of mosses and liverworts. Lichens frequently live in much lighter, drier situations and are able to colonise the most inhospitable substrates such as bare rock, walls and pavements. The combination of the fungus which can penetrate all sorts of materials and make use of rotting organic matter, and the algae which is a green plant utilising sunlight to make food, allows them to survive almost anywhere.

An old beech stump covered with a beautiful green carpet of moss, with the grey candles, the fruiting bodies, of lichens visible behind

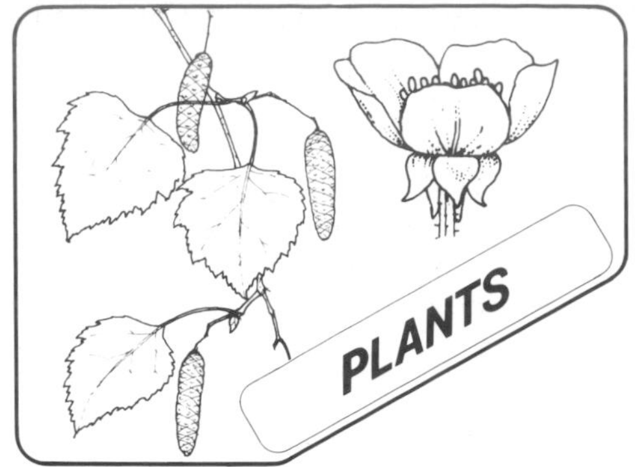

LOOKING AT FLOWERS

Flowers may seem static, even dull, when compared to animals and birds, but in reality they form an ever-changing tapestry with a surprisingly dynamic lifestyle. The closer you look at flowers, the more you will be rewarded by some fascinating discoveries.

Perhaps the first priority before looking at flowers in detail is to work out how to identify them. Although there are very many, the number of common plants in any one area is much smaller, and this book helps to make the process easier by illustrating commoner species separated into their distinctive habitats. To progress further, you need a good colour-illustrated flower book, of which there are many, to give fuller coverage and more information. When trying to identify a flower look closely at features such as the number of petals and the shape of leaves, and carefully read the text accompanying the picture; the information given on flowering time, rarity, distribution and so on will help eliminate any unlikely species. For example, if the species you have found in Surrey looks like one illustrated but the accompanying notes indicate that it is rare and confined to the Scottish highlands, then it is likely that your identification is wrong! It is also a good idea to take the book out with you; not only are memories notoriously unreliable, but often there turns out to be three similar species to the one you found, and you can only separate them by closer examination!

Many plants are very specific in their choice of habitat. We have already looked at the idea that certain plants can 'indicate' the presence of ancient woodlands or old meadows, and as you become more familiar with these species, it is fascinating to be able to use them for historical research. Since most accurate maps only date back to the 17th or 18th centuries, this kind of fieldwork can tell you more about the countryside than is generally known, and there are books available which list the indicator species. In a similar way, many plants are confined to particular situations or soil types; by buying a geological map for your home area you can relate the flowers you find to the underlying rock. It is interesting to be able to drive along and immediately detect the change in soil type by the presence or absence of certain flowers. For example, old man's beard is an excellent and conspicuous indicator of chalk and limestone; in contrast, rhododendrons and heathers will only grow on soil that is acidic and lacking in lime, and there are many other examples to be worked out.

There are many aspects of plant life-histories that are still not fully known, and there are discoveries awaiting anyone with patience to

Pollination

Around 80% of our native flowers are pollinated by insects, with the remainder being pollinated by the wind. Those that are pollinated by insects have developed special mechanisms to attract particular insects, to try to ensure that they regularly visit *their* flowers, thus ensuring that the pollen is transferred from one plant of the species to another. Among British plants, the orchids have the most extraordinary pollination mechanisms, often finely developed to attract one group of insects, or even just one species. The picture shows a small elephant hawk moth, resting on a butterfly orchid (which it visits at night for the nectar), and on its head can be seen the tiny yellow masses of pollen that have stuck to it from previous orchid visits

A group of botanists (right) looking at the plant life around the base of an ancient oak tree. Ancient trees, especially if growing in unpolluted areas, tend to be especially good for epiphytic plants – in other words, plants that grow on them, but do not actually cause them any harm. For example, many lichens, mosses and ferns grow on old trees such as this, and it would be perfectly possible for a 'good' tree to have 40 or more species growing on it, though you would have to look closely to see them! Joining a field course and looking closely at plants under the guidance of an expert is, undoubtedly, one of the best ways of finding out about plants

start looking. For example, the great majority of flowers are pollinated by insects, and there is a fair amount of general information available. Often, there is very little specific knowledge on which insects pollinate which flowers, especially those, such as the butterfly orchids and other pale scented flowers that attract insects mainly at night. If you are fortunate enough to have a population of fly orchids near you, you could watch for the visits of insects attempting to mate with the flowers (pseudo-copulation), and as the flowers go over, you could try to estimate the proportion of the flowers which have been pollinated (and are therefore producing seeds) to discover the success rate of this method.

Rather surprisingly, very little is known about how long individual plants live. The life of economically important species, especially trees, is fairly well documented, but there is remarkable little information on smaller and non-commercial species. Annuals and biennials are well known and the information is readily available in books, but perennials are another matter. A perennial could live for three years or a hundred years. One long-term study of various orchids revealed that, out of the population first investigated, almost all had survived 30 years later and many had flowered regularly during this period. This exploded several myths about certain orchids always dying after flowering, and it was also possible to calculate that some individuals were likely to survive for a hundred years or more! Anyone can embark on studies like this, either by regularly observing an obvious plant or group of plants, such as a small shrub, and seeing what happens; or by a slightly more complicated method of carefully mapping and recording all the plants of one species in, say, a ten-metre square, and seeing which ones can be found each year, if they flower and seed, and whether any new individuals appear. This can reveal an enormous amount about a species, giving information on its average length of life, how successfully it sets seed and how often new plants enter the population. For most species, this is not known, yet it is invaluable information for anyone endeavouring to manage land to conserve flowers.

The possibilites for close observation and discovery with flowers are endless. The first thing to do is find a good wild flower field guide. There are many available, but make sure the one you choose has a wide coverage clear, large illustrations and comprehensive descriptions. Learn to use the keys and you will soon be identifying almost everything.

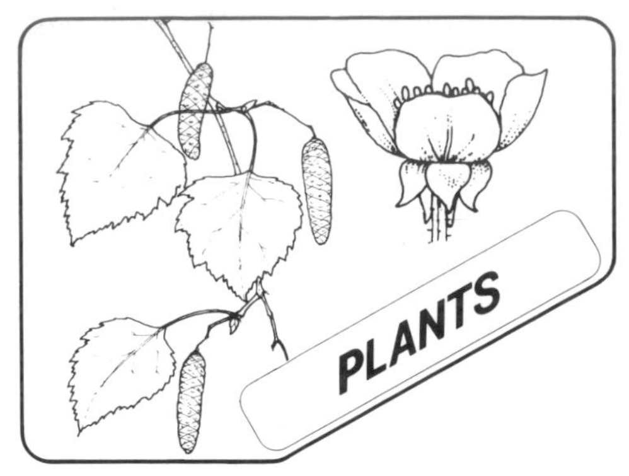

BRITISH DECIDUOUS TREES

It is the trees that give our countryside so much of its characteristic appearance; the stately grace of a mature beech tree, the ubiquitous but beautiful birches, the solid oaks or the fresh green of an ash – all add so much to the beauty of the countryside, whether they are in woods or growing on their own.

In Britain, we have about 35 native species of tree, plus many more that have been introduced but have become familiar sights, like horse chestnuts or cedars. Of the native trees, all bar three (see page 92) are deciduous, losing their leaves each winter, and assuming the characteristic stark winter outlines. Amongst this surprisingly large number of species are some that are very familiar, many that are less known and even some that few people will have heard of.

Everyone knows of the oak, the tree that typifies the English countryside in many ways, but fewer people know that there are actually two native species of oak; the common or pedunculate oak, and the sessile or durmast oak. Of the two, the pedunculate is generally the commoner and favours lower-lying more fertile areas. In contrast, the sessile oak prefers more acid soils and upland areas, so it is the most frequent oak in north and west Britain, through their ranges and habitat requirements overlap considerably. A key difference in their appearance is that the acorns of pedunculate oak have a long stalk, but there is no stalk in sessile oak (that is what sessile means); conversely, the leaves of the latter have longish stalks, whilst those of pedunculate are very short. There are other differences in appearance, too, and the pedunculate oak is more likely to occur in hedgerows and other open places. Also, the main planted oak has tended to be the common oak, so the sessile is a more genuine ancient woodland tree.

Beeches, too, are very familiar trees, and they are certainly native in southern England, though over most of their range they have been planted as a timber tree, especially for furniture making. Even the beautiful natural-looking Chiltern beechwoods were planted on land that was downland about 400 years ago. Birches, like oaks, actually comprise more than one species. The silver birch has the most markedly silver bark and more drooping twigs, whilst the downy birch has brownish bark and tends to occur

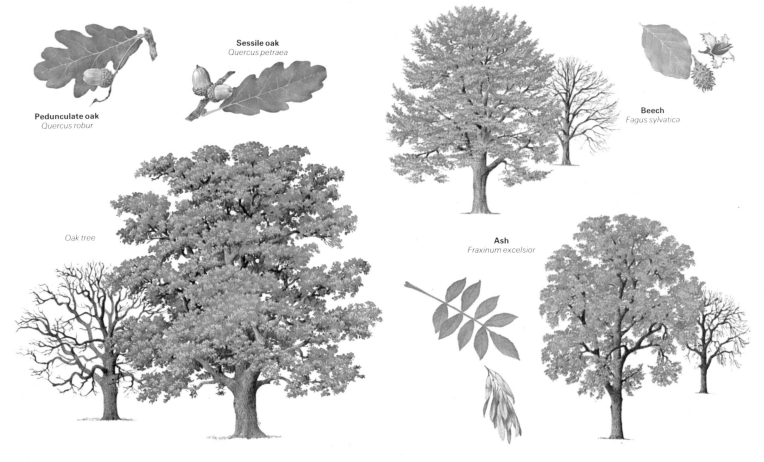

Pedunculate oak
Quercus robur

Sessile oak
Quercus petraea

Oak tree

Beech
Fagus sylvatica

Ash
Fraxinum excelsior

The ash, beech and the oaks are our commonest forest trees. You can identify most trees by their winter silhouettes as well as by their foliage or fruits. The leaves and acorns of the two native oaks are shown in detail

A pollarded beech in the forest of Epping. Pollarding was carried out as a means of providing coppice growth but out of reach of grazing animals such as deer

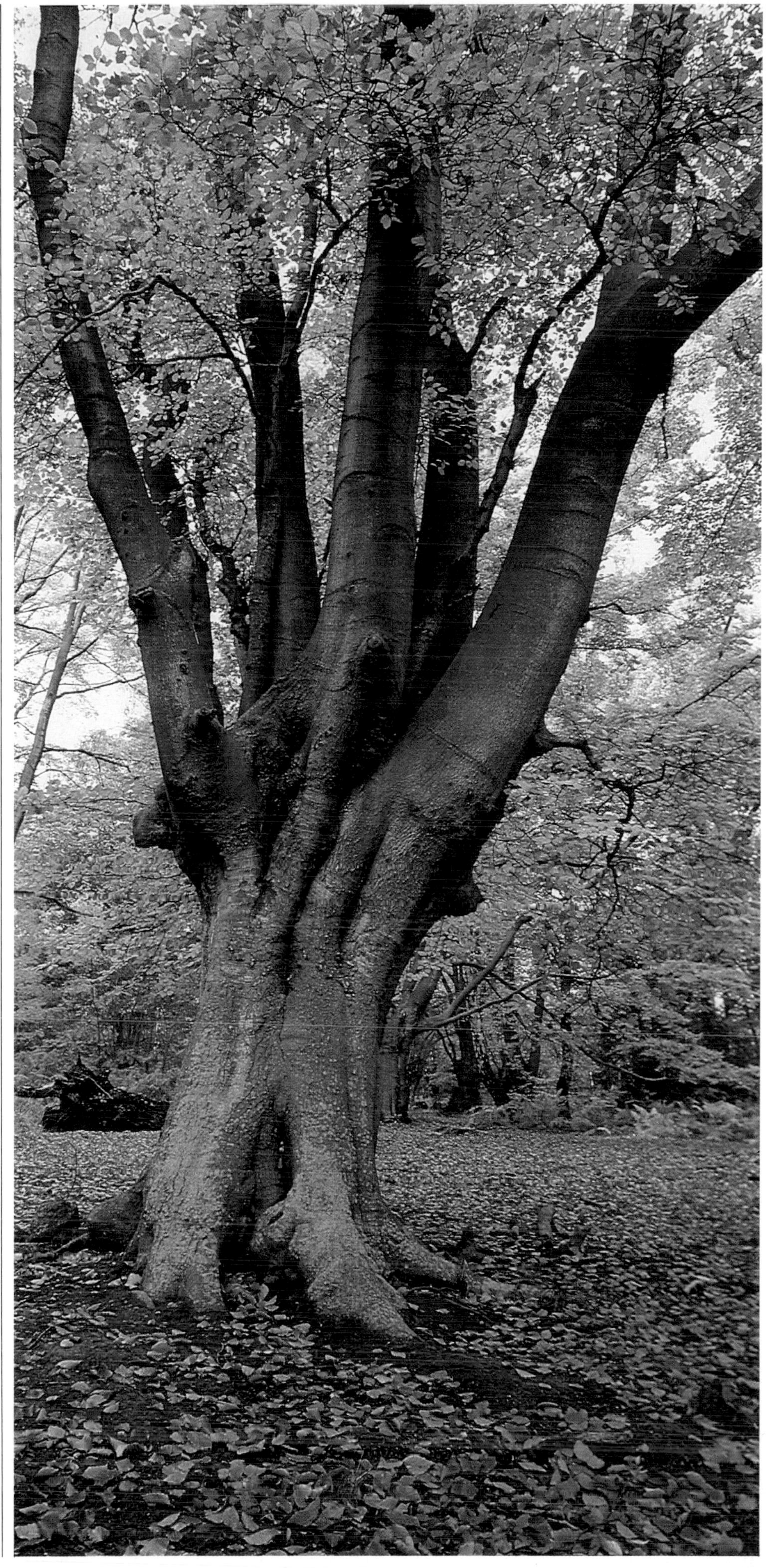

more in damper and upland sites. There is also a third birch, the dwarf birch, though you would barely recognise it as a tree, since it rarely grows to more than half-a-metre high and is only found in mountain areas.

The ash is one of our most beautiful trees, growing in a tremendous variety of places, both in woods and in the open. It is shorter lived than the oaks, but it survives long enough to form ash-dominated woodlands in situations where other trees do less well, such as on hard limestone rock. Its leaf canopy is rather thinner than many trees, so the ground below receives more light; ashwoods are noted for their rich flora as a result.

Elms were once one of the most familiar sights of the countryside, with a characteristic elegantly-shaped tree in almost every hedgerow. Sadly, they have been hit by Dutch elm disease in the last decade or so, which has devastated the populations, killing almost every tree in many areas. Dutch elm disease is a fungus which is carried from tree-to-tree by the elm bark beetle. The female beetle tunnels under the bark of the elm taking spores of the fungus with her. There she lays eggs from which grubs hatch and chew out the easily recognised galleries. The fungus grows into the elm and blocks the tubes which move nutrients around the tree, almost literally starving the tree to death. The English elm was the most familiar hedgerow tree, and it was the one that was hit hardest by the disease; but there are also other elm species, including many closely-related species in eastern England. One very distinctive species is the wych elm, which occurs most commonly in northern and western Britain. It is primarily a woodland tree, reproducing by seed rather than by producing suckers like the hedgerows English elms and with noticeably larger leaves.

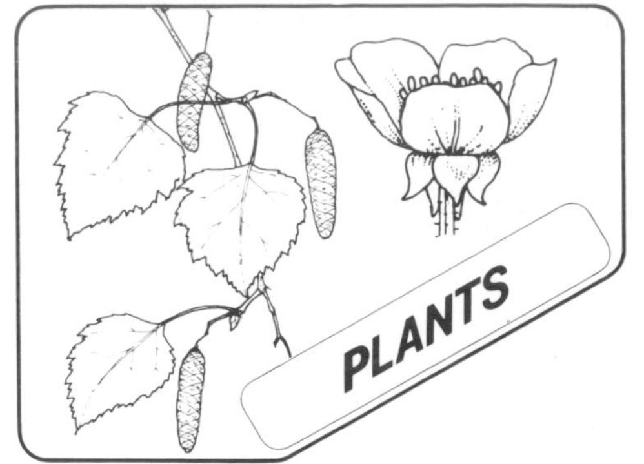

BRITISH DECIDUOUS TREES

As well as the more familiar oaks, ashes and beeches, there are many less familiar or distinctive trees in the countryside, including the native limes, hornbeam, wild service tree, field maple, whitebeam, holly and rowan.

Limes are familiar enough as street trees, though these are nearly always a planted variety of hybrid lime; but there are also two species of native limes both of which are rather rare. By various means, it has been possible to work out that these limes were once very common components of the natural woodland that covered most of Britain. Now the small-leaved lime is uncommon while the large-leaved lime is rare. This has been partly due to climatic reasons, because both are warmth-demanding species and they fail to set seed successfully in our present climate; but they have also been grazed out by domestic stock and selected against wherever new trees were planted. So, they are of interest historically, as well as for being the only sizeable forest trees that are pollinated by insects, rather than by the wind. Most forest trees, such as oak, ash and beech, produce flowers in early summer to allow the best distribution of pollen before the leaves are all open; limes produce their flowers in midsummer to attract the maximum number of insects and a flowering lime literally hums with activity on a warm day.

The hornbeam is a tree of woods and hedges in southern and eastern England, and is often confused with beech as its bark is rather similar. Its leaves, however, are more sharply toothed and ridged than beech leaves, its stem is more fluted when mature and its hanging clusters of fruits are particularly distinctive. Perhaps the best place to see hornbeams is in Epping Forest in Essex, where it is abundant, especially as old pollards. The sycamore is a familiar introduced tree, coming originally from Yugoslavia but finding our climate to its liking; however, it has a more delicate native relative, the field maple. Field maples are beautiful trees, quite common on the more lime-rich soils, but frequently overlooked. In early summer, they have lovely soft green foliage and attractive yellow-green flowers, while in autumn their leaves turn a golden reddish-yellow which can be very striking. Like sycamore, they produce double 'keys' that circle like helicopters as they fall, carrying the seeds away from the shade of the parent tree.

The autumn golds of a field maple. The field maple is found in many ancient woodlands and as a shrub in southern hedgerows

An interesting group of smaller trees belongs to the rose family, and all have lovely heads of creamy white flowers in early summer followed by red or brown berries. These include the whitebeams of which there is one common species, especially on chalk, but also many similar less common species. A few are even totally confined to one small area, such as the Avon Gorge, occurring nowhere else. All the whitebeams have distinctive found on bare mountain sides; its orange-red berries are a fine autumn feature. Also in this group is the wild service tree, a rather uncommon tree that usually occurs in ancient woodlands, often near to the coast. It has more fingered leaves, rather like those of maples, and has brown berries following the white flowers; though, rather like the limes, it is not very successful at producing fertile fruits.

The wild cherry and the bird cher-

leaves that are green above but silver-white below, and the contrast is particularly noticeable when they fall. A close relative is the rowan, or mountain ash, which has more divided leaves without the silver. It is a common tree of acid soil, occurring both in woods and in the open, often to be

Some small forest trees that occasionally reach the forest canopy. They may more usually occur lower down on the woodland edge or in a shrubby habit in hedgerows

ry, both with lovely white flowers, are also in the rose family. The bird cherry is common in the north, while the wild cherry is more frequent in the south, especially on calcareous soils. Other less well-known native trees include the black poplar and its relative – the aspen – the holly and the crab apple.

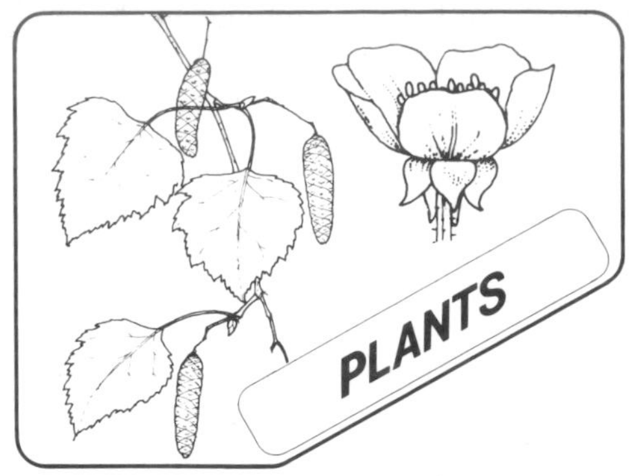

British Coniferous Trees

Although we think of the dark conifers of plantations as being alien trees, imported from other lands, there are also three native species of conifer – the Scots pine, the yew tree and the juniper. The juniper is rarely more than a bush but all three form woods in certain parts of Britain.

Our three native conifers, Scot pine, yew and juniper are all evergreen trees, keeping their foliage through the winter. In fact, most conifers are evergreen, while the majority of other trees are deciduous, though the rule does not always hold good. Conifers also differ from other trees which, in Britain at least, are all flowering and seed-bearing plants, in that they produce cones with the seeds naked on scales. The true flowering plants have the seeds enclosed within a structure that collectively forms a fruit, and thus the conifers are seen as being less highly evolved.

The largest of native conifer is the Scots pine, and in Britain it is a subspecies of a species that is more widely distributed, known as *Pinus sylvestris* var. *scotica*. It was one of the earliest trees to return to Britain after the last Ice Age, forming extensive woodlands across the country that were gradually ousted by deciduous trees as the climate warmed. In Scotland, however, the temperature is cooler, and natural Scots pine would be the dominant native tree still if it were not for the fact that man had taken a hand and cleared and burnt it from almost everywhere. Pine, unlike most deciduous trees, burns readily and fails to regrow from its stumps, so had little hope of recovering from the onslaught. Now native Scots pine woods are confined to relatively small

A plantation of young pines. Most plantations use conifers that are not native species such as larch and sitka spruce

remnants scattered through the Highlands. Elsewhere, it has been grown extensively in plantations, and in many areas it has re-naturalised on heaths and rough ground, often forming woods once more. When allowed to grow to maturity in open conditions, the Scots pine is a most attractive tree, with flaky reddish bark, becoming distinctly red towards the top of the tree, and dark blue-green foliage. Like most conifers, it bears separate male and female flowers: the male flowers are set back down the branch and shed huge quantities of yellow pollen in late spring; the female flowers, the cones, take three years to develop fully, becoming woody by the second year and releasing the seeds in the third. Trees can live for 200 to 300 years and grow to a height of at least 30 metres if left to their own devices, in plantations however they are usually harvested when barely into middle age.

The yew tree is less tall, though it can live for much longer and develop a huge girth. In the wild, it is mainly a plant of chalk and limestone areas, but it also occurs on acid soils such as in the New Forest, Hampshire. In places, it forms extensive woods in which it is the dominant tree such as the huge yew wood at Kingley Vale in Sussex. This is thought to be the oldest and largest yew wood in Europe, dating back at least 500 years and showing little signs of turning into any other sort of woodland. Where planted as specimen trees, as it often used to be in churchyards, the yew lives to a great age and can attain an enormous girth; the famous Selborne yew in Hampshire has a girth of about nine metres, and is certainly of a great age. Yews produce male and female flowers on separate trees, and the familiar fleshy red berry-like cones are the female parts.

The juniper is the smallest of the native conifers, often growing as a low shrub in mountain areas. Here and there, such as in Teesdale, North Yorkshire, or south-west Scotland, it forms extensive low woods. In favourable sites, such as in sheltered valleys on the southern chalk, it can reach six metres or more, though this is rare. The juniper female cones look like purple berries which are used as one of the main ingredients of gin, and the male cones are borne on separate trees as with yew. Juniper seeds appear to require a trip through the gut of a bird or other animal before they will germinate.

In addition to these native conifers, many other species have been introduced to Britain such as larches, spruces, firs, cedars, redwoods and hemlock. Some of these have naturalised, though most have remained in plantations or as specimen trees.

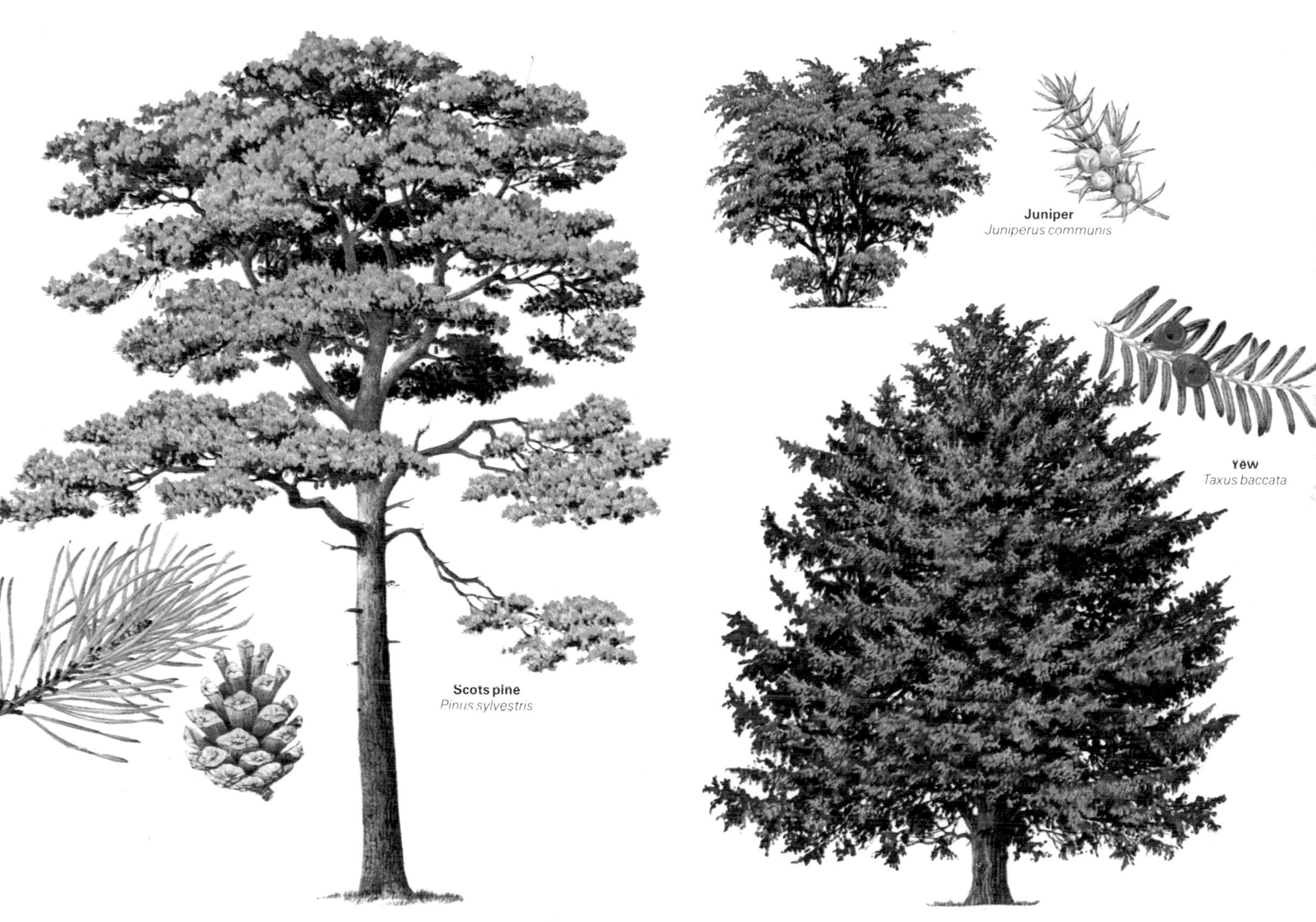

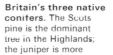

Britain's three native conifers. The Scots pine is the dominant tree in the Highlands; the juniper is more properly regarded as a shrub and the yew is common in woods on chalk and limestone soils

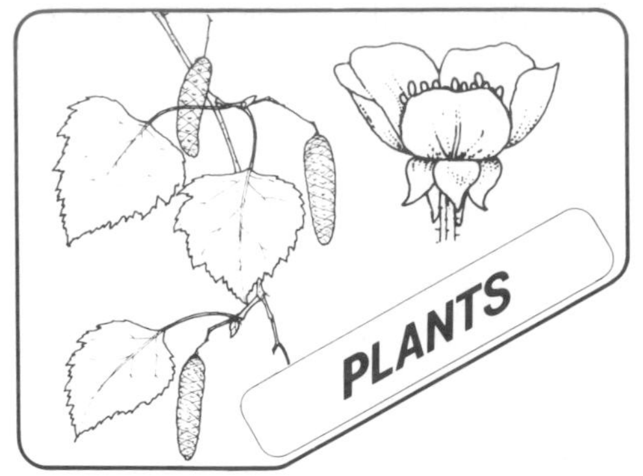

SHRUBS AND BUSHES

Shrubs and bushes form the level below the trees – woody, but not normally tall enough to reach the woodland canopy. We have an immense variety of shrubs in Britain, from knee-high dwarf willows or spurge laurel to shrubs that will readily turn into trees if allowed.

It is difficult to separate trees and shrubs precisely; both are woody, and trees are usually tall and straight, whilst shrubs are shorter and bushier. But there are grey areas, and it is not always easy to know quite where to place crab-apples, holly, rowan or bird cherry.

Of the woodland shrubs, hazel is probably the commonest and most widespread on many soil types, partly because it has been planted and encouraged as an economically-valuable plant for coppicing. It does occasionally form the canopy of woods, as in the hazel woods of western Ireland, but even then it can hardly be considered more than a shrub. It is a marvellous species to have anywhere, giving nesting-cover for birds and dormice, food in the form of nuts for many animals and insects, and even its leaves are eaten by a variety of invertebrates. Its familiar catkins are a great feature of spring when they waft their yellow pollen in clouds. Few people though realise that these are only the male flowers; have you ever wondered how hazel nuts, in ones and twos, come from dangling catkins? The answer is that they do not – there are also tiny female flowers, scattered about amongst the branches, which look like small buds with a tuft of tiny red ribbons on the top. These red 'ribbons' are the receptive parts of the female flower which the male pollen sticks to in large quantities. It is from these that the hazel nuts grow, unless eaten by a weevil or something before they develop that far! Hazel is also a

'Blackthorn winter' produced by the white flowers of the blackthorn or sloe bush. This occurs in March-May. The Hawthorn with which it may be confused flowers later

useful shrub for its crop which is not the nuts in this country, since they do not grow abundantly enough to harvest commercially, but the wood. Hazel will produce crops of poles from cut stumps for century after century, and these poles have found uses in hurdle-making, thatching, fencing and other crafts. The technique of producing young shoots by cutting back shrubs or trees in this way is known as coppicing, which is an ancient art that has been dying out during this century, but is now showing signs of a revival and is making a come back in many parts of the country as an active management regime.

scrub, downs, rough ground and open woodlands; and the woodland or Midland hawthorn, which is confined to relatively few ancient woods in the Midlands and south of England, rarely straying beyond their boundaries. The creamy white flowers of hawthorn are a major attraction to insects in spring, while the berries are eaten by many creatures, and the bushes are used by a range of commoner birds as nest sites. Like most common shrubs, the leaves are eaten by the larvae of numerous insects. The blackthorn is familiar for its mass of white flowers produced in early spring before the leaves appear, and for its purple sloes in autumn. Although there is only one species of sloe, it is closely related to several similar shrubs such as greengages and bullace with which it can readily be confused except in autumn.

The wayfaring tree and the guelder rose are another pair of closely-related shrubs, both in the honeysuckle family. The guelder rose produces lovely plates of frothy white flowers, followed later by almost translucent red berries, while the wayfaring tree is a slightly more mundane version with smaller flowers and less attractive berries and leaves. The elder, familiar both for its clusters of creamy flowers and its tiny purple berries (both of which make excellent wine) is another member of the honeysuckle family. Other shrubs to be found in the countryside include alder and purging buckthorn, spindle, dogwood, box and privet.

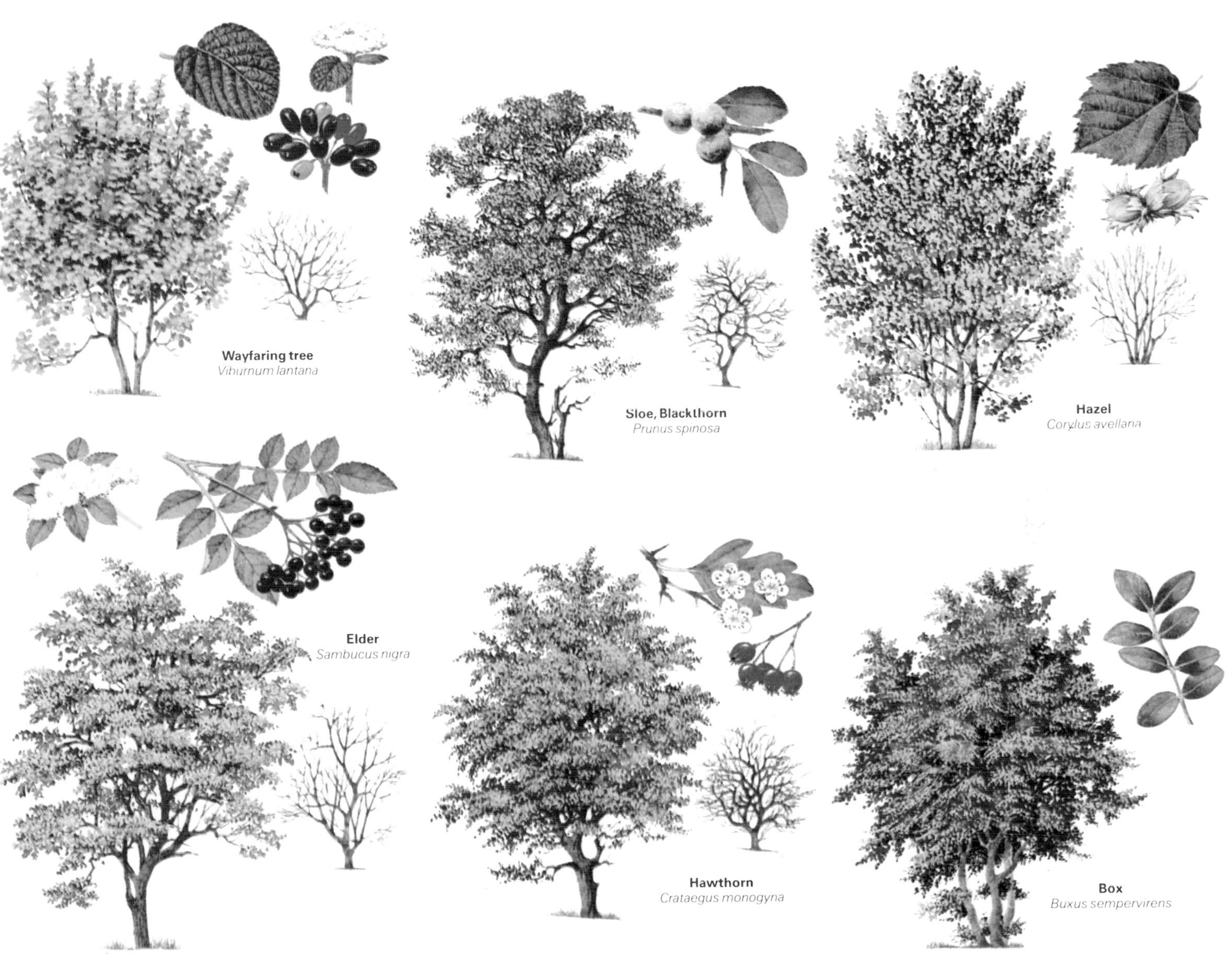

A selection of native shrubs, showing their form, winter shape, and their flowers and berries

The blackthorn and the hawthorn are two closely-related shrubs – both members of the rose family – which contribute a great deal to our countryside. In fact there are two species of hawthorn, the common hawthorn which occurs abundantly in hedges,

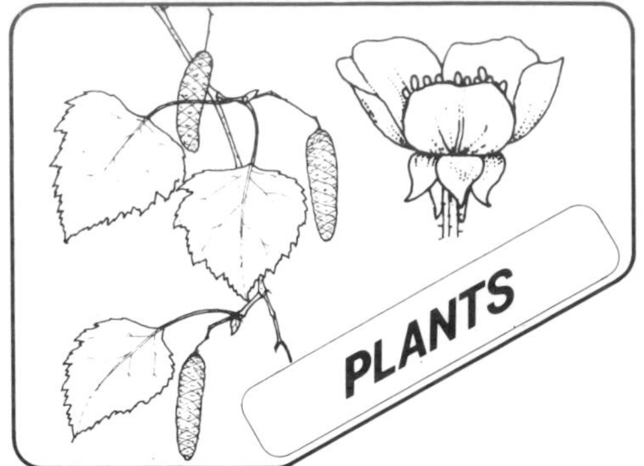
PLANTS

LOOKING AT HEDGEROWS

Hedges and their trees are living memorials to the history of our countryside. Many of them date from Saxon times or before, and their age, their past management and often the soil type can be worked out from a study of their plants.

There are hedges in virtually all parts of the country, in a variety of situations, with a multitude of different origins. They are fascinating to study because so much of this history can be 'read' from their appearance and plant life.

Dating hedges is an interesting occupation, partly because of what it tells you about the hedge, but you can also discover information about the field within the hedges, the process of clearance of fields from woodland, and the history of features that the hedge may follow, such as parish boundaries or ancient droveways. The most accurate way to date a hedge is by the use of maps, though this presents a number of problems. Firstly, it can be a time-consuming business trying to trace the particular map on which a hedge first appears; and, secondly, there are few accurate maps older than the 18th century which leaves a vast gap in the history. Luckily for the student of hedges, a method of dating, based on their plant life, has been worked out. It is not wholly foolproof, but it does give an accurate date in many circumstances, and it can be checked using hedges of known dates for a given area, to test for any regional variation.

The method is as follows. After selecting a hedge, mark it out into 30 metre or 30 pace lengths (the exact length is not too critical) for a long enough distance to give yourself several samples to average. Then, working along one side of the hedge only, walk each stretch and count within it the number of different types of woody plants, including trees, but counting climbers such as roses and brambles as just one. You do not need to know the names of the species you are finding, as long as you can tell that they are different, and you can collect sample leaves to compare as you go along. Having done this for several stretches, you might end up with a list as follows:

Stretch A: Rose, hawthorn, blackthorn, oak, ash, elm, spindle.
Stretch B: Hawthorn, rose, oak, blackthorn, elm, wayfaring tree, species X (unknown).
Stretch C: Bramble, rose, hawthorn, oak, ash, spindle, privet, holly, species Y (unknown).

Thus, making sure you only count rose and bramble together as one, you find seven species in A, seven in B, and eight in C. This gives an average number of countable species per 30 metre stretch of just over seven, actually 7.3. You then multiply this number by 100 to give you a rough age for the hedge, in this case 730 years old. Thus a hedge with about ten species is probably an Anglo-Saxon boundary hedge, while one with just two species will probably date from the 17th and 18th century enclosure movements, when many new hedges were planted.

It is also interesting to look at the shape of hedges around fields; for example straight hedges are probably of enclusure age, very wiggly hedges are often extremely old, while sinuous S-shaped hedges were probably planted on the edges of open fields, early in the enclosure movement. The types of shrubs and trees found in hedges varies regionally, too, depending on what was planted there. For example, beech hedges on banks are

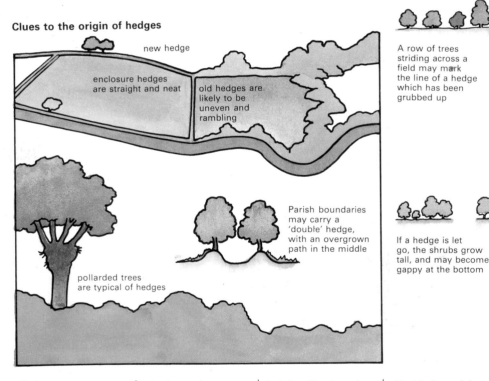

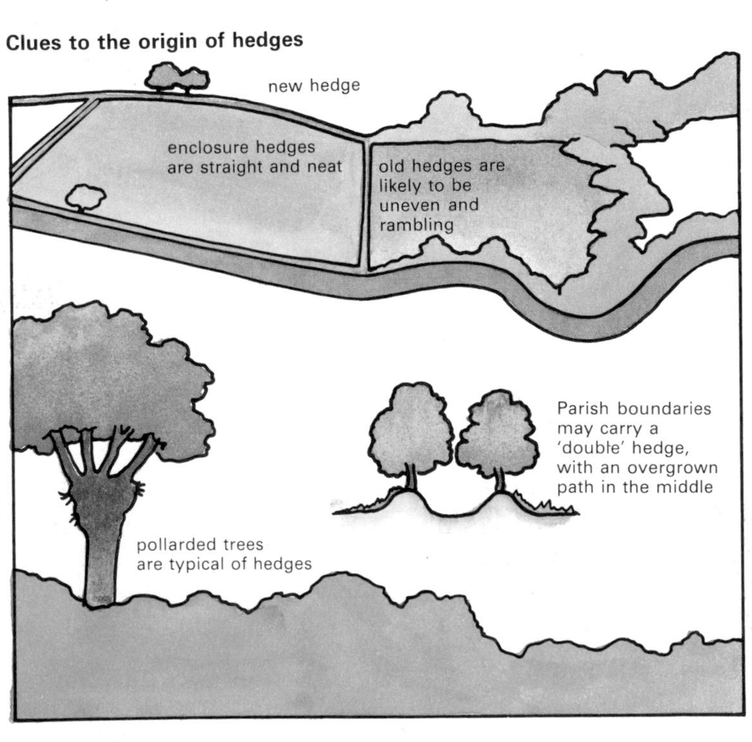
Clues to the origin of hedges
new hedge
enclosure hedges are straight and neat
old hedges are likely to be uneven and rambling
Parish boundaries may carry a 'double' hedge, with an overgrown path in the middle
pollarded trees are typical of hedges

A row of trees striding across a field may mark the line of a hedge which has been grubbed up

If a hedge is let go, the shrubs grow tall, and may become gappy at the bottom

Hedgerows

A great deal of information can be gleaned from a close look at hedges. Their origins and nature are so varied, yet this can often show through in their present day shape, structure and composition. The illustrations show some of the possible clues to look for, either by going out and checking on the ground, or by looking at old maps

Most hedges originated in one of three ways: as parish boundaries, remains of woodland after the wood has been cleared, and as planted hedges

typical of Exmoor, Fuchsia hedges are typical of western Ireland and parts of western Scotland, field maple hedges can be found in the Midlands, whilst the Scilly Isles have hedges found nowhere else, composed of karo and other exotics.

An old hedge that has been cut and laid. Traditionally the uprights or stakes would have been made of cut sticks

There are also regional and historical variations in the way that hedges are managed. If not maintained, the trees within them grow taller and larger, and cease to put out side branches; gaps appear at the base and they cease to function as a stock-proof barrier. Nowadays, most hedges are cut by various types of mechanical flail, but in the past they were often layered, or layed, and this practice still continues in a few areas. The hedge is first cleaned up, leaving a series of tall thin poles, which are almost cut through so only a narrow strip of tissue attaches them. These are known as the pleachers, and they are bent over and interwoven with one another. Because they are still attached, the pleachers continue to grow, in a more or less horizontal position, making a strong thick hedge, which may also be reinfored at intervals by stakes. This is the basic technique but you will find regional variations all of which have the only proviso that they are able to withstand cattle pushing them over.

AN INTRODUCTION TO

INSECTS & INVERTEBRATES

There are at least 20,000 species of insects in Britain, together with about 600 species of spiders and innumerable other 'creepy-crawlies' that make up the invertebrate world. They are the most varied of our groups of fauna, and include amongst them many beautiful and fascinating species. The invertebrates are, as their name indicates, those animals that do not have a backbone. The best-known are the insects which are characterised by having six legs and usually wings, though a few are wingless. The remainder includes the spider, harvestmen, slugs, snails, centipedes, millipedes, crabs, worms, leeches and many other groups, and the following pages attempt to do justice to some of this great variety.

The insects are the most familiar of invertebrates and there are many attractive species. Everyone loves butterflies and we have over 50 different species in Britain, from tiny skippers and hairstreaks that often pass unnoticed to the ubiquitous red admiral or the glorious purple emperor. Dragonflies, too, are harmless beautiful creatures with over 40 different species in Britain, from tiny damselflies to the impressive emperor dragonfly or the lovely golden-ringed dragonfly. Moths are even more prolific with well over 1,000 species if you include the smaller ones. Most of this enormous variety is never seen, as the great majority of moths have developed a nocturnal lifestyle to avoid predation by birds. Amongst the remainder, there are the grasshoppers and crickets, earwigs, lacewings, the large numbers of different bugs (these are the true bugs, though a common name for all insects is 'bugs') and, of course, the beetles. There are more than 4,000 species of beetle in Britain, from the enormous stag beetles that emerge from dead wood to a multitude of tiny species only a millimetre or two long; only a very few are normally noticed by naturalists, but the variety and interest of the group is vast. The true flies form an even larger group, with over 5,000 species known in Britain, but apart from those that bite, they are mostly overlooked, so we introduce some of the commoner and more attractive species in the following sections. Last but not least is the huge group, known as the Hymenoptera which includes the bees, wasps, ants, ichneumon flies and others; between them, they have some of the most fascinating of all insect lifestyles, as parasites, predators, mimics, socially-organised colonies and gall-formers.

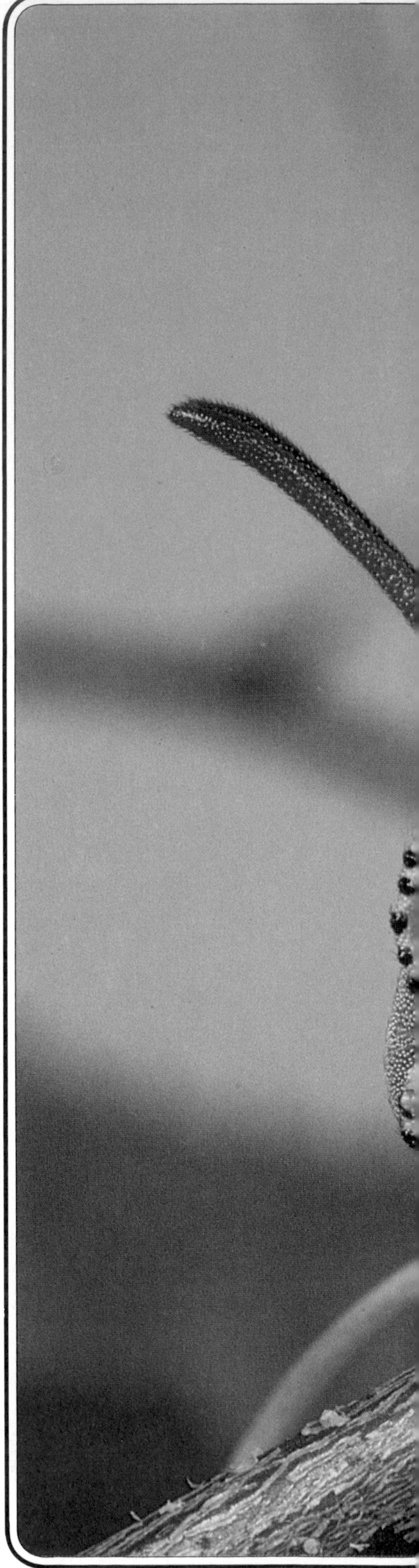

The extraordinary caterpillar of the lobster moth, feeding on beech. Although it looks terrifying it is only about one cm long!

INSECTS AND INVERTEBRATES

INCLUDING: Butterflies • Woodlands • Heathlands • Coasts • Grassland • Dragonflies • Freshwater • Mountain Insect Life • Insects on Farmland • Grasshoppers • Beetles • Spiders • Crabs and Lobsters • Sea-shells • Bees and Wasps • Moths

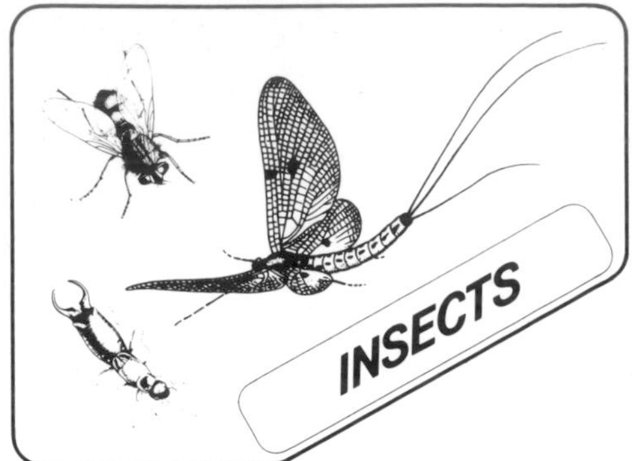

BUTTERFLIES IN WOODLAND

Woodlands are best known for their flowers but they can also be one of the finest habitats for butterflies. There is nothing more exciting than watching a host of beautiful silver-washed fritillaries and white admirals amongst clouds of commoner species on a warm sunny day.

Butterflies abound and it is by no means uncommon for 30 different species to occur; the very best woods have records for over 40 species. In contrast, though, some woods can be very dull, with just a few common species being found around the edges. The main difference between such woods lies in the way they are managed, for butterflies, even woodland species, need sunshine, and they require a range of particular food-plants for their caterpillars.

The best woods have a great range of trees and shrubs; though only a few butterflies actually lay their eggs on these woody plants, the variety helps to create a diverse structure to the wood, with more roosting places, hibernation sites and breeding areas, as well as helping to ensure that the vital ground flora is more varied. It is also important that some system of rides or glades occurs in the wood, because the best places to see most adult butterflies are in the sunny clearings or on woodland edges, and this is where many of the caterpillar food-plants grow, too. These can be straightforward broad rides used for timber extraction, natural clearings caused by tree-fall or deer-grazing, areas where trees have been felled for replanting or areas that have been recently coppiced for hazel products (see page 13). The general effect is similar, in that it produces a flush of plants such as violets and primroses which are important for the caterpillars, and a wealth of nectar flowers such as bugle, yellow archangel and bluebells for the adult butterflies.

Butterflies in woodland

A simple schematic diagram of the way in which different butterflies use different parts of the woodland, as adults. It helps, when out looking for butterflies, to know a little of their habits and where you are most likely to find them. The picture shows a woodland with a marvellous structure for butterflies, with plenty of variety, and obviously such woods are likely to have the greatest number of species. Some, like the speckled wood, prefer dappled shade; others, such as the silver-washed fritillary will be most often seen at head height, visiting brambles or tall thistles. In contrast, the fritillaries which fly in spring (particularly the two species of pearl-bordered fritillaries) tend to feed at ground level, whilst the purple hairstreak and purple emperor are hardly visible at all, since they remain amongst the tree tops

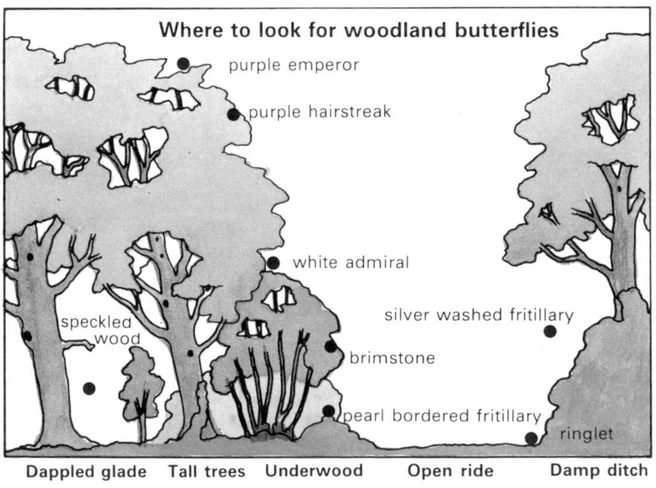

Purple emperor

The beautiful purple emperor can be seen mainly in wooded areas of west Surrey and Sussex. The males are usually found at the top of a 'Master Tree' in each area from where they descend to feed on honey dew. The females lay eggs on sallow leaves in August from which the caterpillar emerges. It overwinters on a silk pad in the fork of a sallow twig. The caterpillar turns into a chrysalis in mid-June to appear as the adult in July.

One of the commonest and most familiar butterflies in woodland is the brimstone. They hibernate over the winter in some sheltered place, emerging in early spring on warm sunny days to feed and mate. The males look like huge flying primroses – they are the origin of the term 'butter fly' – while the females are more creamy-white and can be confused with cabbage whites. The eggs are laid by the female on alder buckthorn or purging buckthorn, and a new generation will emerge by late summer.

The fritillaries are one of the butterfly groups most adapted to woodland, and several species are most likely to be found there especially the silver-washed, the high brown, the pearl-bordered and the small pearl-bordered. The very rare heath fritillary, despite its name, is also most likely to be spotted in woodland, whilst the marsh fritillary occurs in many woods and even the dark-green fritillary strays into them occasionally. There are no woods in which all these fritillaries are found, though it is possible for four or five species to be present together.

The white admiral is a lovely butterfly which typifies summer days in woodlands and, indeed, it is very unlikely to be seen anywhere else. It has a wonderful sailing flight, drifting through patches of sun to land on a bramble flower to feed. Its larvae feed solely on honeysuckle, and it needs to be growing in just the right place, with not too much sun nor too much shade. A close relative is the purple emperor, which is seen much less often, partly because it is rarer but also due to the fact that it feeds less on nectar and stays more around the tree tops, just coming down occasionally to investigate wet areas or light-coloured objects. The only butterfly larvae which feed on oak are, rather surprisingly, those of the purple hairstreak. The butterfly is actually quite common, but rarely seen because it is small and prefers to stay amongst the tree tops, drinking honeydew rather than bothering with nectar. Several other hairstreaks occur in woodland, such as the brown and black hairstreaks, which both use blackthorn, and the white-letter hairstreak the larvae of which live on elm leaves. The black hairstreak is a very rare butterfly found only in the woodland of the east Midland forest belt which runs from Peterborough to Oxford. The adult butterflies usually stay perched at the tops of the trees.

The lovely little holly blue has a strange life-cycle (see page 104 for illustration); the first generation emerges quite early in spring, and indeed almost any blue butterfly seen in woods at the time is likely to be this one. The females of this generation lay their eggs mainly on holly, where the larvae feed on the developing flowers and fruits; the adults emerge in August and these females lay their eggs mainly on ivy, which flowers and fruits in autumn and winter, providing food for this later generation.

Three woodland butterflies. Top: a beautiful male purple emperor butterfly; middle: a female, pearl-bordered fritillary laying an egg beside some violets; and bottom: a fine specimen of the speckled wood, basking on warm dead leaves, where it is well camouflaged. It breeds along semi-shaded woodland edges or cleared rides

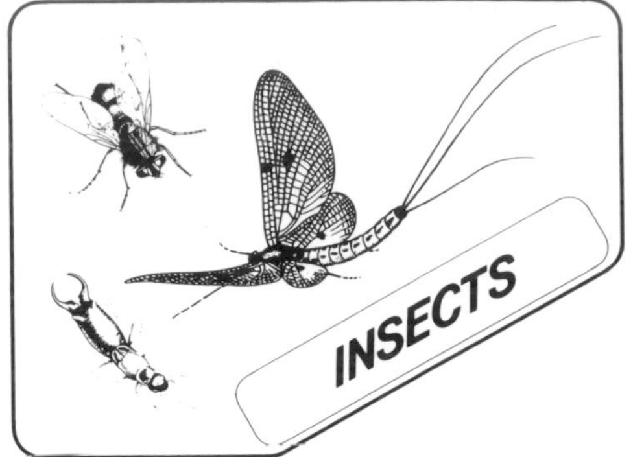

BUTTERFLIES OF DOWNLAND

Chalk or limestone downland in high summer can be a paradise for butterflies, with masses of nectar flowers and all the right larval food plants. On a good piece of downland, it is possible to find over 30 different species, with many of them occurring in great abundance.

Downlands, along with woodlands, are the finest of butterfly habitats, and many beautiful species only occur here. There are several reasons why such places are so good for butterflies. Firstly they are often warm, sunny places, where butterflies can feed and bask readily. Secondly, there is a tremendous range of suitable food-plants for the caterpillars, such as rock-rose, bird's-foot-trefoil and violets. And thirdly, there are masses of nectar-bearing flowers on which the adult butterflies feed.

It is rare for any one downland to be good for all the possible butterflies, because each species has slightly different requirements. Some require very short turf, some prefer long rough grass, some need shelter and bushes, while others need more open conditions. A few large sites contain all the necessary ingredients and these are wonderful places, home to well over 30 different butterflies, but it is more common to find 20 or so species on one site.

Perhaps the most typical and best-known of the downland butterflies are the 'blues'. These have some strange life-cycles, and they are particularly adapted to life on downland. Perhaps the oddest of all was the large blue, which was so specialised in its habitat requirements and its association with one particular species of ant, that it eventually could find nowhere suitable and became extinct in Britain a few years ago. A species with rather similar requirements, that has itself become much rarer recently, is the lovely Adonis blue. This strikingly turquoise-blue species occurs only on warm south-facing downlands with an abundance of its larval food-plant, the horseshoe vetch. However, it also requires the presence of particular species of ant to complete its life-cycle, for the mature larva enters ants' nests when ready to pupate and turns into the chrysalis there. The ants feed on the sugary solution produced by the chrysalis, and protect it by earthing it up in a special cell. When the adult butterfly is ready to emerge, it pushes its way up through the soil, unmolested by the ants, and dries its wings in the sun. The chalkhill blue, which is slightly commoner, has a rather similar life-history, using the same food-plant and also being taken, as a chrysalis, into ants' nests.

There are other blues on downland, too. The common blue feeds on bird's-foot-trefoil and other related plants, and it is the commonest and most widespread of the blue species. The rather inconspicuous smoky-blue coloured small blue lays its eggs on the flowers of the kidney vetch, where the larvae feed on the developing seeds. The brown argus, though neither sex is blue, is one of the blue family with similar habits, and its main larval food-plant is the common rock-rose, another downland plant.

One of the most attractive of downland butterflies is the dark green fritillary which is, in fact, a large tawny-coloured butterfly. It flies fast over open grassland, settling occasionally to feed on thistles, knapweed or other nectar flowers. Its larval food-plants are violets, and it is most often found feeding on the hairy violet which grows vigorously and abundantly on most downs. Similar looking is the smaller Duke of Burgundy fritillary, though it is not a true

The Adonis blue
This is one of our most attractive downland butterflies emerging from May to September on the warmest downs of southern England. Colonies vary in numbers from year to year depending on many factors including the abundance of horseshoe vetch (the caterpillar's food-plant), the weather, length of the sward and level of disturbance. The attractive greenish caterpillar may be seen on horseshoe vetch attended by ants which 'milk' the caterpillar for sugary secretions. The caterpillar is taken down into the ant's nest where it pupates and emerges as an adult a month or so later. It is the male which has the vivid turquoise blue wings. The female's upperwings are mainly brown with orange blotches on the margins

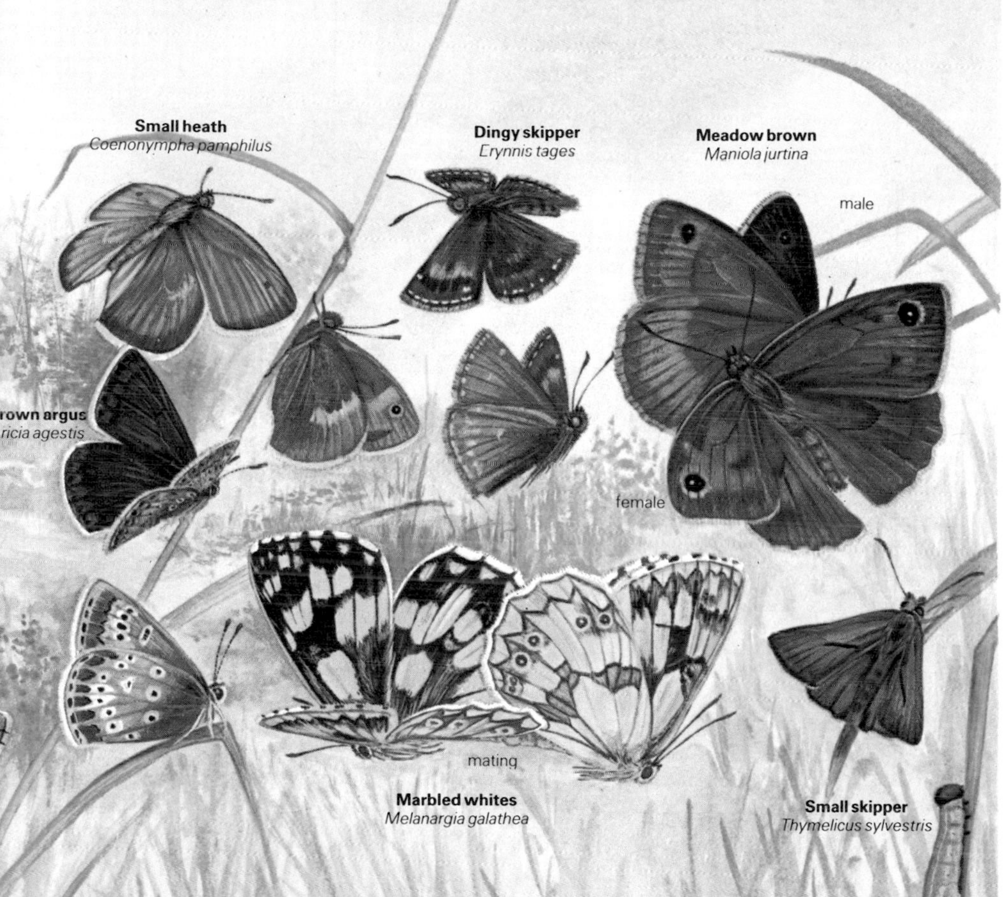

and the decline of sheep farming on downs.

Many of our downland butterflies are ultimately dependent upon the grazing of the turf for their survival. Once grazing stops the butterfly's food plants may be shaded out.

fritillary at all. It has a rather specialised requirement for cowslips or primroses growing in just the right conditions of shelter and humidity, and it tends to occur rather uncommonly in small colonies on sheltered downland with rough grass. A species with the opposite requirements is the attractive little silver-spotted skipper which only lays its eggs on sheep's-fescue grass in very short well-grazed turf, often where rabbits are present. It is rare and declining; a casualty of the effects of myxamatosis

Butterflies of downland. A selection of typical downland butterflies

Right: A male large skipper perched on a rose leaf waiting for a female large skipper to pass by. These attractive little butterflies are common throughout England and Wales, except in higher mountain areas, though they are easily overlooked, and many people have never seen one. The way they hold their wings, with the upper and lower wings separated, is characteristic of the skipper butterflies

BUTTERFLIES OF GARDENS

It is surprising how many butterflies come into towns and gardens attracted by the warmth and shelter, the tremendous range of nectar plants and the food-plants for the caterpillars. It is by no means uncommon for 10 or 12 different butterflies to be seen in a garden.

The butterflies that visit gardens and towns fall into two groups; those that are just visiting for nectar or other food, and those that are able to breed there because their larval food-plant is present. Many butterflies, such as the fritillaries, hairstreaks, most of the blues and some of the skippers, tend to be quite specific about their habitat requirements, and they are unlikely to even venture into gardens to feed, let alone breed, except perhaps in exceptional breeding years when large numbers move around the countryside. Others, such as meadow browns, speckled woods, gatekeepers, marbled whites, small and large skippers and brimstones will readily use gardens for nectar-feeding if there are colonies nearby. Some of them will breed in gardens if the conditions happen to be right, though they rarely are.

The remaining group, however, are the real garden and town specialists, though none are confined to such places. The five common Vanessid butterflies – the small tortoiseshell, red admiral, peacock, comma and painted lady – all occur regularly in gardens and are a familiar sight

A male large white – one of the 'cabbage whites' – visiting a knapweed flower. It is one of the commonest of garden butterflies.

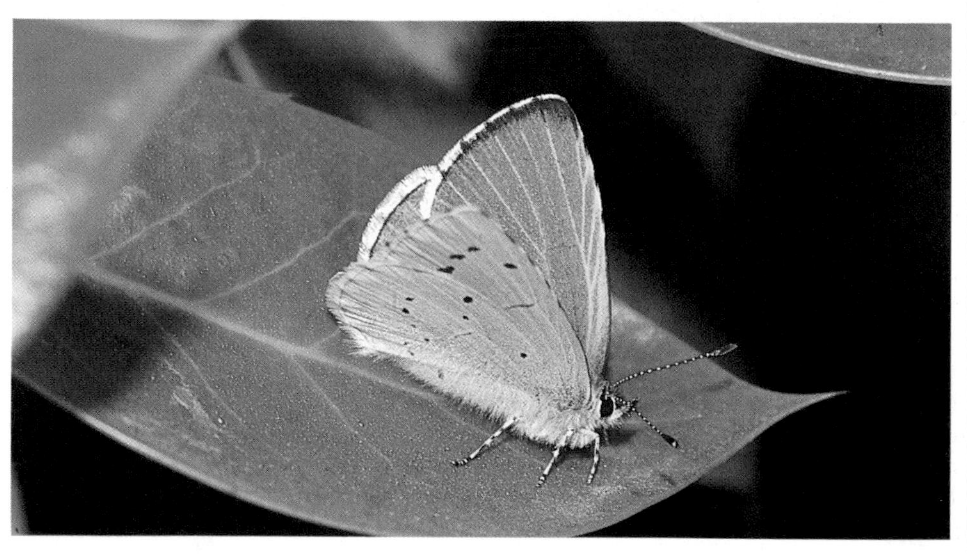

Above: A resplendent male holly blue. The diagram shows how its caterpillars feed on holly in spring and then on ivy in the autumn, as a second generation. The holly blue is confined almost exclusively to the southern half of England where it is common in the summer months even in gardens in central London. Look for them particularly in August

A selection of Vanessid butterflies, which are amongst the commonest and most beautiful of our garden butterflies. Most of them lay eggs on nettles, and the caterpillars can be fairly easily found, and identified as shown. Look out also for the comma with its ragged wings. The comma caterpillar feeds on nettles and has a white patch on its back which looks like a bird dropping

towards the end of the summer. The first four breed on nettles which are frequently found in gardens, waste places and other sites associated with man, as well as in the wilder countryside. Painted ladies breed more often on thistles, but all are so mobile as adults that they can readily seek out new nectar sources from wherever they were hatched.

Gardens are special places in many ways, for they are managed for flowers and fruit, and tend to have a higher density of both than occurs normally in the wild. They also have the extra shelter provided by fences and houses, and are very desirable places for some butterflies. From midsummer into autumn, the flowers of Buddleia, ice-plant, lavender and many other nectar-bearing plants attract the Vanessids, as do plums, pears and other ripening autumn fruit well on into October or even November. Ideas to help to attract more of these beautiful and harmless butterfles into your garden are given on page 155.

Some rather less desirable visitors and residents are the large and small whites, or cabbage whites as they are known. Both species breed prolifically in gardens finding cabbage patches and other Brassicas much to their liking, as most gardeners know all too well, and their numbers may be regularly boosted by migrations from the Continent. There are other whites which visit gardens, though they are much less frequent and do not attack crops. The beautiful little orange-tip and the green-veined white both feed on wild relatives of the Brassicas, and sometimes visit gardens in spring for nectar or in search of egg-laying sites. Look for their caterpillars in damp ditches and hedges where lady's smock or other plants such as garlic mustard and hedge mustard. The adult green-veined white flies from April September and the orange tip mostly in May and June.

Another butterfly which is seen as often in gardens as anywhere, is the little holly blue. It is a frequent sight on warm days in spring, fluttering around holly bushes in towns and gardens where it can find both of its main food-plants – the holly and the ivy – as well as many nectar sources.

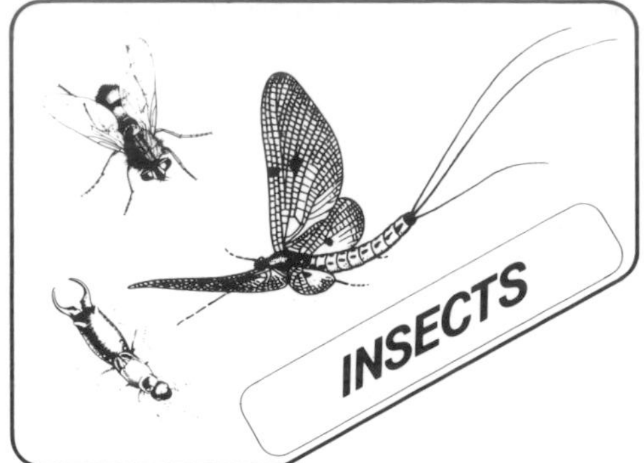

OTHER INVERTEBRATES IN TOWNS AND GARDENS

Towns and gardens are home to a wonderful array of other invertebrates as well as butterflies. These include moths, ladybirds and other beetles, centipedes, hoverflies, honey-bees and spiders. All make use of the extra food, shelter and warmth provided by these man-made habitats.

For the same sorts of reasons that make towns and gardens so attractive to butterflies, they also suit many other invertebrates. Although many of these creatures are specific to more natural habitats, a very large number are able to use towns and gardens for at least part of their life-cycle, and a few have even become dependent on them for their survival.

Moths occur abundantly in towns and gardens. They are the nocturnal equivalent of their close relatives, the butterflies, and more are able to breed in the garden, as they use a wider range of larval food-plants. Others simply move in at night to feed on the abundant nectar sources. Buddleia, for example, may be well-known as a butterfly bush but, if you go and look at it on a warm summer night, you will see that it is also good as a moth bush! Some of the extraordinary hawkmoths have been able to colonise gardens successfully, making use of the fact that their food-plants, or introduced relatives of them, grow here in large quantities. The beautiful pink and brown privet hawkmoth has its larval stages on privet, which is commonly used as a garden hedge, though it is normally a slightly different species to the wild one, and the large horned caterpillars are often found by gardeners. The large elephant hawkmoth, which is a gorgeous pink and green moth, feeds in the wild on willowherbs, but it has transferred successfully to Fuchsia and Clarkia which are in the same family. Its huge larvae normally feed at night, but occasionally appear near the tops of the bushes during the day. Similarly, the lime hawkmoth does well where street limes are commonly planted; poplar hawk are found on ornamental poplars and willows, and the pine hawkmoth lives wherever there are pines.

Other familiar garden and town moths include the garden tiger moth, of which the nocturnal adult is only occasionally seen, but the 'woolly

The striking caterpillar of the large elephant hawk moth, feeding on willowherb. These beautiful insects are quite often found in gardens and towns, because the caterpillars feed on Fuchsias, Clarkias, and rosebay willowherb

bear' caterpillars are often found. The attractive red and grey cinnabar moth flies by day and is often seen; its caterpillars are equally familiar as the yellow and black striped larvae on ragwort or groundsel which they often strip bare.

Honey-bees make frequent use of gardens wherever hives are within reach, for the abundant nectar from flowers of fruit trees, rosemary, Buddleias, marjoram and many others is an attraction right through the summer. Bees are non-specialist nectar and pollen-gatherers, and they can successfully feed from a wide range of flowers. Bumble bees of several different species are common in gardens too, and they frequently nest in hedge bottoms or under garden sheds, as well as visiting the nectar plants. Black ants are relatives of the bees, and become especially obvious in towns and gardens on the hottest days of the summer, when synchronised emergence of the queens and winged males takes place, filling the air with 'flying ants'. Less welcome members of the group are the wasps, which often nest colonially in holes in banks or walls. For much of the summer, they do not trouble us, for their feeding habits do not conflict with ours, but by late summer they turn to sources of sugar for food, and when these include lemonade, jellies, jam and fruit, then the trouble begins. There are also some clever wasp-mimics to be seen in gardens which, though harmless in themselves, rely on their similarity to the aggressive, distasteful wasps to avoid predation. They include several flies and the attractive little yellow and black wasp beetle.

Other beetles that can readily be seen in towns and gardens are the violet ground beetle, that mainly comes out at night, several species of the familiar and welcome ladybirds, and the striking large and impressive stag beetle with its massive 'pinchers' which, for some curious reason, thrives in the southern suburbs of London, though it is never very common elsewhere.

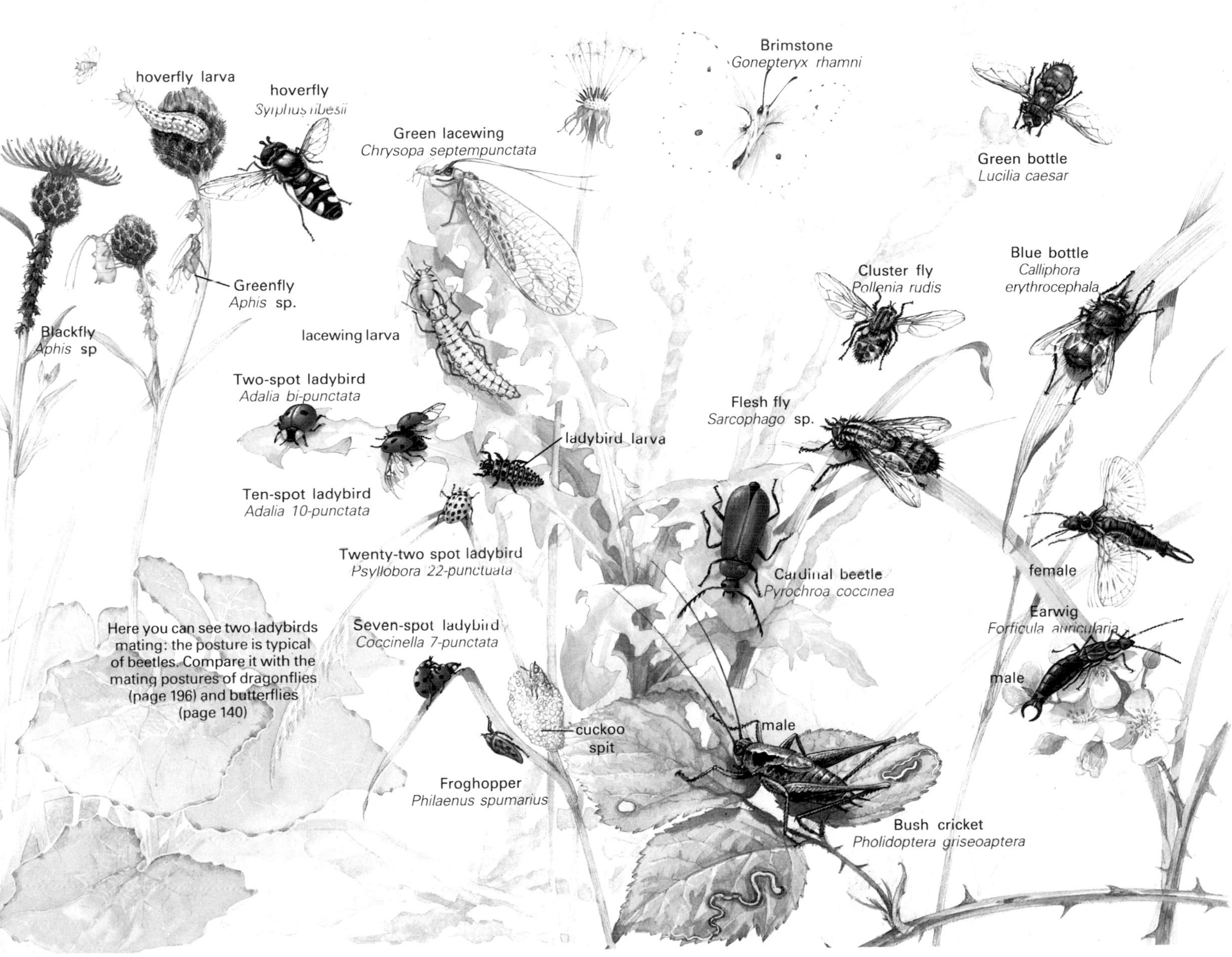

The variety of insects and other invertebrates that can be seen in the garden is extraordinary. Much depends upon what part of the country you are in, what your garden is like, and what surrounds you, but the examples illustrated are reasonably typical

INSECTS IN WOODLAND

We have already seen that woodlands can be one of the finest habitats for butterflies, but they are also wonderful places for other insects and invertebrates. Some larger woods may support literally thousands of species, the great majority of which pass unnoticed.

The warm, sheltered, humid environment of woods is probably the best of all habitats for invertebrates. A suitably managed woodland, with the same structure that is good for butterflies, will be very rich in insects and other invertebrates, because it provides the conditions that so many of them require. The structure of many invertebrates renders them liable to drying out very readily, thus the high, constant humidity of a woodland suits them well. The great variety of trees, shrubs and herbaceous plants provides food for a huge range of larvae, while the varied structure of a good, preferably ancient, wood provides numerous 'niches' for other insects. Dead wood is a favoured habitat for many species such as longhorn beetles, sawflies, hoverflies, a few moths and many others. The three-dimensional layered nature of a wood allows each invertebrate to find its favoured degree of light intensity, warmth and humidity.

Moths are among the most abundant and obvious of woodland insects, with many hundreds of species in a good wood, and they are dealt with separately on page 130. The lovely little hoverflies, of which there are about 260 British species, are especially abundant in woodland; some of the larvae breed in dead or dying wood whilst others favour damp areas. As adults they are attracted to nectar of flowers along sunny rides or on the edges of the wood. Few have English names, but one better-known group is the drone flies which mimic bees. A different, but related, group of flies which is often seen in woodland is the bee-flies. The commonest species, the large bee-fly, is a typical spring species, readily seen hovering in front of primroses or other spring flowers, probing for nectar with its long proboscis. Another woodland insect that is called a fly, but is quite unrelated, is the strange scorpion fly, a familiar sight in woods in early summer. It is so named because the tip of the male's abdomen is reddened and turned upwards, rather like that of a scorpion, though it is quite harmless. It is actually a scavenger, feeding on dead insects, rotting fruit and other decaying material; it is especially good at

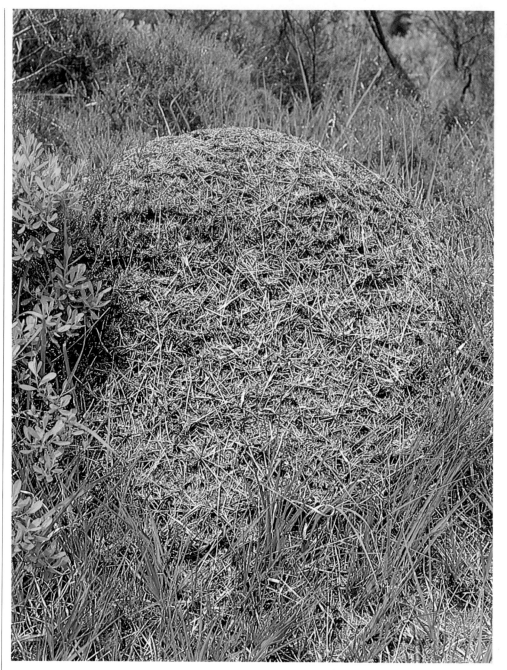

A wood ant nest. One of the most obvious insects of woodland, especially in hilly areas, is the wood ant. They live in huge colonies and build giant heaps of vegetation as nests

creeping onto spiders' webs and feeding on the remains of the spiders' meals.

One of the more obvious and better known woodland insects, because it occurs in huge numbers and builds such large nests, is the wood ant. They are amongst the largest of British ants, and are readily visible as trails of red and brown workers moving along the ground or up trees. They may be ants. They are wide-ranging and voracious predators, occasionally encouraged in commercial forests to help keep down pests, but are considered to be one cause of the decline of butterflies in other woods. When threatened they will turn their abdomen towards the aggressor and shoot a jet of formic acid at them!

The damp, humid habitat of woods is ideal for molluscs, or slugs and snails, as they are better known. About half of the hundred species of British terrestrial molluscs occur in woodland, and the best sites for them tend to be ancient woods, because they are not mobile species and have a poor capability for colonising new habitats. Beech woods on chalk, such as on the South Downs, and ash-elm woods on limestone tend to be particularly favoured because snails

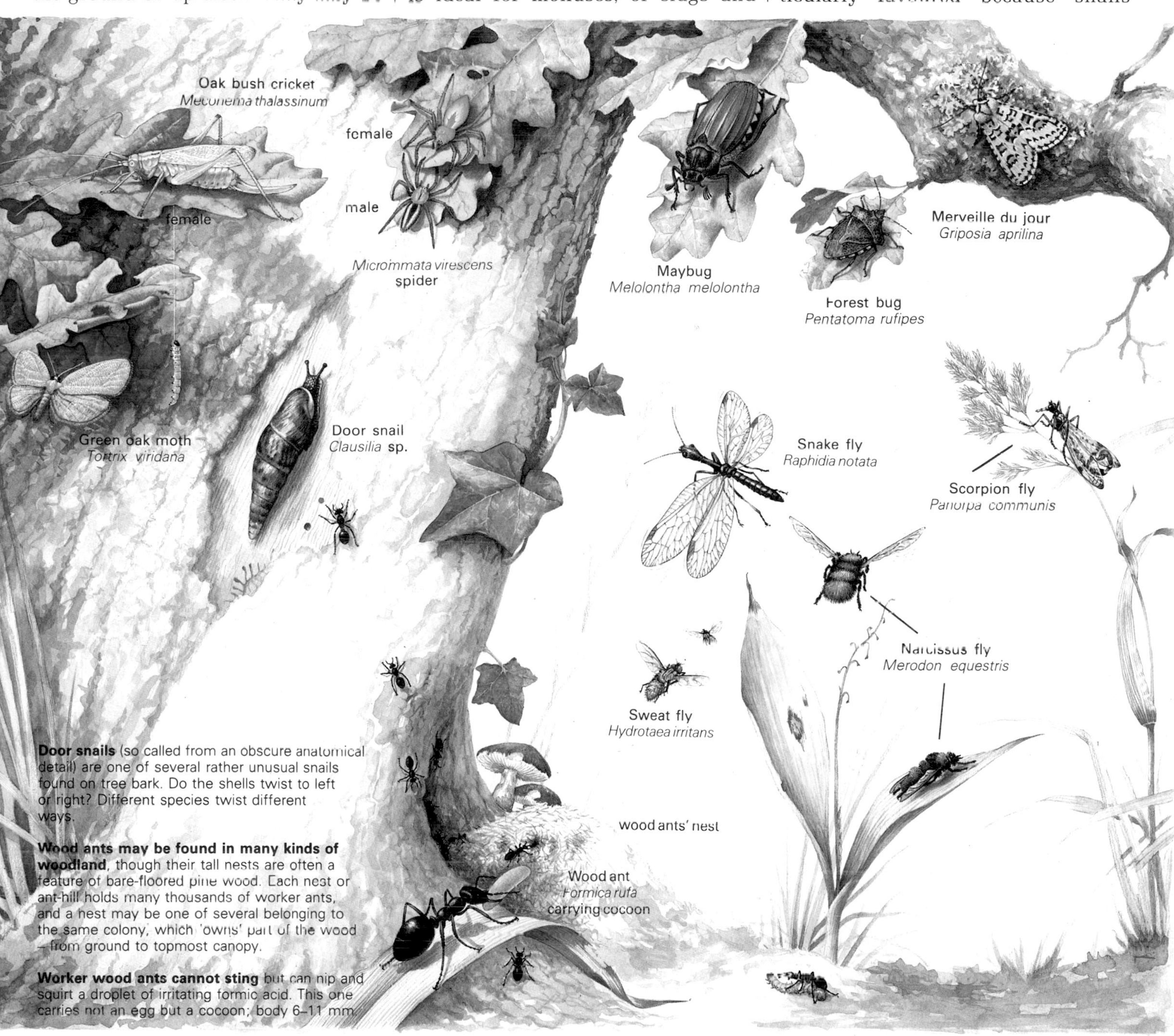

Door snails (so called from an obscure anatomical detail) are one of several rather unusual snails found on tree bark. Do the shells twist to left or right? Different species twist different ways.

Wood ants may be found in many kinds of woodland, though their tall nests are often a feature of bare-floored pine wood. Each nest or ant-hill holds many thousands of worker ants, and a nest may be one of several belonging to the same colony, which 'owns' part of the wood – from ground to topmost canopy.

Worker wood ants cannot sting but can nip and squirt a droplet of irritating formic acid. This one carries not an egg but a cocoon; body 6–11 mm.

more familiar for their nests which are huge piles of leaves and needles up to a metre in height. These may contain 100,000 or more worker ants, and the colonies often last for many years, retreating below ground for the winter, but emerging to forage and refurbish the nest each spring, when its surface becomes a seething mass of

Woodlands are exceptionally rich in insect life of all sorts, and we can do no more here than pick out a selection of some of the interesting species that you are most likely to see when on a spring or summer walk

need the extra lime for shell growth; richest woods may have 40 or more species. Although they are particularly unwelcome in the garden, slugs and snails are not damaging in the wild, as they never eat more than a small proportion of any one plant and a main part of their diet is made up of algae, lichens and mosses.

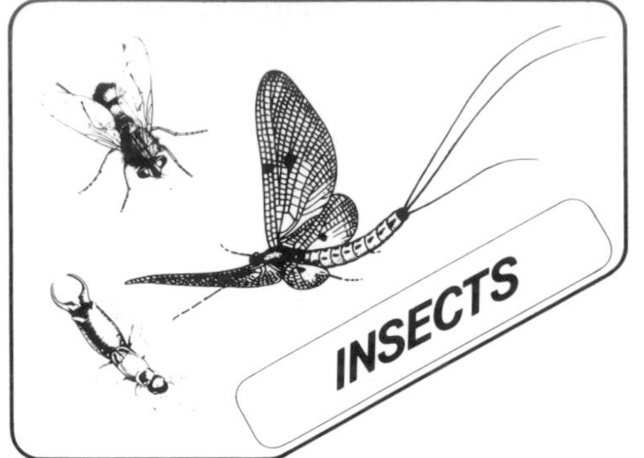

THE INSECTS OF HEATHLAND

Despite their rather barren appearance, heathlands are wonderful places for insects and spiders. Their warm, sunny slopes are home to a wide variety of different species including butterflies, spider-hunting wasps and all manner of strange creatures.

Heathland is not a particularly favoured habitat for butterflies, but there are one or two species that occur regularly there, and one that is now virtually confined to this area. The lovely little silver-studded blue, which is blue in the male and brownish in the female, is frequent on many southern heaths, sometimes dancing in clouds over a patch of young heather. The larvae feed on heather, gorse and other plants, but tend to prefer the youngest growth, so they are common on managed or grazed heaths but rare where the heather is mature and leggy. An attractive large mottled brown butterfly, the grayling, particularly favours heaths, though it is also found elsewhere. The larvae live on grasses, and the adults fly in late summer from mid-July to September. One other regular resident butterfly on heathland is the delicate, orange and brown small copper. Its larvae live on the leaves of sorrels, on heathland it feeds on sheep's sorrel which is common there. Other butterflies, such as green hairstreaks, live on this habitat where conditions are right, while many species visit for the nectar in summer.

There is one heathland moth that might be confused with a butterfly, as it is large, brightly-coloured and flies by day; this is the emperor moth. In spring, the males fly madly about over the heather, looking for sedentary females. The males have very feathery antennae, which are able to sense the tiniest amounts of female scent and hormones, apparently detecting the presence of a female from over a kilometre away. The rather smaller, orange-coloured fox moth behaves in a similar way, whilst other day-flying moths to be found include the heath moths such as the common heath.

Grasshoppers and crickets are familiar insects of heathland, selecting

Here are some commoner or more obvious insects of heathland. The two most specialist heathland butterflies are the grayling and silver-studded blue, both illustrated, while the beautiful emperor moth looks even more resplendent than the butterflies shown here. The other insects are particularly to be found on the ground in warm, sunny sandy or gravelly areas

warm grassy areas. There is a heath grasshopper, so named because it is virtually confined to this habitat. It is now very uncommon, just occurring on a few very warm southern heaths. However, other species such as the delightful little mottled grasshopper are more widespread. This tiny grasshopper has a distinctive call, rather like an old-fashioned watch being vigorously wound up! The bush-crickets are rather like grasshoppers, to which they are closely related, but they have long fine thread-like antennae, often much longer than the rest of the body; the bog bush-cricket is widespread on the damper parts of heaths, especially close to bogs.

The heathland insect community is notable for the number of predators and parasites amongst its number. The adults of the bright green tiger beetle are fierce active predators, but it is the larvae that have the stranger lifestyle; they develop in burrows at the base of little pits, and when anything, such as an ant, falls into the pit it is immediately grabbed and devoured. Some of the many solitary wasps also have interesting ways of life. The sand-wasps, for example, are large red and black species, the females of which hunt caterpillars, paralysing them and dragging them to their burrows, where they are stored, remaining alive but paralysed, as food for the developing wasp larvae. Other species of wasps hunt and catch spiders in a similar way, whilst some catch bugs. Each species of wasp usually specialises in a particular type of prey.

Other insects are parasitic in some way or another. The velvet ant (actually a type of wasp, but wingless and looking more like an ant) crawls around heaths in search of bumble bees' nests, which it enters and lays its eggs. The larvae of the velvet ant then feed on the larvae and pupae of the bumble bees. The beautiful little ruby-tailed wasps have a similar lifestyle, but they are highly mobile and dart around the entrances of bees' nests in the sunshine, waiting for an opportunity to enter and lay their eggs.

A beautiful orb-web of the garden spider, picked out by early morning dew, on a lowland heath covered in heather

Insects of our Coasts

The warm, mild climate of coastal areas and the unusual array of sunny, open habitats support a fascinating range of insects, including many that occur nowhere else. The coast is also the first point of landfall for many migrating insects and is a good place to watch for these.

As an insect habitat, the coast has a number of special features. The climate is milder and more free of frost than inland areas, and often sunnier. The habitats vary, from more widespread habitats such as downland that reach to the coast in places, to special coastal habitats such as dunes and shingle, or crumbling undercliffs. They all tend to be open in nature, with plenty of sunshine and a large proportion of bare ground, and are often unstable. This combination suits a wonderful mixture of insects, some of which occur as frequently inland, but others are true coastal specialists.

Most butterflies that are found on the coast are widespread species, finding nectar or food-plants in coastal habitats as they do elsewhere. One species, though, is totally confined to the coast; this is the attractive little Glanville fritillary, now only found on the coast of the Isle of Wight and in the Channel Islands. It is really a southern European species, so it needs the mild winters and sunny summers of these islands, but also depends on the unstable cliffs producing the right habitat for its food-plant – the ribwort plantain – in the right condition for its caterpillars. The caterpillars are gregarious and spend the winter in hibernation nests, often on grasses, so they are very vulnerable to the hard frosts that occur away from the coast. Another butterfly particularly associated with the coast is the Lulworth skipper, that is especially common on the grassy cliffs in the area of Dorset after which it is named. It also occurs on similar downland areas a little inland, but is never found far from the coast. Several migrant butterflies are also particularly associated with the coast,

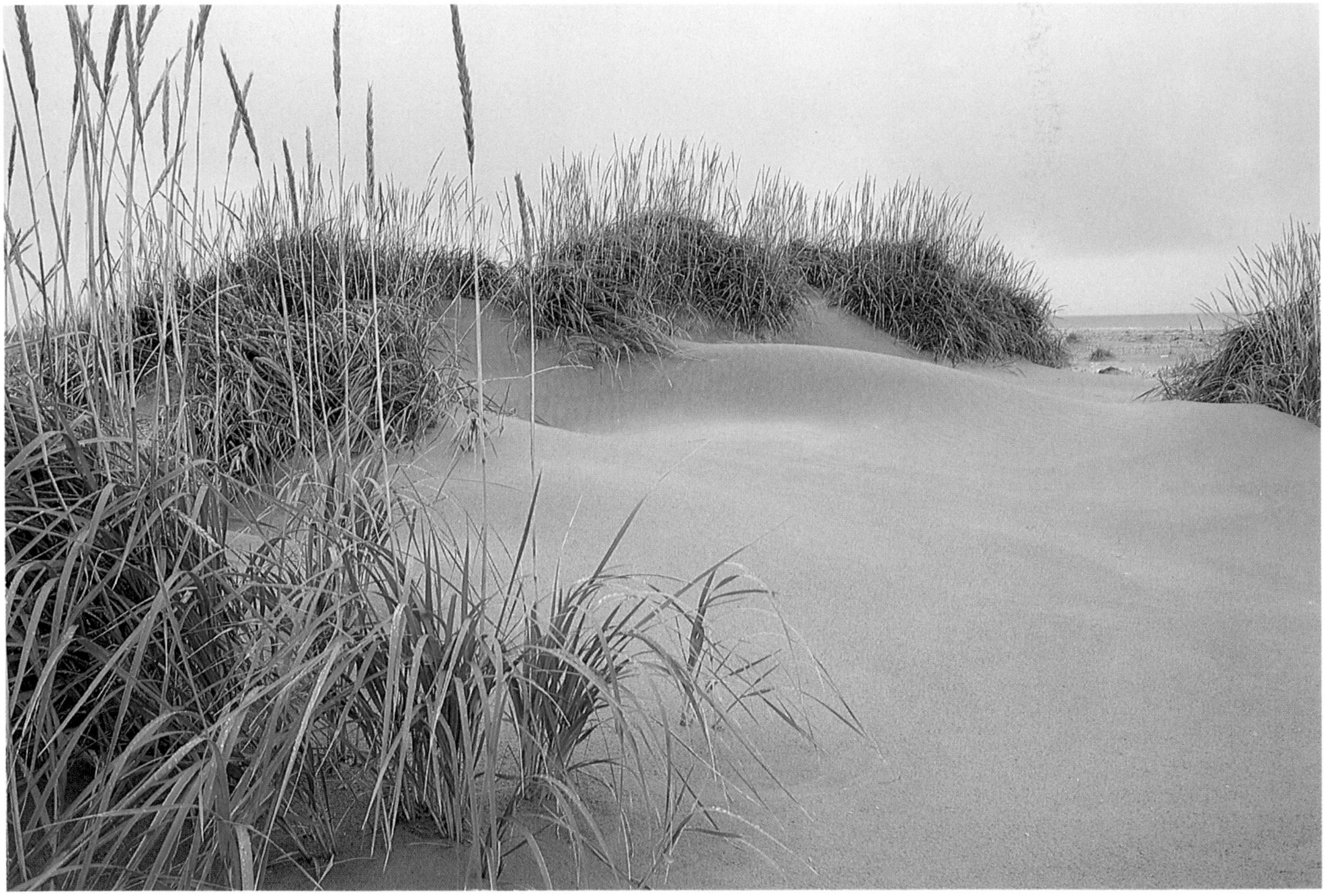

A typically coastal habitat, showing sandy lyme-grass dunes on the edge of a Scottish firth. These habitats are very fragile

A red-tailed bumblebee, feeding on the flowers of sea rocket. It flies April to September. The male has a yellow neckband

including great rarities such as the Camberwell beauty and the Bath white (see illustration). Several moths are most often found on the coast for the same reasons, including the spectacular death's head and convolvulus hawkmoths (see panel).

Grasshoppers and crickets love warm open grassy places, and virtually all the British species can occur somewhere on the coast. The commoner species are dealt with separately (see page 126), but there are also a few specialist coastal species. The grey bush-cricket is only found on warm open cliff areas from Cornwall eastwards, being especially common in Dorset and the Isle of Wight where there is an immense amount of coastal habitat. The same applies to the extraordinary great green bush-cricket, one of our largest insects, which is much commoner along the western parts of our south coast than anywhere else. Its loud continuous singing is a feature of these areas, and it often can be heard well on into the night.

Another bush-cricket, the short-winged conehead, specialises in coastal grasslands, and is quite common on saltmarsh areas, surviving occasional flooding by the sea. Its close relative, the long-winged conehead, used to be virtually confined to the coast, but it underwent a curious population expansion in the early 1980s, and now occurs well inland. The lesser marsh grasshopper lives in rather similar habitats, and another rare bush-cricket, Roesel's bush-cricket, is only found in grassland near the sea in south and east Britain. It produces an unmistakeable call, rather like a tropical cicada. There is also an odd little creature called the scaly cricket, which occurs on the shingle of Chesil beach in Dorset and nowhere else in Britain.

Several snails have a preference for the coast, particularly lime-rich areas such as some sand-dunes and the sandhill and pointed snails only occur in such habitats. The mild climate seems to suit snails, perhaps because they have to overwinter both as adults and young, rather than having a resistant pupa stage like many insects, so are vulnerable to colder weather. Many spiders, too, like coastal habitats, and there are about 30 species which are found exclusively here, together with a spider-relative, the false scorpion. There are also some special beetles that occur mainly on the coast, such as the extraordinary oil beetles, a family of large, predominantly black, beetles; the flightless female crawls about in the sunshine and lays thousands of eggs into holes and crannies where they hatch into tiny long-legged larvae. These only survive if they attach themselves to a wild bee, they are then carried to the bee's nest, and detach themselves to feed on the larvae and the pupae.

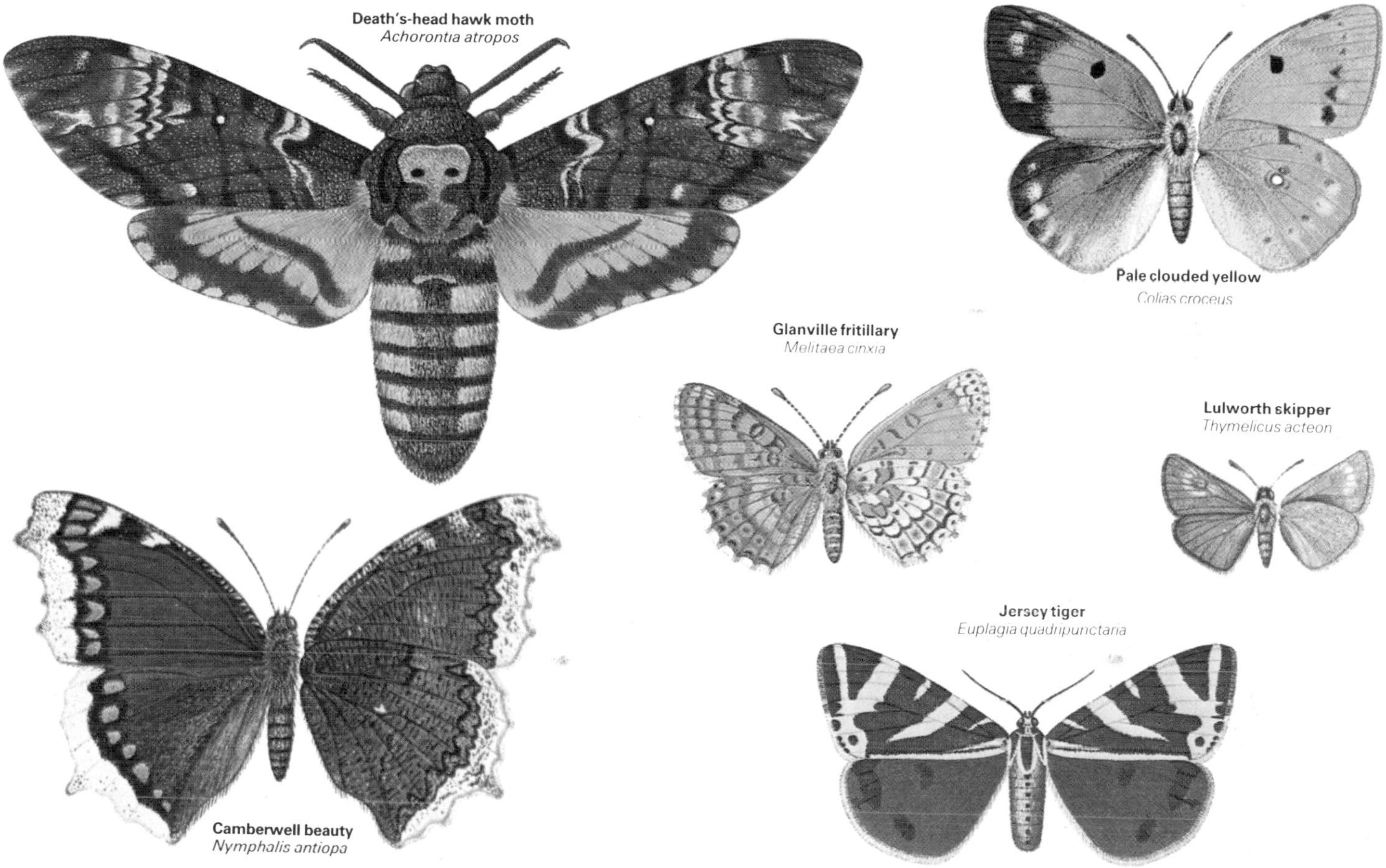

Death's-head hawk moth
Achorontia atropos

Pale clouded yellow
Colias croceus

Glanville fritillary
Melitaea cinxia

Lulworth skipper
Thymelicus acteon

Jersey tiger
Euplagia quadripunctaria

Camberwell beauty
Nymphalis antiopa

Some butterflies and moths that are more likely to be seen on the coasts than elsewhere. The Camberwell beauty is a rare migrant from the Continent seen in late summer or early spring, but it does not brood here

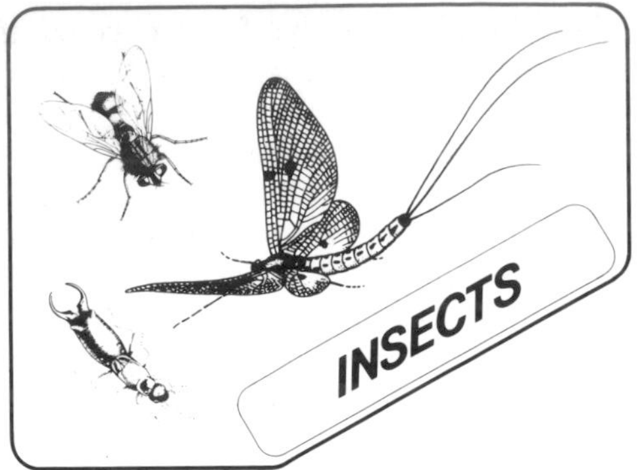

INVERTEBRATES OF GRASSLAND

Flower-rich grasslands hum with activity come midsummer. Not only do the more obvious insects like butterflies abound, but there is also an abundance of less conspicuous invertebrates, often hidden in the grass, such as snails, ants and beetles.

We have looked elsewhere at the butterflies, moths, and grasshoppers and crickets that are all so much a feature of grasslands, especially calcareous ones over chalk and limestone. But, besides these insects, there is a wealth of other invertebrates to be seen in grassland if you look a little harder.

One group of invertebrates that do particularly well in grassland, where there is enough lime in the soil to allow them to grow their shells successfully, is the snails. A surprisingly large number of species can occur in a varied grassy sward, especially if there are plenty of niches for them, such as walls or old chalk pits in addition to the grassland. The best sites tend to be the more humid north-facing or partially-shaded places, especially if the area is not too heavily grazed or mown. Burning can be particularly damaging to molluscs, since they are almost totally immobile. The panel shows a range of different grassland species, including the unlikely-sounding hairy snail and the spire-shaped door snail. Some of these snails, especially the heath snail and its relatives, survive periods of summer drought by climbing up grass or flower stems, closing off their aperture with an impermeable layer to

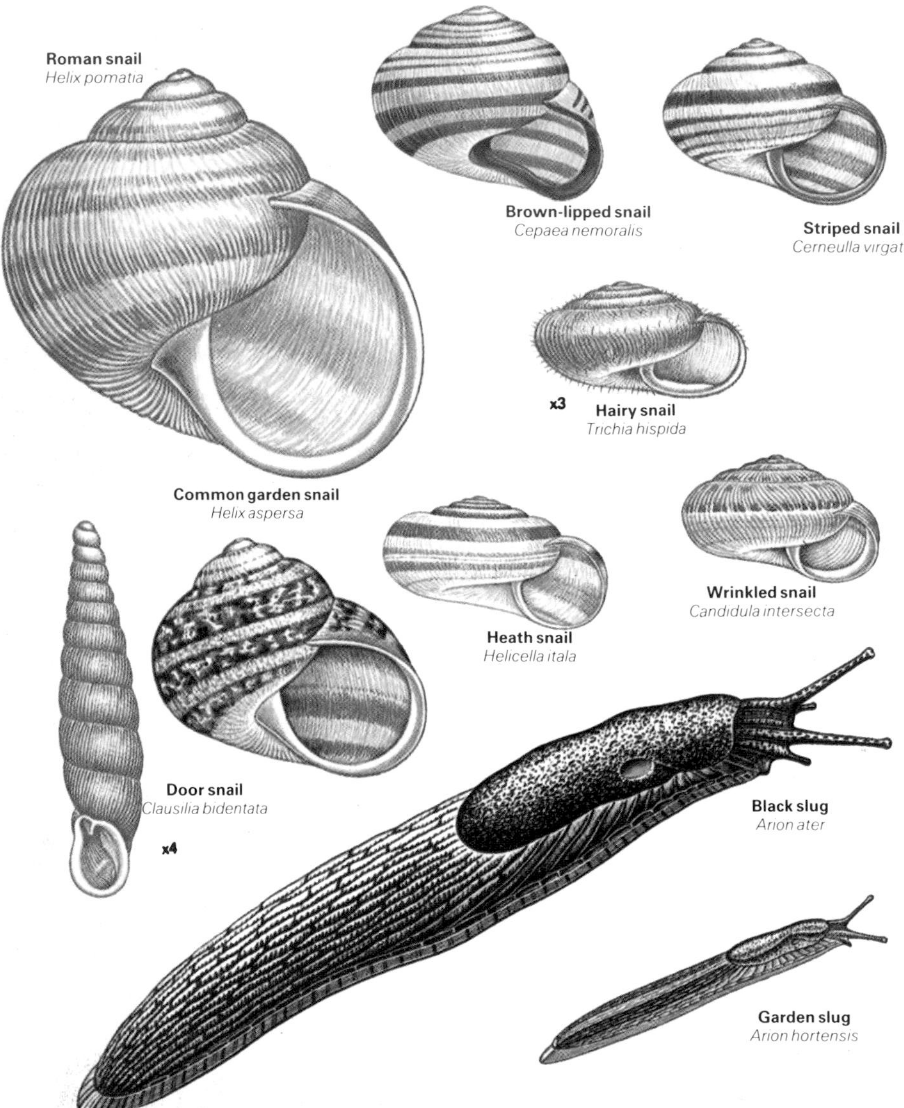

Snails and slugs (which are closely related to each other) are amongst the most conspicuous of grassland invertebrates.

The snails are particularly abundant on chalk grassland where they can get plenty of calcium which they need for their shells

prevent water loss, and aestivating – that is spending the hot period doing virtually nothing, using little energy and conserving all possible water. It may seem strange to see groups of snails attached to the stems of plants, in full view, at the height of summer, but this is the explanation.

One of the most striking and interesting of our grassland snails is the Roman, or edible, snail. It was almost certainly introduced by the Romans, some 2,000 years ago, as a source of food, and has been reintroduced from mainland Europe on several occasions since. Now it occurs over quite a wide area, with its main centres of distribution on the South Downs and in the Cotswolds and Chilterns – all chalk or limestone areas. The snails emerge from hibernation in spring and, in damp weather, they mate, which involves a rather strange snake-like movement with the two partners rearing upwards. It is a process rarely seen by naturalists, partly because the animals are not common, but also because few people venture out onto the downs in wet weather in spring. After mating, the snails lay their eggs in batches through the summer, after rainy periods, and these hatch in about a month into tiny little snails. The young feed on plants as soon as they have eaten their egg-shells. Both animals lay eggs as the Roman snail is hermaphrodite – each individual of the species contains both male and female organs – but they still mate to ensure that cross-fertilisation takes place. The young snails will take several years to reach full size, for the adult snail is quite a large beast, and individuals may live for ten years if unmolested. In France, though, where they are avidly eaten, they would have less chance of surviving for so long! Each autumn, in about September, the snail digs a burrow in the soil, which it enters and seals up with a plug of chalky soil. The snail is thus kept warm and dry, and simply pushes off the top the following spring when a new year begins.

The presence of yellow ants is a good indicator of old, even ancient grasslands. The meadow ants construct mounds of soil which provide protection and an improved microclimate as well as a place to store food. The yellow ant *Lasius flavus* is found throughout the British Isles but it is most common in the south. They can be seen throughout the summer going into hibernation deep in the soil as winter draws in. They have the habit of 'farming' aphids for their honeydew. Honeydew is a sweet sugary substance which aphids secrete.

Ant hills in an old orchard. Yellow meadow ants build these hummocks of soil in old grazed pastureland, and become quite a distinctive feature of ancient grassland as shown here

MOUNTAIN INSECT LIFE

As you would expect, our mist-clad cold hills and mountains are not home to an enormous range of insects and other invertebrates; yet they have their own specialities, creatures that have learnt to live with the harsh winters and short summers, and it is surprising what can be found.

Mountains are undoubtedly one of the most inhospitable places for insects and other invertebrates. The temperature is almost invariably low, even in summer, making activity difficult, for invertebrates need warmth to mobilise themselves. Furthermore, there are often high winds, extremely harsh winters and very short summers. To add to this, there is the problem of acid, infertile rocks which make life particularly difficult for those species requiring lime, as well as lowering the productivity of plants which are essential food. Nevertheless, some species do survive there, in the most unlikely situations, and the very harshness of the environment means that they face little competition.

Butterflies are hardly conspicuous in the mountains, but there are a few to be found. The hardiest of them all, a real mountain specialist, is the mountain ringlet, which only occurs above about 250 metres and goes as high as 1,000 metres. Its larvae feed on mat-grass, though the butterfly is unfortunately by no means as widespread as its food-plant, and the adults fly for a short while in summer. In dull weather, they virtually all disappear down into grass tussocks but, as soon as the sun comes out, they become active, and their dark wings are specially adapted for absorbing warmth rapidly from the sun's rays. Another similar, though slightly more brightly-coloured species is the Scotch argus, which occurs in similar habitats, though not at such high altitudes. The northern brown argus which, despite its name, is not related to the Scotch argus (it is one of the blue family, while the Scotch argus is a relative of the meadow browns), occurs on hills and mountainsides, but only in lime-rich areas, where its food-plant, the common rockrose, occurs. This type of habitat was very widespread in Britain just after the Ice Ages, and the northern brown argus is believed to have been one of the earliest butterfly colonisers of the country, though now it is confined to relatively few northern mountain areas. Other mountain butterflies include the large heath, another brownish species, that feeds as a caterpillar on various sedges and grasses, though it is not an upland specialist as it also occurs on lowland bogs in the Midlands. The lovely little chequered skipper is now confined to the lower, more sheltered parts of mountains in Scotland (though it used also to occur in lowland woods in central England), and the marsh fritillary finds its way well up onto mountains if the habitat is suitable.

The Scotch Argus

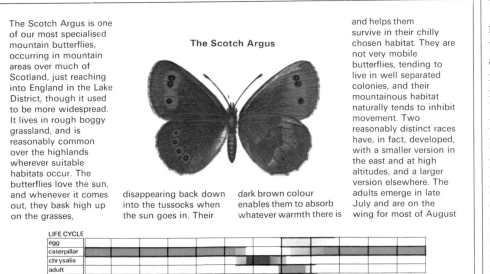

The Scotch Argus is one of our most specialised mountain butterflies, occurring in mountain areas over much of Scotland, just reaching into England in the Lake District, though it used to be more widespread. It lives in rough boggy grassland, and is reasonably common over the highlands wherever suitable habitats occur. The butterflies love the sun, and whenever it comes out, they bask high up on the grasses, disappearing back down into the tussocks when the sun goes in. Their dark brown colour enables them to absorb whatever warmth there is and helps them survive in their chilly chosen habitat. They are not very mobile butterflies, tending to live in well separated colonies, and their mountainous habitat naturally tends to inhibit movement. Two reasonably distinct races have, in fact, developed, with a smaller version in the east and at high altitudes, and a larger version elsewhere. The adults emerge in late July and are on the wing for most of August

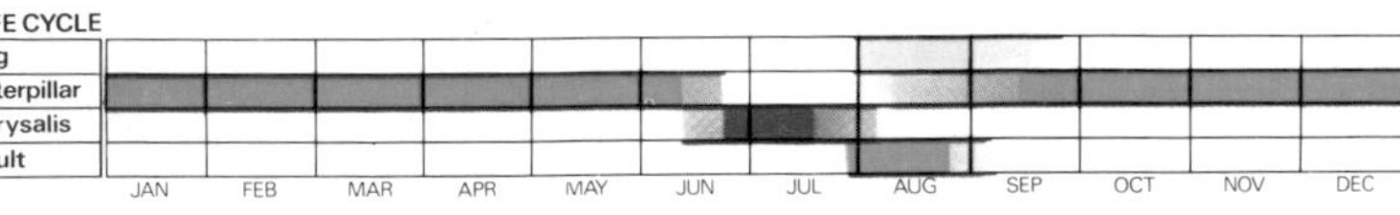

Mountains share many species with heathlands, especially where there is extensive moorland habitat because many of the plants are the same. The emperor moth, for example, is frequent on high moorlands as well as on heaths, while the large dark-brown northern eggar moth is a common sight on many moors. Both are day-flying moths, so they tend to be noticed more than the nocturnal species, though the caterpillars of some nocturnal species, such as the fox moth, are conspicuous during the day.

Dragonflies do surprisingly well in mountains. There are several species that are virtually confined to these areas, breeding in acid, boggy pools or rivulets, and flying over the heather or in woodland rides as adults. The beautiful azure hawker, which is a large blue and black species, is a purely Scottish insect, occurring here and there over most of the western highlands. The rather similar common hawker is found throughout the country, but is equally at home in the mountains, being common all over the Scottish highlands and in other mountain ranges. The rare and beautiful northern emerald dragonfly which, as its name suggests, is a shiny bronze-green colour occurs only in the highlands, where it breeds in peat bogs. The much more common black darter is widespread wherever there are heathy or moorland areas, and on some wet northern moors where conditions are right it is abundant.

Typically, mountain species from

whatever group tend to be darker in colour than their lowland counterparts, and are often smaller. This helps them to absorb and conserve what little heat is available. Some widespread species show gradual changes in size, colour and habits as the altitude increases, though they are not sufficiently distinct, yet, to be called different species. These are a clear illustration of the strong pressures that the mountain environment is putting on these creatures and of the ways in which they are able to cope.

A male golden-ringed dragonfly, one of our largest and most impressive insects, this magnificent individual is resting by an upland stream while waiting for a female

Netted mountain moth
Semiothisa carbonaria

Small dark yellow underwing
Anarta cordigera

Twin-spot carpet
Perizoma didymata

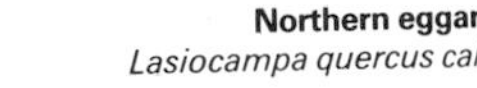

Northern eggar
Lasiocampa quercus callunae

Rannoch sprawler
Brachionycha nubeculosa

The male mountain ringlet is basking in the sun, making use of whatever warmth is available. This species is virtually confined to mountain areas, in England and Scotland, where its caterpillars feed on mat-grass. It is a rare and inconspicuous species, only occurring in small well-defined colonies in a few areas.

The mountain ringlet is very similar to the Scotch argus but it is rather larger and the markings are much better defined. Their self contained colonies may be made up of many thousands of adults which fly only when the sun is shining and even then merely fluttering just above the grass tops. They emerge almost exclusively in July spending most of the year as a caterpillar which hibernates throughout the winter in the densest parts of the grass. They are found mainly at high altitude in the lake district and Grampian Mountains

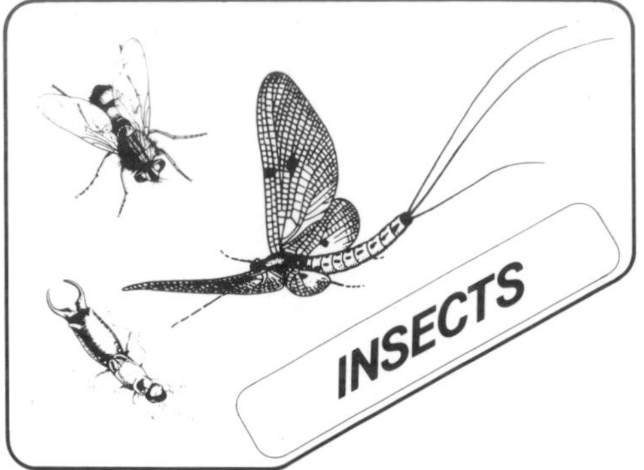

THE DRAGONFLIES OF BRITAIN

Dragonflies are the most exciting of insects. They have been called 'the birdwatchers' insect' because they are so conspicuous and active, flying to and fro over ponds and lakes catching insects. We are fortunate to have some 40 species in Britain.

Dragonflies are large, very mobile and active, winged predators, spending much of their adult life in the air catching other flying insects as prey. The general name 'dragonflies' actually includes two related groups of insects – the true dragonflies and the damselflies. The most obvious differences are that the dragonflies are usually bulkier and stronger, and when they settle, they hold their two pairs of wings out at right angles to the body; the damselflies, by contrast, are rather delicate creatures, with a weak flight, and when they land they close their wings down the length of the body, making them look quite different (see illustrations). Dragonflies are much stronger fliers, and they travel and migrate long distances, often spending virtually all day on the wing; whilst the damselflies are usually very sedentary, and much of the time is passed settled on vegetation.

In fact, the adult dragonflies that we see are only a very small part of a rather complicated life-cycle. Males and females pair up, often on the wing – when they are sometimes described as being 'in tandem' – and soon afterwards the female lays eggs into her chosen habitat. This is always wet, or very close to water, but it varies according to the species from still, acid waters to fast flowing streams or heavily vegetated bogs and fens, with each species having slightly different requirements. The eggs may be laid into plant stems or leaves, or simply scattered on the surface of the water, to sink or drift to the bottom; a few species carefully insert the eggs directly into mud. In due course, the larvae hatch out and soon become voracious predators catching any prey that they can find in their watery environment. They possess an extraordinary feature, unique in the insect world, called a 'mask'. This is a hinged mouthpart that is normally held closed but can be shot out violently when prey is sighted within range, and retracted to bring the prey back to the larvae's mouth. The larvae grow gradually, changing their skin as they outgrow it and eventually become mature. Amazingly, this process usually takes at least a year (though it is less in some damselflies), but can take up to five years in some larger species, especially when they live in colder, rather unproductive waters. This means, of course, that the adult insect – what we think of as the dragonfly – may only represent a tiny

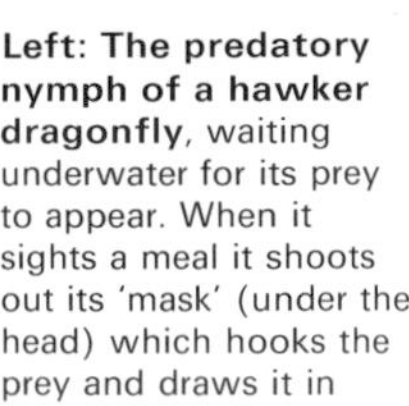

Left: The predatory nymph of a hawker dragonfly, waiting underwater for its prey to appear. When it sights a meal it shoots out its 'mask' (under the head) which hooks the prey and draws it in

Right: A pair of common blue damselflies mating in the wheel position that is characteristic of this group

proportion of the life-cycle of the animal.

When the larva become mature, it crawls towards the shallows of its aquatic home, and climbs out onto a piece of vegetation, such as a waterside reed or sedge, though some species, such as the emperor dragonfly, prefer to climb up trees. Here, the larva attaches itself firmly by its front legs, and then begins the extraordinary transformation into the winged insect. From out of the drab, rather unattractive larva, there emerges a shrunken insect, which gradually expands as it takes in air, then spreads its glorious shiny wings to dry, finally becoming ready to fly. The process takes several hours, depending on the temperature, and it is a very vulnerable stage in the dragonfly's life, because it is totally unable to move and can be easily picked off by birds or mammals looking for a quick meal. This is why many species emerge at night, or very early in the morning, becoming ready to fly, at least a little way, soon after it is light. It is worth getting up early in midsummer and going out to a suitable nearby pond to watch this extraordinary process.

There are about 40 regular British species of dragonflies and damselflies, though additional ones appear in the country occasionally as migrants from the Continent where there are many more species. In any one area, you could easily expect to see ten or more species, especially if there is a good range of unpolluted ponds or lakes, or a bog, and these insects are not too difficult to identify if you concentrate at first on the more common ones. As one becomes more experienced most dragonflies can be identified in the field, even on the wing, by their behaviour, size, and general colour.

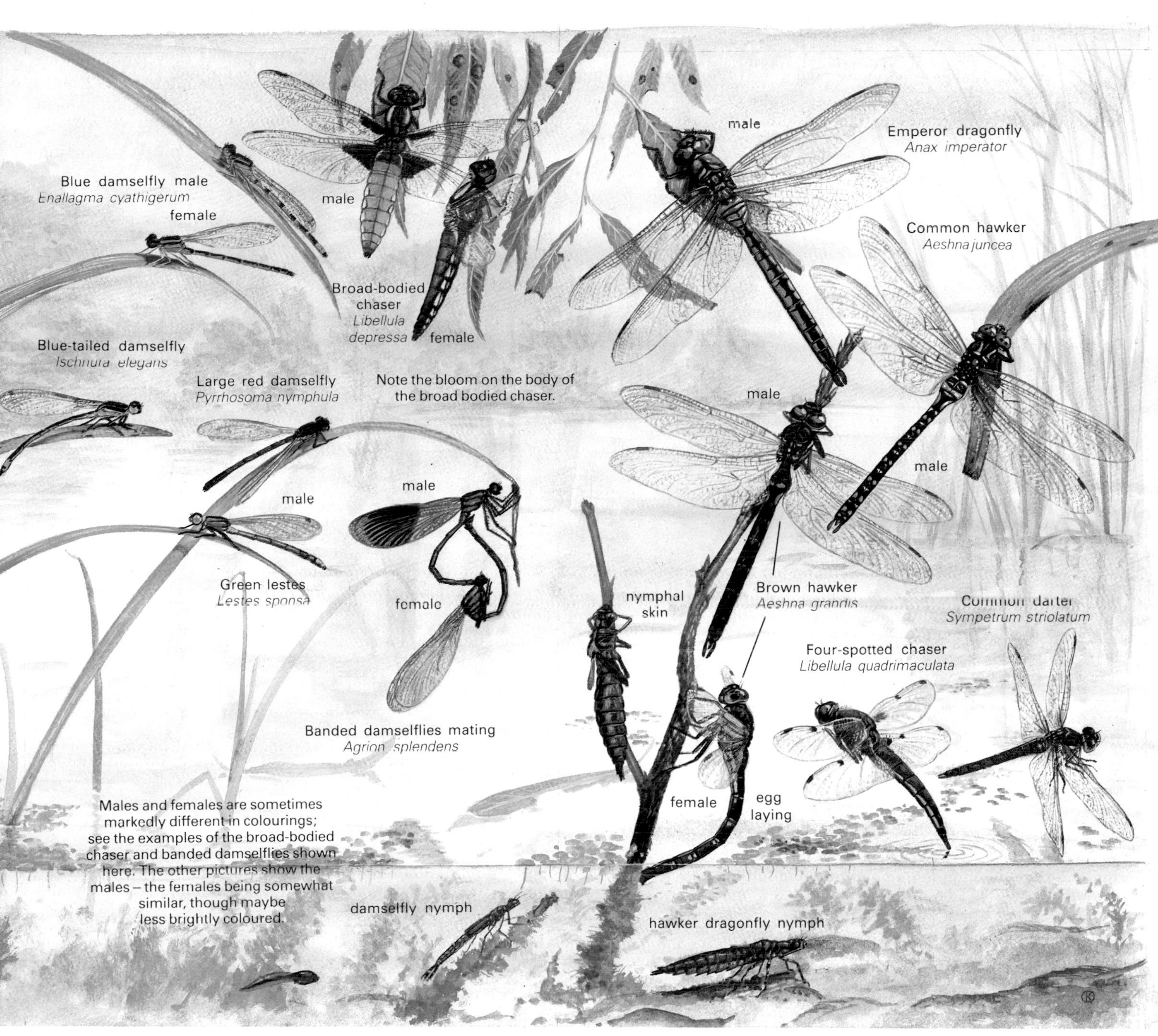

The life-cycles of our native dragonflies and damselflies are shown in this composite picture. Notice the females laying eggs, the nymphs living underwater, and the adults mating in the so called 'wheel'

INSECTS IN STILL WATER

The calm, mirror-like surface of a pond or lake conceals beneath it a totally different world. Any warm, nutrient-rich water body is a seething mass of unfamiliar life-forms, living together in an almost perfect environment.

Still, freshwater is a wonderful environment for invertebrates. There is no danger of desiccation (except when the whole pond dries up), little need to produce supporting tissues because of the buoyancy of the water, easy mobility in all directions and a continuous supply of nutrients. But because freshwater is such an ideal place for invertebrates, it is also a cut-throat world of predator and prey, where anything that moves is liable to be eaten.

Any still freshwater is alive with a multitude of tiny animals, many of them too small to see with the naked eye. If you take a droplet of pond-water in summer and place it under the microscope, a teeming mass of tiny bodies is revealed. These are generally known as the zooplankton, in contrast to the tiny plants, the phytoplankton (see page 20), and most of them feed on the tiny floating plants that also abound in freshwater. The zooplankton include water fleas, protozoa, such as Amoeba, and the tiny larvae of larger animals. This mass of tiny creatures forms the food for numerous animals just one step up the food-chain. For example, there is a small animal called Hydra, of which there are several related species, that looks just like a tiny plant attached to other plants or rocks. It consists of a hollow tube with tentacles at the mouth, which waft water into the tube and trap any suitable prey items. It is not only shaped rather like a plant, but may also be green; this is because some species support colonies of minute green plants – algae – within them in a mutually favourable relationship.

Amongst the larger predators, many larvae of insects are prominent. The larvae of dragonflies and damselflies are both common and voracious predators on anything that they can catch, including small fishes and tadpoles. Equally fierce are the larvae of some of the water beetles; the

Toothed pondskater *Gerris odontogaster* x2½

Common water boatman *Corixa punctata* x2

Common backswimmer *Notonecta glauca*

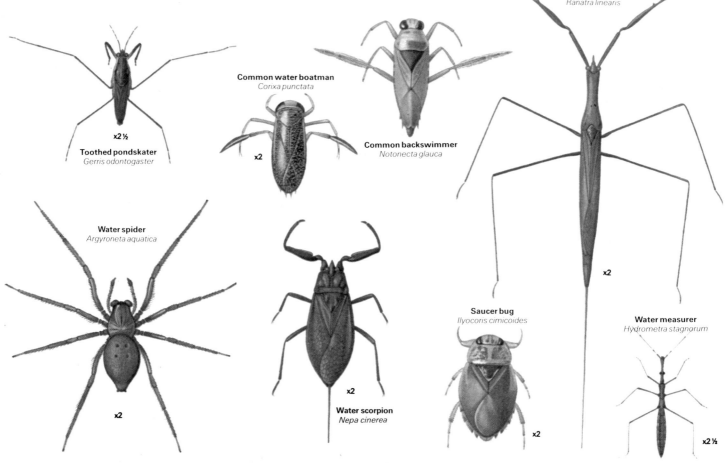

Water stick insect *Ranatra linearis* x2

Water spider *Argyroneta aquatica* x2

Water scorpion *Nepa cinerea* x2

Saucer bug *Ilyocoris cimicoides* x2

Water measurer *Hydrometra stagnorum* x2½

Some of the various invertebrates that have taken to living in water. All of them are insects except for one spider

fearsome-looking larva of the great diving beetle is a sizeable creature that will attack almost anything, including animals much larger than itself such as tadpoles and even fingers if you are unwary! Unlike the dragonflies, which have terrestrial adult stages, the water beetles usually remain in water as adults, still as active predators; however, most of them can fly if necessary and they colonise new ponds by this means.

A group of insects that have taken to pond life in a big way is the true bugs. Many of them have become highly-adapted wholly aquatic animals, such as the water boatmen and the backswimmers. The latter are extraordinary animals that spend their lives swimming upside down, both submerged or at the surface, actively seeking other animal prey. The bugs differ from many other aquatic insects in that they do not have clearly separate larval and pupal stages; instead they grow up as a series of enlarging replicas of the adult – the nymphs – which successively shed their skins and turn into the next, slightly larger one. The whole life-cycle is aquatic, but many of the bugs can fly strongly to colonise new sites. They often take to the air at night, and may be mistakenly attracted down to shining car-roofs or other artificial objects. Other aquatic bugs include the so-called water scorpion with a long sharp tail and rather fearsome-looking pincers, the water stick insect, water cricket and pond skaters. The first three are not related to the creatures they are named after, but they all bear some resemblance to them by chance. The pond skaters are surface-dwellers, familiar for their skilful abilities in skating about the surface of any pond, lightly denting the surface-tension film. There, they act as scavengers and predators, eating anything that becomes trapped on the water.

There are many herbivorous invertebrates, too, typified by the freshwater molluscs. These include about 36 species of the snail-like gastropods, and about 30 species of the freshwater bivalves. The latter includes species such as the swan mussel, which may grow up to 20 centimetres long and has strange little larvae that live part of their lives as parasites on fishes; curiously enough, there is also a fish that lays its eggs into mussels, but that is another story! (See pages 160–161.)

The beautifully marked male great diving beetle, an aggressive carnivore which will attack anything it can handle, and much it cannot, including small fishes!

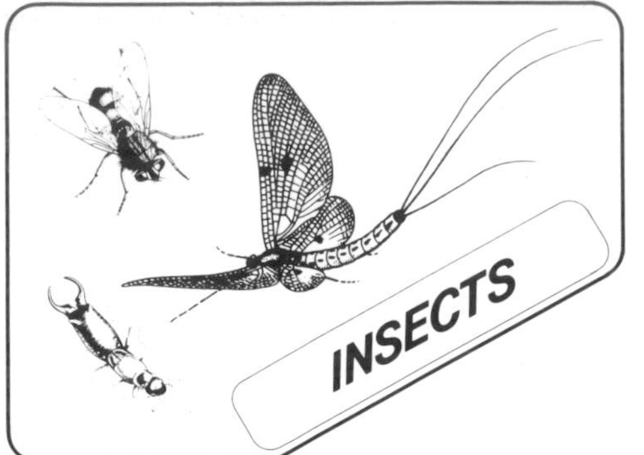

INSECTS IN FLOWING WATER

Life in fast-flowing water is rather different from that in ponds. Though some of the advantages remain, there is the constant danger of being swept away which reduces the number of species able to survive, and forces the remainder to adapt.

Running water has many of the benefits of still water as an environment for invertebrates, except the current picks up anything that is not firmly anchored and carries it away, ultimately to the sea. Consequently, life in the faster flowing rivers is impossible for many free-floating species, and a relatively small assemblage of animals remains, precisely adapted to the more difficult habitat. One advantage of flowing water, though, is that there is little likelihood of dissolved oxygen – a vital ingredient of life in water – running short, as it occasionally does in still water. Similarly, the periodic shortages and excesses of nutrients, that characterise still waters and cause the algal 'bloom' on ponds and lakes, are evened out.

Amongst the British dragonflies and damselflies, the vast majority are adapted to still water, or very slow-flowing water in canals and lowland streams. A few, however, are specialist flowing water species. For example, the curious and rather uncommon club-tailed dragonfly occurs almost exclusively in large river systems such as the Thames and Severn. In contrast to the still-water species which may become very abundant, this species tends to be found in quite small numbers, reflecting the difficult nature of the habitat. The water of large rivers is almost invariably turbid, so visibility for any predator is greatly reduced; thus the frequency with which it can catch prey is reduced, and its length of life as a larva is correspondingly increased as it grows more slowly. A specialist of clearer, often more acid rivers, especially in hilly areas, is the beautiful golden-ringed dragonfly. The female is the longest of all the British dragonflies, with a dagger-like egg-laying spike at the end of her abdomen, which she thrusts into the mud in suitable places to lay her eggs. This behaviour probably helps to prevent the eggs from being washed downstream in the fast-flowing waters that this species favours. There are also several damselflies that like flowing water, including the lovely demoiselle or agrion species, which have broad colourful wings and can look more

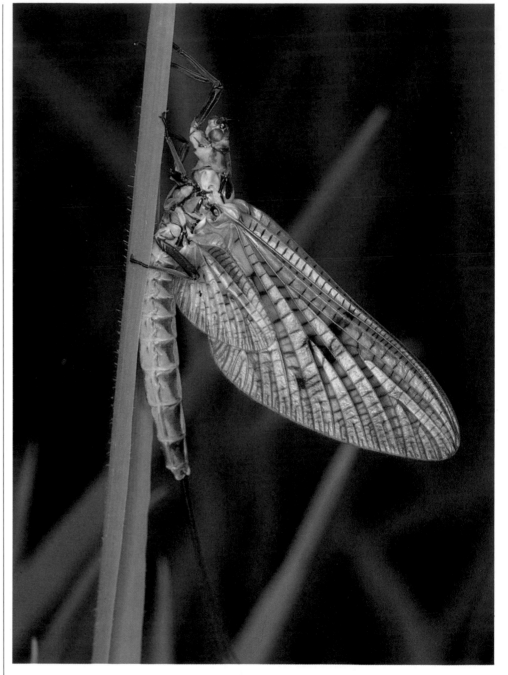

This mayfly 'spinner' is the fully mature insect. A short-lived less spectacular adult called a 'dun' first emerges from the water which after a few hours sheds its skin to become the marvellous insect shown here

like aquatic butterflies than damselflies.

Mayflies occur abundantly as adults around water, and many of them spend their larval stages in rivers and streams. They are famous for the fact that the adults live for a very short time, just a day or so, and this is reflected in the scientific name for the group – the Ephemeroptera. They are also unusual in that it is the adult and that as an aquatic larva; some mayflies spend two to three years as a larva in the river, to be followed by just one day as an adult – if they are not eaten by a fish or bird just as they are emerging!

Stoneflies look rather similar to mayflies, though they are usually rather heavier insects, and the larval stages have two long 'tails' in contrast to the mayfly larvae which have three. Some species of stonefly in upland streams, which they tend to favour, grow very slowly and one species is known to pass through some 30 skin moults in three or four years before becoming an adult. The curious caddis flies are also habitual river-dwellers, with the larvae of numerous species to be found in flowing water. Many species are noted for their strange habit of collecting various

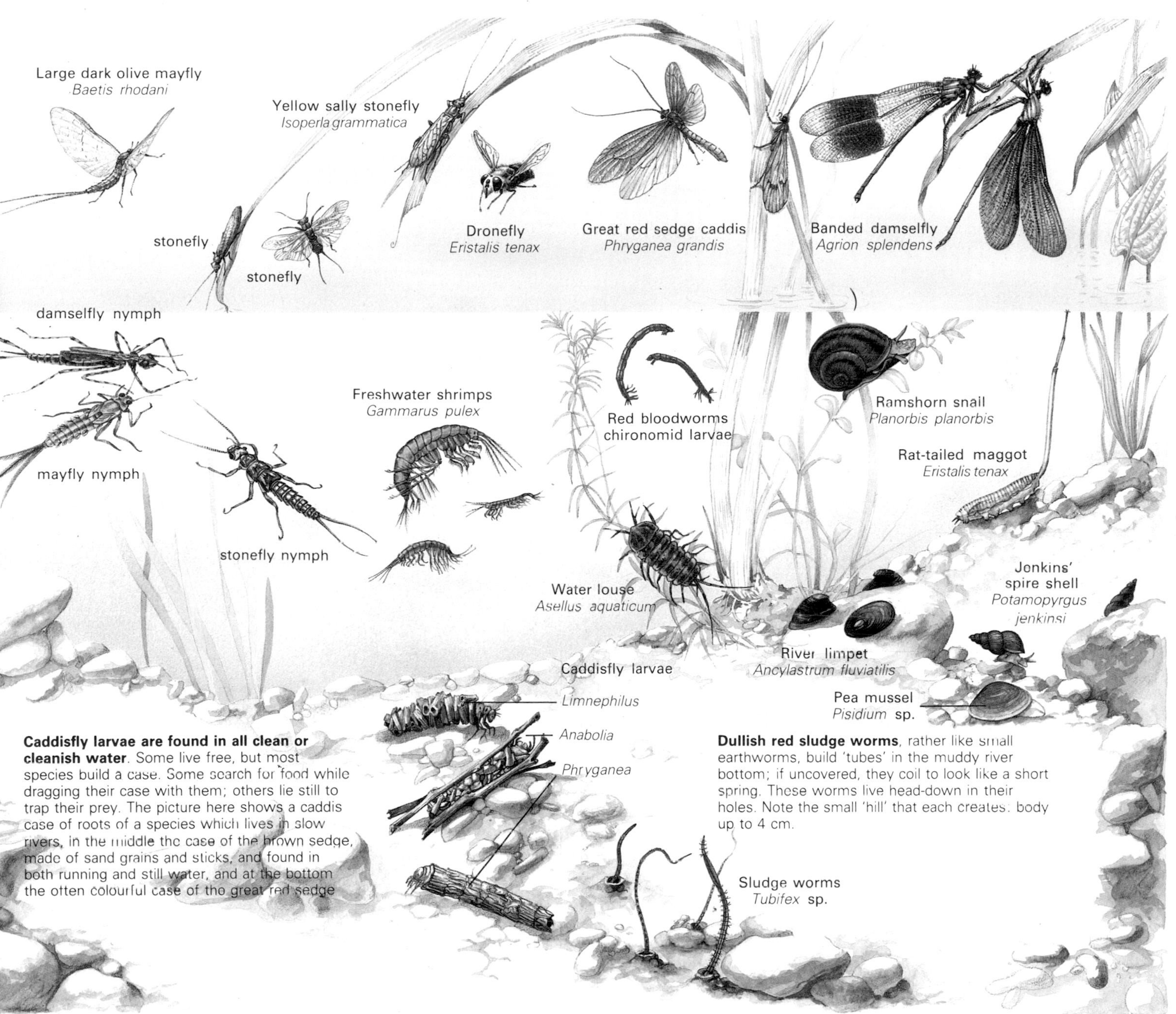

Caddisfly larvae are found in all clean or cleanish water. Some live free, but most species build a case. Some search for food while dragging their case with them; others lie still to trap their prey. The picture here shows a caddis case of roots of a species which lives in slow rivers, in the middle the case of the brown sedge, made of sand grains and sticks, and found in both running and still water, and at the bottom the often colourful case of the great red sedge

Dullish red sludge worms, rather like small earthworms, build 'tubes' in the muddy river bottom; if uncovered, they coil to look like a short spring. These worms live head-down in their holes. Note the small 'hill' that each creates. body up to 4 cm.

last larval stage that becomes winged and leaves the water, moulting again after this to turn into the adult insect. The pre-adult winged stage is known as the 'dun', while the fully adult stage is called the 'spinner'. Like the dragonflies, there is a marked imbalance between the length of life as an

The variety of life living in a clean river or stream is enormous, with some species spending their whole lives there, while others live out their larval stages in water to emerge as winged adults

forms of local debris, and adorning their cases with it. They carry the resulting structure around with them and, not surprisingly, are well camouflaged. Indeed, the name caddis comes from an old word for tinker, who used to carry their wares hung about their bodies!

INSECT LIFE ON FARMLAND

Despite the sprays and the disturbance by ploughing, an amazing amount of insect life is found on farmland. Some are pests of farm crops, but most are harmless wild species surviving along the hedges and in the rougher corners of the farm.

Farms can be hostile places for many insects, particularly those that need certain food-plants which only occur in more natural habitats, or those that are sensitive to pesticides. However, they are also the home to an enormous number of other insects which can tolerate the conditions, especially where the farming is a little tolerant of the requirements of wildlife.

Arable fields are almost totally useless for insect life, since there is only one species of plant – the crop – and no nectar sources, other than the occasional weed. In addition, many crops are sprayed regularly with insecticides and other pesticides which are lethal to many insects. However, that incredibly resilient insect, the aphid, not only manages to survive all this, but even does well and becomes a real pest in certain conditions. Aphids, the group that includes greenfly and blackfly, have virtually no natural defences, but succeed by being able to reproduce incredibly fast without even mating. In warm weather, aphids produce young at an extraordinary rate, and a proportion of these are winged, so they immediately start to move around, often in vast numbers. Consequently, any crop or other edible plant is liable to be colonised, and their numbers will rapidly build up in these new areas. Thus, however often a crop is sprayed, in favourable warm weather, aphids will soon re-establish themselves. They are eaten by a vast array of other insects, including ladybirds as both adults and larvae, hoverfly larvae, lacewings and also by many birds, but their reproduction rate is so prodigious that they always produce enough offspring to outstrip the effects of the hords of predators.

Arable fields also support other insect life such as ground beetles, which come out at night and seek food on the bare ground. The vital factor for almost all insects, other than the crop pests, is the hedgerows that surround fields. These are the operational bases for the insects and their density tails off markedly away from the hedge. Some recent experiments have shown that the insect life is greatly benefitted by leaving an unplanted strip around the crop, adjacent to the hedge, where no spraying is carried out and plenty of wild flowers can grow. This benefits birds, especially gamebirds such as partridges which depend on insects to rear their chicks, and even butterfly numbers increase considerably.

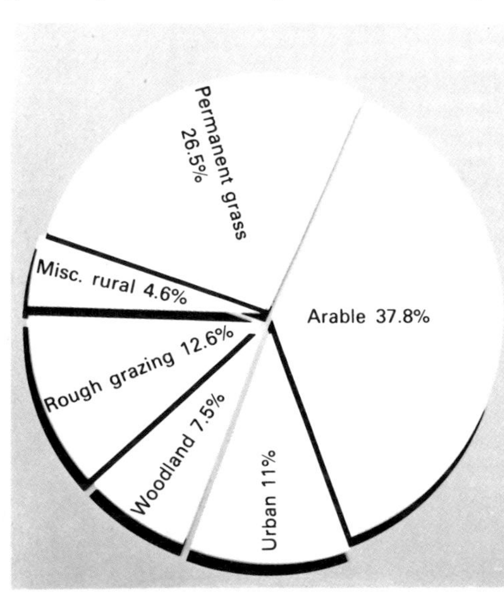

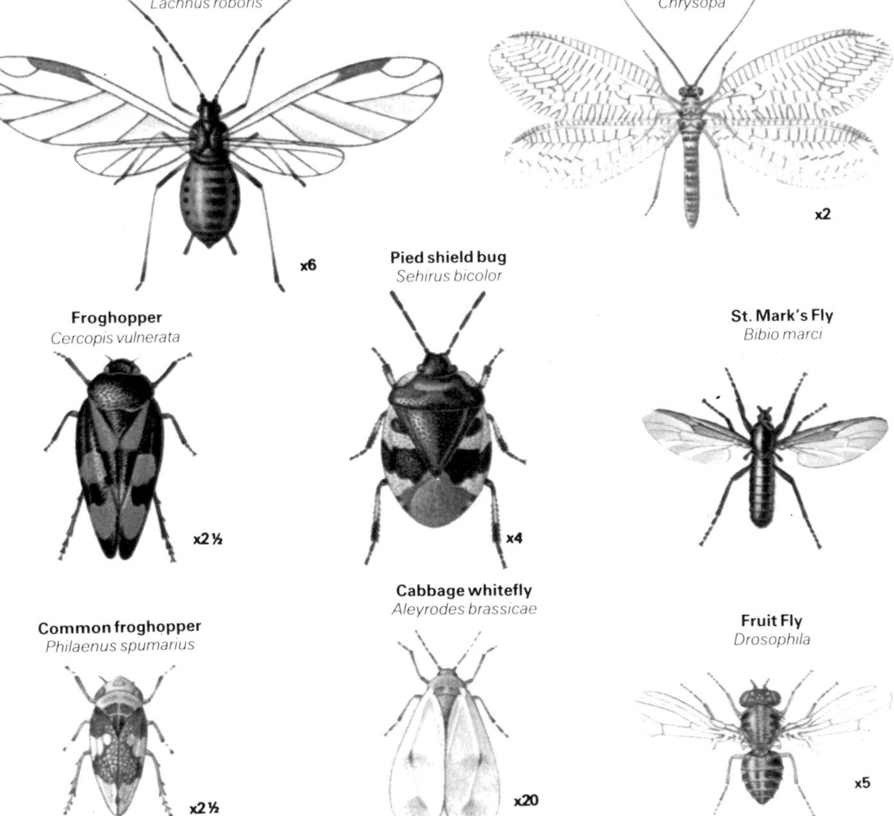

Above left: A pie diagram showing the proportions of different categories of land in England and Wales

Above: A selection of bugs and other insects likely to be found in the more natural parts of farms

The hedge itself is a fine insect habitat, as long as it does not receive too much spray drift. There is a good array of plants, both as shrubs in the hedge and as herbaceous plants in the hedge bottom; common hedgerow from the winds. The spider-like dark bush-crickets creep amongst the undergrowth, emitting their distinctive single-note chirps late into the night; hoverflies whirr up and down seeking nectar flowers or looking for egg-laying sites; the attractive hedge-brown or gatekeeper butterflies feed on bramble blossom, whilst ladybirds gorge themselves on aphids on the plant stems. If there is much old wood at the base of the hedge or old tree

A pair of yellow dung flies mating on cow dung, in which the female will subsequently lay her eggs and the larvae develop

shrubs such as hawthorn and blackthorn are excellent for insects both in leaf or in flower. The bank of the hedge, if there is one, provides a good place for bumble bees to nest and other insects to hibernate, and the hedge itself always gives some shelter stumps, then dead-wood feeding species like the lovely red cardinal beetle or the yellow and black wasp beetle appear; and there will be innumerable thrips, flies, aphids, lacewings and an extremely wide and varied array of other insects everywhere.

GRASSHOPPERS AND CRICKETS

In summer, grassland areas are alive with the buzzing and ticking of a myriad of unseen insects. The great majority of these strange noises are made by the grasshoppers and crickets belonging to a dozen or more species, each with a different, recognisable song.

The grasshoppers and the bush-crickets are two related and rather similar groups of insects; indeed the bush-crickets are sometimes known as the long-horned grasshoppers. Grasshoppers have short antennae and a great ability to jump and to produce a song which is often very loud. Bush-crickets are also good songsters, have the same enlarged back legs (though they are rather less good at jumping), but they have long fine thread-like antennae, and the female bush-crickets have a dagger-like ovipositor (egg-laying organ) at their rear end which is lacking in female grasshoppers.

Out of the 11 species of grasshopper in Britain, most of them occur in grassland, though one is confined to bogs, whilst others are only found on coastal grasslands or heathlands. The noise that they produce is called stridulation and, like most insect noises, it is made by rubbing one surface over another. If you are close enough to see a singing grasshopper, you will notice that it is making small movements with its legs, and it is this that produces the noise. On the inner surface of the enlarged thighs of the rear legs, there is a row of tiny pegs or teeth, made of very hard material; these are rubbed against the prominent veins of the forewings on either side, causing them to vibrate and produce the 'song'. The males are better developed for stridulation, and each species produces a quite distinct song; this is the easiest way to identify grasshoppers if you have a reasonably good ear.

The common green grasshopper, which is abundant in dense grassland everywhere, is one of the earliest to start singing, often in June; it produces a prolonged rapid ticking sound, gradually increasing in intensity, and lasting about 20 seconds. The common field grasshopper, though, which is also widespread but generally prefers more open areas, produces single chirps at intervals and sounds quite different. The field grasshopper is also easily recognisable when adult, by its long wings which reach well beyond the end of its abdomen, and it is one of our strongest fliers. The third common species is the meadow grasshopper, notable for its very short wings, and it produces a song which is comprised of little bursts of stridulation, each lasting two or three seconds, about ten or 15 seconds apart, though it is not quite as obvious as some of the other species. Some other examples of songs include the distinctive rising and falling 'wheeze' of the stripe-winged grasshopper, and a sound like the winding up of a watch made by the mottled grasshopper.

There are ten species of bush-cricket in Britain, several of which occur in grassland, though one is tree-living (the oak bush-cricket) and others live in particular habitats like bogs or cliffs. As a general rule, they prefer thicker, taller vegetation than grasshoppers, being most often found in rough grass, hedges, nettlebeds and so on, rather than in short turf. Although they all stridulate, or sing, like the grasshoppers, and each species has a clearly-recognisable sound, they produce the song in a rather different way. Again it is the males that sing, and they do so by rubbing a

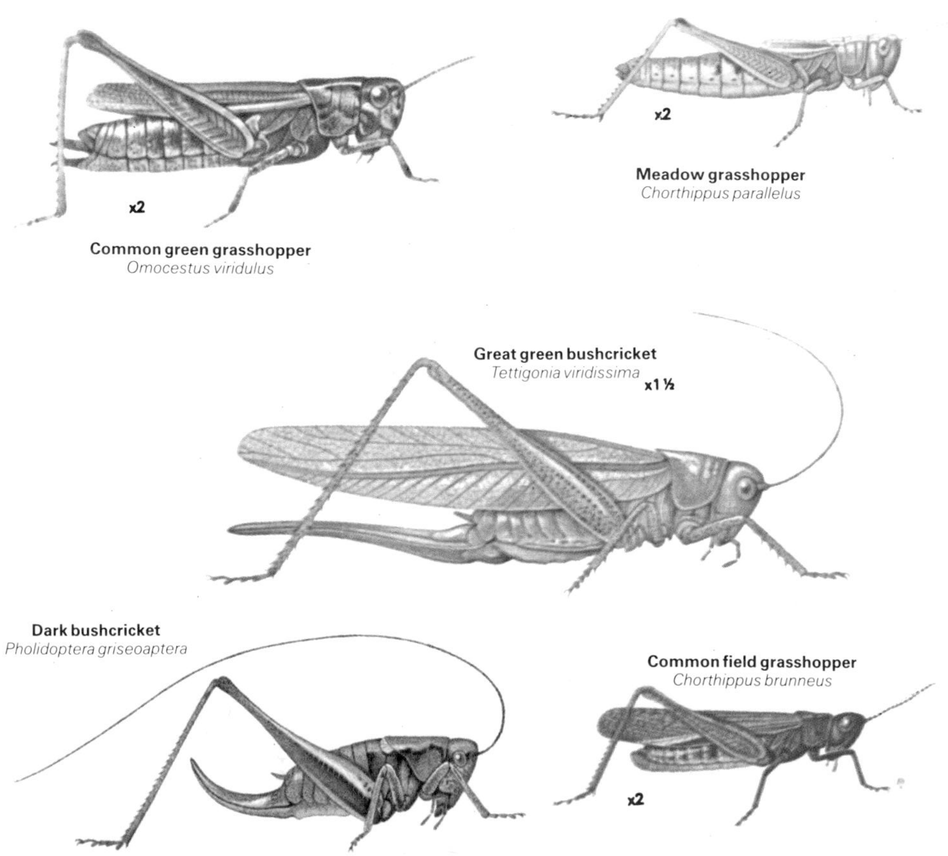

A selection of the commoner grasshoppers and bush-crickets of grassland habitats.

Although very elusive each has a characteristic 'call' which, when learnt, allows easy identification

strengthened vein covered with teeth on the base of the left forewing against the thickened hind-edge of the right forewing. There is also a small area known as the mirror on the right forewing that acts as a resonator, increasing the volume of the sound. Thus, in the bush-crickets, the legs are not involved at all in producing the sound, only the wings. The very abundant dark bush-cricket produces very short guttural bursts of song, each lasting about half a second, from deep within the vegetation; the great green bush-cricket often sits on top of the vegetation to make its loud, almost continuous purring call, so familiar to holiday-makers in south-west England; whilst the common speckled bush-cricket utters such a quiet noise that you have to be within about a metre to hear its song.

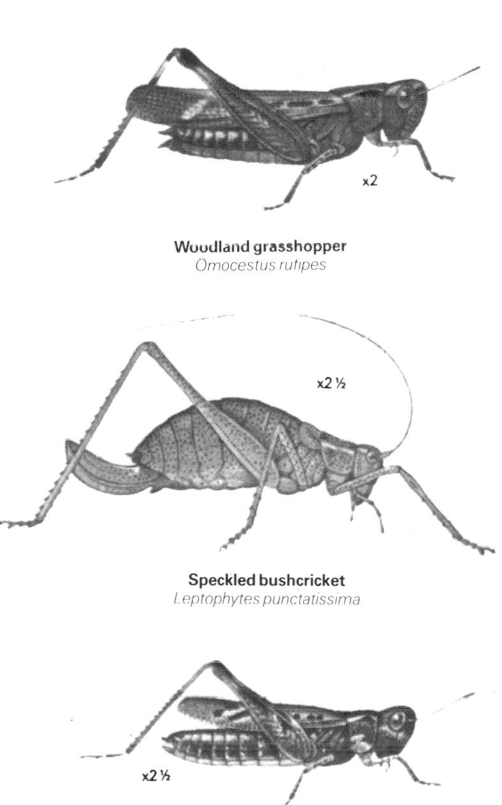

Woodland grasshopper
Omocestus rufipes

Speckled bushcricket
Leptophytes punctatissima

Mottled grasshopper
Myrmeleotettix maculatus

A striking picture of a meadow grasshopper resting on a yellow hawkbit in grassland in a late summer afternoon. They are found in dampish grassland throughout Britain. The adults are flightless and active from June to October.

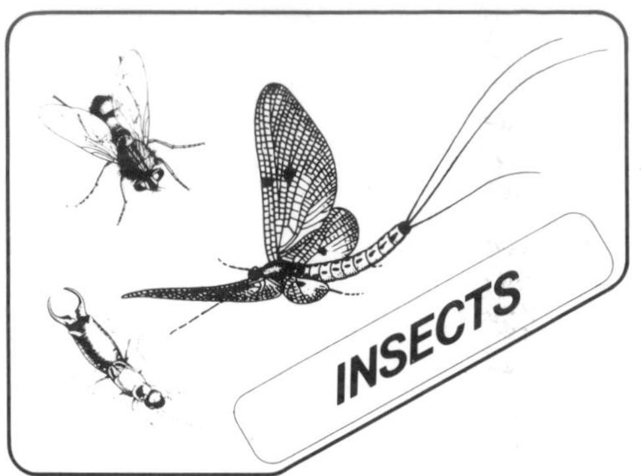

PLANT GALLS

If you have ever noticed those strange outgrowths or swellings on plants, that look as though they should not be there – oak apples or the robin's pincushion – then you have been looking at plant galls. Their causes are as varied and unusual as anything in British natural history.

If you look at an oak tree in early summer, you may wonder why it appears to have more than one type of fruit. There are not only developing acorns, as you might expect, but also apple-like growths, others like hard marbles and even outgrowths which resemble redcurrants! These are just some of the 35 or so different galls that infect oak trees, and there are many more on other plants, too.

Galls are the host plant's reaction to some kind of infestation, usually caused by an insect, but also occasionally by fungi or mites. The presence of the invading creature causes the tree or other plant to grow in a particular way, and this gives protection to the developing larvae of the gall-forming species. Most galls are caused by tiny insects known as gall-wasps, related to true wasps, but looking quite different. When the female lays her eggs in the developing bud or fruit of her chosen host-plant, she also leaves a quantity of a substance similar to the plant's own growth hormones. This causes the cells of the tree adjacent to the eggs and developing larvae to grow abnormally and out of the plant's control, to provide a home for the larvae which are protected inside in a series of chambers.

One of the most familiar types is the oak apple, which is a large soft greenish structure, looking like a slightly deformed apple on an oak tree (it is sometimes confused with marble galls which are the hard woody spherical galls on oaks). It is caused by a gall wasp called *Biorrhiza pallida*, one of several such insects with a strange double life-cycle. After the wasps have mated in summer, the females burrow down into the soil to seek out the finer roots of the tree on which to lay their eggs. The developing larvae produce root galls, in which they live and develop slowly, eventually emerging in the following winter. The insects that develop from these larvae are wingless females which climb back up the tree and lay their eggs in the dormant winter buds; these eggs are capable of developing without being fertilised by a male. When the buds start to grow in spring, those that have been infected grow rapidly to produce the spongy oak apple instead of leaves, and inside there is a series of chambers, each containing a developing larva. By late summer, they leave the gall, through a series of clearly visible exit holes, as winged males and females, which will later mate to start the cycle again.

The story of currant and spangle galls on the oak is equally strange, because they are both caused by the same insect. You may have noticed strange redcurrant-like strings hanging from the trees in spring, often mixed up with the male flowers. These are galls, and from them emerge winged males and females of another gall wasp species which meet and mate shortly after emerging. The female then lays her eggs, in June, on the undersides of the developing oak leaves, and each one causes a spangle gall to form. These are a familiar sight in autumn when the fallen leaves are often covered with orange or red spangle galls. The larvae overwinter in these on the ground, protected by resistant layers of tissue and covered by other leaves. In spring wingless females emerge to crawl up the tree

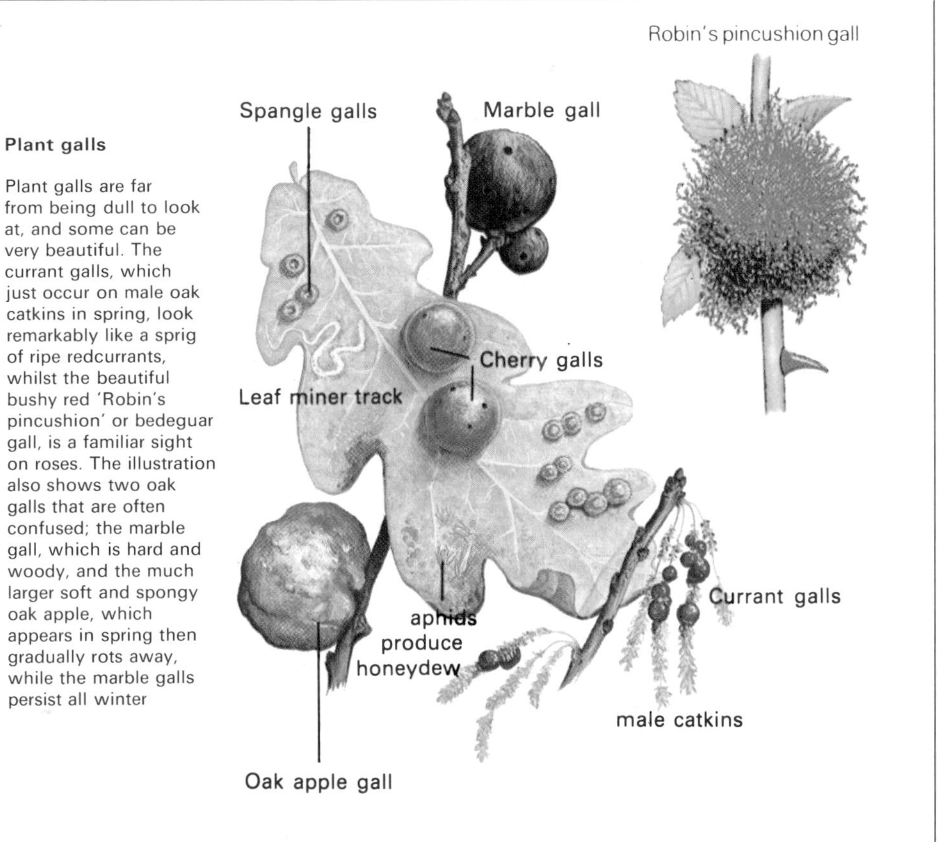

Plant galls

Plant galls are far from being dull to look at, and some can be very beautiful. The currant galls, which just occur on male oak catkins in spring, look remarkably like a sprig of ripe redcurrants, whilst the beautiful bushy red 'Robin's pincushion' or bedeguar gall, is a familiar sight on roses. The illustration also shows two oak galls that are often confused; the marble gall, which is hard and woody, and the much larger soft and spongy oak apple, which appears in spring then gradually rots away, while the marble galls persist all winter

and lay a new batch of eggs in the male oak catkins, which will once again cause the redcurrant galls to form.

Oaks are more affected by galls than any other plant, but they can be found on many other trees, shrubs and herbs, and, once you start to look, the more you realise how many there are: the red swellings on willow roses. It has the appearance of a large greenish or reddish mossy ball and is caused by yet another gall wasp, *Diplolepis rosae*. The females lay their eggs into unopened rose buds in spring, and these then develop into the gall, which contains 50 or so chambers each with its own larva inside. They feed and develop here, spend the following winter in the gall, still on the bush, and then emerge the following spring. The robin's pincushion is also the focus of an extraordinary sub-community in itself: another gall-wasp frequently lays its eggs in the gall, without causing any extra swelling, but simply using the existing gall; there are some wasps that eat the larvae of the gall wasps, and other parasites that lay their eggs

leaves, the furry buds on speedwell plants, the artichoke-like swellings on yew trees and the little red 'nail-galls' on maple and sycamore leaves caused by mites. One of the best known, and certainly most attractive, is the robin's pincushion or bedeguar gall on

A female of the gall-wasp that causes knopper galls, shown here investigating the buds of an oak tree.

Knopper galls can seriously affect the growth of even the largest oak tree if they become very numerous

into these larvae. On top of this, there are also parasites that attack the parasites themselves, and even ones that attack them – the phrase 'big fleas have little fleas on their backs to bite them' has never been more appropriate!

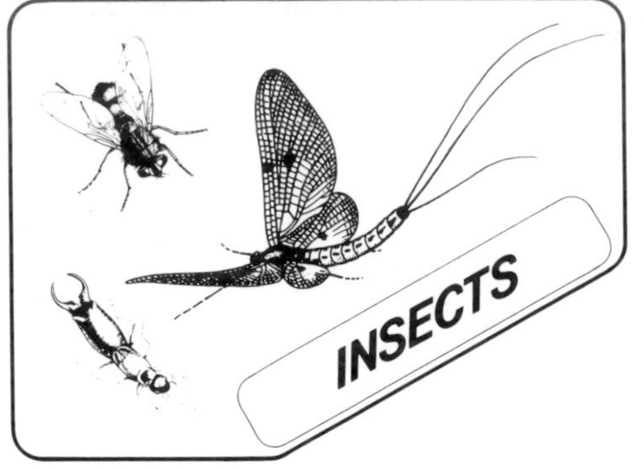

THE MOTHS OF WOODLAND

Woodland is the best habitat of all for moths but you rarely see any of them because they are almost all nocturnal. In late spring and summer, woods are literally alive with the sound of moth caterpillars chewing at the leaves; by midsummer there are huge numbers of adults about.

Just as with butterflies and other insects (see pages 100 and 108), woods are a marvellous place for moths. A good varied deciduous woodland in southern England can easily support some 300 to 400 species of moth, or many more if you include the smaller 'micromoths' that are much more difficult to identify. Only one butterfly, the purple hairstreak, feeds directly on a forest tree (oak), but numerous moths use them as their larval food-plants, and in some years the numbers of caterpillars may be so great as to totally defoliate large areas of woodland.

Oak, as always, supports the largest number of species. The leaves, as with many other trees, are most palatable when young, because they gradually harden with age, and the content of tannin and waste products gradually rises through the summer. Most moths therefore time their egg-laying and hatching to coincide with the bursting buds and the developing new leaves. Far fewer species feed on the late summer or autumn leaves, though some have a smaller second brood at this time. One of the most abundant moths on oak is the green oak roller moth, a pretty little silvery-green moth that occurs in vast numbers in some years, and can defoliate oak single-handed. The breeding behaviour of insectivorous woodland birds, such as the tits, tends to be timed to coincide with the superabundance of these caterpillars. In good moth years, even the demands of numerous birds feeding their young cannot keep pace with the army of growing caterpillars! Other moths tend to be less damaging and more moderate in their feeding behaviour; the oak hook-tip, the buff-tip moth and the vapourer, for example, are all larger moths that feed on oak. A few moths use dead or even live wood as food for their caterpillars, though nowadays these tend to be rare species. The extraordinary goat moth, for example, has larvae that grow within the timber to a huge size, perhaps 10 to 12 centimetres long, taking several years to do so. When they are mature, they often leave the tree in autumn to find a more suitable pupating site underground, and this is when they are noticed by naturalists. Because they are so large and mobile they have even been mistaken for slow-worms! The moth itself is mottled brown in colour and large, though not as impressive as the larva.

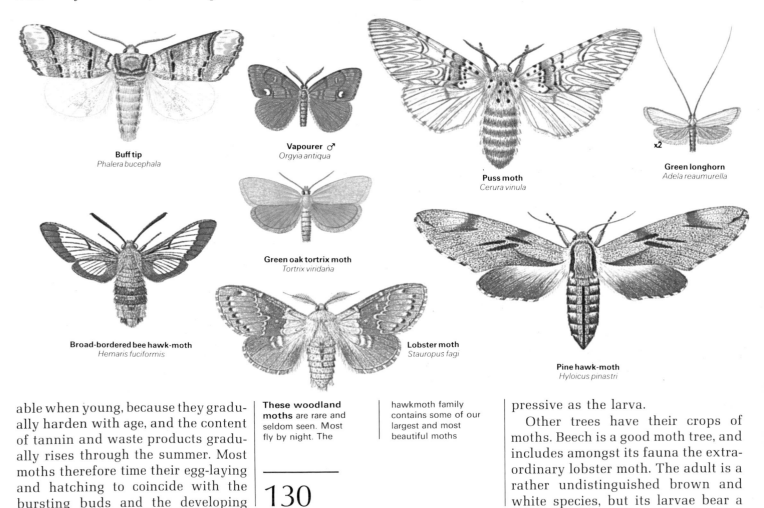

These woodland moths are rare and seldom seen. Most fly by night. The hawkmoth family contains some of our largest and most beautiful moths

Other trees have their crops of moths. Beech is a good moth tree, and includes amongst its fauna the extraordinary lobster moth. The adult is a rather undistinguished brown and white species, but its larvae bear a remarkable resemblance to a small arboreal lobster, and its behaviour when disturbed adds to the illusion of it being a fierce predatory animal, though it is in fact a harmless beech-leaf eater! Unlike most moths, the lobster moth does not leave the trees to pupate in the soil, but instead spins a silken cradle up amongst the twigs where it spends the winter before hatching the following year. Similarly, the puss-moth, which has an extraordinary large green caterpillar with face-like markings and false antennae, pupates on its food-plant tree – usually willow or poplar. It does so by constructing a wooden cocoon on the trunk which appears to be simply a bump on the tree, completely invisible unless you know what you are looking for!

The hawkmoth family does well in woodland and includes some of our most attractive moths. The poplar hawkmoth feeds on poplars and willows, the pine hawk occurs on pines, and the attractive little broad-bordered bee hawkmoth has caterpillars which feed on honeysuckle. It is one of the few resident hawkmoths that flies by day and, where it occurs, it can be seen visiting rhododendron, bugle, or other early summer woodland flowers, sipping nectar from each flower briefly, more like a humming-bird than a moth, then darting off to the next bloom, its long proboscis like a fueling pipe.

A marsh tit with a mouth full of tortrix moth caterpillars. Oak trees can be almost smothered in these caterpillars at certain times in the summer providing plenty of food for hungry chicks and their assiduous parents

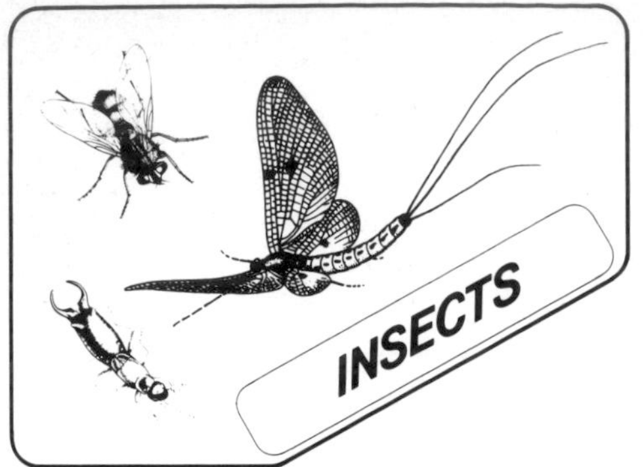

GRASSLAND MOTHS

If you walk through a flowery grassland in summer, just as evening falls, you will notice great quantities of moths stirring into life as they begin their nocturnal activities. Grasslands that have not been ploughed or sprayed are amongst the best places to see moths.

Any grassland that has a good mixture of herbaceous flowering plants amongst its sward – and, in practice, this usually means areas that have not been agriculturally improved – will almost certainly be very rich in moths of many species. The problem with moths is that they mostly fly at night, roosting deep in the grass by day so, unless you go out with a torch after dark, or better still, run a moth light, you are unlikely to see this great variety. Occasionally you come across a nocturnal species roosting somewhere conspicuous, such as the small elephant hawkmoth shown in the photograph, resting on a butterfly orchid. This is one of our most attractive moths with a lovely combination of pink and gold, and its larvae feed on various bedstraws that are frequent in unimproved grassland. It acts as pollinator for certain nectar-bearing, long-spurred flowers such as the orchids, though you are unlikely to see this happening as it only occurs under the cover of darkness.

However, there are quite a number of moths in grassland that do habitually fly by day, and they make a welcome addition to the insect fauna on sunny days in summer. The most conspicuous are the attractive velvet black and red burnet moths, which are unusual amongst moths in being rather colonial in their habits, with several hundred often breeding together in a loose group. They are very slow at moving and flying, and tend to stay together, making no effort to fly away when approached. The reason for this is that, like many other brightly-coloured insects, they are highly distasteful and are even rather poisonous. For a long time, it was known to insect-collectors that burnet moths were rather resistant to the normal method of killing by using cyanide, but it has only quite recently

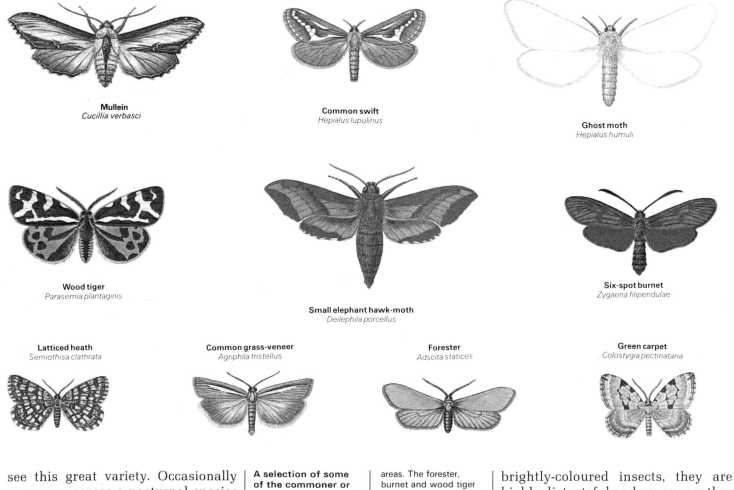

Mullein
Cucillia verbasci

Common swift
Hepialus lupulinus

Ghost moth
Hepialus humuli

Wood tiger
Parasemia plantaginis

Small elephant hawk-moth
Deilephila porcellus

Six-spot burnet
Zygaena filipendulae

Latticed heath
Semiothisa clathrata

Common grass-veneer
Agriphila tristellus

Forester
Adscita statices

Green carpet
Colostygia pectinataria

A selection of some of the commoner or more conspicuous species of moths to be found in grassy areas. The forester, burnet and wood tiger moth regularly occur on chalk grassland during the summer

been shown that these moths emit two substances when attacked; one has a very unpleasant taste, the other contains the highly poisonous hydrocyanic acid, or cyanide, as well as some histamines. A bird or other predator may kill one or two burnet moths when they first see them, but they very quickly learn to associate red and black 'warning' colorations with the unpleasant taste, and all other burnet moths will henceforth be left strictly alone! Other insects that resemble burnet moths will also be avoided, whether they taste nasty or not, which is why it benefits certain insects if they evolve to resemble the distasteful species. Burnet moths are almost equally conspicuous at other stages of their life-cycle, for their brightly coloured caterpillars feed openly by day on their food-plants, such as bird's-foot-trefoil, and the pupa attaches itself high up on grass stems in the most conspicuous of positions. It seems that birds find it difficult to settle and remove them in this position, though the pupae are also unpleasant-tasting which aids their survival. They are such sluggish moths that it is by no means uncommon to find a mating pair immediately below the pupal case from which one has just emerged!

There are seven species of burnet moths in Britain, all looking rather similar, and several are common; the transparent burnet, however (with rather transparent wings) only occurs in the north, and the New Forest, mountain and slender Scotch burnets are all rare or local. Some close relatives of the burnets, which are also day-flying grassland species, are the forester moths. These pretty little metallic green moths feed openly by day on flower heads such as knapweed or ragged-robin. There are actually three species of forester moth, of which only the common forester is at all frequent, though they are rather difficult to distinguish from each other.

Other moths that you often see in grassy areas by day include the curiously-named Mother Shipton moth, so-called because the wings have a dark shape on them that supposedly resembles an old witch's head. Look out for the rather similar looking heath moths, such as the small and easily overlooked latticed heath which is an attractive speckled brown and cream coloured moth.

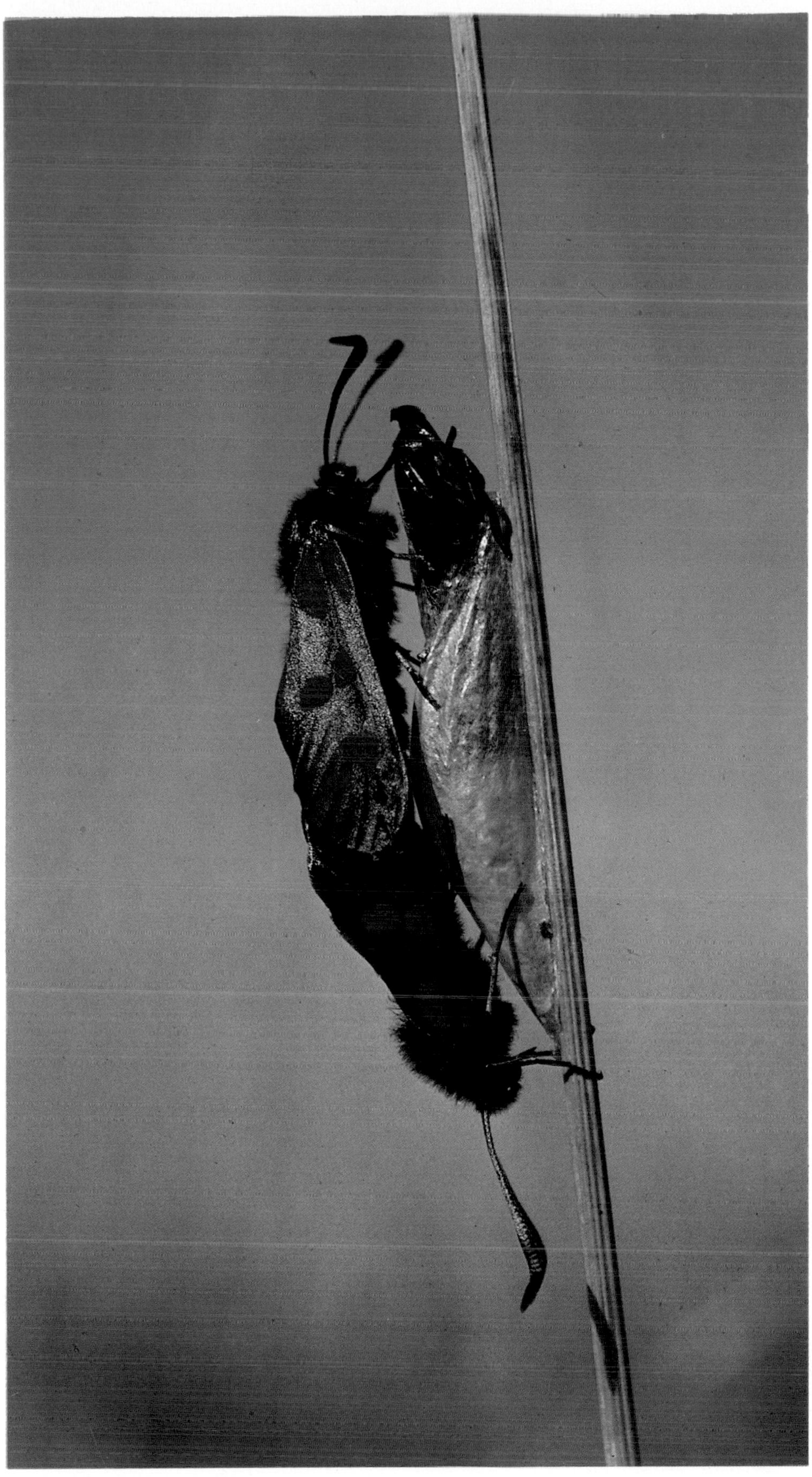

A pair of six-spot burnet moths mating on the emergence cocoon of one of them in grassland. Burnets are day-flying moths which deter predators with their red warning colour and horrible taste. The pale green caterpillar feeds on kidney vetch and other 'pea family' plants and when full grown spins a papery cocoon which is stuck to a grass stem

BEES, WASPS AND THEIR MIMICS

Far from consisting simply of honey-bees and aggressive sugar-seeking black and yellow wasps, there is in fact a vast range of bees and wasps with an extraordinary range of life-cycles. Their aggressive stinging ability has led to a number of other insects mimicking them.

Bees and wasps are closely-related groups of insects that are particularly familiar in the form of the honey-bee, bumble bees and the wasps which crowd aggressively around anything sweet in late summer. These species are, however, only the tip of the iceberg of an enormous group of species.

They fall basically into two groups: the colonial or social species, living together in large colonies which often have specialised groups within them, and the solitary species which live on their own. Honey-bees are amongst the most highly developed of the social species, as well as being the most familiar. A colony can hold about 60,000 worker bees, which are sterile females that perform all the routine tasks of the hive, together with a much smaller number of males or drones, and a single breeding female, the queen. The workers collect nectar and pollen, feed all the developing larvae and produce honey to maintain the colony over the winter. Not surprisingly, the worker bees only live for a few months, whilst the queen lives for several years. The sole function of the drones is to mate with the queen, which is fertilised once and then lays eggs for the rest of her life. All three classes of bee work together to make the colony successful and to help to found new colonies. The survival of individual workers becomes unimportant in relation to the continuation of the colony.

Bumble bees have a rather similar, though smaller organisation, in underground colonies; though in this case only the queen survives the winter to start a new colony in spring, whereas the whole honey-bee colony overwinters. There are five species of social wasp, all looking somewhat similar in their bright yellow and black colours, and in fact the familiar wasps seen around the house include more than one species. Early in the year, a queen which has survived the winter makes a small nest and lays a few eggs in it. These soon hatch into larvae and develop into worker wasps, which take on the task of enlarging the nest and feeding the larvae from the eggs that the queen continues to lay in very large numbers. By late summer the colony may be several thousand strong. During the greater part of the summer, the workers are fully occupied catching insect prey for the developing carnivorous larvae, which in turn produce a sweet substance for the workers to eat. When there are no more developing larvae, the large numbers of workers seek out sweet food from flowers or fruit, or from man-made produce, in the absence of the sweet larval secre-

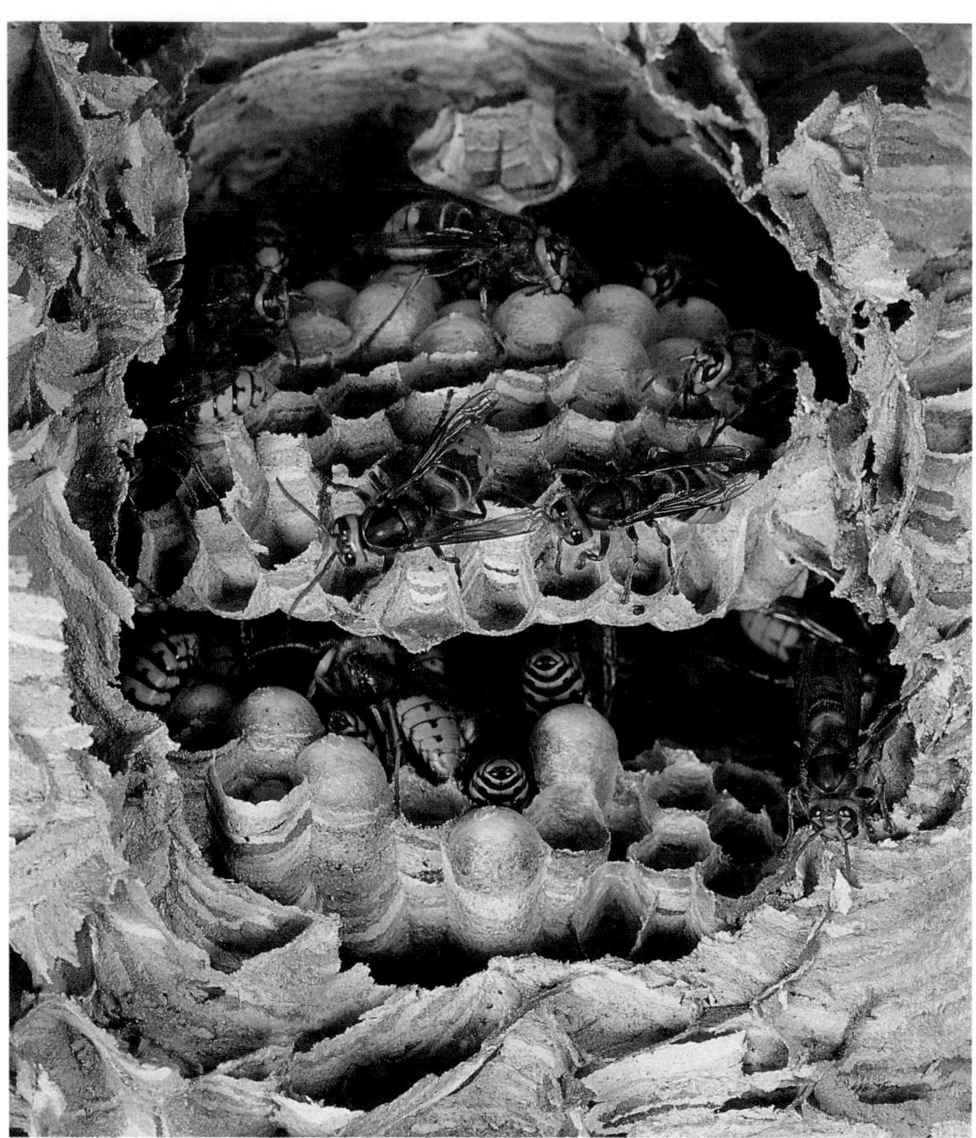

The interior of a hornet's nest, showing the worker hornets tending the larvae, in their 'honeycomb' nursery

tions, and it is then that they come into conflict with us!

Amongst the other lifestyles, the cuckoo bees are of interest; rather like the bird, these bees take over an existing bumble bee nest, oust the queen, and persuade the workers to look after their own developing larvae. Ruby-tailed wasps, which are brightly-coloured jewel-like wasps, have similar habits.

The majority of the solitary wasps lay their eggs in small nests which they then provision with live food; some species collect caterpillars which they paralyse and carry to the nest, whilst others catch spiders, bugs or various specific sorts of prey. In each case, the developing larvae are provided with an adequate food source which keeps fresh because it is alive, but paralysed. Solitary bees, such as lawn bees, work in a similar way, except that they leave a supply of nectar and pollen in each chamber.

Because bees and wasps are aggressive insects, armed with a powerful defence, they are largely avoided by predators, so it is hardly surprising that a number of unrelated species have evolved to look like them. These mimics include the attractive black and yellow striped wasp beetle, the drone-fly (actually a hoverfly), the bumble-bee hoverfly that even occurs in different colour forms – just like the bumble bee it is mimicking – and a number of other species, which vary a great deal in the exactness of their mimicry.

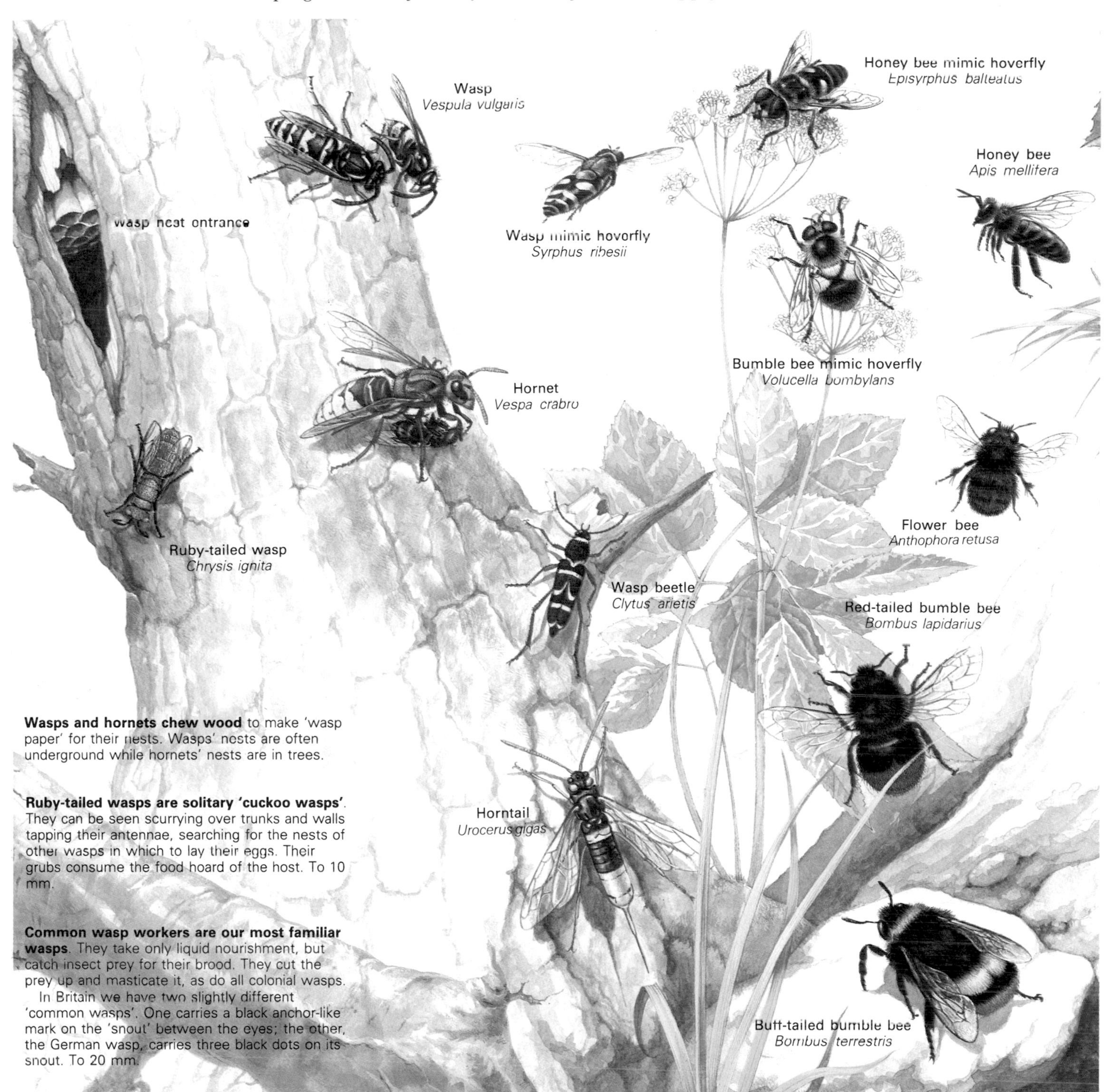

Wasps and hornets chew wood to make 'wasp paper' for their nests. Wasps' nests are often underground while hornets' nests are in trees.

Ruby-tailed wasps are solitary 'cuckoo wasps'. They can be seen scurrying over trunks and walls tapping their antennae, searching for the nests of other wasps in which to lay their eggs. Their grubs consume the food hoard of the host. To 10 mm.

Common wasp workers are our most familiar wasps. They take only liquid nourishment, but catch insect prey for their brood. They cut the prey up and masticate it, as do all colonial wasps.
In Britain we have two slightly different 'common wasps'. One carries a black anchor-like mark on the 'snout' between the eyes; the other, the German wasp, carries three black dots on its snout. To 20 mm.

Many insects mimic the warning colours of bees and wasps. This strategy of survival is aimed at fooling prospective predators into thinking they can sting

BEETLES IN BRITAIN

From the giant stag beetle with its forbidding jaws, one of Britain's largest insects, to tiny creatures that are so small you can hardly see them, Britain's beetle fauna consists of some 4,000 species inhabiting almost every habitat.

Beetles are the largest group of creatures in the animal kingdom, with about 350,000 different species known in the world, and probably many more waiting to be discovered. In Britain, we have a meagre total of just under 4,000 species, though this is quite enough if you are trying to identify them! They vary incredibly from huge species like the stag beetle with males of at least six centimetres long, to tiny species only a millimetre or so in length. Their lifestyles are enormously varied too. As adults they may be predatory, flower-feeding or non-feeding; the larvae may feed on dead wood, dung, rotting material or they may themselves be highly carnivorous. Most beetles are terrestrial, but a few are even aquatic, so overall the variety is immense.

Amongst the larger species, the longhorn beetles are particularly attractive. Their larvae feed on dead wood, living in rotting stumps, old branches or dying trees. Like most dead-wood feeders, they remain in the larval state for several years because of the low nutritional value of their chosen food. They hatch into beautiful insects which are more conspicuous than many groups because some of them are active by day and feed on flowers. The strikingly-coloured black and yellow Strangalia species are particularly frequent on summer flowers such as hogweed, angelica or hemp agrimony. Other dead-wood

One of the longhorn beetles (*Rhagium mordax*) with its long antennae, collecting pollen; longhorn grubs feed in timber

feeders, in different families, include the blood-red cardinal beetles with their prominent serrated antennae, and the stag beetles themselves of which there are three British species. The large stag beetle is an extraordinary beast, for the huge male has a pair of large antler-like horny outgrowths which he uses for sparring with other males in the presence of a female; she is smaller and possesses no such outgrowths. Stag beetles are generally uncommon, and probably declining, though in a few areas, such as south London and the New Forest in Hampshire, they may be reasonably abundant.

The burying beetles or carrion beetles form an interesting group. They fly, mainly at night, in search of carcasses which they locate by smell and, on finding one, they immediately begin to bury it by removing the soil from beneath, at the same time chewing it into a more compact shape. Their eggs are laid into the rotting material, which provides an immediate food-supply for the developing larvae. In a similar way, the dung beetles, including dor and scarab beetles, seek out dung which they bury as food for the larvae. Both these groups perform a useful service in their own ways!

Other beetles include the strange click beetles, which are generally brown or reddish, undistinguished insects, but they share the ability to jump some considerable distance from any position, even lying on their back, by means of a peg-and-loop spring mechanism, which surprises predators and human observers alike. Ladybirds are also beetles, familiar residents found in towns and gardens and they are highly carnivorous in both the adult and larval stages, feeding mainly on aphids such as greenflies.

A few beetles have taken to water. These include the carnivorous diving beetles, which are aggressive predators both as larvae and as adults, and the water beetles, such as the great silver water beetle, which is herbivorous as an adult but carnivorous in its larval form. The extraordinary little whirligig beetles, which spend much of their time gyrating madly about on the surface of the water, have some strange adaptations to their aquatic life, including split eyes for seeing both above and below water. They live mainly as scavengers seeking out any form of animal life trapped on the water surface, diving below the surface if danger threatens.

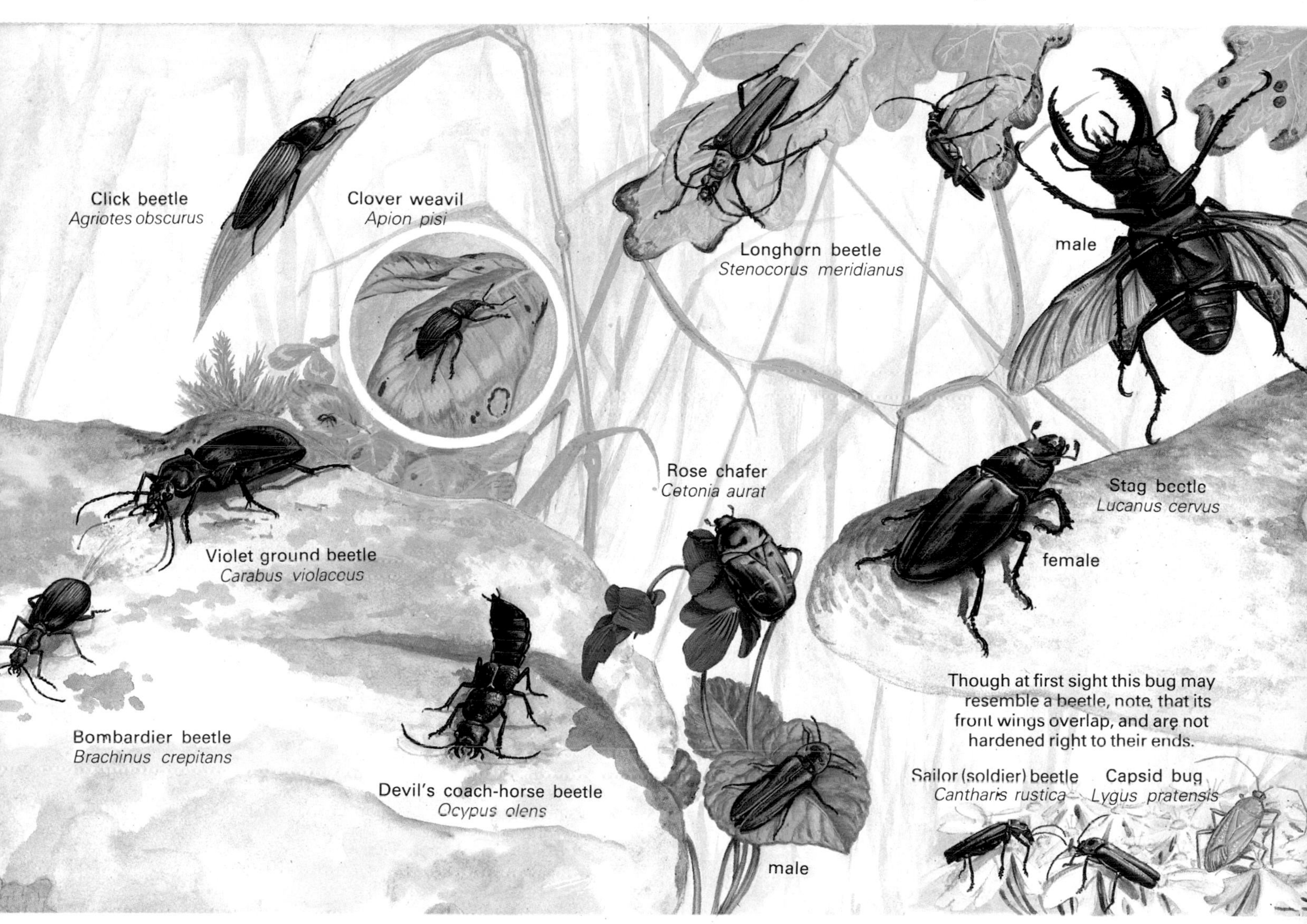

A few of the 4000 or so species of beetle found in Britain. Beetles have only one pair of functional wings, the second set forms the wing case which often forms a horny covering to the back. Note that beetles usually have biting mouth parts. Weevils are plant-feeding beetles which have a long snout for piercing and sucking up the sap

CRABS & THEIR RELATIVES

Around our shores, from close to high water-mark down into deep water, there is a surprising array of crabs, lobsters and other crustaceans to be found, including such strange creatures as the hermit crab, the spider crab and the porcelain crab.

The crustaceans are a kind of marine equivalent of the insects or the spiders. All three are anthropods sharing the same tough outer skeleton and jointed limbs, with a segmented body plan, though they do not look very similar because of the different pressures imposed by life in the sea. In fact, crustaceans come in many forms, and they are the dominant group of marine arthropods. Their numbers include such diverse creatures as barnacles (probably the most modified of all the crustacea), goose barnacles, sandhoppers, sea-slaters (large marine relatives of the woodlice) and the more familiar forms of crabs, lobsters and prawns.

Barnacles have similar tiny free-living larvae to other members of the group – they are all constituents of the zooplankton in their larval stages (see page 21) – but when they settle onto a rock or other surface, they develop a shell composed of calcium carbonate plates and look superficially like a mollusc. Goose barnacles have long stalks, and are most often attached to unstable substrates such as boats or driftwood; while a third type of barnacle is parasitic on crabs and looks quite different from either of the others.

The largest and best known of the crustaceans are undoubtedly the decapods – the lobsters, crabs and prawns – and it is this group which contains all the economically important species. A typical member is the edible crab, which is the largest of the common crab species in Britain, weighing several kilos when fully-grown and living (if unmolested) for eight or ten years. Young edible crabs tend to stay near the shore line, hiding and feeding amongst rocks and seaweeds, but as they grow and mature they move into deeper waters, so that the larger individuals are unlikely to be seen by the casual swimmer or beachcomber. Like all members of this group, the crabs shed their skins regularly as they grow, to allow the body to expand, and young rapidly-growing crabs moult several times a year. The females mate when they are about five years old and, as with most crustaceans, this takes place just after

A group of barnacles, relatives of the crustaceans which feed by filtering drifting plankton out from sea water using their feeler-like legs. At low tide they pull in their feelers and close-up revealing a jagged carpet on rocks

moulting while the body is still soft. The male detects the female's readiness to moult and stays with her even assisting her with the skin removal. Millions of eggs may be laid but obviously only a very few survive and these at first join the floating zooplankton, gradually sinking to the bottom as they grow. The adult crabs are catholic predators and scavengers, living off other crustaceans together with anything else they can find.

Hermit crabs, though related, have a rather different lifestyle. They live inside the disused shells of molluscs, especially whelks, which offer them better protection than their own shell, and they are often active by day. They have adapted to this peculiar way of life by developing smaller back legs which grasp the shell and hold the rest of the body inside, and a large pair of front legs with which it walks dragging its shell behind. Like other crustaceans, the hermit crab has to moult the harder parts of its skeleton periodically, but is also has to move to a bigger home occasionally. It frequently has to share its shell with other animals, and it suffers from the parasitic barnacles already mentioned.

The largest of the well known crustaceans is the lobster, which can grow to about half a metre long, weighing many kilos. It is blue when alive and, though it may occasionally wander into rock pools on the upper shore, it spends most of its time in deeper water moving slowly and hiding amongst rocks; if alarmed it can shoot backwards rapidly. It differs from the crab in that the eggs when laid are carried for many months in a mass under the body; they eventually hatch into tiny shrimp-like larvae about a centimetre long. If not caught in traps, lobsters can live for up to 30 years.

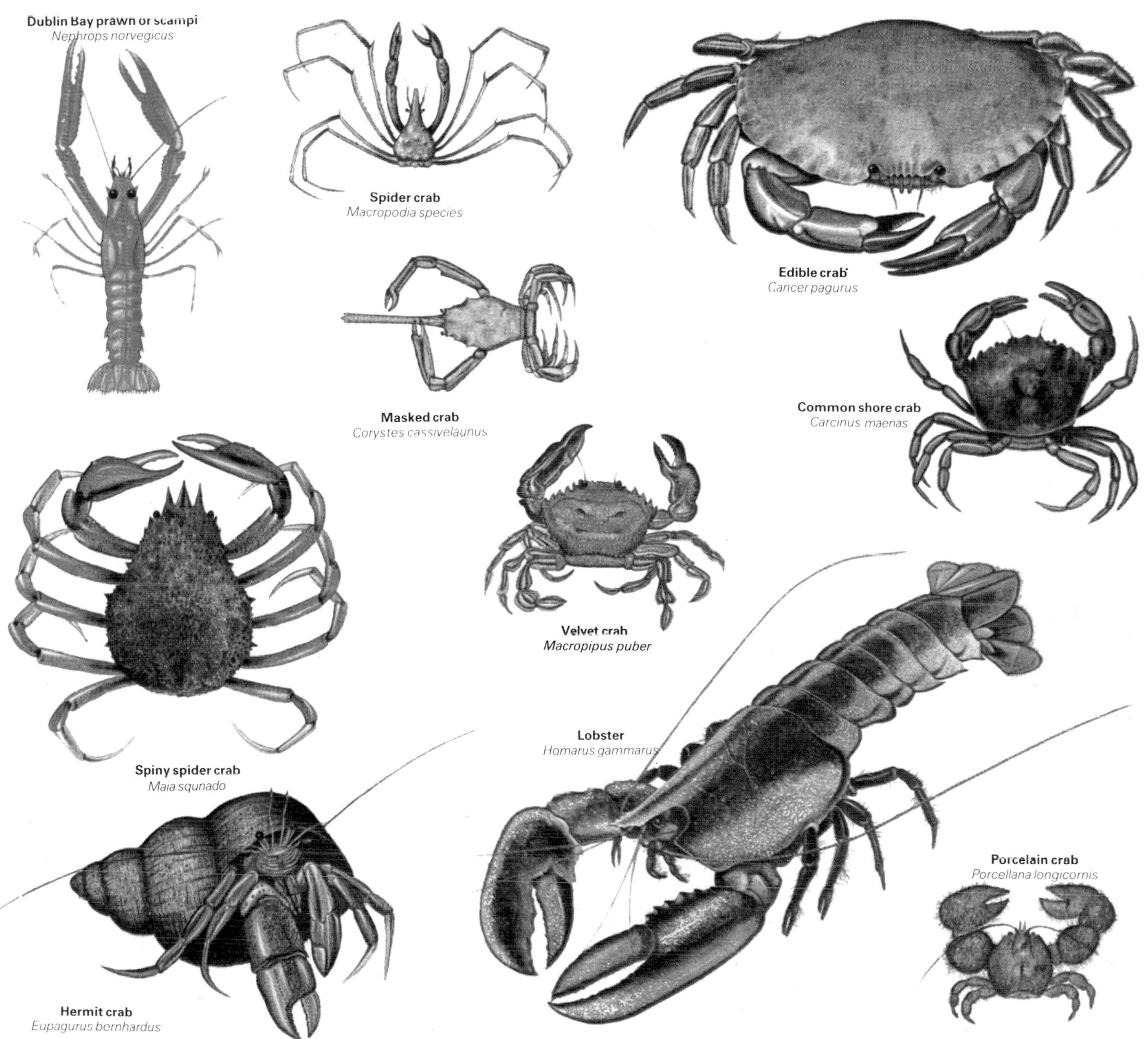

Many species of crabs and lobsters find a home around our coasts; they are all closely related. The commonest are shore crabs and the tiny (6mm long) porcelain crab which lives under stones in the intertidal zone

SEA-SHELLS

You do not have to go to the tropics to find attractive sea-shells, for the waters around our coasts are full of animals living in shells, many of which are washed up on the shores, and the variety of types to be found is endless.

Virtually all the shells that we find belong to members of the molluscs, the group which includes terrestrial snails and slugs. Molluscs have taken to the sea very successfully, and they occur in large numbers in a huge variety of forms. All the main groups of molluscs are found around our coasts; these are the slugs and snails (Gastropods), bivalves, chitons, squids and octopuses (Cephalopods) and tusk shells. Some of the molluscs do not have obvious shells, and they are dealt with on the following page, whilst conversely there are a few shelled animals, like the barnacles, which are not molluscs (see page 138).

The plates show the marvellous variety of types of sea-shells to be found, and should help to identify most 'finds'. Collecting empty shells can be a pleasant and fascinating occupation that obviously can do no harm to the life of the sea, but please do not collect live shells or those with hermit crab lodgers, as they will certainly die.

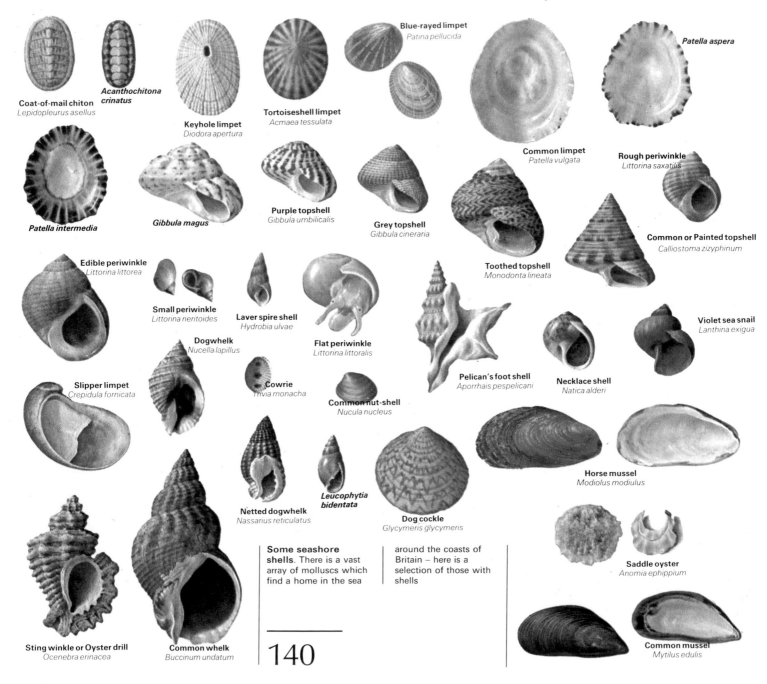

Coat-of-mail chiton *Lepidopleurus asellus*

Acanthochitona crinatus

Keyhole limpet *Diodora apertura*

Tortoiseshell limpet *Acmaea tessulata*

Blue-rayed limpet *Patina pellucida*

Common limpet *Patella vulgata*

Patella aspera

Patella intermedia

Gibbula magus

Purple topshell *Gibbula umbilicalis*

Grey topshell *Gibbula cineraria*

Toothed topshell *Monodonta lineata*

Rough periwinkle *Littorina saxatilis*

Common or Painted topshell *Calliostoma zizyphinum*

Edible periwinkle *Littorina littorea*

Small periwinkle *Littorina neritoides*

Laver spire shell *Hydrobia ulvae*

Flat periwinkle *Littorina littoralis*

Pelican's foot shell *Aporrhais pespelicani*

Necklace shell *Natica alderi*

Violet sea snail *Lanthina exigua*

Dogwhelk *Nucella lapillus*

Slipper limpet *Crepidula fornicata*

Cowrie *Trivia monacha*

Common nut-shell *Nucula nucleus*

Horse mussel *Modiolus modiulus*

Netted dogwhelk *Nassarius reticulatus*

Leucophytia bidentata

Dog cockle *Glycymeris glycymeris*

Saddle oyster *Anomia ephippium*

Sting winkle or Oyster drill *Ocenebra erinacea*

Common whelk *Buccinum undatum*

Common mussel *Mytilus edulis*

Some seashore shells. There is a vast array of molluscs which find a home in the sea around the coasts of Britain – here is a selection of those with shells

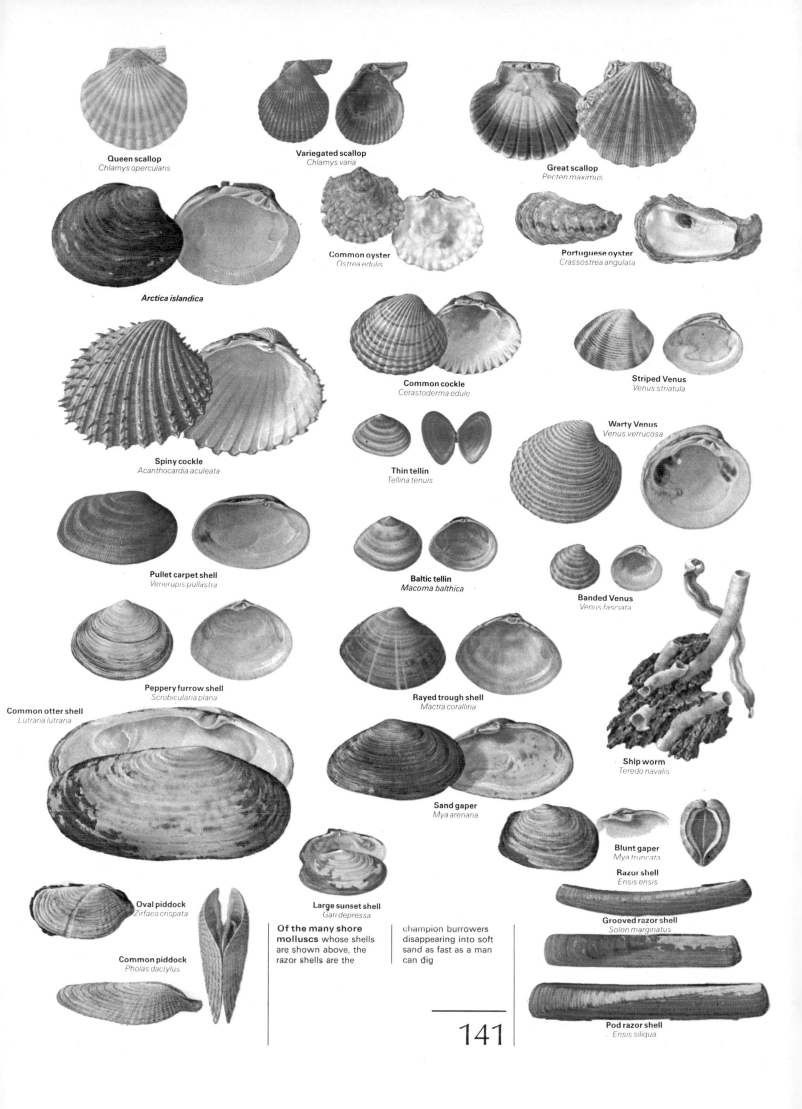

Queen scallop
Chlamys opercularis

Variegated scallop
Chlamys varia

Great scallop
Pecten maximus

Arctica islandica

Common oyster
Ostrea edulis

Portuguese oyster
Crassostrea angulata

Spiny cockle
Acanthocardia aculeata

Pullet carpet shell
Venerupis pullastra

Peppery furrow shell
Scrobicularia plana

Common otter shell
Lutraria lutraria

Common cockle
Cerastoderma edule

Striped Venus
Venus striatula

Thin tellin
Tellina tenuis

Warty Venus
Venus verrucosa

Baltic tellin
Macoma balthica

Banded Venus
Venus fasciata

Rayed trough shell
Mactra corallina

Ship worm
Teredo navalis

Sand gaper
Mya arenaria

Blunt gaper
Mya truncata

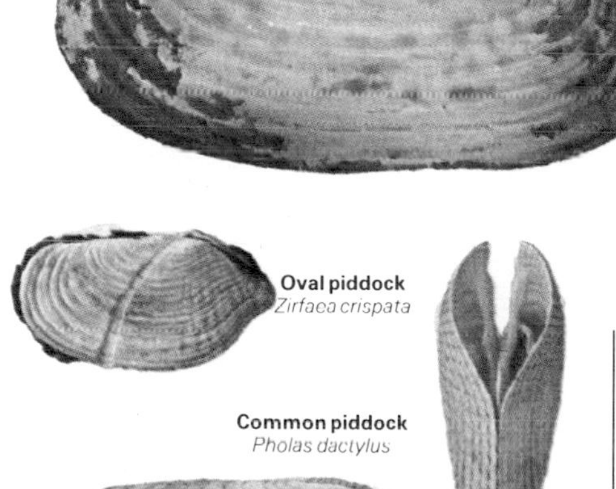

Oval piddock
Zirfaea crispata

Common piddock
Pholas dactylus

Large sunset shell
Gari depressa

Of the many shore molluscs whose shells are shown above, the razor shells are the champion burrowers disappearing into soft sand as fast as a man can dig

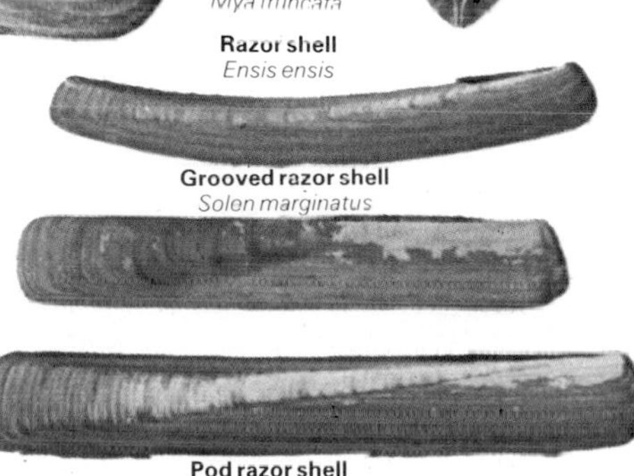

Razor shell
Ensis ensis

Grooved razor shell
Solen marginatus

Pod razor shell
Ensis siliqua

MARINE MOLLUSCS WITHOUT SHELLS

Besides the familiar sea-shells, there are also some molluscs that look quite different – the octopuses, squids, cuttlefish and strange animals like the sea-slug and sea-hare. They are a bizarre group – the epitome of marine animals.

Amongst the molluscs, there are a number of marine types totally lacking shells or in others they are much reduced, giving them all a very different appearance. The opisthobranchs are wholly marine relatives of the snails which have lost their shells in varying degrees allowing them to take on more varied forms and habits such as swimming. They include the sea-hare, the sea-slugs and sea-lemon, all names which give some idea of their variety of form!

The largest and most familiar group of molluscs without shells are the decapods, or the squids and octopuses. There are two species of octopus to be found in British waters, the lesser octopus and the much larger common octopus. In fact, the lesser octopus is the most frequent of the two, and the large octopus probably rarely breeds here, but its larvae (which are planktonic) are brought in regularly by southerly currents. The octopods have lost all trace of a shell, and have a bag-like body and a ring of eight tentacles around the mouth from which, of course, they derive their name. The tentacles have rows of suckers along them, one row in the case of the lesser, two rows for the common octopus. They live, usually in

The Cuttle bone or shell, shown above, is filled with 'gas' which keeps it 'afloat' as it swims. When alarmed the cuttle-fish forces water through its 'siphon' which jet-propels it out of danger. At the same time, it may also squirt out an inky 'smokescreen' which distracts the attackers attention. This 'ink' is used as the main ingredient of the artists colour sepia

deeper water, amongst rocks or in a lair and may re-arrange the stones around them to enhance the camouflage. Like all the decapods, they are predatory animals, feeding on crustaceans and other marine creatures which they pounce on and envelope in their tentacles. The eggs are laid in large bunches, rather like grapes, in rock crevices, and the emerging larvae become part of the zooplankton for a while before gradually sinking to the bottom.

The squids are mainly deep water species, occasionally brought up in nets or found washed ashore. They are as strange looking as the octopods, with a torpedo-shaped body and large, paired triangular fins along the rear half of the body. At the front, they have eight short tentacles, but they also have a pair of longer tentacles which can be extended to seize prey. Unlike the octopus, which has a very soft formless body, the squid has a rigid part which acts like a backbone, and enables it to swim more effectively. Cuttlefish are rather similar, with the same elongated shape and an eight plus two tentacle arrangement, though they differ in having a special internal shell, which has many gas-filled chambers that make it much easier for the cuttlefish to float above the sea-bed. This means it can swim, with little effort, just above the bottom in search of prey moving with the aid of broad, flattened paired fins which run from behind the head to the tip of the body. Although cuttlefishes are primarily deeper sea creatures, except for the tiny lesser cuttlefish which lives on sandy shores, they do come close inshore to lay their eggs. Their cuttlebones, the buoyant internal shell of the animal, are a familiar sight on the beach and are often seen in budgerigar cages! They are washed up in large numbers as they last for a long time after the death of the cuttle. The lesser cuttlefish is only four to five centimetres long, and occurs abundantly in some places, swimming over or burrowing in sand, and, if you are very eagle-eyed and very quick may even be caught in handnets. It is very variable in colour depending on the substrate.

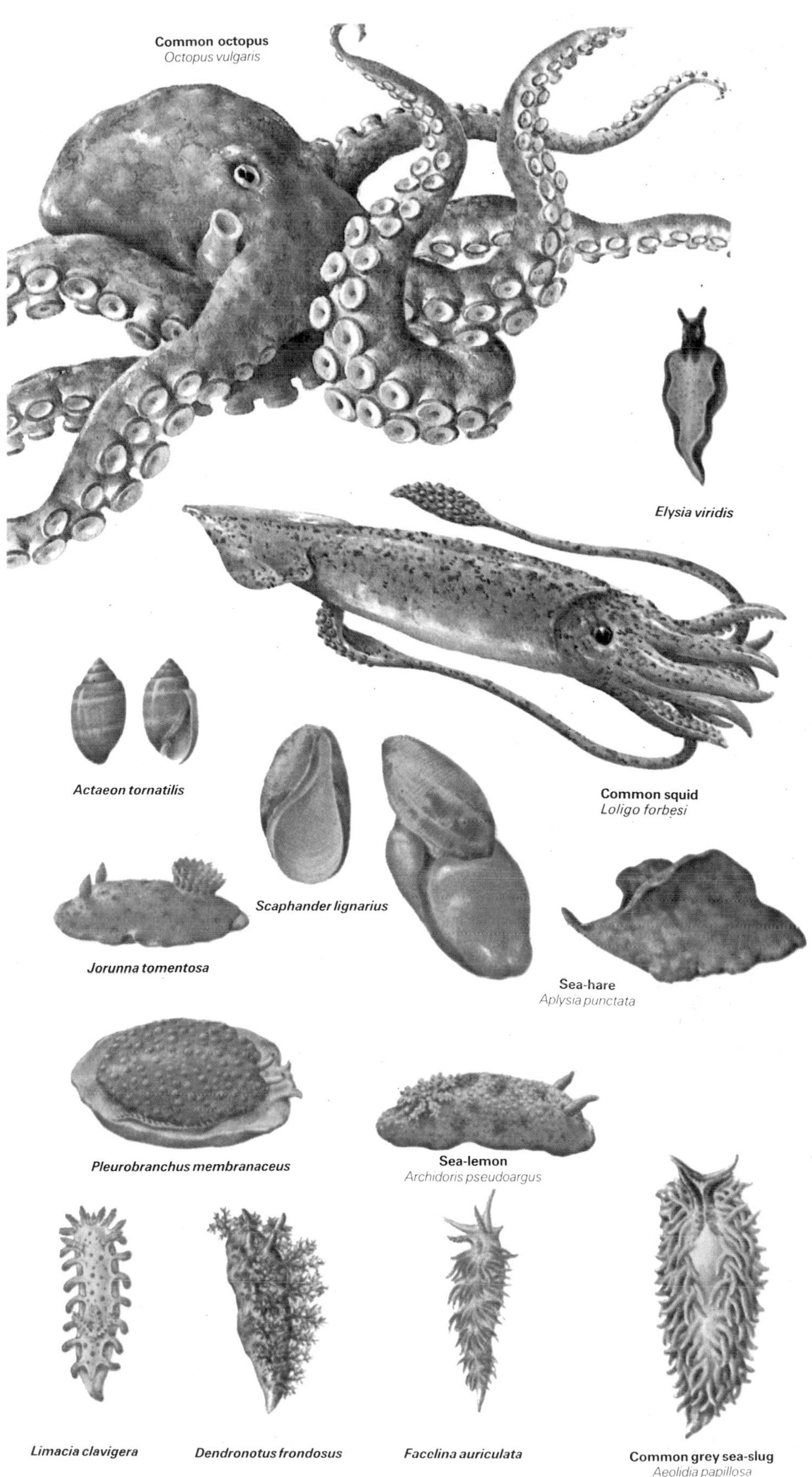

Here is a selection of 'opisthobranchs' and 'cephalopods'. The squid and octopus which are in the second group have eight sucker bearing arms (the squid has two extra extendable tentacles). The opisthobranchs include the sea-slugs and sea-hare

Other Marine Invertebrates

The sea around our coasts is full of numerous creatures other than those already described – jellyfishes, sea-anemones, star-fishes, sea-urchins, marine worms and many others. They include large numbers of fascinating and beautiful creatures.

The great and surprisingly attractive variety of marine worms is illustrated and described opposite, as are some of the echinoderms – the familiar starfishes, sea-urchins and brittle-stars. Besides these groups, there are many other forms of marine life, some familiar and some less well known, but all extremely interesting.

The coelenterates are a large, rather primitive group of invertebrates, and consist basically of a bag-like body enclosing a stomach with a mouth surrounded by tentacles, these are covered with stinging cells which can stun the prey. Many of the coelenterates are colonies of these basic individuals, the polyps, acting together as one organism. There are also special reproductive polyps which grow on the colonies and produce mobile free-swimming medusae that look like miniature jellyfishes. These medusae are not themselves the young stages, but they join the zooplankton and in due course produce fertile eggs. These hatch into planktonic larvae which eventually settle on the sea-bed and start new colonies. Amongst this group of hydroids there are some species that have cells modified for different functions, and these include the extraordinary Portuguese man-o'-war. This looks very like a bluish inflated polythene bag, with tentacles and polyps hanging down below it, extending for several metres. Like their relatives the jellyfish, they can give quite a painful sting.

In the true jellyfish, which are also coelenterates but in a different group, the medusae have become the dominant part of the life-cycle as a free-swimming large animal, though some still have a polyp phase. Jellyfishes consist of a large bell with tentacles hanging down from below it, and they can swim to an extent by pulsating the bell, but not strongly enough to avoid the effects of currents. As a result, they arc at the mercy of tides and winds, and are quite often washed up in large numbers onto beaches, where they soon die.

The other group of coelenterates is the sea-anemones, which are probably the most familiar because they live well above low tide mark, and are often found in rock pools. There are many different sorts; the most familiar is the beadlet anemone, which extends its tentacles when submerged, but retracts them when exposed to the air and ends up like a blob of reddish jelly! They are more attractive when seen in pools with their waving tentacles ready to close over any suitable prey item, including small fishes if they are too slow. A colour variety of the beadlet anemone, now recognised as a separate species, is the strawberry anemone; it is similar but is an attractive yellow-spotted red colour and looks somewhat like a strawberry. There are also snakelocks anemones, with attractive green tentacles tipped with pink; dahlia anemones looking remarkably like pink dahlia flowers amongst the rocks, and the little jewel and gem anemones which are rarely seen as they live in shadier, deeper water.

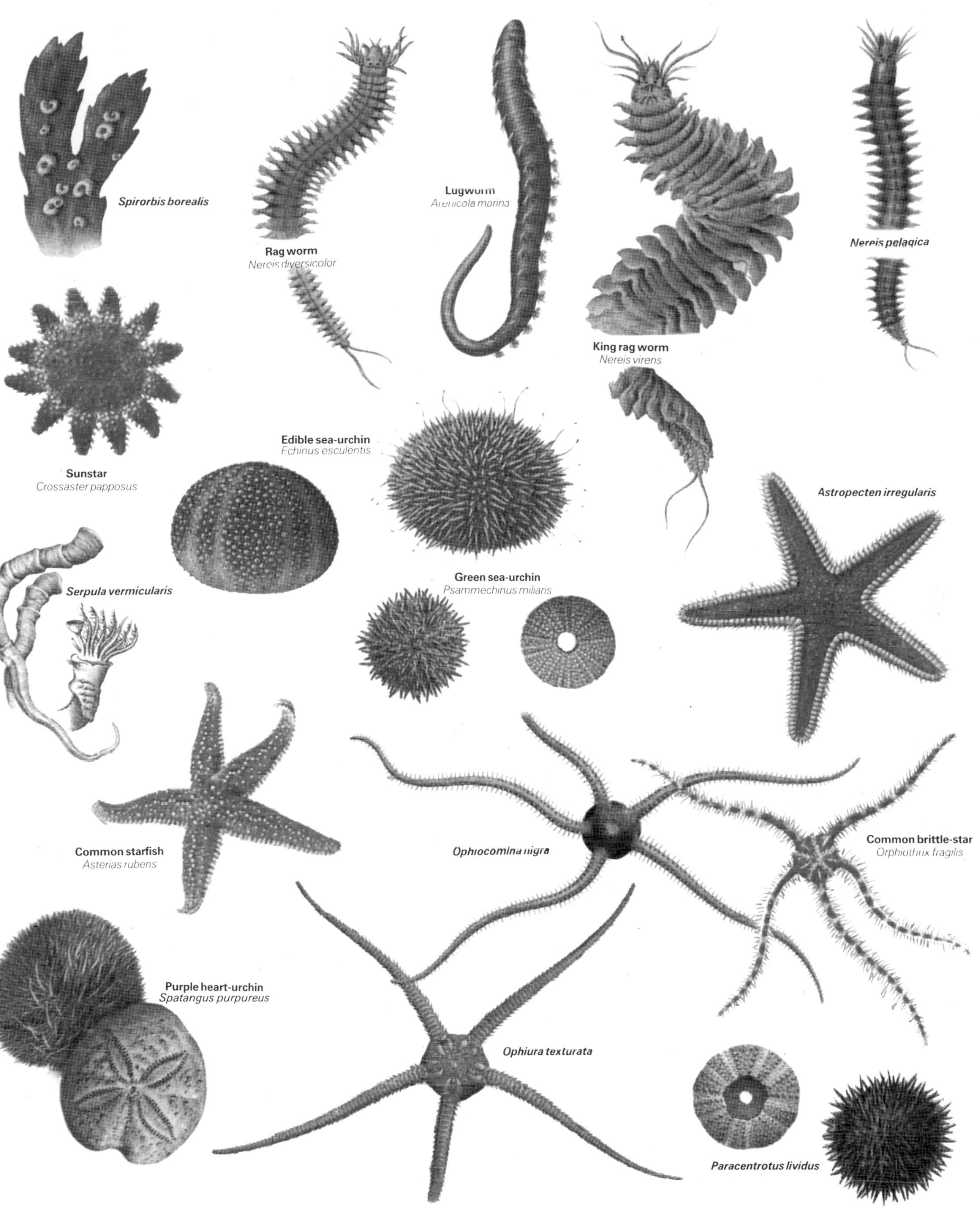

The beadlet anemone, left, withdraws its tentacles when the tide recedes revealing a red jelly-like blob with a ring of 24 bright blue dots around its oral disc. It is found in the middle shore, on rocks and in crevices

Marine worms and echinoderms. The echinoderms comprise the starfish, brittle-stars and sea-urchins. The brittle-stars have a small central disc and long, jointed arms

MESSING ABOUT ON THE BEACH

Messing about in rockpools is a familiar and pleasant summer holiday acivity. But, it can be more enjoyable with a little planning and knowledge to help you find the best pools and recognise the animals and plants you see.

The shore is the meeting place of two worlds – the sea and the land. Because it is not possible for us to see very much of the marine world directly, the shore provides our best opportunity for looking, at least, at the tip of the marine 'iceberg'. The sea is a remarkably rich place, with a tremendous range of species in a wide range of unfamiliar life-forms, and even the tiny proportion that we can watch on the shore can provide a lifetime of study.

There are really two groups of creatures and their signs that we will come across on the shore. Those that are resident because the conditions suit them as they need light or some other factor; and those that are from deeper sea areas, and are washed up by freak conditions or after their death. This group also includes interesting beach-combing 'finds' like the egg-cases of whelks, dogfishes or skate.

If you are planning to look closely at the animals and plants that live on the sea-shore, the first thing to do is to consult a tide-table. Rock-pools and similar habitats become steadily richer the further down the shore they are, and low tide will be the most revealing time. However, tides vary considerably in how low they go, and you will find it best to select a spring low tide (irrespective of the season), when high tides are highest and low tides lowest. These occur when the moon is full or new. Better still, though less well timed for summer holiday work, are the low tides around the spring and autumn equinoxes, when the moon and sun are pulling almost together, on March 21st and September 21st and a few days either side. These are the lowest tides of the year, and they make for much more exciting research. Some parts of the country tend to have their lowest tides in the evening and early morning, while in other places they

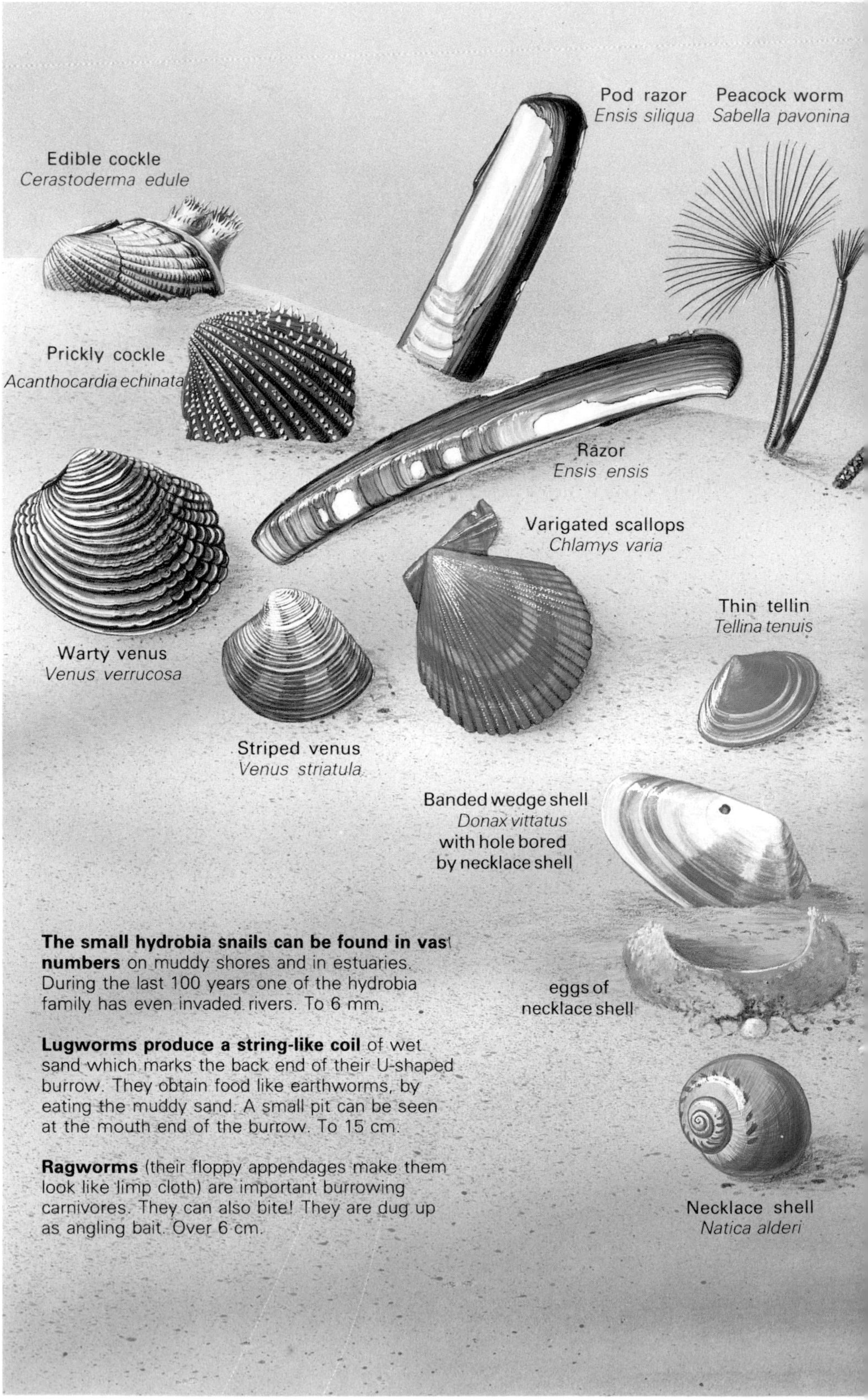

Pod razor *Ensis siliqua*

Peacock worm *Sabella pavonina*

Edible cockle *Cerastoderma edule*

Prickly cockle *Acanthocardia echinata*

Razor *Ensis ensis*

Varigated scallops *Chlamys varia*

Warty venus *Venus verrucosa*

Thin tellin *Tellina tenuis*

Striped venus *Venus striatula*

Banded wedge shell *Donax vittatus* with hole bored by necklace shell

eggs of necklace shell

Necklace shell *Natica alderi*

The small hydrobia snails can be found in vast numbers on muddy shores and in estuaries. During the last 100 years one of the hydrobia family has even invaded rivers. To 6 mm.

Lugworms produce a string-like coil of wet sand which marks the back end of their U-shaped burrow. They obtain food like earthworms, by eating the muddy sand. A small pit can be seen at the mouth end of the burrow. To 15 cm.

Ragworms (their floppy appendages make them look like limp cloth) are important burrowing carnivores. They can also bite! They are dug up as angling bait. Over 6 cm.

are close to midday, so you will have to check the times for where you are going! Generally speaking, the September equinox is more rewarding, as the weather is usually better, all species are active in the warmer water and many species have bred during the summer so there are plenty of young stages to be seen.

The best sort of habitat to visit to see a good range of plants and animals is the sheltered rocky shore, preferably in the west or south-west of Britain, where marine life is most luxuriant and varied. This type of shore has more opportunities for static species to become attached, and more rock-pools to look at. Some rock types are better than others for forming rock-pools, and the soft ones, like chalk, usually erode too quickly to be well colonised. A rock-pool is a rather specialised place in which to live. It is not simply a temporary refuge for marine animals whilst the tide is out. A pool high up on the shore will, for example, be subject to many hours of possibly hot sunshine which will reduce the water volume and concentrate the salts; it will also warm the water considerably which increases the oxygen requirement of many of the residents, but at the same time decreases the amount of oxygen that the water can hold. Conversely, when it rains heavily, the salt content of the water will drop dramatically, almost to freshwater in very heavy rain, which many marine orgnisms cannot tolerate. At night, if the pool is exposed, the concentration of carbon dioxide gas rises considerably as the plants respire and this can also reach damaging levels. So, the rock-pool is not the easy option that it might appear to be, and it becomes obvious why larger pools are better (because these changes take place more slowly), and why pools further down the shore are better than those near the high water-mark. On exposed areas, the effects are not quite as serious, as waves will tend to keep topping up the pools, but on sheltered rocky shores the problems are acute.

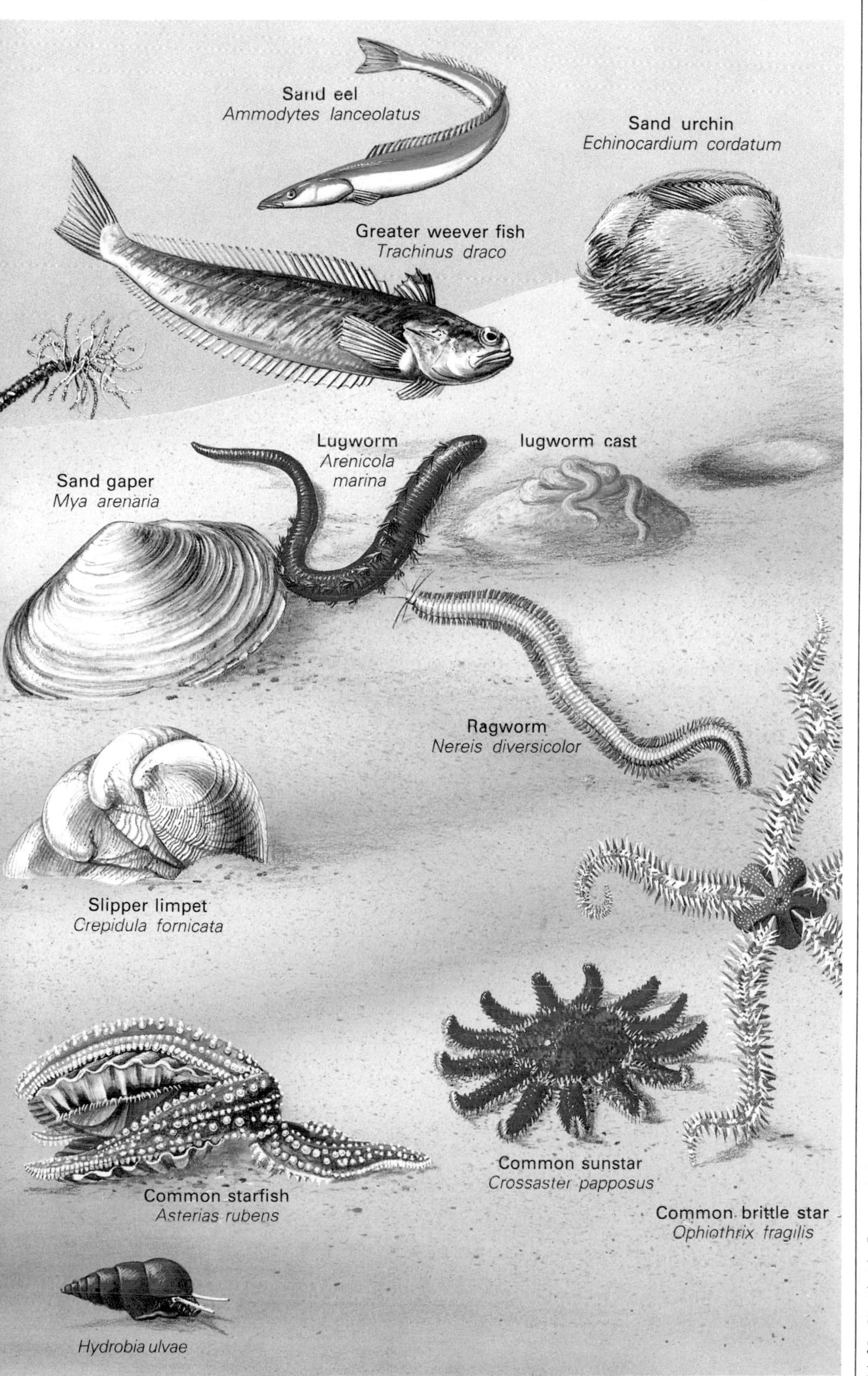

Once you have determined where to go and when to be there, you can start. The equipment needed for looking at rock-pools can be very limited. A good field-guide (see bibliography) is essential, a notebook is always useful and a net will help you to collect anything you cannot reach or idenitify because it is moving too fast. The weak children's-type nets are unsuitable, and you need something more sturdy, with several mesh sizes if you are serious. An enamel tray, or more conveniently and cheaply, some translucent margarine or ice-cream containers are ideal for observing creatures. Unless you really know what you are doing, it is unwise to try to take marine life home as it will almost certainly die. Nevertheless, there is plenty to be seen *in situ*, and a good field-guide should ensure that you can identify everything you find.

It is wise to take care when beachcombing. Try to find out the times of the tides and always keep an eye towards the shoreline. Above all make sure someone knows where you are going and when you are likely to return.

SPIDERS OF THE BRITISH ISLES

Spiders must be amongst the most feared and least understood examples of our native wildlife. Yet, they are totally harmless to man, and are beneficial in many ways. There are over 600 species of spiders in Britain, in a bewildering variety of colours and forms.

Spiders hardly have the best reputation amongst our native fauna, yet the fear and loathing that surrounds them is totally unjustified. They are harmless to man and, despite their highly carnivorous habits, it is exceedingly rare for a spider to bite a person. They occur commonly in virtually all habitats, though there is only one truly aquatic species.

One of the most familiar things about spiders is their webs, or cobwebs as they are called when attached to the ceiling! Most spiders build webs which act as traps for catching food. They come in all shapes and sizes, and obvious examples are the regular near-circular webs of the orb-web spiders, and the three-dimensional, tangled sheet-webs of the sheet-web spiders. Webs have different functions according to their structure and where they are built. Ones built as sheets close to the ground are generally designed to catch crawling insects by enmeshing them in their sticky threads, whilst ones hung from bushes are placed in insect 'flyways' and trap anything that flies into them. Some species build tiny webs close to the ground when they are young and small, thus catching smaller, more manageable prey, and then build successively larger webs as they grow, each one being placed higher in the vegetation to trap bigger prey items.

The silk for the webs is produced through little organs called spinners, and is extruded as a liquid from the silk glands, but rapidly solidifies when stretched out in the air. It is extraordinarily strong for its size and weight, and even quite heavy insects become totally entangled in it. The silk also acts as a lifeline for the spider, attached at one end and reeled out as it moves, or keeping the animal suspended if it drops from its perch.

It is fascinating to watch a spider as it quickly spins its web. Young spiders do not need to learn the ability from their parents, but are able to spin neat webs, often more perfectly constructed than those of the adults, straight away!

All sorts of insects are trapped in webs. A few, such as moths, have such scaly wings that they quickly slip out of the mesh leaving a few scales behind, whilst lacewings can twist into an upside-down position and slip out downwards, if they are quick enough, before the resident spider pounces. Bumble bees or wasps are usually too strong or aggressive, but almost everything else is caught. The spider, which may be in the middle of the web or just off it but touching a 'trip-wire', immediately senses the presence of a victim by the vibrations, and rushes over to inject a poison and wrap the prey up in silk. It

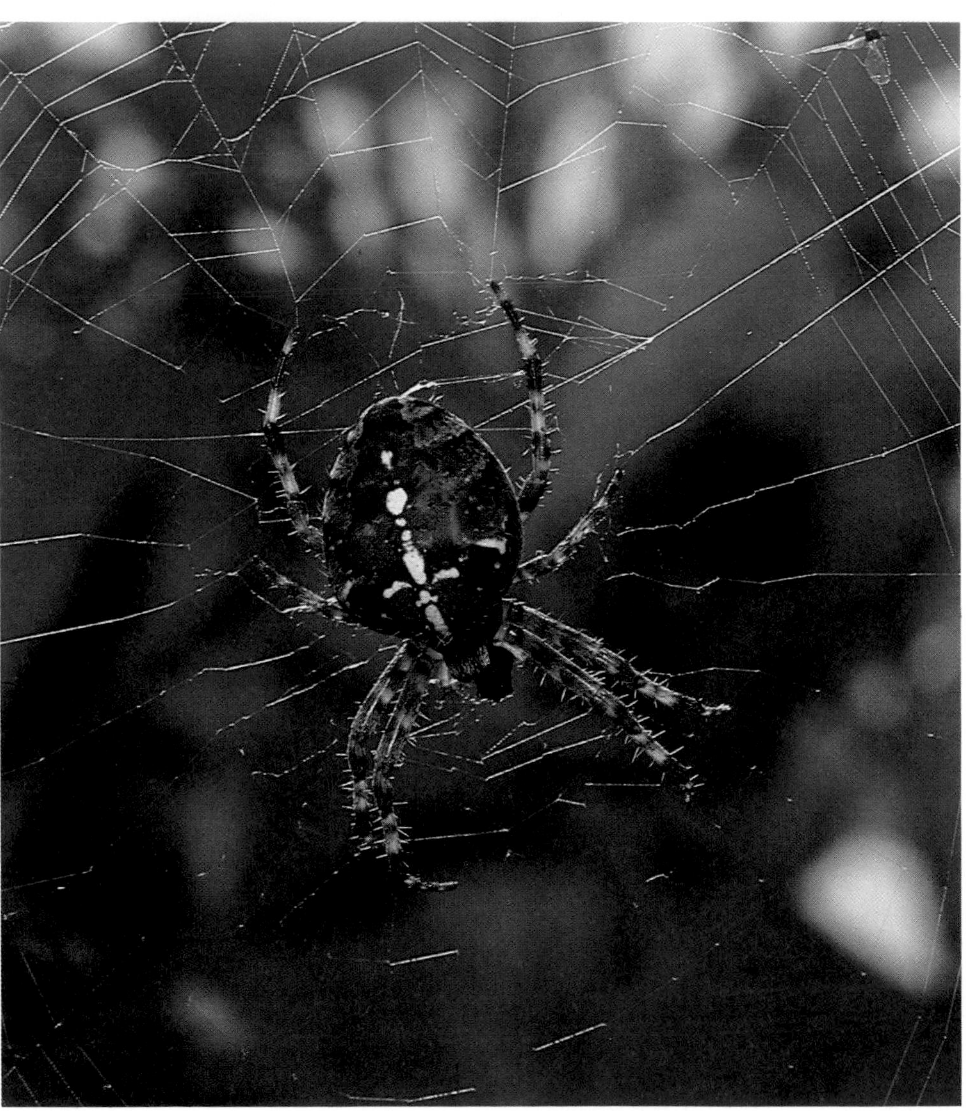

A garden spider waits at the centre of its web. An average orb web contains about 20 metres of silk which weighs less than 0.5 milligrams yet has over 1000 junctions

may be eaten straight away, or saved until later. Spiders have no internal digestive system, so they inject digestive juices into the prey and suck up the resulting, easily-ingested liquid.

Some spiders do not make webs at all but catch their prey by hunting. Such spiders include the wolf spiders and the spitting spider. The former stalk their prey and pounce on it, immobilising the victim with a poisoned bite; whilst the spitting spider sprays a jet of mixed glue and poison over its intended prey from a distance which sticks it to the ground. The extraordinary water spider uses its spinning abilities in a quite different way. It constructs an underwater diving bell from silk, which it provisions with bubbles of air and then lives in, periodically darting out underwater to catch prey. It returns to the home-base with any prey, eating it in the bubble of air. As the air supply begins to run out, it collects more by a series of trips up to the surface returning to its underwater home.

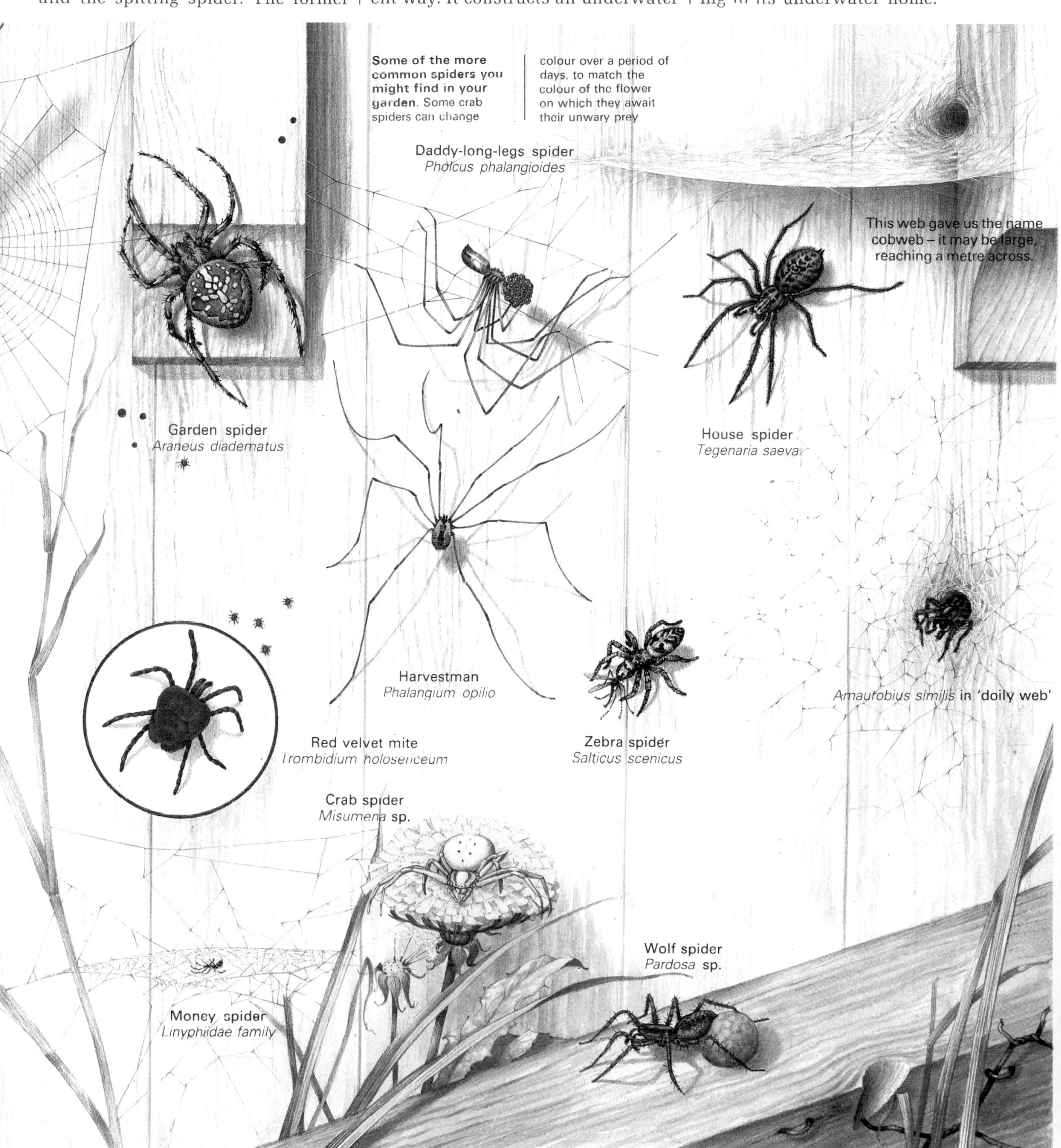

Some of the more common spiders you might find in your garden. Some crab spiders can change colour over a period of days, to match the colour of the flower on which they await their unwary prey

Life on the Ground

Hidden amongst the leaves, or deep in the grass, there is another world of life, that we rarely see or hear. Millipedes, centipedes, pseudoscorpions, springtails and all manner of other creatures live out their lives as predators, scavengers and herbivores almost unnoticed.

Besides insects and spiders, which we have already looked at in detail, there is a whole host of other invertebrates that live on the ground or in similar habitats. Their particular structure means that they dry out readily, so they tend to be confined to damp, shady, humid places, and are rarely seen out in the open.

Millipedes and centipedes are somewhat similar looking animals that are often confused, though in fact they are very different, and have quite separate lifestyles. Centipedes are highly active carnivorous species – they are the ones which disappear quickly when you lift a log or stone – and they have anything up to 100 pairs of legs, though the more common species have 15 to 20 pairs. They hunt down almost any form of animal prey within their size range, including slugs, insects and even other centipedes, which they capture and bite with their poisonous fangs. They are mainly active at night, and shun any light areas, living mostly in leaf-litter, under logs and stones or in the soil. Millipedes, in contrast, are slow-moving vegetarian creatures. They generally have smaller legs than centipedes, and there are two pairs on each segment, whereas centipedes only have one pair. They live in the same sorts of places as centipedes, but need rotting or live plant material as food, so tend to live deeper in the soil. Some species can cause considerable damage to crops and garden plants when present in large numbers, but most are harmless and simply help to break down the remains of plants and recycle the nutrients. A few millipedes construct little nests lined with silk produced from glands, in which they lay their eggs and rear the young. Species found in Britain include the pill-millipedes, which can roll into a ball when threatened, and these are sometimes confused with woodlice.

A number of spiders and spider-relatives live mainly on the ground. The little wolf spiders run about over the leaf-litter chasing their prey though they rarely catch very much. In early summer, the female lays eggs which she carries in a large white ball under her abdomen, and it is so conspicuous that it makes her look like a different species! When the young hatch, she continues to carry the spiderlings around for a while, all perched in a little pile on her back, with individuals gradually falling off as she runs about! The harvestmen are relatives of the spiders and look rather similar; they have eight legs, but only have a one-piece body, and do not possess poisonous fangs or the ability to produce webs. They move around on very long thin legs, scavenging and catching anything they can; like spiders, they are totally harmless to man. The pseudoscorpions are much smaller relatives of the spiders that also have eight legs, but are most notable for their greatly enlarged front 'claws', which give them their resemblance to true scorpions. Although these claws contain poison glands and are used to capture insect and mite prey, pseudoscorpions are also totally harmless – they are only about half a centimetre long!

Many insects occur in the soil or on the surface in their larval or pupal stages, but some spend their whole lives here. The springtails are primitive insects without wings that live in the ground or amongst leaf-litter and eat rotting material. The name springtail comes from the folded spring that they have at their rear end that is normally clipped under the body, but can be released causing the animal to jump suddenly and thus escape any predator. Another primi-

A banded snail on a pine trunk after a downpour of rain.

Snails like damp, cool conditions and are rarely seen in the open

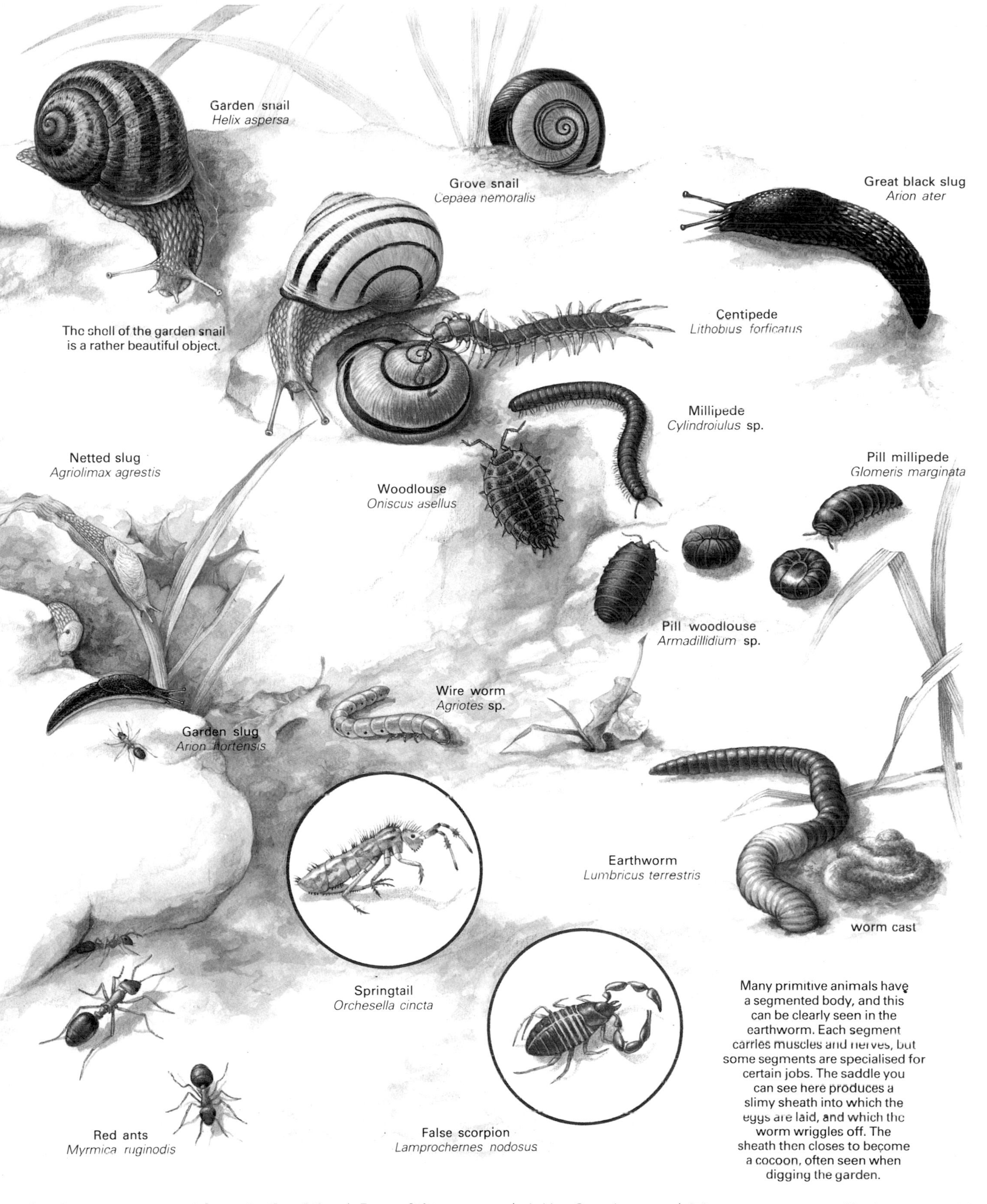

Many primitive animals have a segmented body, and this can be clearly seen in the earthworm. Each segment carries muscles and nerves, but some segments are specialised for certain jobs. The saddle you can see here produces a slimy sheath into which the eggs are laid, and which the worm wriggles off. The sheath then closes to become a cocoon, often seen when digging the garden.

tive insect group, with a similar lifestyle, is the two-pronged bristletails – like the springtails, these are very small and usually overlooked. Much more obvious members of the ground insect fauna are the ground beetles; these are a group of beetles that have taken to an active predatory life. If you lift a stone, you will often see a black or purplish beetle scurrying rapidly away, for they are very active and dislike the light. One of the commonest is the attractive violet ground beetle, which is two to three centimetres long and very noticeable (see page 137).

Some of the many creatures that live on the ground, with an indication of the way in which they use the habitat. Go and turn over a few stones in the garden and see what you find in amongst the leaf litter and soil

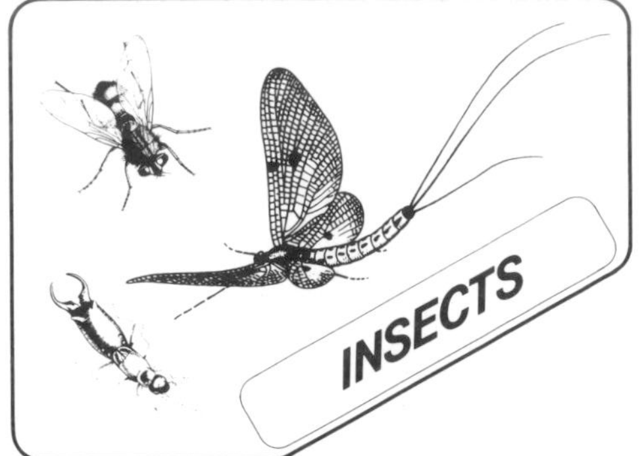

LOOKING AT INSECTS

With over 20,000 species of insects in Britain, there is no shortage of subjects for study, and it is amazing how little is known about even the more common varieties. Their huge range of life-cycles and fascinating behaviour make insects an ideal group to investigate.

For a long time, all studies of insects tended to concentrate on identification and classification – taxonomy, as it is called – and the ecology and habits were left largely unexplored. With our native wildlife under so much pressure – and insects are affected just as any other group – it has become necessary to manage areas for the survival of particular species, or groups of species, and this has revealed enormous gaps in our knowledge of what insects do and what they need. Where does that butterfly go to pupate? Why are certain butterflies absent even though their foodplants are plentiful? How long does this species live for? What really pollinates that rare orchid? There are so many questions and so many interesting lines of observation, that the difficulty lies more in where to start than what to do!

An obvious starting point lies in getting to know insects' life-cycles and how to identify them. There is no one who can recognise all the British species, so initially it is a question of learning the main characteristics of each group, such as beetles, dragonflies and butterflies, and then teaching yourself to distinguish the commoner species from the groups that interest you. Most people find the larger, more obvious ones such as butterflies or dragonflies the most rewarding; but others find the challenge of the more difficult groups irresistible and the attraction of being an almost instant expert cannot be ignored. It helps to join a suitable society with an interest in field entomology, and to go to evening classes or join residential courses, as well as obtaining suitable books. You will need a good net to catch insects and something to put them in, preferably a clear plastic container that you can easily see into. For all the groups of larger insects, there is no need to kill specimens, because they can be identified by close scrutiny while still alive. If you become interested in the more difficult groups with numerous species, such as the ichneumons or the beetles, then you will inevitably need to kill examples to identify later, often using a microscope or lens, the specimen can then be kept as a reference.

Once you have become familiar with the range of insects, you will begin to realise some of the possibilities and notice some of those 'unknown' entries in books. You can begin by filling in a few gaps in the known distribution of some species. Whilst the distribution of butterflies may be well documented (at least, in the lowlands), information on even such obvious groups as dragonflies is still very poor. In the last few years, a great deal of effort has been put into studying the distribution of dragonflies and damselflies, and numerous hitherto unknown sites have been discovered simply because people began to look harder. For less common groups such as moths, grasshoppers and crickets or hoverflies – all of which are covered by good identification books – the possibilites for new discoveries are much greater.

A very pleasant activity involves watching insects visiting flowers. As already mentioned under 'flower-watching', there is much still to be discovered about which insects pollinate which flowers, especially at night, and anyone who is able to identify both these groups will find plenty to do. It is also interesting to watch the 'pecking-order' that develops on a popular nectar flower, such as hogweed or angelica, when a number of insects are visiting. Some insects are quite aggressive and will drive away other species, whilst others keep feeding regardless. You can start by noting down the insects that are driven off and which was the victor. You can then gradually work out a form of hierarchy, with the most aggressive insects at the top. Little is known about this, but you can be

fairly sure that, like blue tits driving off starlings from the bird-table, you will be in for a few surprises! It is also worth compiling a total list of all the insects that visit a particular flower, and trying to see whether they are sucking nectar, eating pollen or whatever. You could also look at a range of different flowers and list the insects visiting them, and work out which ones are best overall – this can be done readily in the garden, too, using cultivated flowers and any weeds that you may have. Or you could watch one species of insect, such as honey-bees or a butterfly, and count the number of different flowers it visits and which it seems to prefer.

There is much to be discovered about insect behaviour, too. They are easier to watch than birds, as you can often get closer to them, but a pair of binoculars that can be focused on near objects will still be useful. Dragonflies exhibit a form of territorial behaviour, with males establishing and defending particular areas, but do other insects do this? Do any insects warn each other of the presence of predators? Some insects are known to have pre-breeding courtship behaviour, but what about the smaller insects? Do they do the same, and if so, what form does it take?

If you begin by looking closely at the insects in your garden or somewhere that you can visit regularly, it is amazing what you can discover; much of it will be unknown or may even contradict established information.

One of the best ways to learn about insects is to photograph them. Here, the photographer is taking a picture of a small tortoiseshell butterfly with a complicated flashgun arrangement

GARDENING FOR WILDLIFE

There are over 750,000 hectares of private gardens in Britain, more than all the formal nature reserves put together. If these were all managed with animals and plants in mind, it would make the most marvellous bonus for our hard-pressed wildlife!

Not all forms of wildlife can occur in gardens, because many are simply too demanding in the type or size of habitat that they require. Nevertheless, if you ignore golden eagles, wildcats and Adonis blue butterflies, there is still an enormous range of plants and animals that can live in, or benefit from, a garden managed for wildlife; and they can be wonderful places for the human residents as well as the animal visitors.

Gardening for wildlife docs not necessarily mean leaving the area to go totally wild, nor do you have to stop growing fruit, vegetables and flowers. It is more a way of looking at the garden, and changing your practices and layout to help wildlife to co-exist with your activities and the cultivated plants. There are many sorts of levels at which it can be attempted, from just leaving a wild corner to having a whole nature reserve around the house.

Gardens are not natural situations but with a little thought they can be managed to provide supplementary habitat for wildlife. If we look first at insects, which are not only attractive in themselves but will also help to attract many birds and mammals, we can build up a picture of what is required. Insects, including butterflies, like the shelter and warmth that a garden provides, and if your garden is exposed, it can be immediately improved by putting up fencing or, better still, planting a hedge. Most insects need particular larval food-plants. Some groups will simply benefit by there being a wide range of plants in the garden, and these should include as many native plants as possible; for example the native birches or rowans make lovely small trees, whilst hawthorn, guelder rose, spindle, crab-apple, privet and many others are most attractive shrubs that will all support an enormous range of wild, harmless and beneficial insects.

A well-established garden pond, designed and planted with wildlife in mind. There is a tremendous variety of plants around the edge or emerging from the water, and plenty of floating plants to provide cover and food for fish, amphibia and invertebrates. This particular pond is in a garden in Shropshire

To encourage breeding butterflies, you will need the specific food-plants of the ones most likely to occur. The easiest to attract are the Vanessids – red admirals, tortoiseshells, peacocks – because four out of five of the species lay their eggs on stinging nettles. This may not be the most attractive of flowers but, if you leave some to grow in a reasonably sunny corner of the garden, you may establish a breeding colony of at least one of these lovely butterflies. Similarly, a good holly tree and some ivy will soon be found by the beautiful little holly blue butterfly which is a welcome addition to any garden.

Insects, especially butterflies, also require a range of nectar-bearing flowers. These need not be native plants, and many of the familiar and attractive garden plants are excellent. Try to have a range of flowers that will provide nectar right through from spring to autumn; primroses make a good start in spring, whilst such plants as rosemary, buddleia (the deservedly famous butterfly bush), ice-plants and cotoneasters will all be welcome; attractive wild plants like hemp agrimony or angelica are excellent for a wide variety of insects. Fruits are good, too, and the more apples, pears and crab-apples you have, the better. To broaden the range of insects that you attract, you can also try such practices as leaving piles of rotting logs or cut tree stumps, keeping a couple of compost heaps, not weeding all the garden too assiduously, and generally avoiding too many areas of bare ground by planting creeping plants. Try minimising or even abandoning the use of insecticide sprays to help maintain the lacewings, ladybirds and other insects that all eat aphids; and why not allow a few other flowers like daisies and speedwells to come into the lawn? All these devices will help to diversify the fauna to include stag beetles, ground bees, bumble bees, ground beetles, hoverflies and so many more. They all help to keep the pest numbers down, and will themselves provide food for birds.

Birds and mammals can be attracted easily by putting food out, and a garden that is managed as described, to produce more insects and more fruit, will inevitably attract more birds and mammals; tits will feed on the caterpillars, spotted flycatchers will catch flying insects, hedgehogs love slugs, and goldfinches may visit your teasel and thistle heads if you leave them to seed! You can put up artificial bird and bat boxes, but do not forget the natural homes in bushes, mature trees, rough vegetation, earth banks, open outbuildings and so on.

Finally, a pond will attract and keep a wonderful range of extra species. Even a small one, if carefully planned and with a little rough vegetation around it, will attract birds to drink and feed, many insects such as dragonflies to breed and resident frogs, newts or toads are a possibility. Choose the range of plants for your pond carefully with lilies and other floating plants, a good array of surrounding plants and where possible reeds. For more ideas and details, look at the books mentioned in the bibliography.

Although you would be unlikely to have a garden that looked like this. Illustrated here are many of the species that you could expect to see, at some time or other, in your own garden

An Introduction to

Fish, Amphibians & Reptiles

Although there are over 50 different species of fish in freshwater and many more in the seas around our coasts, most people know very little about fish, other than that you can eat them and numerous people set out to catch them! But there is much more to fishes than that!

If you include the waters of the sea around the coast down to a depth of 100 metres, we have about 235 different species of fish in British waters, of which some 55 occur in freshwater. Fish are all vertebrates – that is they have a backbone of some sort, though in several groups, this is made of cartilage rather than bone. To give an indication of just how varied fish are in form, there are four different classes of fish, whilst the whole of the world's mammal and bird faunas each fit into only one class. All fish live in water, and are highly adapted to aquatic life, though some of the freshwater species are temporarily able to leave water.

The four classes of fish are the lampreys, hagfish, bony fish and those fish which have jaws but no bones. The lampreys and hagfishes have neither jaws nor bones. They have very little in the way of a skeleton except for a thin cartilaginous 'backbone', and their mouths are usually just a sucking disc or a slit. There are three species of lamprey in British waters, and just one hagfish.

The fish which have bony cartilage, rather than bones, but do have jaws (very noticeably so, in some cases) include amongst their number the sharks, rays, skates and rat-fish which are all widespread marine fish. By far the largest group, both for Britain and in world terms, is the bony fish. About 200 of our total fish fauna fits into this group, and it includes virtually all the familiar fish like trout, salmon, pike, perch, carp and the eels. All the freshwater fish, with the exception of the freshwater lampreys, fall into this group.

The variety of forms and life histories amongst the British fish is immense, as the following pages show.

Also covered in this section are the amphibians and reptiles. There are only eight species of amphibians found in Britain and even fewer – only six – species of reptiles.

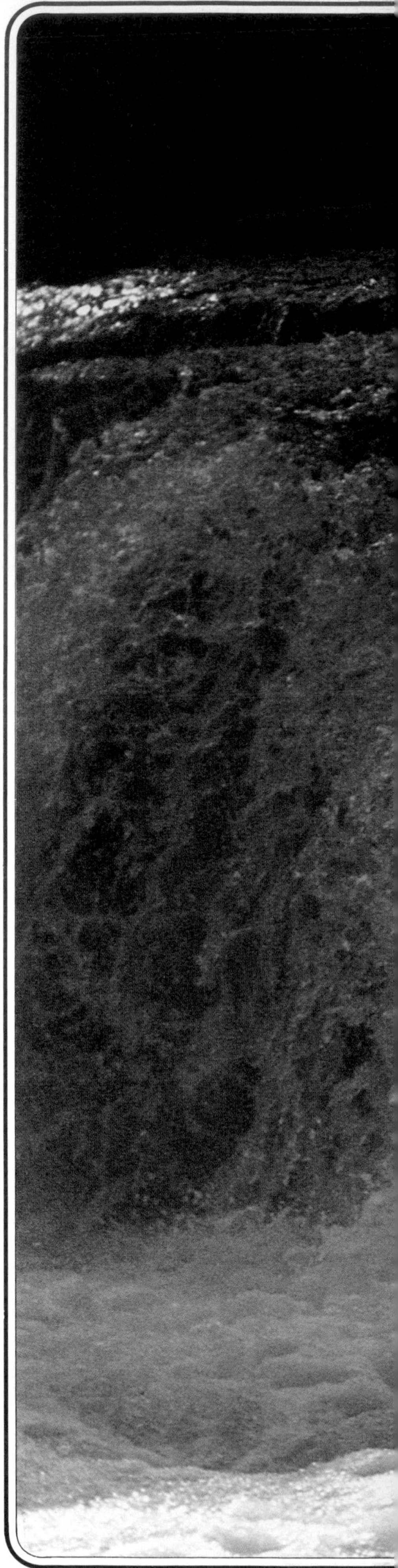

An Atlantic salmon negotiating a crashing waterfall on its way upstream to its spawning grounds

FISHES AND AMPHIBIANS

INCLUDING: Fish in Rivers • Fish in Lakes and Ponds • Fish Around our Coasts • Sharks, Rays and Dogfishes • The Life of the Salmon • British Reptiles • British Amphibians : Frogs and Toads • How to go Pond dipping • British Newts • •

FISH IN RIVERS

Of all the British fish, those that occur in our rivers must be the most familiar and exciting; to see salmon jumping up a waterfall, a shoal of brown trout in a clear stream or to hear the snap of a pike's jaws are amongst the most evocative experiences for the naturalist.

Rivers are excellent habitats for fish, and most of our freshwater species occur in them at some time or other. One of the reasons for this is that rivers vary considerably in where they arise and the land they flow through, but they also divide into a number of sections with different ecological characteristics, each with their own particular fish species.

In the upper sections of rivers, especially where they arise in hill or mountain areas, the waters are clear, cool, fast-flowing and well-oxygenated, and the base is usually stony or gravelly. This is the region where trout are particularly common and indeed it is sometimes known as the trout zone; other fish such as minnows, dace and grayling also occur. Because of the currents, which may be very strong in places, only the most athletic of fishes are present, and there is a tendency for the young or smaller species to occur in calm stretches or amongst sheltering rocks. The gravelly stretches are also the areas where the salmon spawn, cutting themselves spawning sites in mid-winter.

In the middle reaches of a river, the current is somewhat slower, and there are more calm stretches. The base is a mixture of rocky and gravelly areas, and silt or sand where the current slows, such as on the inside of a bend. The water is reasonably warm, usually averaging about 15° centigrade, and there is generally more weed growth than higher up, which gives more cover and food for fish. Naturally, this section shares fish with both the upper and the lower stretches, but the relative abundance of species changes. Common middle-river fish include dace, barbel, chub, perch and pike, with gudgeon in deeper pools on the river-bed. The pike and perch prefer calmer stretches within this zone, whilst along the many shallower stretches you will find sticklebacks, minnows and stone loaches.

A traditional angler's hut in the Test valley, Hampshire. The chalk stream rivers, of which the Test is one of the best-known examples, are famous for their excellent trout fishing, though they also have wild populations of pike, grayling and many other fish

The lowest freshwater reaches are familiar to everyone, and most towns tend to occur here. The water is slow-moving, usually cloudy and generally quite warm, up to about 20° centigrade in summer. There is a reasonable amount of weed growth, but oxygen levels tend to be lower than further up stream, and may be almost lacking at the bottom of the river. Overhanging trees are frequent, and the rivers tend to pass through intensively-used agricultural land, which contributes considerably to their silt and chemical load. Typical fish of these stretches include bream, roach, the bleak, often feeding at or near the surface on drowning insects, and the pike is still present here.

Towards the mouth of the river, where the estuary forms, the river becomes affected by the variable influence of salty tidal water, and fish which live here have to tolerate the physiological changes that this brings about. There tends to be a mixture of inshore fish and lower reach fish, though there are some estuary specialists, too. The flounder and the smelt are typical estuary species, though they may not spend all their time there, whilst many migratory species such as sea-trout, salmon and eels pass through this stretch.

All these natural changes are complicated nowadays by the effects of man. Most rivers are managed for fishing of one sort or another, and they may also be used for other purposes such as water supply, flood alleviation or navigation, all of which affect the fish populations. Rivers managed for fly-fishing tend to have high numbers of fish but of rather few species, while rivers, such as the Hampshire Avon, by virtue of their less concentrated management for coarse fishing have a richer variety of species. The plates show river and still water fish together; turn the page for further illustrations of both types.

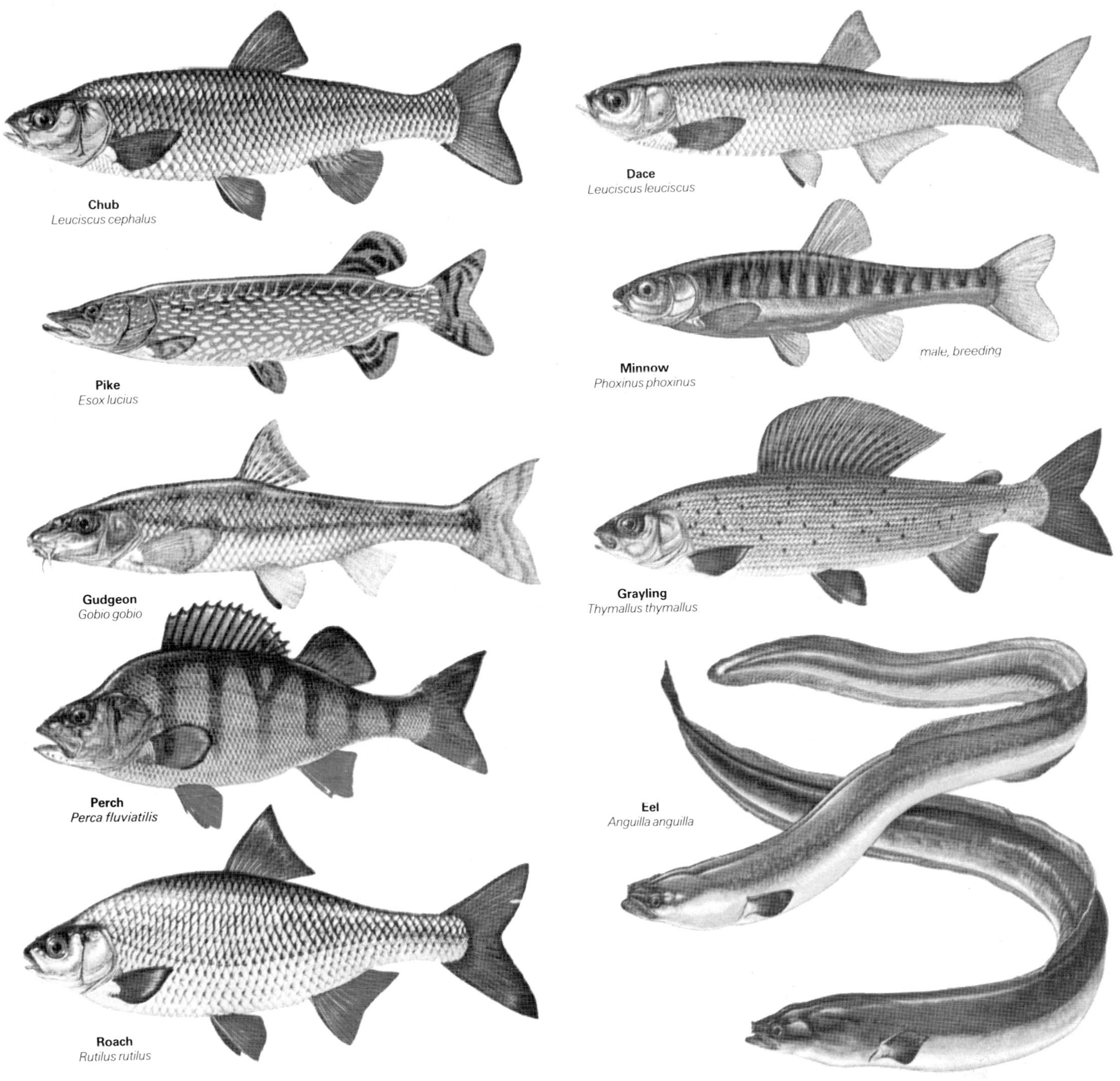

Chub
Leuciscus cephalus

Dace
Leuciscus leuciscus

Pike
Esox lucius

Minnow
Phoxinus phoxinus

Gudgeon
Gobio gobio

Grayling
Thymallus thymallus

Perch
Perca fluviatilis

Eel
Anguilla anguilla

Roach
Rutilus rutilus

Unless you are an angler, you are unlikely to be familiar with more than one or two of the fish that can be found in our rivers. Yet the variety is considerable and fascinating

FISH IN LAKES AND PONDS

Although lakes and ponds share many fish in common with rivers, they have their own special fish too which are found only in still waters. For example, the mysterious char or the bizarre bitterling which lays its eggs into mussels.

The great variety of freshwater fish of both rivers and still waters is shown in the plates, and many fish occur in both types of habitat. Some have fascinating natural histories, like the char of our upland lakes.

Char are members of the trout family, and it is believed that they used to be migratory, like their relatives, but became trapped after the last Ice Age in a series of upland lakes. In fact, migratory char still occur in Scandinavia, but in Britain we have hundreds of separate isolated populations in hill lakes in north Wales, western Ireland, the highlands of Scotland and a few of the Scottish islands. Although rarely seen, it is one of the most colourful of fish and the males, in particular, in the breeding season are very bright with an intense red belly. Because the char became isolated in many different lakes, with various characteristics of acidity, nutrients and food supply, they evolved in a variety of ways, and at one time some 15 different subspecies or races were recognised. Now, it is generally considered that the differences are not sufficiently marked to warrant separate names, though they may become so one day as evolution continues to make them more distinct. Few char reach any great size in mountain lakes, because of the poor food supply; in other parts of the world where they migrate and have ample food available to them, they may reach lengths of a metre or more, but in Britain they rarely exceed 30 centimetres and a kilo or two in weight.

Char spawning behaviour tends to fall into one of two groups; some spawn in winter, in November or December, whilst others breed in spring. Most lakes contain either one population or the other, though a few have some of each. They usually spawn at about eight years old, but this depends on the food supply and their rate of growth; in a more nutrient-rich lake like Windermere in the Lake District, for example, they breed at about five years old, whilst in poor upland lakes they reach 12 or more years old before spawning. Sadly, the isolated populations of char are under threat, and they have disappeared from several lakes that once contained distinct populations.

Freshwater fish have some strange adaptations to aquatic life. A fish that is not actually native, but is now well established in many ponds and lakes, is the bitterling. It is a small inconspicuous silvery member of the carp family, but the odd fact about it is its method of egg-laying. The female bitterling depends on the presence of the large freshwater swan mussel for its survival. When the female is ready to lay eggs in spring, she develops a long tube, which she will use to insert the eggs inside the gills of a mussel; but before she can do this, she has to find a suitable mussel and condition it to her presence to make sure that it does not snap its shell shut on her

A stone loach in clean unpolluted water in the Isle of Wight. The loaches are mainly nocturnal creatures, spending the day hiding amongst stones or weeds, emerging at night to feed on aquatic crustaceans and other invertebrates. They have six long barbels round their mouths

ovipositor when she starts to lay. So, she gently nudges the mussel regularly with her snout, until there is no longer any reaction to her, then she inserts the egg tube. After the first few eggs are laid, the male bitterling appears and ejects a quantity of sperm by the mussel, which will be taken into the gills and fertilise the eggs. Several mussel shells will be used before the female has finished laying.

The eggs of the bitterling are relatively large, and they sit in the gills of the mussel until hatching, where the young fish remain for a few days until their own food supply has been exhausted, then they leave. They are not parasitic on the mussel at all, but they gain shelter, a continuous supply of oxygen-rich water, protection from predators and the advantage that the mussel will move if conditions become locally unsuitable, and will close its shell if the water body becomes dry. The system obviously works well because the bitterling lays far fewer eggs than most fish – a sure sign of successful survival. The only possible disadvantage is that the mussels themselves have minute parasitic larvae, the glochidium, and close association increases the chances of the bitterlings picking some up. But they are not a serious problem to the fish and they rarely do any harm to them since they really only serve to disperse the mussels, so this seems to be a good mutually beneficial relationship between two aquatic animals.

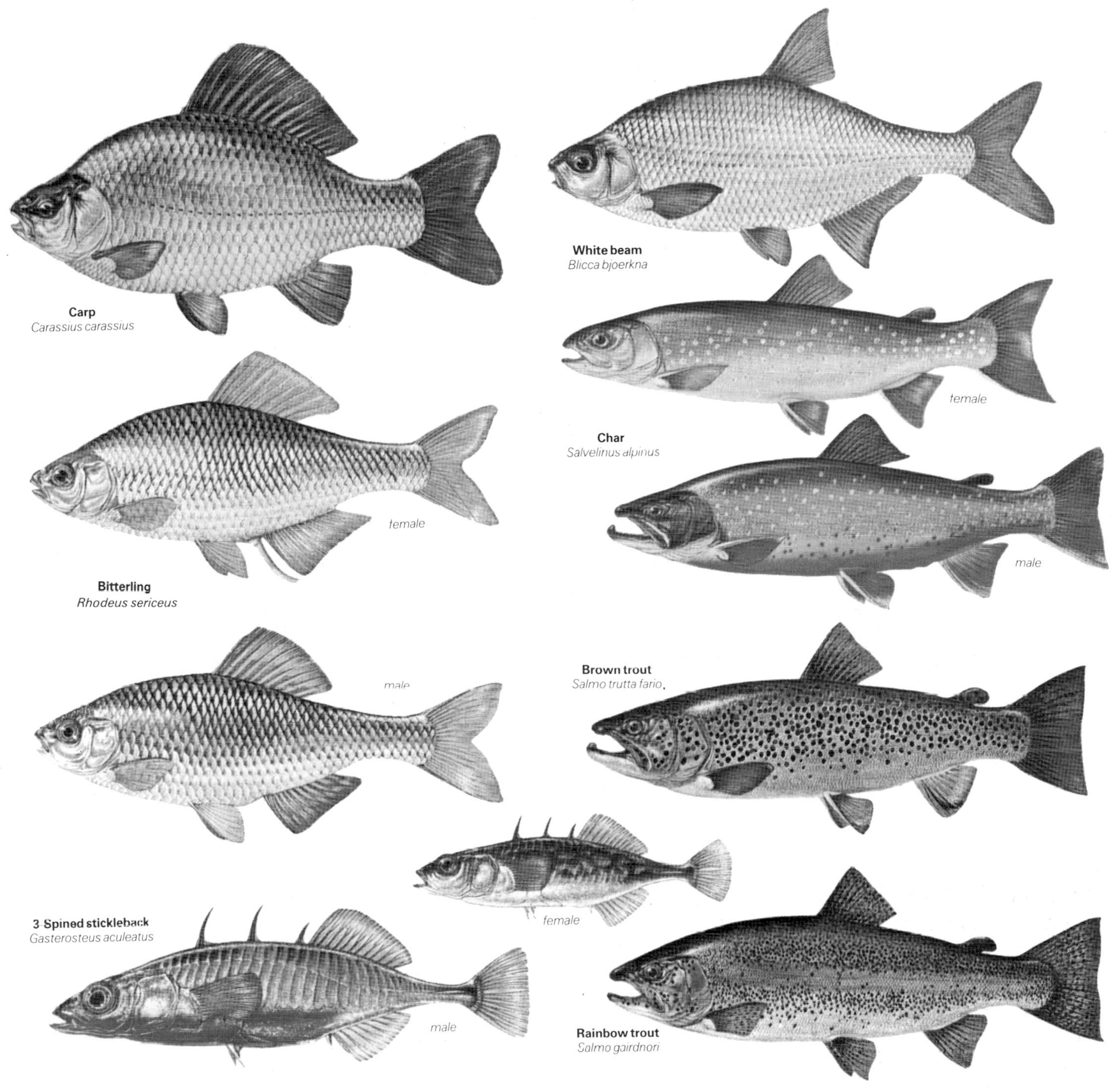

Our lake and river fish tend to be something of a mixture of native and introduced ones, thanks to a long history of man bringing in foreign edible or sporting fish. The picture shows a selection of those fish you are most likely to find

FISH AROUND THE COAST

Besides the more familiar sea-fish that are caught for food around our coasts, such as herring and mackerel, there are a tremendous number of other species of all sorts of shapes and sizes ranging from little gobies and blennies to the huge basking shark.

There are about 50 different species of fish that are caught commercially around our coasts, and many more than this that are inedible or not considered for food. Some are resident all the year round, whilst others move northwards from warmer waters during the summer, and are found around our southern and western coasts.

Amongst the familiar commercially-caught fish are the mackerel, herring, pilchard and cod. The mackerel is an abundant fish, especially in the North Sea and English Channel, but like most commercial species it has suffered from over-fishing and has declined considerably. During the year the fish move and change their feeding habits considerably. In autumn, they begin to descend from the surface to the sea-bed where they remain until January, often in dense concentrations. At this time of year, food is usually in short supply, and this is probably the time of highest natural mortality for this species. After January, the fish begin to move towards the surface and start to head for the spawning grounds, which for most British mackerel means a trip to the Celtic Sea, to the south of Ireland, on the edge of the deep ocean water. After spawning, they move back to coastal waters in shoals, where they feed hungrily on the increasing populations of zooplankton. It is during this period that they are most likely to be fished for, and caught in huge numbers. In midsummer, their behaviour changes again, and they begin to split up into smaller groups, feeding on young fish or smaller species. In October, they again gather to head for deep water.

The cod is the most important of the British commercial fish, supporting a multi-million pound industry. It is primarily a northern species, extending well up into the Arctic, and occurs throughout British waters. In March and April, the North Sea cod collect together in shoals to spawn in deep

The spotted goby, seen here in a shallow rock pool on the Dorset coast, is one of a number of gobies and related fish that occur in rock pools or shallow waters just offshore. They are invariably well-camouflaged and difficult to see, until they move

water, mainly off East Scotland. The eggs float to the surface, where they become part of the zooplankton, and when the young fry emerge, they remain planktonic for a while, feeding on other minute creatures. At about

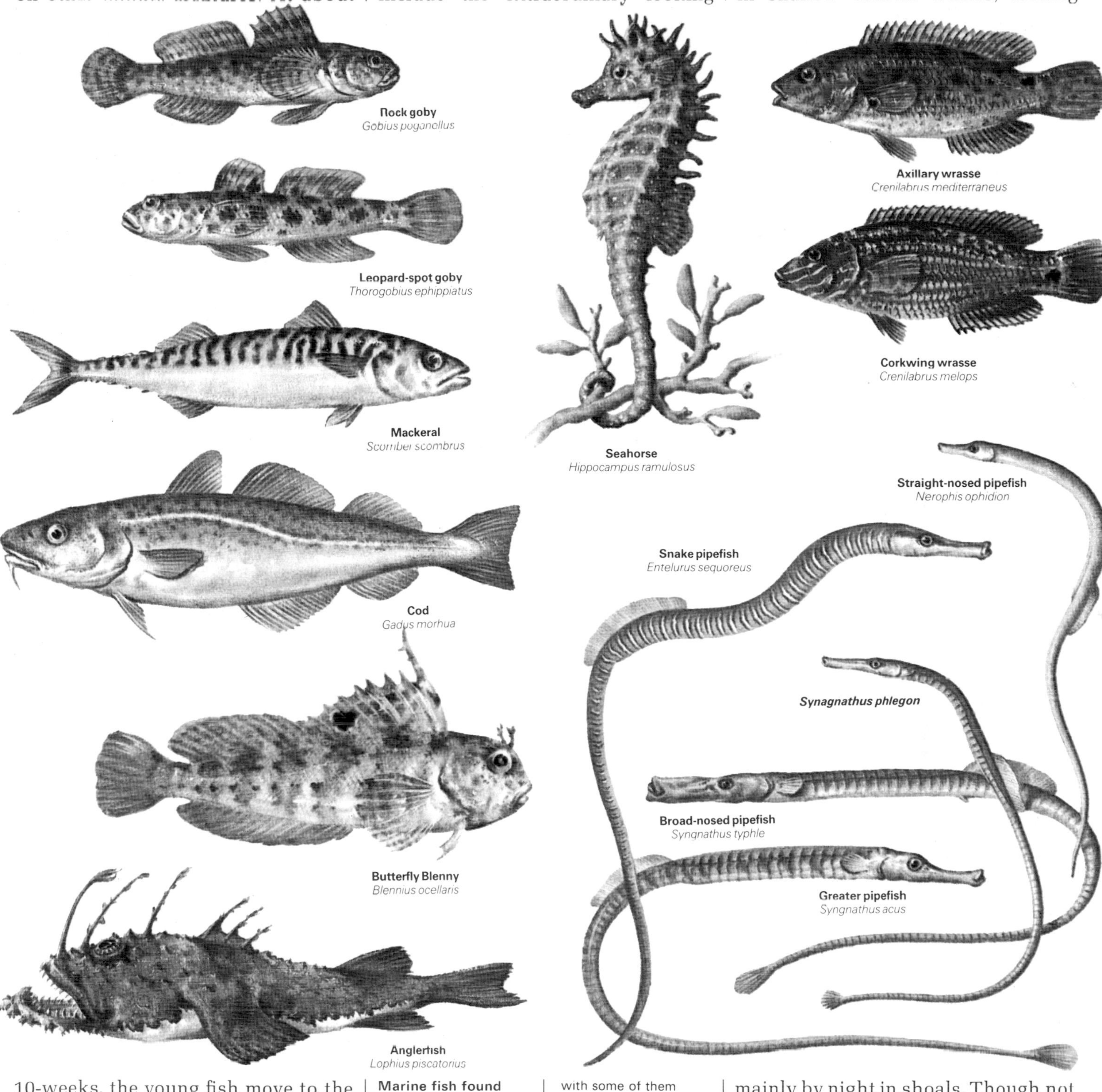

10-weeks, the young fish move to the sea-bed where their diet changes to bigger invertebrates, particularly small crustacea. As they grow, they feed on larger and larger organisms, both on the bottom and in mid-water, and when fully-grown they include a wide range of other fish in their diet, for they become sizeable animals when mature.

Most of the non-commercial fish species are unfamiliar to most people, both in appearance and name, though the emergence of marine aquaria as a tourist attraction has shown some of them to a much wider public. They include the extraordinary looking elongated pipefish, the angler fish, the attractive and aptly named sea-horses, gobies, blennies, Wrasses, clingfish and many others. Sand-eels are small fish that occur abundantly in shallow coastal waters, feeding mainly by night in shoals. Though not of economic significance directly, they are the food of many commercial fish, and they are taken in large quantities by many coastal birds such as terns and puffins. It is a familiar sight to see a puffin standing on the clifftop possibly near its nest with several sand-eels arranged crosswise in its beak, and their importance to these bird populations is enormous.

Marine fish found around Britain's coasts, especially those that spend most of their time in deeper water, are a bizarre collection, with some of them bearing little resemblance to the traditional idea of a fish. The picture illustrates a small selection of these

SHARKS, RAYS AND DOGFISH

The thresher, porbeagle, and the starry smooth-hound are all types of sharks to be found in British waters, just three of the 20 or so species that occur around our coasts. Together with the rays and skates, they make up the group of fish without bones.

One of the main groups of fish to be found in the sea is the cartilaginous fish (those without bones) which have jaws; these are the sharks (which include dogfish) rays and skates. They make up a fascinating group, and as far as our species go, they belie their reputation for viciousness and aggression. In fact, a few, such as the basking shark, are even plankton-feeders. This huge shark grows to about 12 metres long, and is the second largest of the world's sharks, occurring as a summer visitor to the north and west coasts of Britain. The rest are highly predatory, and closely adapted to this way of life, but despite this the species around our coasts are all harmless to man.

Many of the sharks have an interesting reproductive feature in that they retain their fertilised eggs within the body, and the young are born live; in some species, such as the spiny dogfish, the gestation period is up to two years, longer than any terrestrial mammal. This clearly has advantages to the sharks as the young are born with a good chance of looking after themselves, though it limits the number that the mother is able to carry to about 12, in contrast to the hundreds of thousands of eggs laid by many species of fish. The problem is made worse when populations are fished, because the gestation period of over a year means that there can be no effective 'close season', and a proportion of pregnant females will always occur in any catch, thus reducing the population's capacity to withstand exploitation. Some of the dogfishes, which are really just small bottom-living sharks, lay their eggs in shallow water, protected by a hard horny egg-case.

Sharks are amongst the most perfectly adapted of all fish to swimming. They are able to swim all their life

The lesser-spotted dogfish, rough hound or rock salmon is found on sandy or muddy shores from shallow water down to 100 m or more. It may reach over 70 cm when adult

without fatigue, as well as being able to move very fast when the need arises. They have an enormous oil-filled liver, which serves the same purpose as a swim-bladder, and are effectively almost weightless in water. This makes them elegant and effortless swimmers. British sharks include species with fascinating names such as the porbeagle, the starry smooth-hound, the tope, the thresher and the spurdog.

The skates and rays are in the same group, though superficially they look very different. They share the same cartilaginous skeleton and the same carnivorous habit as most sharks, but are a very different shape. They are strongly flattened, and from above appear diamond-shaped with a long tail. They swim by undulating through the water, though they spend much of their time near the bottom. Most of them are caught, at least occasionally, and the wings, or pectoral fins, are eaten. Electric rays have part of their pectoral fins modified to produce electricity, up to a remarkable 220 volts, fortunately they are rare in British waters. Sting rays have a long whip-like tail with a strongly poisonous spine on the end, whilst commoner species include the pale ray and the thornback ray. The skate is actually a type of ray, which is more diamond-shaped than most. Rays like some dogfish lay eggs encased in a horny capsule which are washed up on the strandline and are known to beach-combers as 'mermaid's purses'.

Although sharks and rays tend to be most often thought of as exotic fish of warmer waters, there is a considerable variety to be found in the coastal waters of Britain

THE LIFE OF THE SALMON

Just off the coast of Greenland, there is an area where all the north Atlantic salmon gather to feed. The migration of salmon, from their hatching places in British rivers, across the north Atlantic and back again, is one of the most extraordinary events in natural history.

Each autumn, in the high, clear gravelly stretches of our less polluted rivers, exhausted salmon begin to breed. In early November, the female salmon begins to cut exploratory depressions in the gravel to see if they will make suitable nests for her eggs, using her tail and the strength of her body to dislodge the stones. When she has made a nest that is to her liking, she crouches in the depression, or 'redd' as it if often called, and lays her eggs. The male salmon, who is in close attendance keeping away rivals and intruders, sheds his sperm or milt over the eggs before the female covers them with gravel and moves upstream to excavate another redd. This is the start of an extraordinary life-cycle.

The exertions of reaching the spawning grounds may often prove fatal for the salmon, especially the female, as they become particularly susceptible to predation and disease, though many also return to the sea and come back the following year for another spawning. The eggs that are left behind lie under the gravel, perhaps 15 centimetres or more deep, washed by cool well-oxygenated water, until the following spring, though development takes place within them during this period. In March or April, the young salmon or alevins, break out of the eggs to begin their free-swimming life. At this stage they hardly look like fishes at all, with their large yolk-sacs suspended beneath them. Whilst they have these food reserves, they do not need to feed, but within a few weeks, they have exhausted the supply, and begin to look more like young salmon. They are then called 'fry' for the first year of their life, after which they become 'parr'. At some stage after this, usually in spring when the parr have become 10 or more centimetres long, they start to change colour, becoming more silvery and losing the distinctive grey marks along the side. This precedes a downstream migration by the young salmon, now called a 'smolt', which makes its way to the river's estuary, where it may feed for a while, fattening up and growing accustomed to salt water. In the estuary and the open sea, the young salmon feeds voraciously, growing more in a few months than it did in the period of years spent in the river of its birth.

For a long time it was a mystery where the majority of adult salmon fed in the sea, but the major feeding grounds are now known to be south of Greenland. When they are ready, the now mature salmon leave this area and begin to return towards the country of their origin, using currents, and perhaps the stars, to help them navigate, though much remains to be discovered about this migration. As they near the coast of their 'native' land, it is believed that they can detect their river of origin by scent, possibly responding to minute amounts of hormones, pheromones, exuded by their brethren in the river. Whatever the

The salmon goes through various stages, each with its special name, before reaching adulthood. The eggs are laid upstream where they hatch, move down stream to become a 'parr' and then out into the open sea

means, the regular return of salmon to the river where they were spawned is one of the most remarkable events in nature, and there is still a great deal to be learnt about the story.

colours, and the male becomes red and mottled, with an enlarged head and hooked lower jaw, whilst the female becomes dark brown or purple. They gradually make their way upstream towards the spawning grounds, and the sight of salmon negotiating waterfalls and rapids on their way to the upper reaches is a familiar and magnificent spectacle.

The eggs and hatchlings of the salmon. The eggs are laid at the headwaters of the stream in the middle of winter. As they grow they move down the river developing all the time until they emerge at the sea

Salmon return to the rivers at various times of year, after spending one year or more at the feeding grounds, though spawning always takes place in the autumn. After the salmon have been in the fresh river water for a month or so, they lose their silvery

As the female swells with eggs, she becomes less able to negotiate obstacles, so she needs to arrive in the spawning area before she is too swollen, and it is little wonder that they are exhausted by the time spawning is over and many die.

BRITISH REPTILES

Many people are surprised to learn that there are six British reptiles, three snakes and three lizards. They are a most attractive group of animals with some fascinating lifestyles.

Reptiles are vertebrates, like mammals and birds, as they have backbones, but they differ in a number of ways including the fact that they are cold-blooded and have no fur or feathers. Being cold-blooded means that unlike the mammals, for example, which maintain their own body temperature at a constant level, the reptiles are much more dependent upon the temperature of their surroundings for warmth. Consequently, reptiles tend to be much more common in warmer climates than our own and even within Britain there is a very marked difference between the fauna of the south and north of the country.

Their cold-blooded nature also affects their behaviour. All the British reptiles hibernate spending the cold period, when they would have to be inactive anyway, in burrows well protected from both the cold and likely predators. Similarly, their daily cycle is governed strongly by the weather. On a sunny morning they emerge to find a suitable basking site where they warm themselves up; during this period they may be very sluggish. Later in the day, if it is hot, they will need to move to cooler, shady places where the heat from the sun is not too intense because they can also overheat. In spring and autumn, when the days may be sunny but the air temperature is cool, they often spend much of the day basking.

Two of our British reptiles bear their young live – these are the adder and the common lizard. The remaining four all lay eggs. Sand lizards lay

The gorgeously-marked and exotic-looking male sand lizard, basking on a rock in warm sunshine. Sand lizards are now very rare in Britain being only found in localised areas in the southwest and northwest.

their eggs in covered depressions in sand on warm, south-facing slopes where the heat from the sun will help them to develop; while grass snakes lay in warm rotting vegetation, and they have taken to using compost heaps, which are ideal, where they are available.

Most of our reptiles tend to occur in heathy, sandy places, probably because these sites are normally warm and have adequate hibernation and reproduction sites. The rare smooth snake is confined to heathland in southern England, whilst the almost equally rare sand lizard is found almost entirely on southern heaths, mainly in Dorset and Hampshire, but there are a few on some northern sand-dunes. Adders are most frequent in heathy areas and in open woodland, where they particularly favour clearings, margins and the edges of rides. They tend to move seasonally, preferring drier sites in autumn, winter and spring, moving to damper sites in summer, if they have the choice. Grass snakes are less associated with heathlands, occurring in quite a variety of rough habitats with long grass, but they have a particular affinity for water, and spend some of their time swimming and hunting actually in water. It is quite an impressive sight watching a grass-snake undulating its way rapidly across a pond or lake!

Common lizards can occur almost anywhere, though they prefer reasonably warm sunny places with plenty of basking sites. Heaths are good, but so are such places as old railway lines, open woods and other habitats. Slow-worms, which are actually legless lizards, though they look more like snakes, occur in all sorts of places, but they prefer well vegetated sites, with plenty of cover. They tend to bask under stones or, nowadays, under corrugated iron, rather than in the open, perhaps because their slower movements make them vulnerable to birds and other predators.

Of all the British reptiles, only the adder is venomous. None of the lizards are, nor are the smooth or grass snake, though they are often mistaken for the adder. In fact, the venom of the adder is by no means as dangerous as often suggested. Adders are frightened of any large animal, and will always flee rather than fight if they can. If they do bite, it is highly unlikely to be fatal, and there have only been a few deaths this century from adder bites, and they are normally children because of their lower body weight. The chances of getting seriously injured by a snake in Britain are very small indeed.

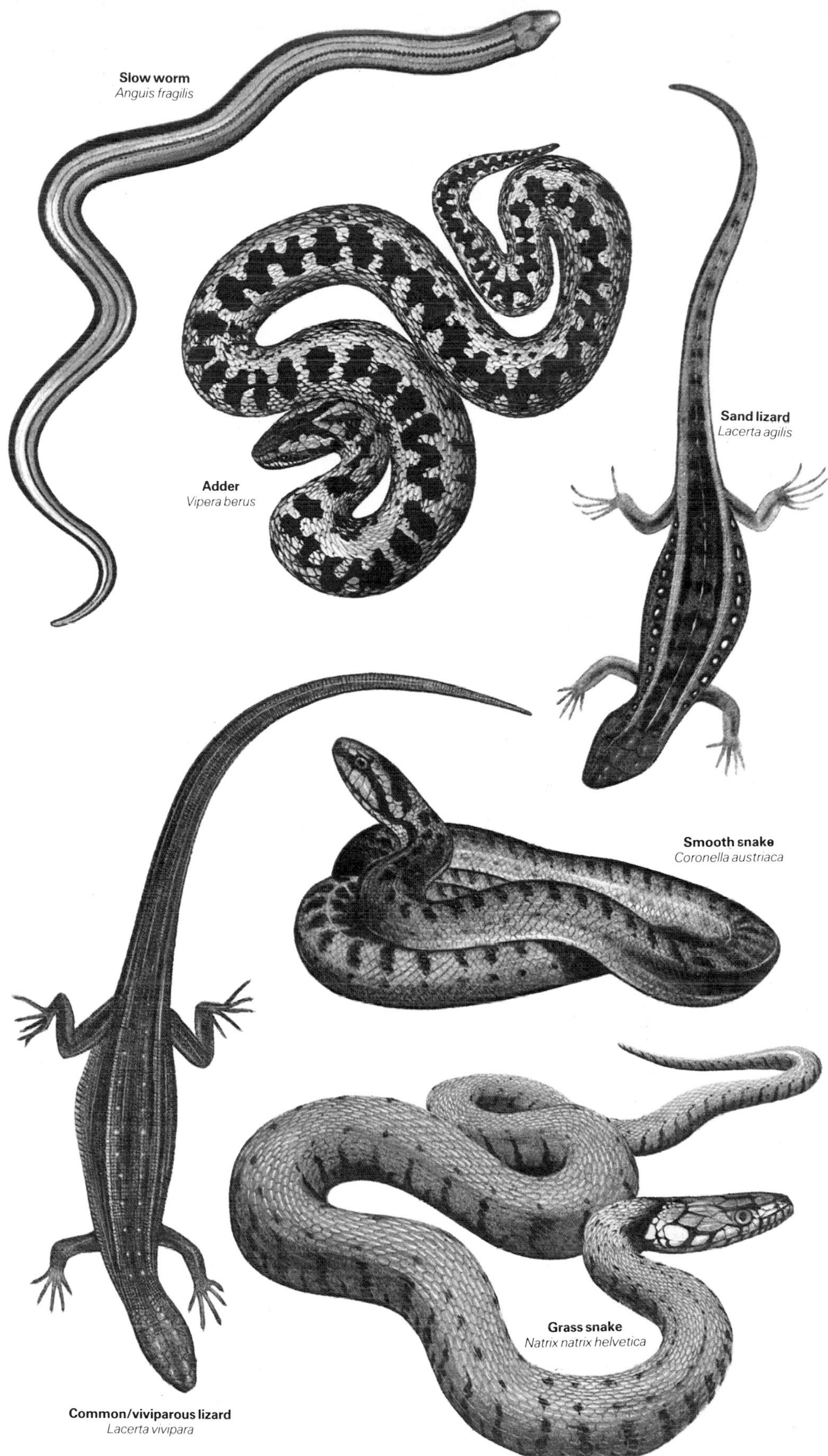

All six of our native reptiles are shown here, from the inconspicuous slow-worm to the beautiful sand lizard. Only the 'diamond' backed adder has a venomous bite but is rarely fatal to man in this country

FROGS AND TOADS

Tadpoles and frogspawn are familiar sights in spring but few people see the adult frogs and toads, which are secretive and mainly nocturnal creatures. There are two native species of toads and one frog species, though several introduced frogs have gained a foothold in the country.

Frogs and toads are amphibians – cold-blooded vertebrates that are adapted for life both on land and in water. However, their skins are unprotected (unlike reptiles which have scales), so they lose water readily in a dry environment; they tend therefore to be mainly nocturnal and to remain in damp habitats. Their eggs are laid in water, and the developing young spend their first few months there, before coming out onto land. The adults vary in their tolerance of dry conditions, but all species spend much of their time, out of the breeding season, away from water.

In the spring, the adults begin to make their respective ways to their breeding grounds. Frogs may start to breed as early as February in mild areas, though March is more usual; whilst toads are generally a little later. Frogs are very catholic in their tastes, and will use almost any area of water, acid or neutral, including very small areas such as ditches or winter ponds. Many of their spawnings fail through being placed in unsuitable waters which dry out, or are too disturbed like cart ruts but, despite this, they have a considerable ability to colonise new areas. Toads, by contrast, are inclined to be more specific in their tastes, choosing larger, more stable, reasonably deep water bodies, with the right chemistry. This tends to mean that they are more traditional in their breeding habits, with all the toads from a wide area gathering together to breed in the same place annually. It is at this time that frogs and toads are most noticed, and toads, in particular, may be killed in large numbers if they have to cross a road to reach the breeding site. The same happens, less often, to frogs because their sites are more widely dispersed. Natterjack toads are very much rarer than the two commoner species, with just a few colonies scattered through the country on heaths and sand-dunes. They are largely active at night, 'running' rather than hopping, after beetles and woodlice. They sometimes use rabbit burrows for hibernation. They seem to require shallow ponds that warm up quickly, yet are not so shallow that they dry out before midsummer, so it is not surprising that they are rare!

The eggs of our frogs and toads are laid, as most people know, in gelatinous masses known as spawn. It is easy enough to tell the spawn of frogs from that of toads because the frogspawn appears as the much more familiar rounded masses, while toadspawn occurs as long strings of eggs encased in jelly. The spawn of natterjack and common toads is rather similar, though that of common toads always contains double lines of eggs, whilst that of natterjacks comes out double, but very quickly becomes a single line of eggs as it swells. Also you are far less likely to find the spawn of natterjack toads than either

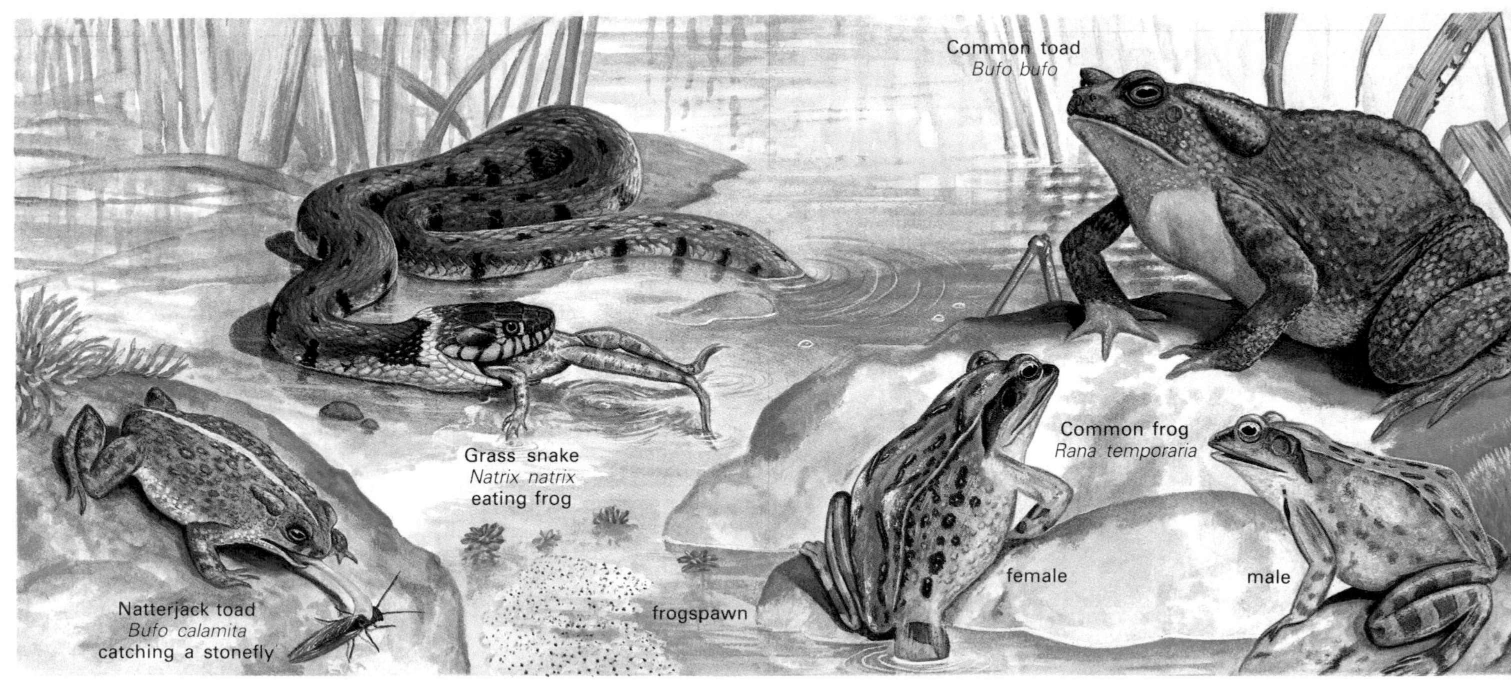

Our three native species of frogs and toads. The natterjack is now very rare and is confined to a few sand dunes and heaths throughout the country; the others are widespread

of the other two, as it is now a very rare species.

The eggs hatch and gradually separate from their encasing jelly to become tadpoles. At first, these are pest-controllers. The tadpoles of different species are rather difficult to distinguish, as they all look very similar, but there are minor differences in colour and structure that allow an experienced amphibian-watcher to identify them.

There are also several non-native species of frogs that have become established in Britain over the years,

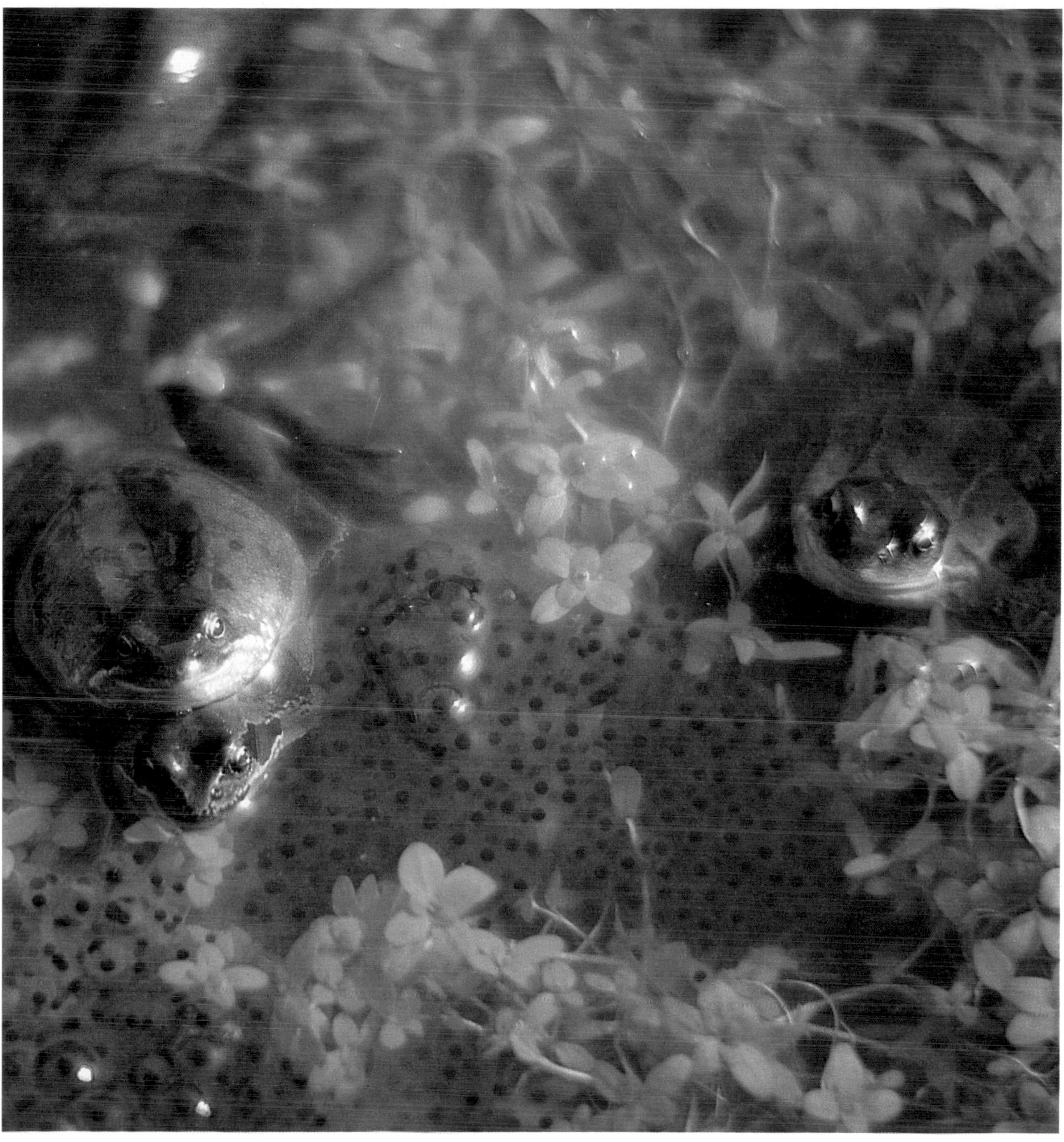

Frogs
Common frogs mating in a favoured pond in spring, amongst the jelly-like masses of newly-laid frogspawn

wholly vegetarian, eating algae and other plant material, though they gradually become more carnivorous, eventually eating only animal prey. The adults are predators on a wide variety of invertebrates and are (or should be) welcome in any garden as

either accidentally or deliberately. These are all mainland European species, and the most established ones are the pool frog, edible frog and marsh frog with one small, but very long established colony of the European tree-frog.

NEWTS

Besides the more familiar frogs and toads, there is another group of amphibians that are rarely seen and seldom heard of; these are the newts, and we have three species, all with intriguing semi-aquatic habits.

Newts, though closely related to frogs and toads, look superficially more like lizards, and indeed are often confused with them. Like the other amphibians, though, they lack the protective scales of the reptiles, but unlike the others they have retained their tails which gives them such a different appearance. It is interesting that tadpoles of all our amphibians have tails but those of frogs and toads lose them as they develop.

There are three species of newt found naturally in Britain (see illustration). These are the crested or warty newt, which is by far the largest; the smooth newt which is generally the commonest, particularly in the lowlands; and the palmate newt which can live under all sorts of conditions, and is more frequent in the north and west of Britain. The crested newt is specially protected by law, since it has declined considerably in recent decades, though it is not exceptionally rare, whilst the other two species are usually common in suitable habitats. The crested newt earns its other name of warty newt after the nature of its skin which also gives off an unpleasant, acrid liquid that deters predators. The other two species have this defence mechanism during the breeding season, but their skin becomes dry and velvety for the rest of the year, and they have to rely on other means of defence such as concealment.

If the newts are so common and widespread, why are they so infrequently seen? The answer is that they have a very inconspicuous lifestyle which rarely brings them into contact with man. Like the other amphibians, they are mainly nocturnal to reduce the dangers of water loss and predation, and spend much of their time well-hidden under vegetation or stones. Except for the breeding season, they are mainly terrestrial, but rarely venture out into the open. The two smaller, commoner species will quite readily colonise garden ponds if conditions are right, though great-crested newts very rarely do. However, not only do they move and hunt at night but, unlike frogs and toads, their breeding activities also occur after dark, so you are unlikely to notice masses of them in a pond in spring. In fact, the best way to find newts is to go to a suitable pool at night with a torch, especially in spring or early summer.

The breeding season for newts begins in spring, like all amphibians. The adults gradually return to water from their terrestrial hibernation sites (though a few may hibernate in water), and courtship, mating and egg-laying then takes place over a

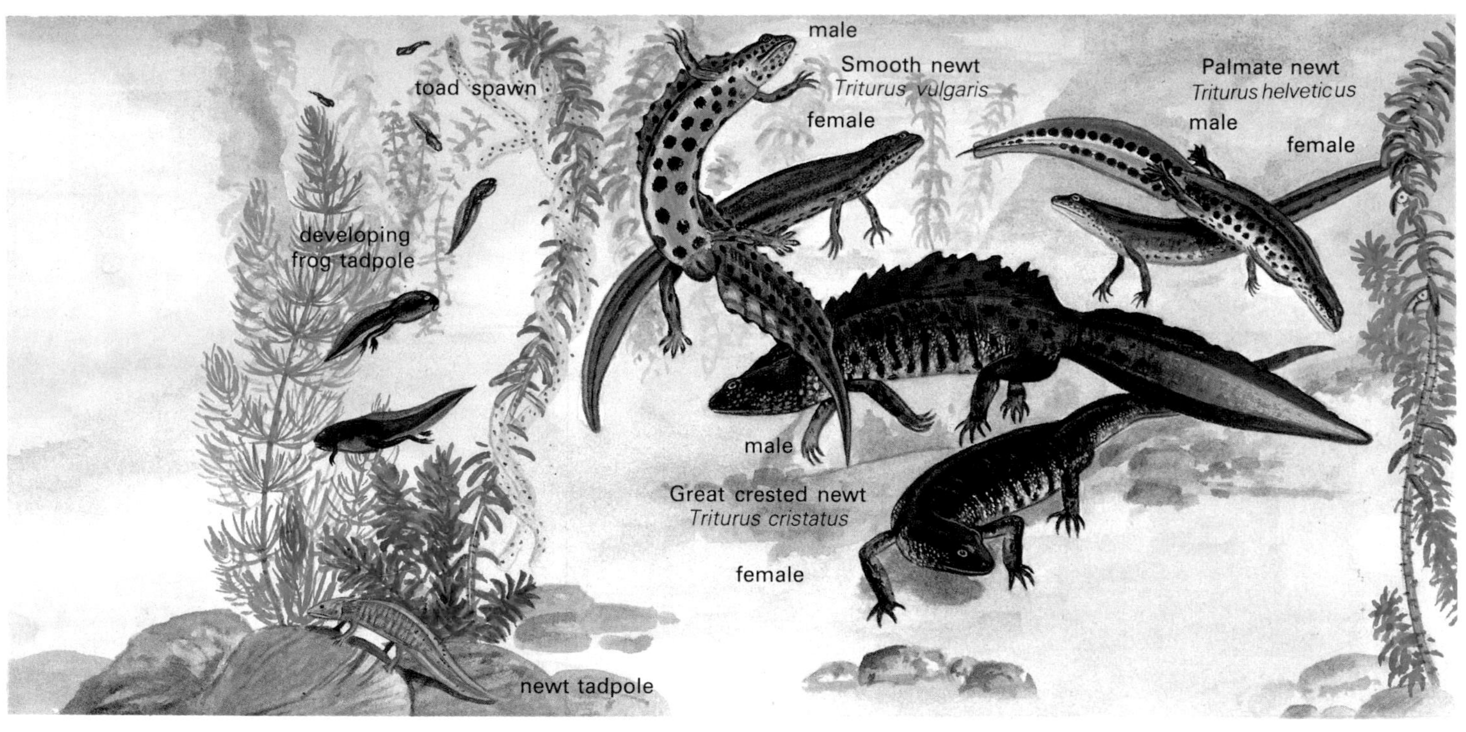

Britain's three native newt species are shown here in their strongly-marked breeding colours. All male newts sport a crest when breeding but lose it soon after

period of several weeks or months. The males of all species become much more colourful, though those of the crested newt become particularly striking, with their elongated raised crest and bright orange-red belly. All process is very slow and laborious and the female may easily take a week or so to lay her 200 to 300 eggs. The eggs are never laid together in masses, like those of frogs and toads, so they are easily overlooked. limbs at first, so it moves randomly and sticks itself to anything with its two protruding adhesive organs. Gradually it develops front legs and the gills become enlarged and feathery, while later the back legs develop,

species have a prolonged and deliberate courtship dance underwater then, after mating, the female stores the male's sperm in a special chamber until her eggs are ready to be fertilised; the sperm may come from one of several males, as both sexes mate several times. When the female is ready to lay, she seeks out broad-leaved water plants and lays each egg, individually, under a leaf, which she curls carefully around the sticky egg, concealing it from predators. The

After a few weeks, the developing tadpole eats its way out of the egg and emerges into the water. It is equipped with gills for breathing, but has no allowing it to crawl around underwater. It may, however, be several months before the newts are ready to leave the water, and indeed in some cold or food-poor ponds, they may remain in the young aquatic stage for their first winter before emerging the following spring. After coming out onto land, it may be several years before the newt is ready to breed, and those that survive predation can live for up to 20 years, breeding each year after they are mature.

A pair of common smooth newts, during the spring breeding season, with the more crested male below

After breeding the male looses its crest and the female becomes a bland brown/grey colour until the next season

HOW TO GO POND-DIPPING

One of the most fascinating and absorbing activities for naturalists of any age is that of pond-dipping. The closer you look in any pond, the more you begin to find, and there is always something interesting to see. Here, we suggest how you can start out on this fascinating hobby.

Almost any pond, or even puddle, will support a tremendous array of life and it is possible, with a little planning and equipment, to sample this variety and examine it closely. Even with the naked eye, it is perfectly possible to watch much of the aquatic life, though with the aid of a simple lens even more is revealed.

What do you need? The equipment required for pond-dipping is simple and cheap, and much of it can be found or made at home from bits and pieces. First, you need a net or two; you can use a simple aquarium net from a pet shop, or a fishing net, or you can make one yourself from muslin and a wire loop – whatever you use, the mesh should not be too coarse. For catching and examining very small creatures, the plankton of the pond, you may find it best to use a special net made from an old stocking with a small jam-jar fixed into the toe – this concentrates the tiny animals so that you can see them more easily. A drag hook is a very useful piece of equipment for hauling in strands of floating water weed to examine the multitude of creatures that will come with them. You can make one by tying together several pieces of strong wire, each with an outward-facing hook at the end, and attaching the resulting structure to a length of thin rope, strong enough to bear the weight of a load of very wet weed.

To examine your catch white shallow trays are needed; plastic two-litre ice cream containers are ideal, and free. Jam-jars and similar containers are not as good, as it is difficult to see things clearly in them, though you can buy or make thin glass-sided observation tanks which give a much better view. If you plan to take anything home (and you should be sure that you can look after it before you do), a small glass or plastic aquarium is ideal, especially if you stock it well with oxygenating weed and clean it regularly. It is best to return the contents quite soon, though, with some effort, you can establish a successful self-sustaining community. A $\times 5$ or $\times 10$ magnification hand lens will be useful for looking at the smallest creatures in shallow water or water droplets.

How do you get started? First, find a pond which, of course, vary in the amount of life that they contain. A sheltered, well-vegetated, unpolluted pond will be better than an exposed or polluted one, but most ponds contain something. They vary seasonally, too, and summer undoubtedly yields the richest harvest, but you can go pond-dipping at any time of the year provided the water is not frozen. A garden pond is a good place to start (so why not consider making one, see page 156) because it is convenient and you can easily take things inside to examine them.

It is best to sweep the net through the water, and then turn out the contents into your tray or container. If you have picked up some bottom mud you will find it difficult to sort out the catch as everything will be murky and some pond-life feigns dead for a few minutes after being caught. Unless you are especially looking for bottom-dwellers, it is best to sweep only the upper layers away from any mud. The areas around water weeds can be particularly productive, as many invertebrates and small fishes gather there for shelter or feeding. If you pull in weed with a drag hook, immerse it in water to see what emerges, and then examine it more closely to discover what has remained attached. In spring, you may be lucky enough to find the eggs of newts (see page 175) rolled up in leaves though, of course, these, like everything else, should be put back unless you have the right conditions to rear them.

There is also a considerable amount of life actually on the surface of the water – pond-skaters, whirligig beetles and water-crickets for example – which can be caught and examined with a little care, though some surface-dwellers can fly if they need to, so you may not be able to watch them for long. If you look carefully into any clear water, preferably before you disturb it by netting, you may see larger creatures such as newts, fishes or water stick insects which you can carefully catch and examine. If you are interested in dragonfly larvae – those extraordinary aquatic predators, with their fearsome 'mask' that shoots out to catch prey – you will probably do best by delving in the bottom mud and carefully sifting the contents, though some species do occur up amongst the weeds.

Whatever you do, please treat everything carefully, put all animals and weed back unless you are sure you can look after them – never leave them lying on the bank; be careful not to destroy bankside vegetation or disturb breeding birds. You will be well rewarded with a rich variety of creatures and plants.

Pond-dipping can be one of the most exciting of pastimes. Here is the specially-created 'dipping pond' at Woods Mill in Sussex

Pondskaters (top) live on the surface tension of the water. It uses its long middle legs to row across the surface

An Introduction to

British Birds

Birds are undoubtedly our most popular form of wildlife, with more people watching birds that any other group. Although the birdlife of Britain is not exceptionally rich when viewed on a world, or even European, scale, we do have a wealth of birdwatching opportunities. The birdlife of our coasts is quite exceptional by any standards, and the teeming colonies of gannets, guillemots, kittiwakes and many others are a fascination for birdwatchers from all countries. Equally, the winter spectacle of hundreds of thousands of wintering waders and wildfowl in our estuaries all around the coast is difficult to surpass. And birdwatchers in Britain are better catered for than anywhere else, with a tremendous variety of nature reserves, hides and viewing facilities to be visited.

Wherever you are and whatever the time of year, there are always birds to be seen in the British countryside. Woodlands are probably the richest breeding habitats overall but heaths, downs, wet meadows, coasts, mountains, moorlands, lakes and even towns and gardens all have their own birds, often in large numbers. Many species will breed in one habitat, but spend the rest of the year in another, whilst others move regularly to exploit varying food sources. Thus there is always something new to be seen which is one of the pleasures of birdwatching in Britain.

British birds divide roughly into those that are resident all the year round, for example the robin, blackbird and rook, and those that are seasonal visitors. Some seasonal visitors come just to breed, such as the swallows, cuckoo and various tern species, leaving as soon as breeding is successfully completed, whilst others from colder areas come here to feed in winter, like the brent geese. The position is actually more complicated than this; numbers of our resident species are often swollen at certain times of year by an influx of migrants, whilst others that are primarily winter visitors may also breed here in small numbers. The number of birds on the British list – those which have been reliably recorded in Britain at sometime or other – is now not far off 500 species, though the number of breeding birds is only about half this, and many of these are very rare. Still, the variety of birds to be seen is immense, especially when you take into acount the different appearance of males, females and juveniles, and the changes in plumage through the seasons.

A blizzard of gannets on Grassholm island off the rocky coast of Pembrokeshire

BIRDS

INCLUDING: Coast • Uplands • Woodland • Woodpeckers •
Conifer Plantations • Hedgerows • Open Farmland •
Scrubland • Lowland Heaths • Downland •
Wet Meadowland • Birdwatching •
Freshwater • Gardens •
Signs of Birds
Towns

BIRDS OF THE COAST: TERNS, GULLS AND SKUAS

Of all our seabirds, the terns are almost certainly the most graceful – the swallows of the sea – while the gulls are undoubtedly the most familiar. Together with the voracious predatory skuas, they make up a fascinating group.

The word 'seagull' is used frequently to describe almost any large white or grey seabird, but in fact there are six different types of gull which can be commonly seen, and five different sorts of the rather similar terns (or six if you include the black tern which breeds occasionally).

Gulls, in general, have done well in their last few decades, increasing their numbers and extending some of their ranges. Herring gulls breed in large colonies on cliffs, but have also moved to various urban sites in recent years, where they are far from popular. They are scavengers, like most gulls, and their population expansion may have resulted from the greater availability of food from man in rubbish dumps and other places. Herring gulls are the most typical of gulls, and they fulfil the epitome of a seagull, but other gulls may be almost as common. The black-headed gull has increased in numbers and has moved into towns, where noisy flocks may raid bird-tables. Their greedy feeding and squabbling is usually unwelcome, though they are difficult to get rid of once they have discovered a food source!

The common terns shown here may be distinguished from the Arctic tern by its dark red orange bill with a black tip: the Arctic tern has *no* black tip and has longer tail ends

Terns, though they may look a little

like the smaller gulls, have quite different habits. They only come to Britain to breed, and their lifestyle owes little to man. They are amongst the most beautiful of birds, with a graceful flight, delicate colours and the appearance of large pale swallows with their forked tails. They breed mainly on the coast, on sand and shingle in particular, though there are some inland groups of the common tern. They are colonial nesters, with large numbers of the same species – and often several species – nesting together in one place. They lay their well-camouflaged eggs in depressions on the ground and often the nests are so close together that it would be difficult to walk between them (though nowadays it would be illegal to do so, as they are strictly protected by law on their breeding grounds). Despite their graceful appearance, they defend their eggs and young aggressively and the common and Arctic terns, in particular, will dive-bomb intruders repeatedly, often actually hitting them.

The migration of terns is one of the wonders of the bird world, and the Arctic tern makes one of the most remarkable journeys of all. It breeds in northern Britain and beyond, well up into the Arctic, arriving in early summer, and in late summer it leaves to head southwards down the coasts of Europe and Africa, to eventually spend the winter (their summer) in South Africa and even into Antarctic regions. This represents a journey of about 16,000 kilometres, which is then retraced soon afterwards in the following spring! Over its whole life, an individual Arctic tern could easily fly half a million kilometres. The journey is a hazardous one for, although it keeps the tern in areas of constant food supply, they are also trapped mercilessly and this is undoubtedly one of the reasons for its decline in recent years.

The skuas, of which there are two species breeding in Britain, are piratical birds that live by raiding the nests in the breeding season, and by robbing other species of food. They are highly skilled fliers, and will chase and harry any other seabird with food in its beak until it eventually gives up its food to the skua, though of course they are not always successful. The two breeding species in Britain are the Arctic and the great skuas, though the long-tailed and the pomarine skuas pass through occasionally. All are primarily northern in distribution, and the two breeding species only nest in northern Britain.

The gulls and skuas shown here are the ones that you are most likely to come across

BIRDS OF THE COAST: WADERS

Every autumn and winter, our coastal estuaries and mudflats are the feeding and roosting grounds for vast numbers of attractive birds known as waders. Many of these birds have moved here from their breeding grounds in the Arctic, though some also breed in Britain.

The term wader or wading bird is a general one used to describe a number of loosely-related birds, from several families, that share the habit of feeding in estuaries or on the seashore. Most of them are medium-sized birds, often with long legs and beaks, like the avocet, curlew and snipe (see illustration).

During winter, huge numbers of waders congregate in coastal areas around Britain, often making really spectacular displays of thousands, or even tens of thousands, of birds in one place. The reason that they all gather on the coasts is, of course, for the food which is readily available. Estuaries, intertidal muds and strand-lines are immensely rich in invertebrates, such as molluscs and worms, and generally the mild climate and the high salt content of the seawater prevents the feeding grounds from freezing up in winter. In very hard weather, most inland feeding sites are likely to be frozen solid, so all the birds move to the coast. The amount of invertebrates that they remove must be enormous. For example, it has been estimated that even a tiny bird like the dunlin may consume as many as 700 Macoma molluscs in a day. So if you multiply this up by thousands, then add on the numbers consumed by all the other waders, every single day, you begin to realise the amazing pro-

A habitat picture showing many of our commoner waders, including both winter and summer species, showing the many different ways in which they exploit the coastal habitat in search of food

ductivity of the invertebrate fauna in the mud.

Our winter waders come from a variety of places, though most of them breed in the Arctic tundra in large numbers, and start to move southwards from late summer onwards. The tiny dunlin, for example, or the knot, which can both occur in very high numbers, mainly breed in the high Arctic, making the long journey south to British coasts in the autumn. Species such as sanderling, grey plover and turnstone do not nest in Britain at all, though others including the curlew, snipe, golden plover and greenshank do breed in relatively small numbers on our northern uplands. A few black-tailed godwit nest in wet meadows in Britain, while the redshank is relatively common in similar situations. Ringed and little ringed plovers, oystercatchers and the avocet are all primarily coastal breeders, in small numbers, though some will nest inland where suitable habitat exists, and the oystercatcher has moved inland to many northern river valleys in recent decades. With all these species, the relatively small numbers of home-bred birds are boosted by immigrants from elsewhere. A few species, like the whimbrel, are regularly seen on passage when stopping off briefly on their way from the Arctic, where they have nested, to their African wintering grounds. Small numbers do however breed in northern Scotland.

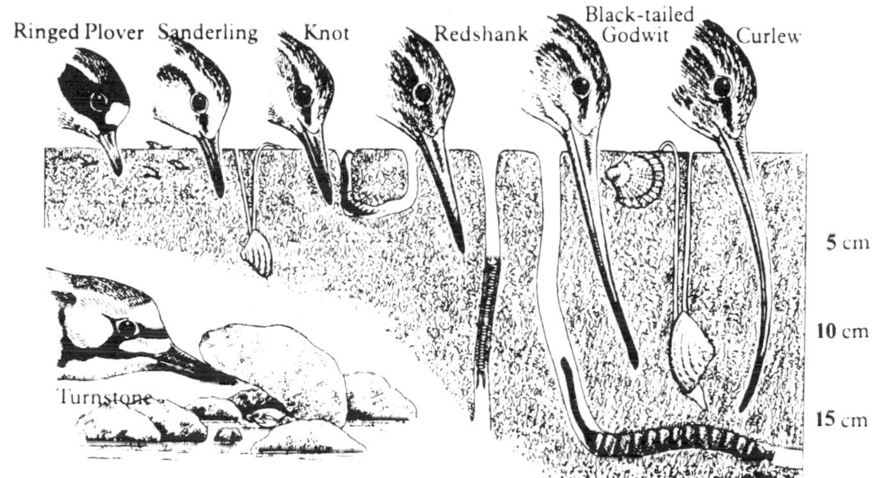

The relationship between length of bill and food in waders

The beaks of wading birds come in a fascinating variety of shapes and sizes. Almost all of them are long and thin, adapted for probing in the mud, yet each has its own special features. For example, the long straight beak of the woodcock has an expanding tip allowing it to grasp prey whilst deeply stuck into thick mud; the little turnstone has a short strong bill to overturn stones (hence its name). The long blood-red bill of the oystercatcher is used for prising mollusc shells from rocks and crushing them (which is why it was given its name), whilst the redshank has an all-purpose, medium-length bill. In general, waders have long legs and those with the longest legs often have the longest bill, like the godwits or the curlew. This allows them to stand in shallow water, for example when following the tide down a muddy beach, and still probe for invertebrates without getting their head or body wet. This gives them a greater chance of finding invertebrates.

A massed flock of waders over the Beaulieu estuary, including dunlin, redshank and grey plover amongst others

BIRDS OF THE COAST: DUCKS AND GEESE

Ducks and geese are the most conspicuous birds of all those that are found on the coast. They occur in very large numbers, and many of them are brightly coloured and noisy, making a welcome splash of colour and life in our winter-drab estuaries.

Ducks and geese are all closely-related members of the same family, the Anatidae, and most of them congregate on the coast at some time or other. Like waders, many are winter visitors to our shores, whilst others are resident here.

The geese are amongst the most attractive of birds. To those who are only familiar with noisy farmyard geese, they may not seem to be anything special, yet the sight of a skein of geese flying into an cstuary one evening, calling to each other as they circle down, is a memorable experience. Although some geese do breed in Britain, most of our winter species come in from elsewhere and, like many of the waders, the majority breed in the far north. Greylag geese, which are probably the most familiar genuinely wild geese and the most closely-related to the domestic varieties, breed in the wild in north-west Scotland, and there are 'escaped' populations elsewhere. The Canada goose was an introduction from North America, but is now so well-established as a breeding bird (mainly inland) that it has become our most well known goose, with its striking black and white plumage and its loud honking call.

The other species of geese are, perhaps, less familiar but they are all beautiful birds. The small, dark-coloured brent goose, for example, comes to Britain for the winter from its Arctic breeding grounds. Its numbers vary enormously according to the breeding success but, in the last few years, it has been increasing steadily after a period when very few birds came here. In fact, we get two distinguishable races: most of our birds are the dark-bellied brent geese, which come from Arctic Russia; though there are smaller numbers of pale-bellied Greenland brents which winter mainly in Ireland. They are amongst the most coastal of geese, rarely venturing far inland; their main food is the eel-grass species which grow just around the low-tide mark and they graze away often clearing the whole sward before the end of the winter. In fact, one of the reasons that the brent goose population dropped so dramatically was because of a severe disease that attacked eel-grass populations here and elsewhere, but both the eel-grass and the goose have recovered remarkably. When eel-grass swards become exhausted by over-grazing, the brent geese have taken to moving just inland onto playing fields, meadows and even arable land, and they become very tame at this time of year.

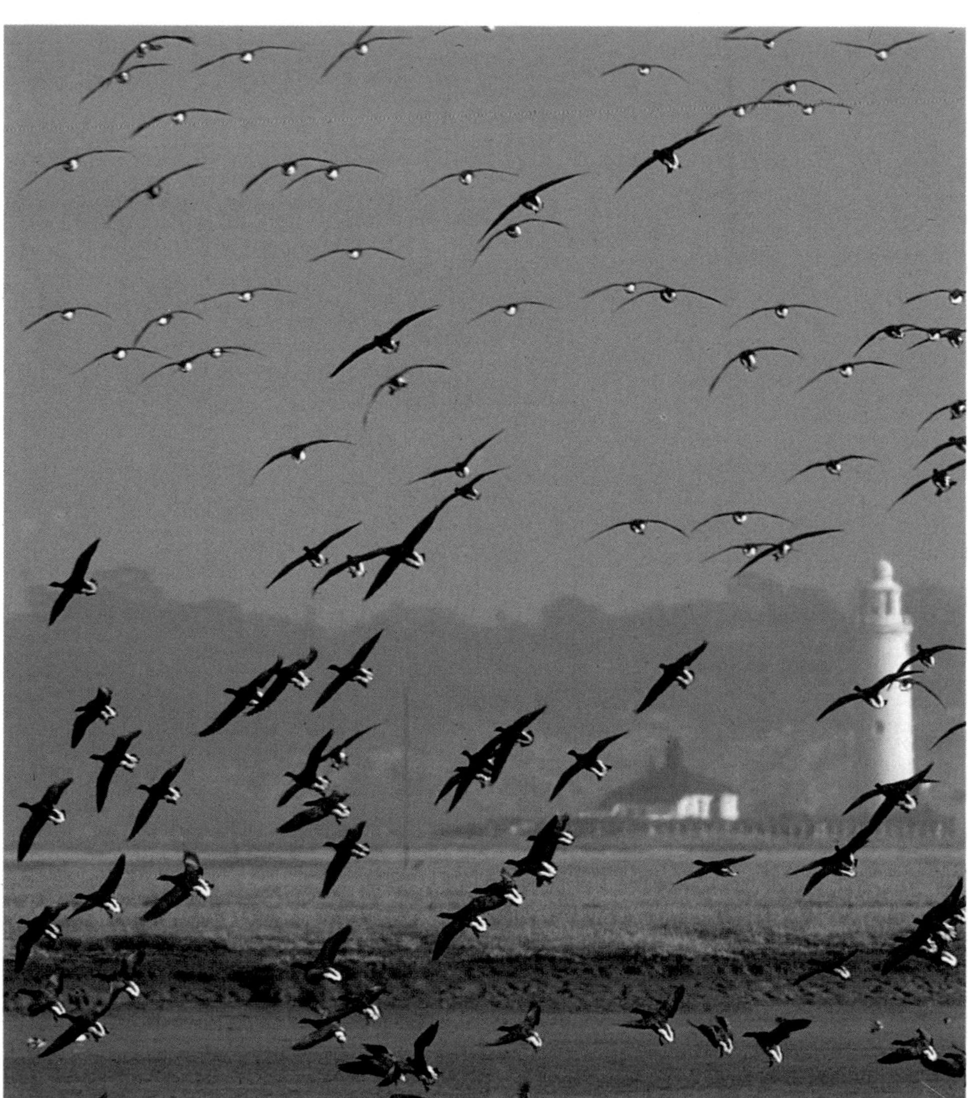

Brent geese in flight over Keyhaven in Hampshire. These are the dark bellied race.

The light bellied race overwinter mainly in Ireland and parts of the North Sea coasts

The shelduck is a duck with a slight of the look of a goose in it. It is a large, very brightly-coloured species, strongly marked with black, white, orange and red, and for once the female is as bright as the male (the female, ducks, are usually far less brightly-coloured than the resplendent drakes). They breed all round the coasts, in a range of different habitats, in burrows below ground. Occasionally they breed inland, though more usually close to the sea. In July, almost the entire population of our shelduck pied plumage is a familiar sight on the coast for the rest of the year.

Ducks are more often thought of in association with inland lakes and ponds, and many species do both breed and winter inland. However, the rich feeding of coastal areas, especially in very hard weather when other waters are frozen up, makes an irrestible attraction. Huge flocks of ducks such as wigeon, teal, scaup and even the ubiquitous mallard gather on the coasts. Some, like the scaup, come down from the far north where they breed, whilst others, like the mallard, are partially resident and are just

moves eastwards to the Heligoland Bight, off north-west Germany, for their moult; a small flock also gathers in the Bristol Channel area. Some juveniles and a few adults remain scattered around the coasts but by autumn they are all back, and their

Here are some ducks and geese commonly seen around our coasts. Most geese are grazers and may be seen in flocks plucking at the grass around saltings or elsewhere near the shoreline. They may even stray into farmland

moving within Britain. In contrast, the lovely eider ducks are coastal residents *par excellence*, breeding near the sea in northern Britain where they collect their young into crèches looked after by a few attendants. They remain close to the sea all their lives.

OTHER COASTAL BIRDS

There are many other birds that we particularly associate with the coast. Some, like the shearwaters, spend most of their life at sea and just come to land to breed, whilst others, like the rock pipit, spend all their lives at the edge of the sea, feeding and breeding there.

In addition to the gulls and terns, and wintering ducks and waders, there are quite a few other birds that particularly favour coastal habitats for at least some part of their lives. These include the highly oceanic petrels and shearwaters – our closest cousins to the albatrosses – all the auks, such as puffins and guillemots, and various other mainly maritime birds like gannets, shags and cormorants.

The petrels and shearwaters are a fascinating group of birds. They are very poorly adapted to life on the land, and many are barely able to walk when they come ashore to breed. To make up for this, they are remarkable fliers, with an endless capacity for graceful flight, often just skimming the wave-tops. Nowadays, the commonest of this group is the fulmar petrel or, as it is more often known, the fulmar. About 100 years ago, the fulmar was a very rare breeding bird in Britain, with just one colony on the tiny northern island of St. Kilda, in the Outer Hebrides. Then, some 80 years ago, they colonised Foula in the Shetland Isles, and so began a remarkable expansion of range and numbers which has carried on ever since. Now, they are one of our commonest coastal breeding birds, with colonies in all suitable parts of the country. Although they appear rather like

The seabirds shown here nest on cliffs or close to them. They divide the cliff into preferred levels. Generally the puffins are at the top with the guillemots and razorbills setting up home towards the bottom

gulls with which they are often confused, they differ in their characteristic straight-winged stiffer flight, with the flap-glide style of flying that is typical of this group. They are highly skilled in the air and have an impressive way of circling in, at high speed, to land on the cliffs of their breeding colonies, or skimming low over the wave tops of even the roughest sea. They nest mainly on cliffs and on rough coastal land, and one of their less appealing habits is the regurgitation of their last fishy meal, mixed with a foul-smelling fluid, over any intruder! Research has shown that some birds may be remarkably long-lived, as they were still alive at the end of the studies.

The related Manx shearwater, though reasonably common on western coasts in the breeding season, is a much more unfamiliar and enigmatic bird. They only come to land to breed and spend the rest of the year at sea, often travelling half way round the world, passing much of our winter in the south Atlantic ocean. When they breed, they nest in burrows and normally only enter and leave the holes at night, so are very rarely seen except offshire. When the non-brooding partners arrive in the night with their catch of fish, the whole colony sets up the most weird, unearthly wailing sound, which has given rise to all sorts of ghostly legends! The homing instinct of shearwaters is quite remarkable. Not only do they return to the same breeding grounds each year from the other side of the world, but one individual taken from its breeding site in Wales and released in Massachusetts, USA – well outside its normal travelling range – found its way back home to its mate and chick in just 12 days!

Gannets are amongst our most impressive birds. They have a striking plumage of bright white with black wing-tips and a yellowish head, and their wingspan may reach two metres. Because they usually nest in large colonies, they are highly conspicuous. Indeed, Britain's islands are the main breeding ground for most of the world's gannets. Huge colonies exist on places like St. Kilda, the Bass Rock in the Firth of Forth, or Grassholm off West Wales and, with their cacophony of noise, are amongst the most remarkable of our wildlife spectacles. The fishing habits of gannets are very impressive, too. These huge birds fly to about 30 metres above the sea, then, on spotting a suitable fish, they close their wings and plummet straight down into the water, like an ornithological harpoon. Their precision is so great that they rarely miss.

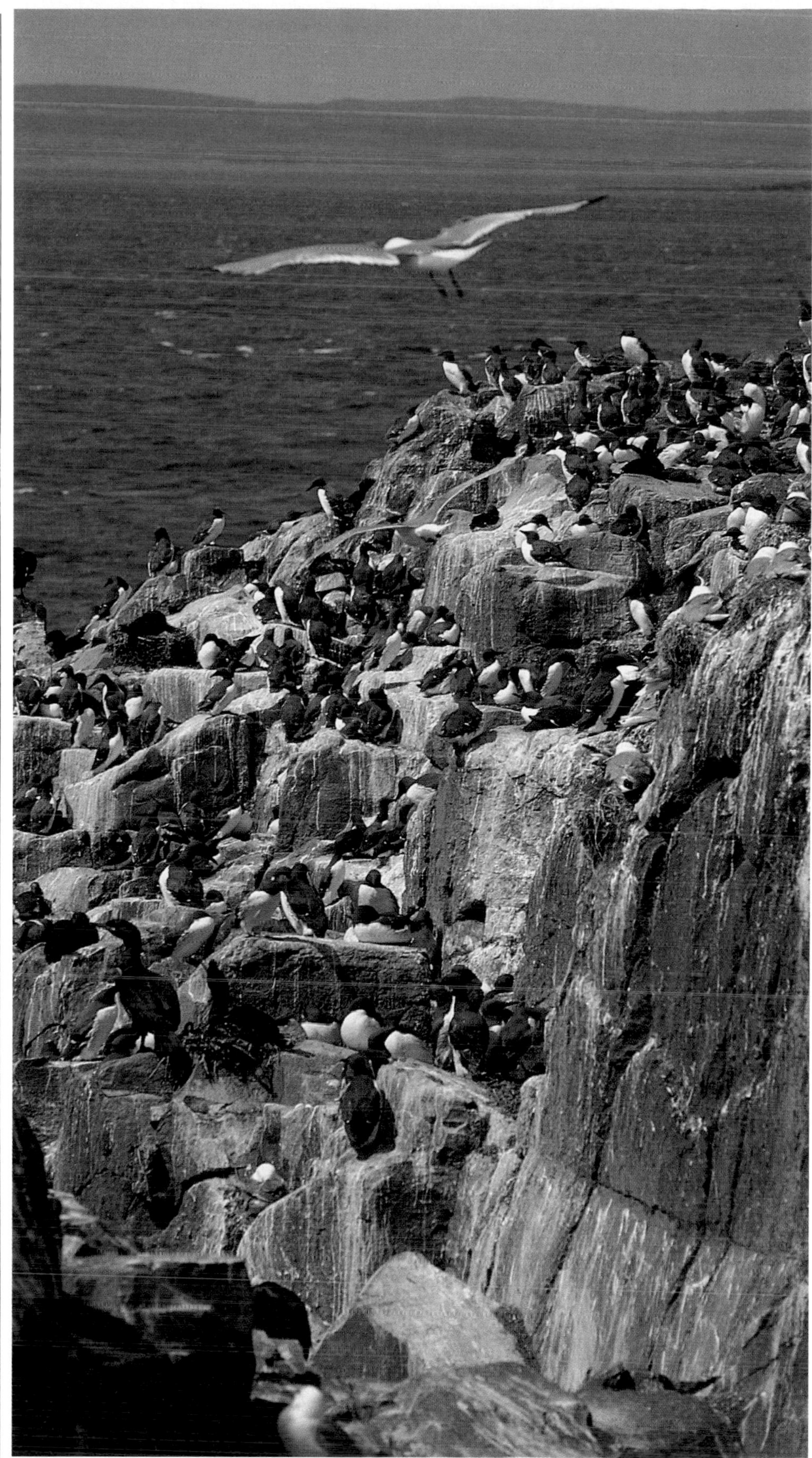

The Farne Islands off the coast of Northumberland are home to all manner of cliff nesting seabirds.

Here you can see fulmers flying and below on the cliffs guillemots and a pair of shags

Birds of the Uplands

Some of our most magnificent birds occur appropriately in our finest scenery. The wild, open spaces of the hills and mountains of the north and west are the only places suitable for birds like the golden eagle, merlin and ptarmigan.

Although the uplands are cold, bleak and unproductive, with short summers and long winters, there are a surprising number of birds that live there at one time or other. Some, like the ptarmigan or snow bunting, are real mountain specialists, choosing only the highest and wildest areas in which to breed, whilst others would be more widespread but have retreated to the mountains which are now the only refuges left to them from farming and development. Other upland birds are common and widespread generally, like the meadow pipit, and can survive almost anywhere. In a similar way, some birds only visit the mountains to breed, making use of the mass hatchings of insects that take place in summer, leaving again as soon as the young have been reared. Such birds include the delightful dotterel, one of the tamest and most confiding of all birds, the golden plover and the ring ouzel, which looks like a blackbird with a white bib. Other birds, however, stay around the hills for the whole year, while some move downwards to less harsh conditions during the worst of the weather. The hardiest and most montane of these birds is probably the ptarmigan.

The ptarmigan is a slightly smaller, mountain relation of the red grouse, and lives in broadly similar habitats but in higher and wilder situations. They have some remarkable adaptations to their mountain habitat. Firstly, they are one of the only British birds to undergo a marked colour change in winter for camouflage reasons. They moult three times a year, changing from mottled brown in summer, through greyish in autumn, to almost pure white in winter which helps them blend into the background whatever the season. Obviously, changing to white in winter would only be successful if their habitat becomes completely snowbound for this period, and this plumage change is an indication of the severity of their winter conditions. Secondly, the ptarmigan has heavily feathered legs and toes, unlike the red grouse, and this helps it to conserve heat during the winter. Their diet is vegetarian, consisting largely of heather and bilberry shoots, and they continue to find food in areas blown clear of snow, or even beneath it if necessary. They are very selective feeders, taking only the most nutritious parts of the plants, so their territories have to be large. Only in the very worst weather, with deep snow lying everywhere, do they descend from the highest ground, and even then they do not come down far.

A very different mountain bird, that is one of the chief predators on ptarmigan, is the majestic golden eagle. In Britain, these birds are confined to mountainous or very hilly country, though they would be more widespread if it were not for the activities of man. They are huge birds, with a wingspan of over two metres, and the strength to kill and carry animals as large as full-grown hares. To survive, their territory needs to be vast – as much as 50 to 80 square kilometres in mountain country. The number of pairs in Britain has declined steadily over a long period, through persecution by keepers and farmers, and as a

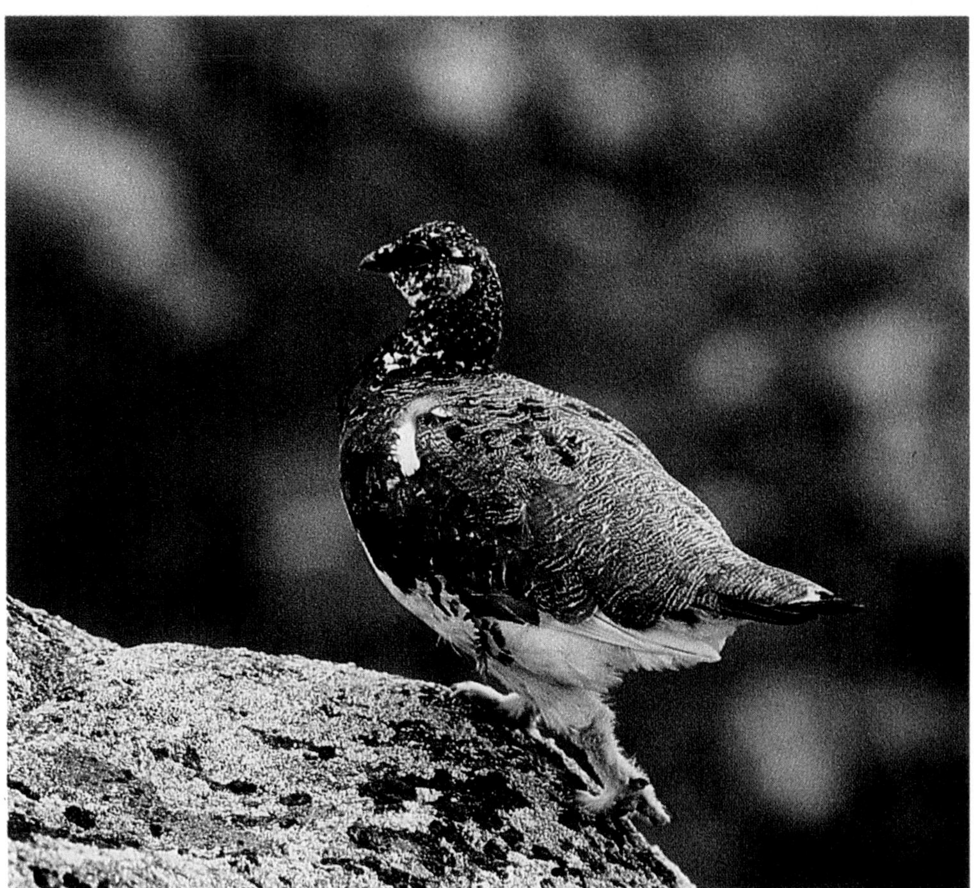

A beautiful male ptarmigan photographed on a rock some 1,230 metres up in the Cairngorm mountains in Scotland

result of pesticide residues a few years ago. The population is roughly stable now, at an estimated 250 to 300 pairs, and they have recently recolonised the Lake District in a small way. Nevertheless, there are still many vacant territories in Scotland, and the birds are not yet increasing as much as hoped. They are a wonderful sight, as they soar above wild peaks and valleys, being over one and a half times the size of the common buzzard, and it would be marvellous if they were to become more common in our mountain areas.

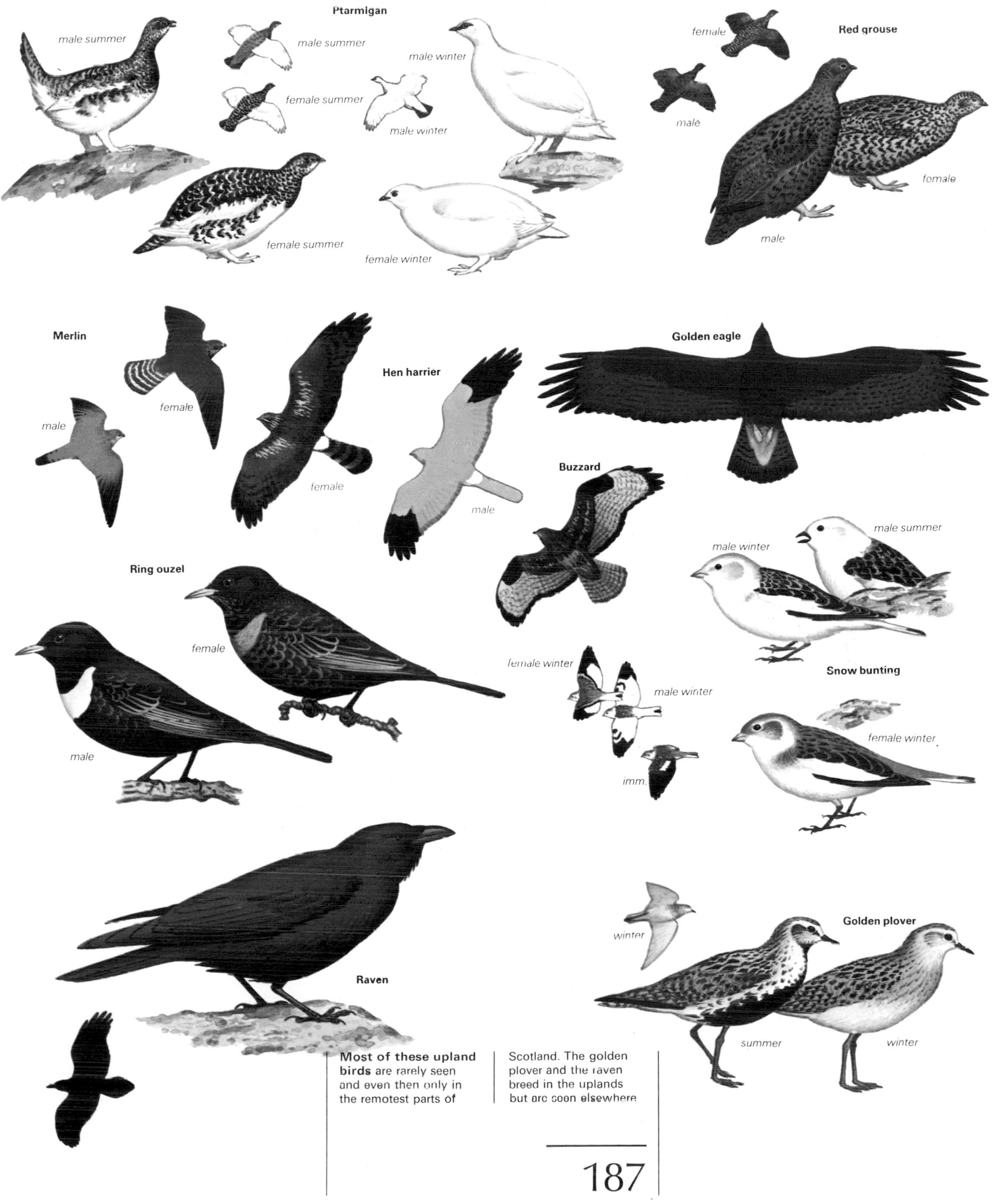

Most of these upland birds are rarely seen and even then only in the remotest parts of Scotland. The golden plover and the raven breed in the uplands but are seen elsewhere

BIRDS OF OLD WOODLAND

Woodlands are probably the richest of all habitats for breeding birds. A suitable ancient woodland, with plenty of cover, can support very high densities of breeding birds of many different species which will all contribute to a deafening dawn chorus in spring and early summer.

Woodlands are an exceptional habitat for breeding birds and the numbers to be found there are very large. Different sorts of woods vary in the birds that they can support, and each region of the country may have its own specialities but, by and large, the same birds occur in most woodlands.

For really varied communities of breeding birds, a woodland has to have a structure that provides nesting-sites for a wide range of species, and sufficient different plants to supply them all with food. Some birds nest on the ground, either directly on it, like the woodcock, or at the base of tree-stumps, as the robin will often do. Others, such as many of the warblers or nightingale, require thick undergrowth of various sorts in which to breed, whilst there are those that particularly favour nest-sites high in trees. Quite a few species also nest in holes in trees; inevitably such species tend to be rare of absent in plantations or younger woods, and most abundant in ancient woodlands that are not intensively managed, and have

The wonderful cryptic camouflage of the woodcock, a 'wader' that has taken to life in damp woodland. In spring and early summer the male performs a display flight called 'roding' at dawn and dusk

plenty of old trees with holes. Such birds include redstarts, nuthatches, woodpeckers, some tits and pied flycatchers. Naturally, a good diverse old wood with all these elements will have a much richer bird fauna than one with less variety.

There are, however, many regional variations within the country, and some birds do not occur in places where there is ample, apparently suitable, habitat. For example, the pied flycatcher is primarily a western species and, though it passes through eastern counties on migration, it fails to nest there. The beautiful redstart will nest further east, but it tends to be commoner in the west because there are more suitable woods. In contrast, the nightingale is now almost exclusively a south-eastern species, though it did once exend more widely. The size of a woodland can affect the birds that breed there, too, and a number of species are not found in small woods at all. Tawny owls and nuthatches, for example, both do best in woods that are at least 100 hectares, which is larger than the vast majority of woods.

Old woodlands are not just of great value because of the large numbers of potential nesting places, but also due to the fact that there is so much food available at the critical period in early summer when birds are raising their young, and incredible quantities are consumed. An old wood is a multi-dimensional place, and various foods are available in different places. Some birds feed on seeds, which they may seek on the trees, on shrubs or on the ground; other birds, like the flycatchers, will catch flying insects, so they will be drawn to sunny glades. Many birds feed their young on the growing caterpillars of moths and sawflies, which may abound in the canopy of broad-leaved trees like oak and ash. Thus the way in which birds feed is quite structured within the wood (see illustration), though there are, of course, the inevitable opportunist feeders that range more widely, taking whatever is available. A few birds which breed in woodland may spend some or all of their time feeding outside the wood, like the woodcock. In the case of herons, which nest colonially in the tree tops but feed on fishes and amphibians from wetland areas, the habitat difference is very marked. Many rooks, too, breed in woods (though they will also nest in more isolated trees) but feed mainly on farmland. Their colonies are called rookeries where nests are built close together at the top of trees forming gregarious and noisy groups that rise in the air when disturbed.

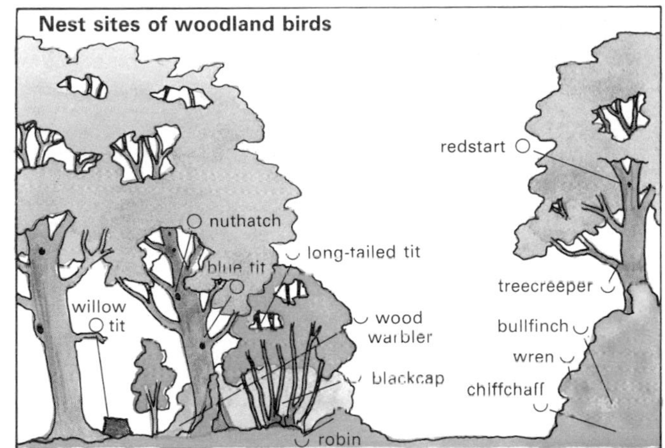

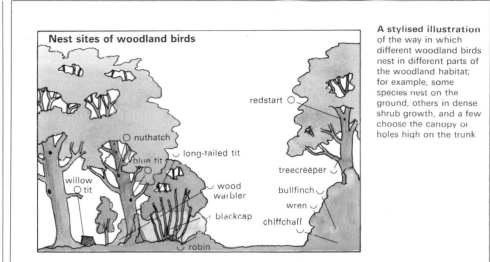

A stylised illustration of the way in which different woodland birds nest in different parts of the woodland habitat; for example, some species nest on the ground, others in dense shrub growth, and a few choose the canopy or holes high on the trunk

A male pied flycatcher bringing a juicy hoverfly to the young in their nest-hole high in the trees in old woodland

BIRDS OF OLD WOODLAND

The variety of different species that can occur in woodland is immense. Colonies of herons, tiny blue tits, several different warblers, flycatchers, nightingales and many more all breed there. Most are elusive characters usually heard rather than seen.

The canopy – the upper parts of the trees – provides a suitable breeding habitat for a number of birds, as well as being the prime feeding area for others. The grey heron, for example, which is one of our most striking birds, nests in large colonies which are almost invariably in woodland, and often well away from the watery areas where they feed. The largest colonies contain well over 100 nests tightly packed together but, on average, there are 20 or 30 pairs. Herons begin breeding well before most other woodland birds, laying their first eggs in February. Other birds that may nest up near the canopy include the wood pigeon, the tiny goldcrest and the jay.

Many woodland birds choose the relative safety of nest-holes in trees, either excavating their own or using ones that already exist. Two specialist hole-nesters, with similar habits, are the nuthatch and the treecreeper. The treecreeper, which is always rather smarter when seen closely than it appears in illustrations, is brown above and white below. The bird feeds by working its way steadily up a trunk to the top often spiralling round the tree in the process; when it has gone far enough, it flies to the base of another tree. The lovely slate-blue, white and orange nuthatch, however, is able to move both up and down tree trunks, so its feeding pattern is rather different. The nuthatch usually takes over other holes to nest in, and it has the distinctive habit of using mud to wall up the entrance of the hole if it is too big, to keep out larger birds. The beautiful redstart nests mainly in tree-holes, or occasionally in a hollow on the ground. The male redstart is a resplendent bird, with his white cap, black bib, chestnut breast and fiery red tail, though sadly it is not a common bird, and is easily overlooked even where it is frequent.

A selection of woodland breeding birds, showing some of the situations where you are most likely to see them

Blue tit
In springtime, the male wood warbler is often seen displaying to the female, spiralling down to perch beside her, singing while he does so
Wood warbler
Treecreeper
Chiffchaffs, like other warblers, may sometimes be seen 'fly-catching' on the wing.
Chiffchaff
male
Redstart
Blackcap
This is the male blackcap, the female has a brown crown
Great tit
Long-tailed tit
Nuthatch
The nuthatch can be seen running head first down tree trunks
Marsh tit
male
Bullfinch
Robin
Wren

Both sexes of robin sing a liquid song from a small tree or other lowish song post, even in winter, for they each hold a 'territory' throughout the year, flaunting the red breast in aggressive displays. Common garden birds in Britain (you can watch them feeding, darting to the ground from a perch), they are shy deep forest birds in Europe, where only their *tic tic* alarm note gives them away. 14 cm.

Another selection of woodland breeding birds, including common and widespread species like the great tit, robin, and chiffchaff, and more local species like the beautiful redstart, which is only frequent in the woods of western Britain

Another traditional hole-nester is the pied flycatcher, with its smart black and white plumage. The female chooses ready-made holes, and builds a nest of oak leaves and grass, often in a tree near running water, perhaps to make feeding easier on the abundance of aquatic insects that swarm above streams.

Some surprisingly large birds nest in holes. The tawny owl – familiar by virtue of its 'tu-whit-tu-woo' call though rarely seen – normally nests in holes in trees, though it will occasionally use old squirrels' dreys and other nest-sites. Its relative, the attractive little owl, which was introduced into Britain from the Continent about 100 years ago, is also a frequent hole-nester, but by no means always in woodland. The stock dove, which looks very similar to its unpopular relative the wood pigeon, is a much less conspicuous bird that nests most frequently in tree-holes in woodland, though it also occurs elsewhere. Almost all hole-nesters, of whatever size, can be encouraged to nest in boxes, and there are specially-made ones available for most species up to and including owls. By putting up boxes birds can be encouraged to nest in woods where there are no natural holes, indicating that it is often a shortage of nest-sites that limits where birds breed.

In an average lowland woodland, probably the greatest number of birds nest in low thick cover, and some species even nest on the ground. Many of the contributors to the dawn chorus, which is so impressive in a wood, nest in these areas but sing from higher song perches and feed in yet another place. Blackcaps, garden warblers, willow warblers, chiffchaffs, blackbirds, nightingales, robins and many others all nest in these lower regions.

The mix of birds one is likely to see will change from wood to wood. The geographical location, the mix of trees, the age, management and size of the wood all have a bearing on the number and type of species present. A large wood will conceivably support more species than a small wood which not only has less space and diversity of tree species, but will also tend to lose resident breeding species through disturbance and bad winter weather. Birds that nest in woods may forage in surrounding hedgerows and fields and species which use the woods in winter may never be seen there in summer.

BRITISH WOODPECKERS

Besides the woodland birds we have already looked at, there are three species of woodpecker and a strange related bird called the wryneck. All four species build their nests in tree-holes. Look out also for the treecreeper with its curved bill for winkling out insects from under bark.

All of our four woodpeckers have strong beaks and long tongues suited to their particular feeding habits and share the habit of breeding in holes in trees.

The green woodpecker is undoubtedly the most conspicuous and familiar. At rest, it is a beautiful green bird, with lighter underparts and a red cap, together with a fine black 'moustache', though it is most often seen flying away with a characteristic undulating flight. When on the wing, it appears to be more yellowish in colour, and is often mistaken for other birds, though its characteristic loud laughing call is totally distinctive and has given rise to its country name of the yaffle. Although the green woodpecker nests in holes in trees, it feeds mainly on the ground on its favourite food – ants. It has a long sticky tongue which is used to lap up the ants, either from the ground or after the woodpecker has excavated the ants' nest, and in grassland ant-hills which have been broken open by green woodpeckers are quite a common sight. You will often find their tell-tale cigar-shaped droppings, too, filled with ant remains.

The wryneck, on the other hand, is seen only very rarely. It is an inconspicuous bird anyway but, in recent years, has declined to the point of extinction as a breeding species. Once, it was widespread throughout England, but its numbers decreased all through this century and, by the early 1960s, it was confined to one or two south-eastern counties of Eng-

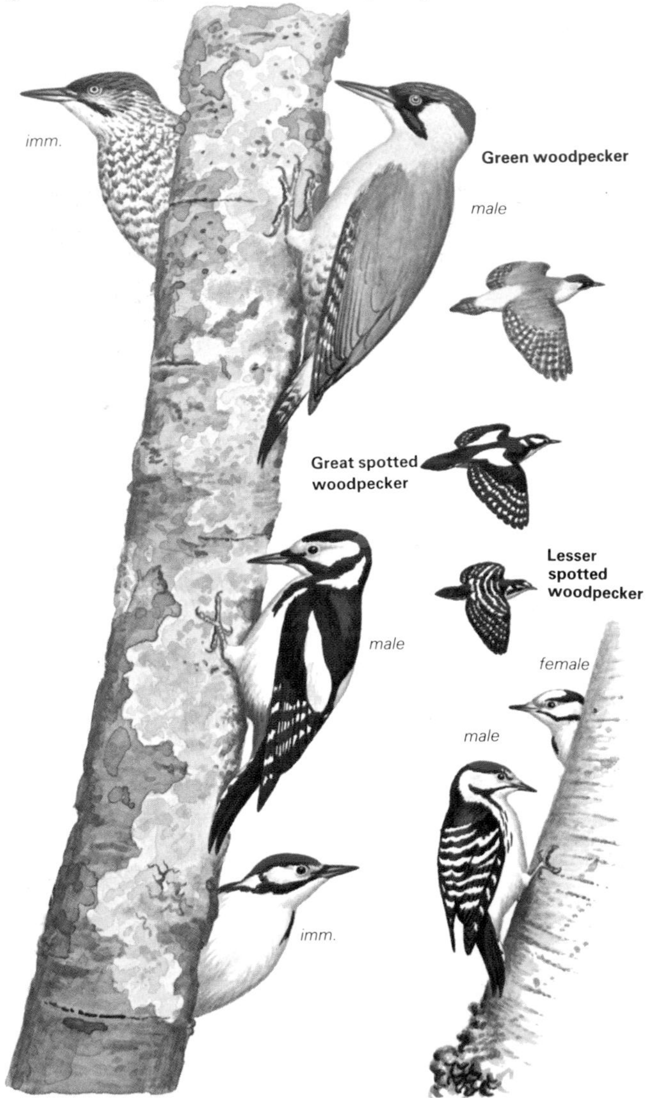

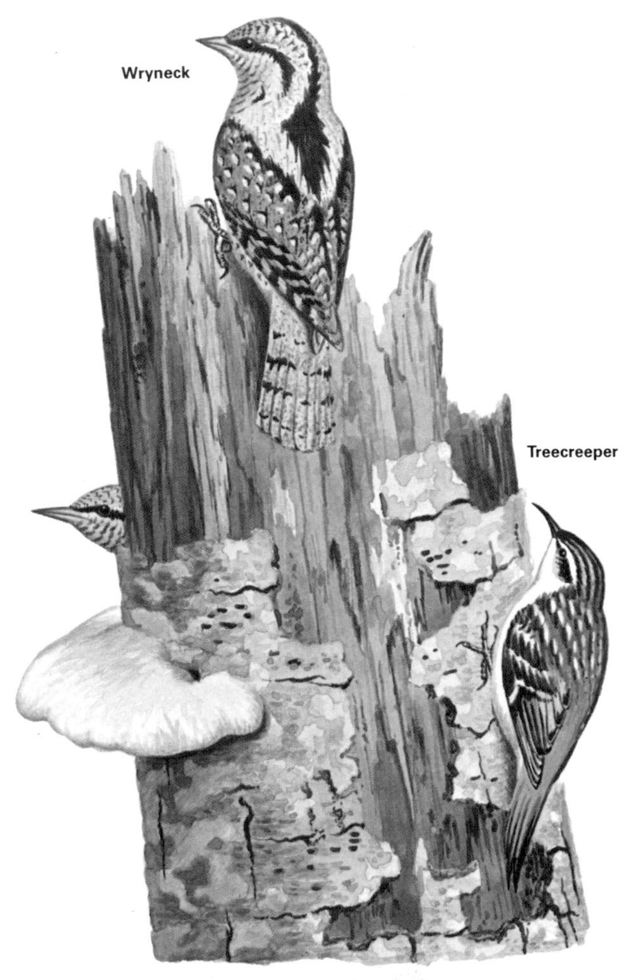

Woodpeckers commonly seen in Britain. Also shown is the elusive wryneck and the dainty treecreeper with which it may conceivably be confused

land where it bred in very small numbers. This was followed by hopeful signs as new breeding colonies, almost certainly of Scandinavian origin, became established in north-east Scotland; unfortunately the decline continued and it must now be considered extinct. The only wrynecks likely to be seen are those on passage in autumn or, to a lesser extent, in spring. It is a fascinating bird, and we can only hope that one day it will re-establish itself. Although similar to woodpeckers in having the same hole-nesting habit and the same strong beak and long tongue; it differs in several other respects. It feeds mostly on the ground, and when it does climb trees has a very different posture, because it lacks the stiff tail of the woodpeckers; it tends to spend more time in a horizontal position, using its long mobile neck almost like a snake. The reasons for its dramatic decline are not known exactly, but the most likely causes are a change in the climate, making Britain a little less suitable, and a gradual loss of its preferred habitats – old grassland, heathland and open parkland with scattered trees. It used to breed in orchards with old trees, but the current preference on the part of the fruit-growing industry for young trees, with fertilised grassland below, has deprived it of both nesting-sites and food.

There are two spotted woodpeckers, the great and the lesser spotted. Of the two, the great is the most familiar and common. It is a very attractive bird with black and white plumage, bright red under the tail and a red nape in the male. Its loud drumming, which is made by rapid striking of a particularly resonant branch, is well known and often heard, especially in spring. It is a form of territorial display and is used in a similar way to singing, marking out the pair's breeding area. The two spotted woodpeckers are the most likely species to be found in woodland, as they nest and feed in trees, though both will use isolated ones in gardens or parks. The great spotted is more adaptable of the two, often coming to bird-tables for fat, nuts, fruit and other food. The lesser spotted though not rare is never abundant, and its small size and retiring habits mean that it is unlikely to be seen unless specifically looked for, or detected by its call. Both species are highly adapted for removing insect larvae from wood, with very strong beaks for making holes, and a long sticky barbed tongue for removing the grubs from insect galleries once they have been found.

The great spotted woodpecker is sometimes seen in gardens and parks but is more often heard 'drumming' against a tree in short bursts

BIRDS OF CONIFER PLANTATIONS

The dark and gloomy corridors of conifer plantations support a surprising array of birds, many of which specialise in living in such places. They include such diverse birds as long-eared owls, goldcrests and crossbills.

Conifer plantations are far from being ideal places for wildlife of any sort. The trees are usually alien and support far fewer insects, there is little or no undergrowth for feeding and nesting, and the trees are not left long enough to become fully mature so never provide a good supply of holes and crannies for nest-sites. Nevertheless, they do offer shelter and freedom for disturbance, a limited range of places to nest in the foliage or close to the trunk, and a food supply in the form of cone seeds and some insects. For the few bird species that do use plantations, they are something of a haven.

There are a number of native birds that have long been adapted to life in pine woods, depending either on the supply of seeds or on the particular insect life associated with the native Scots pine. The dwindling acreage of native pinewoods (see page 92) in Scotland meant that such birds had become rare, but some have been able to stage a revival, using the extensive commercial planting of conifers as a

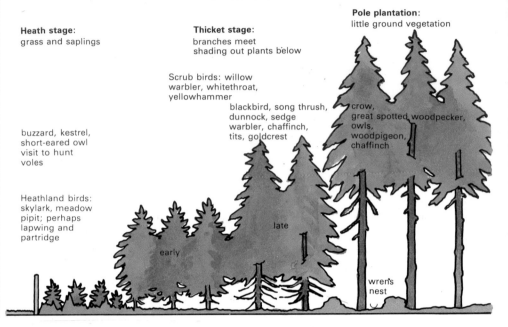

Where to look for birds in coniferous plantations

Heath stage: grass and saplings

Thicket stage: branches meet shading out plants below

Pole plantation: little ground vegetation

Scrub birds: willow warbler, whitethroat, yellowhammer

blackbird, song thrush, dunnock, sedge warbler, chaffinch, tits, goldcrest

crow, great spotted woodpecker, owls, woodpigeon, chaffinch

buzzard, kestrel, short-eared owl visit to hunt voles

Heathland birds: skylark, meadow pipit; perhaps lapwing and partridge

early

late

wren's nest

Above: A picture of rather ill-designed conifer plantation on the slopes of the Brecon Beacons, Wales. The lack of light below the dense canopy of needles drives out most species of birds leaving those that have evolved a special relationship with this rather alien environment. Crossbills feed almost exclusively on conifer seeds and may provide a brood with over 100,000 seeds before they fledge. Other birds, such as the coal tit, feed on insects in summer and seeds in winter. You may even see siskins visiting bird-tables in winter

springboard. Specialised birds like the crested tit seem to have failed to take much advantage of these changes, but others, like the crossbill, have been able to expand their range greatly, though our current crossbill populations are not necessarily originated from the Scottish ones.

The crossbill is a highly specialised and fascinating bird. It has a very large beak with crossed-over ends, like a curved pair of scissors. This extreme adaptation reflects its almost total dependence on the one food source, conifer seeds. In fact there are several races of crossbills, each one tending to specialise in one group of conifers, and most of ours are the spruce-feeding common crossbill, though of course the native race feeds on pine seeds. They differ primarily in minor beak characteristics, with each adapted to the different cones, but all feed by cutting through the cone and scissoring out the seeds. The males, in particular, are very attractive birds with a brick-red and brown plumage. Their habit of feeding in the topmost branches makes them easily missed, though they are most readily detected by the sounds of eating and falling cone-scales. They nest in the conifer branches, often well out towards the ends, and rear their young on a diet of partly-digested conifer seeds. Crossbill young take much longer to fledge than those of other finches, and it may be two months before they are able to feed themselves. This is largely because conifer seeds are a poorer source of protein than the insect-rich diet of most young finches.

Siskins are lovely canary-like finches that are also particularly associated with conifers and have spread even more widely with the extension of maturing conifer plantations. They breed mainly in northern areas, though their range is still extending, and they are now quite common in, for example, the New Forest in the far south of England. In winter, our resident birds are joined by many migrants, and they feed on a wide range of seed including those of conifers but also alder, birches and others. They spread out all over the countryside at this time of year and often visit gardens for peanuts, but tend to return to plantations for the breeding season. Their nests are often high in the trees and far out on the branches, making them exceptionally difficult to find, though the resplendent yellow-green male, with his smart black cap, will often be seen singing nearby.

Other small birds such as coal tits, goldcrests, firecrests, redpolls and chaffinches are all frequently associated with conifer plantations. One very different bird that also makes its home here is the long-eared owl. Although by no means confined to conifer plantations, this attractive and secretive owl does have a particular affinity for them, and this is where it is most often seen or heard. The long-eared owl is highly nocturnal, and is virtually never seen in the day, spending all the daylight hours roosting deep in a wood. It is wonderfully adapted to the dark, with very sensitive and accurate hearing, which is believed to be aided by the shape of the facial disc, which directs sound towards the ears. The long ear tufts are actually nothing to do with the ears and are used mainly in display. They prefer isolated plantations surrounded by open countryside where they can hunt, returning to the trees before dawn.

A small selection of characteristic conifer-loving birds, including the crossbill – the most specialised one of all

BIRDS OF HEDGEROWS

As far as birds are concerned, hedges are like long thin woodland edges, ideal for scrub-nesting birds, and filled with an abundance of insect and plant food. Our huge network of hedges makes a tremendous contribution to the number of birds in our countryside.

Hedges vary enormously in their structure and mixture of plants but, if the combination is right, they can be wonderful places for birds. Old hedges are generally the best, for they tend to have a much more varied mix of shrubs and trees (see page 96), and a more complicated structure, with ancient stools at the base, more of an earth bank, greater variation in the thickness of cover, and generally more trees for nests and song-perches. This sort of hedge provides quite a variety of nest-sites that will all be well-hidden when the hedge comes into leaf, in addition to plenty of insect food and an abundance of fruit and berries in autumn. Equally important, though, is the type of farmland that the hedge passes through, and an intimate mosaic of flowery meadows, ponds, small copses and so on will be infinitely better than a highly-sprayed arable farmscape.

From early spring onwards, the hedge begins to come alive with song as males start to stake out their territories, and the number and variety of birds can be quite surprising. Although hedges may support fewer species than a true woodland, the birds are very visible in hedges, giving the impression of a greater number. Yellowhammers are amongst the most characteristic birds of hedges and they are almost totally dependent on them. The bright yellow-breasted male will perch on a protruding twig and deliver his familiar song 'a little bit of bread and no cheeeeese' with the emphasis on the last syllable, whilst the duller female incubates the eggs on her nest down at the bottom of the hedge. Like many finches and other birds, the yellowhammers are strongly territorial in the breeding season, but feed together in large flocks of one or more species at other times.

One bird takes its name from the hedge – the hedge sparrow or dunnock which is not a true sparrow but a relative of the accentors. It is not entirely dependent on hedges but is very common there, and its nondescript monotonous song is a great feature of hedged landscapes. If you look closely at a dunnock, you will see that it has the thin, sharp beak of an insect-eating bird, rather than the

A male blackbird, a typical hedgerow nesting bird, bringing food to his young. The density and variety of birds that will nest in a varied, well-managed thick hedge is astonishing as shown on the right

broad bills of the seed-eating true sparrows. Other birds that nest in hedges in very large numbers include greenfinch, blackbird, linnet, chaffinch and whitethroat – an attractive little warbler. One bird that uses hedges in the breeding season, though can hardly be said to nest there, is the cuckoo. The female cuckoo, as most people know, seeks out the nests of other birds in which to lay her eggs; when the cuckoo hatches, in rather less time than the rightful inmates, it evicts them and acquires the undivided attention of the beleaguered mother! Dunnocks are amongst the favoured hosts of the cuckoo, hence the cuckoos interest in hedges.

A bird that specialises in feeding on hedgerow birds is the sparrowhawk. This is a rather unobtrusive hawk, quite common and widespread but easily missed. It has a habit of flying along one side of a hedge then suddenly swooping up and over it, catching any birds on the other side unawares and knocking one down in a cloud of feathers. Other birds that may hunt along hedgerows, looking mainly for mammals, include the ghostly barn owl and the kestrel, which hovers above the rough grass at the base of the hedge waiting for a mouse or vole to make a move.

Come autumn, the hedgerow harvest matures, and the hedges are often laden with haws, rosehips, blackberries, crab-apples, hazel-nuts and other types of seeds and berries, depending on the soil and the age of the hedge. These provide food for a fine array of birds, and the resident species, are augmented by mixed flocks of thrushes – redwings, fieldfares and blackbirds, most of which have come to Britain from areas to the north and east to feed on these rich pickings. They will roam the fields in flocks gathering the remains of the harvest of gleening the hedgerow berries.

Yellowhammers sing a persistent, hammering song, really hitting home its message – a *chitti-chitti* song with the rhythm *a-little-bit-of-bread-and . . . noooo . . . cheese*. The song is delivered from the top of a bush. Yellowhammers are buntings, with a heavy beak adapted for seed eating. They form flocks in winter, often with other birds. The nest is usually on the ground hidden in grass against a bush or hedge. They are birds of open farmland. 16.5 cm.

Kestrels are our commonest bird of prey – they can be seen hovering with fast beating wings, tail dropped. They are a common sight along motorways, for the long grass often carries a fair number of the voles they hunt. They fall in stages until within striking distance of their prey and then finally drop. They also sometimes attempt to take small birds. They possess a high *kee* or *kek* call. The nest is on a ledge on a rock outcrop, tree, or sometimes on a building far into town. 38 cm.

You may not see a hedgerow quite as busy as this one, but all of these birds could reasonably be found in a hedge, either nesting there or visiting for food

BIRDS OF OPEN FARMLAND

Although large numbers of the farmland birds live or feed in hedgerows, there are also many birds to be seen feeding, and even nesting, in the open fields, often well away from hedges. These include such birds as the skylark, two species of partridge, lapwings and rooks.

Intensively-used agricultural land is inhospitable to birds in many respects. Most fields, especially if arable, are ploughed, rolled or sprayed too frequently for birds to rear any broods between tractor visits; the variety of plants is small and few invertebrates can survive in the hostile climate of pesticides. Nevertheless, many birds feed on the crop itself or its residues, and on such invertebrates as there are. Some birds do manage to breed successfully, despite all the difficulties.

Two birds that epitomise open farmland today are the skylark and the lapwing. The skylark must be one of Britain's best-loved birds, constantly celebrated in poetry and other writings for its evocative song. It is a real open-country bird, needing no song-post or nesting cover. The nest is always made on the ground, in grassland or other crops, and they will nest in more intensively used areas of farmland. The song, though not especially melodious, is wonderfully sustained, starting when the bird begins to ascend, carrying on as the bird flies and hovers for five minutes or more, and then continuing as it descends. The sound of several skylarks singing from high in the air, often almost out of sight, is one of the finest sounds of the countryside.

Lapwings are equally typical of open farmland and they are, perhaps, more at home here than any other bird. In winter, they will gather in large flocks, hundreds of birds strong to feed on stubble, plough and pasture, eating worms, insect larvae and other invertebrates. Many of the birds are migrants from the Continent, though they are common breeders in this country too. It is an amazing sight to see a flock of such apparently conspicuous birds land in a field and virtually disappear. Their secret is that though they may look predominantly black and white in flight, espe-

A rookery in beech trees in the spring. Although much less common than in the past, rooks and rookeries are still a familiar sight – and sound – in villages throughout the British countryside

cially from below, when they land and close their wings they are more of a greenish-black colour which blends in with anything. In fact, one of their other common names is green plover, reflecting this colour, and a third is the peewit, referring to their melancholy double-syllable call. At any time of year they are attractive birds, though perhaps they are best seen in the breeding season, when the individuals fly close to you to draw you away from the nest, and tumbling display flights take place constantly above their territories. Although they nest in wet meadows and on moorland, they have also taken to breeding successfully on farmland in large numbers, either in arable fields or in permanent pasture. The nest is just a mat of grass in a depression (though this is more than most waders make) containing four well-camouflaged eggs. It is estimated that there are around 200,000 breeding pairs of lapwings in Britain, though their numbers fluctuate according to the severity of the winters.

Partridges are a great feature of farmland, as a covey of dumpy birds takes flight and whirrs off to another field. But in fact, there are two species of partridge that are widespread in Britain; the common partridge and the red-legged partridge or Frenchman. The common partridge is a native bird, though it is difficult to regard it as such, because populations have been constantly introduced from abroad and existing ones maintained by breeding – all in the interests of shooting. The red-legged partridge was first introduced from France about 200 years ago, and is now common in many areas, especially in eastern England. Both occur in similar habitats, especially on farmland, though the red-legged is easily distinguished as it is larger and has prominent black and white eye-stripes, barred flanks and red legs.

Crows have for hundreds of years been regarded as vermin. They have been poisoned, trapped and shot to the extent that their natural habitat is not clear and now they survive where they can. They usually nest high in the fork of a tree, taking a variety of food, including birds, eggs and carrion; but, contrary to folklore, rarely (if ever) attacking living young lambs. They have a rather laboured flight and the call is a hoarse *kraah* repeated three or four times. The all-black crow is resident in western Europe, and is the one most often seen in England, Wales and southern Scotland. However, the hooded crow, with the bulk of its body greyish and with black head, neck and wing feathers, can also be seen in Iceland; in Scotland north-west of the Caledonian Canal; and on the Continent. Where the range of these two races (subspecies) meets, they interbreed. In winter, hooded crows sometimes fly some distance south. To 47 cm.

Red-legged partridges were introduced (from France) a couple of centuries ago and have colonised in places, especially in the drier south and east. The call is a *chuka chuka*. The bird is slightly larger than the grey partridge. To 33 cm.

A habitat picture showing most of the commoner birds of open farmland, in the various situations where you are most likely to see them

Birds of Scrub

Somewhere in between the two habitats of grassland and woodland, there is a bushy mixture known as scrub. Such places, with their abundance of food and cover, are often alive with a wide variety of birds for most of the year.

Scrub can best be described as an area of ground with a partial, or occasionally total, covering of bushes and young trees. It is nearly always a temporary habitat, in the sense that it is usually a stage between open land and woodland, though certain situations can maintain scrub for a long time. Any piece of land in Britain, except for the highest, most exposed or most infertile sites, will quickly become covered by invading scrub if it is no longer ploughed, grazed or mown, so much of this habitat derives from abandoned fields, old ungrazed downland or railway lines no longer cut annually. The mixture that makes up the scrub will depend both on the range of trees and shrubs to be found locally, since their seeds tend not to disperse far, and on the soil and situation. A chalk downland scrub will, for example, probably have a mixture of dogwood, hawthorn, spindle, wild clematis, wayfaring tree and others, whilst in the upland it would be more likely to contain downy birch, juniper, rowan and possibly young pines. Another situation that produces a scrub habitat is enclosed land planted with trees; although more regimented than naturally occurring scrub, the effect is very similar for a few years, and may be very good for certain birds.

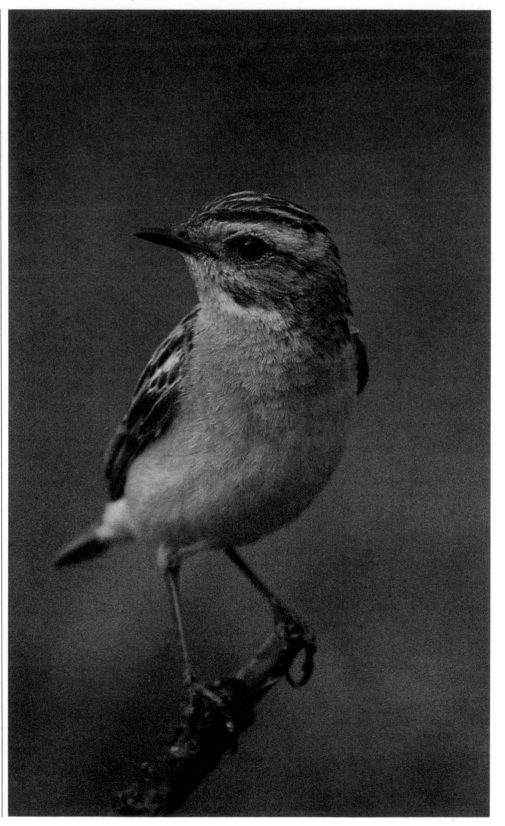

The birds that are found in scrub depend upon the structure of the habitat – the density, the height of the trees and how much open land there is – and, to a lesser extent, on the types of bushes and trees present. Some of the birds that frequent scrub are the same as those found along hedges, whilst others are woodland birds, though there are a few that frequently breed here much more than anywhere else. The warblers, as a group, particularly favour scrub; there are, for example, two species of whitethroat which both nest regularly in this habitat – the whitethroat and the lesser whitethroat. The whitethroat is one of our most visible and attractive warblers, often seen singing its short melodious song from the top of a bush, where its white throat and breast stand out in contrast to its brown back. Whitethroats have an unusually aggressive looking courtship, in which the male seems to attack the female by rushing at her, singing, and often follows her around with a piece of grass in his beak. The female responds by spreading her wings and tail and leaping at the male, as if to drive him away, though he always avoids the assault. The male frequently builds several nests, working on two or three at once, but often none of them will be completed.

The lesser whitethroat is a much less familiar bird, usually detected by its song emanating from a dense patch of scrub, but even this can be overlooked. Occasionally, the male will sing from a perch when defending territory, but usually they remain hidden; they are generally less common than their larger cousins. Other warblers to be found in scrub include the ubiquitous willow warbler, which is very undistinguished in appearance but has a highly recognisable song, consisting of a high-pitched, wistful cadence of notes – one of the most characteristic sounds of high summer wherever there are bushes. The grasshopper warbler, which unfortunately is much less common that it was, is another regular bird in scrub, and its strange song can often be heard though the bird itself is rarely seen. It sounds more like an old-fashioned sewing machine, or perhaps a free-wheeling bicycle, than a grasshopper, and it continues reeling for long periods of time, turning its head from side to side to spread the sound. Besides the warblers, the other characteristic breeding birds of scrub include tree pipit, whinchat, yellowhammer and many common hedge and garden birds, such as robin, dunnock and blackbird.

At other times of year, too, the scrub is good for birds. Migrants will use it for feeding up before they leave, or roosting and shelter, and as their first landfall if patches occur near the coast. Most bushes bear good crops of berries, like haws, hips and elderberries, and these attract many birds in autumn and winter, especially thrushes such as redwings and fieldfares. These two species migrate to this country in autumn from Scandinavia.

Left: A female whinchat perched on a twig on the way to her nest on the ground. Whinchats are often seen in this characteristic pose and will stand upright on low bushes, thistles, fences or barbed wire, occasionally flicking their tails and making their alarm call when they sense danger

Here is a selection of the birds most likely to be found nesting in amongst scrub and bushy areas. Blackbirds are often heard rummaging around in the undergrowth sounding like small rodents. The garden warbler is very elusive and stays well inside bushes from where it may be heard singing its song. The willow warbler may be glimpsed in the trees and nightingales nest on or near the ground with a preference for coppiced groves. Nightingles are summer visitors from central Africa and are restricted to the south-east of Britain

BIRDS OF LOWLAND HEATHS

The seemingly barren heathland wastes are actually home to a fascinating variety of birds, some of which occur nowhere else in Britain. They range from the tiny, secretive Dartford warbler to that dashing falcon, the hobby.

The birdlife of a heath is undoubtedly sparse; there are relatively few species and they tend to occur in quite small numbers for the habitat is not a particularly productive one. Nevertheless, the birds which are present are an interesting collection and many of them are rare and unusual.

The bird that, in Britain, has come to symbolise heathland more than any other is the Dartford warbler. For this is its only regular habitat and it is therefore totally dependent upon our dwindling heaths for its survival. It is, in addition, one of the very few warblers that remain in Britain all the year round, continuing to live on a diet of insects right through the winter, in contrast to the majority of its relatives that leave for warmer areas. In fact, it used to be considered the only resident warbler, but the advent of Cetti's warblers and the increasing numbers of overwintering blackcaps has altered its unique status. This demanding requirement inevitably means that the Dartford warbler is confined to heaths in the warmest English counties, notably Dorset and Hampshire, and it is on the northern edge of its range here. It spends the winter seeking out spiders, insects, larvae and other invertebrate food in the heather and amongst gorse; it has a particular requirement for a mixture

Here are a selection of birds you are likely to see on lowland heaths. Listen out for the churning call of the nightjar at dusk

of heather and moderately mature gorse in its territory. Not surprisingly, its numbers fluctuate considerably according to the severity of each winter, and a very hard year with prolonged freezing weather can lead to severe population crashes. For example, after the winter of 1962/63, which was particularly cold in the Dartford warbler's stronghold, the numbers crashed from around 460 pairs to just 11 pairs.

Perhaps the most dashing of heathland birds, though by no means only confined to this area, is the hobby. The main two habitats in Britain of this most attractive falcon, are heathlands and downlands. It is only a summer visitor to this country and never occurs in large numbers. It arrives late in the spring and, instead of making its own nest, takes over the deserted nest of a crow, squirrel or even sparrowhawk, often high in a pine tree, and the female lays her three white eggs in June. Although not large birds, hobbies are impressive by virtue of their strongly back-swept wings, which makes them look rather like a large swift, and their powerful agile flight. They catch all their prey on the wing, and can outfly house martins, swallows and even bats. Most heathland hobbies tend to move towards wet, boggy areas for feeding where they catch dragonflies in the air, and often eat them without a pause. Their mastery of flying is shown to greatest advantage in the courtship flights, where the male catches a suitable small bird, climbs high into the air, then dives down towards the female and passes her the prey at full speed.

A nocturnal bird of heaths, that is quite often heard but very rarely seen, is the curious nightjar or goatsucker as it is sometimes known. During the day, the nightjar lies up amongst bracken or bushes, superbly camouflaged by its colouring, so that you could easily walk within centimetres of the bird and not see it. As night falls, they take to the air on their softly-feathered wings in search of moths and other insects, which they trap in their large gaping beaks. It is only after sunset that they produce their song, an eerie churring (from which the name nightjar comes) that rises and falls in volume as the bird turn its head from side to side. During courtship, they fly up into the air and clap their wings together making a sound like a cracking whip. It is sad that so strange and beautiful a bird should have decreased to the point of rarity in recent decades, through loss of habitat, declines in its insect food and difficulties on its migrations to and from Africa.

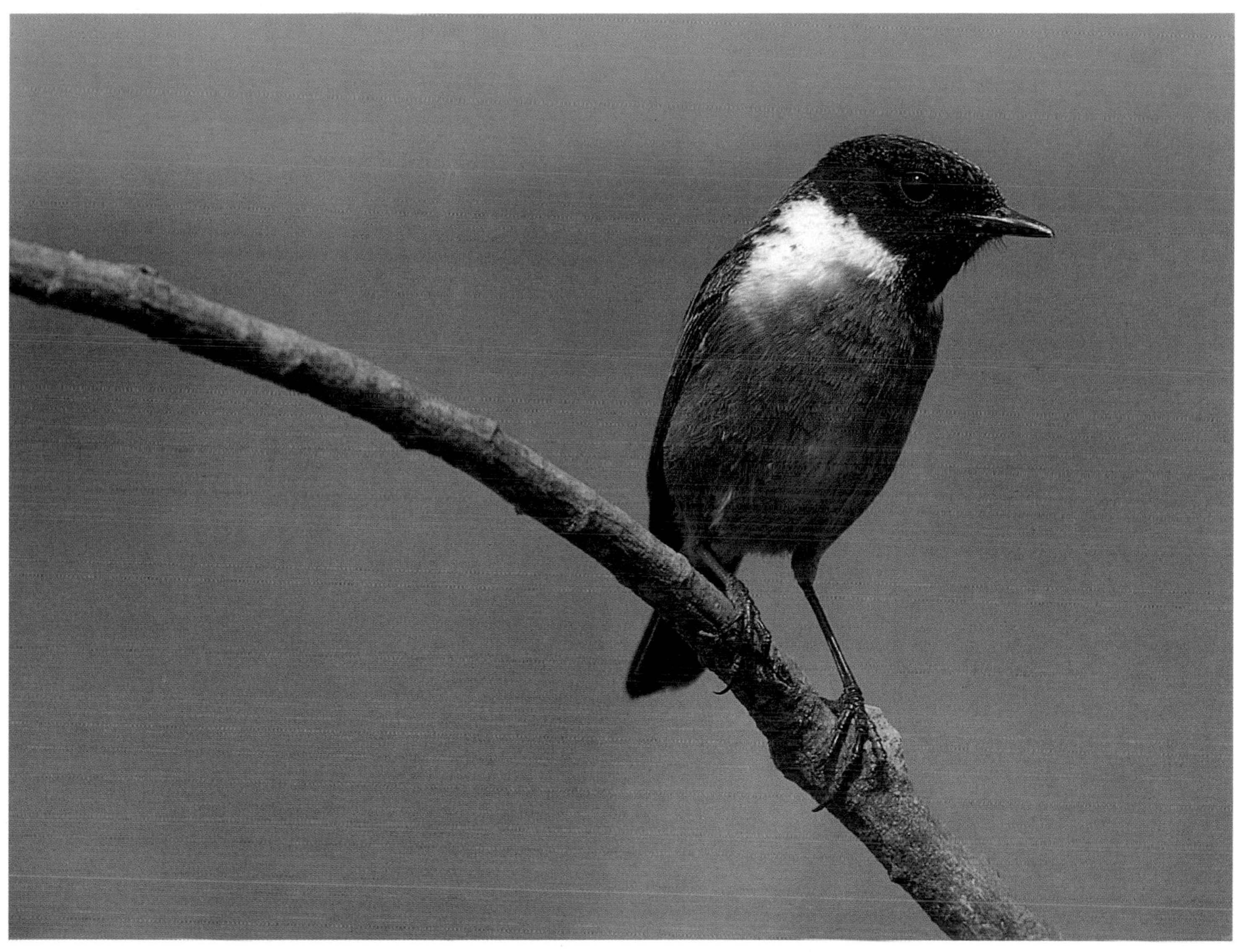

A male stonechat perched characteristically upright, flicking his tail and wings restlessly. They are most likely to be seen on heaths and commons near the coast in the south and west of England

BIRDS OF DOWNLAND

The high chalk and limestone uplands are home to several rare and strange birds in addition to the commoner skylarks, meadow pipits and finches that are found in large numbers there. Of these, the stone curlew is undoubtedly the strangest of them all.

Downlands are, contrary to their name, actually uplands, usually of chalk or limestone. Over many centuries, such areas have been managed almost exclusively for sheep-grazing, producing an open unfenced countryside carpeted with a fine turf, rich in flowers and insects – 'champagne' country, as it is sometimes known. More recently, however, changes in agricultural methods have meant that vast acreages of downland have been lost under the plough, and barley stands in its place. Such areas are exceptionally rich in plants and insects and they also have their own special birds. If the downland is sheltered or well-covered with scrub then the birds include many that occur in woods, hedges and bushy areas in general, though they will often include such unusual species as nightjars. Wide open downs, in contrast, attract fewer species, though some of these are of special interest.

Skylark

Meadow pipit

Tree pipit

song flight

imm.

Quail

female

Red-legged partridge

rear flight view

male

female

male

rear flight view

Partridge

imm.

female

male

juv.

Wheatear

Corn Bunting

Of the downland birds shown here look out for the skylark and meadow pipit. The skylark sings hovering high in the air, the meadow pipit flies high up only commencing singing as it floats down to earth

The stone curlew, or thick-knee, is a most extraordinary bird. It is related to the waders, but its life-cycle is completely adapted to dry conditions, and its primary home is in the deserts and dry areas of southern Europe and the Middle East. In Britain, we are on the extreme north-western edge of its world range – one of the reasons that it is so rare here. The habitats in Britain that most closely match its normal desert home are heathlands and downlands, and it has always bred in small numbers on both, mainly in southern and eastern England. However, the clearance of these areas for agriculture has led to the birds moving to open arable land from their more natural habitats. Newly-ploughed or planted land is as similar to desert as anything, and the birds can easily select a nest-site with a good view and plenty of opportunities for feeding, and many birds have bred successfully here. Unfortunately, autumn has tended to mean that the farming activities coincide more with the birds' breeding cycle, and the number of successful broods has gone down dramatically. Now small numbers of pairs breed in a mixture of places, such as the few remaining open downs, some heaths and arable fields helped along by schemes to find and mark their nests to prevent them from being destroyed by agricultural machinery.

Stone curlews are shy, secretive birds but are most often detected by their calls which are mainly heard in the evening and at night. It mixes its normal rather curlew-like call (hence its name) with a weird assortment of other noises, quite unlike any other bird in this habitat. The cries carry for at least a mile on a still night, and in one area they were once thought to be the voices of hanged criminals calling to each other in the night!

Other rare birds that occasionally nest on downland, or have done so in the recent past, include the beautiful bird of prey the Montagu's harrier and the red-backed shrike. Their flight pattern is elegant and floating on their long pointed wings. Both the Montagu's harrier and red-backed shrike also breed on heathland, like the stone curlew, but are now exceptionally rare and seldom seen, though Montagu's harriers have been breed-

Stone curlews like the one above only occur in small numbers in southern and eastern England but are very striking and unmistakeable when seen

though, most farmland is more disturbed than natural habitats, and it seems that regular rolling, spraying or other activities have been one of the main factors contributing to the bird's decline in Britain. In chalk areas, a change of planting time from spring to

ing on downland in southern England in the last few years. In winter, a relative of the red-backed shrike, the great grey shrike may return regularly to the same area of downs though, on the whole, downs are rather lacking in birds in winter.

Birds of Wet Meadows

As spring comes to the wet meadows along our river valleys, they come alive with the calls and courtship of many attractive birds. Among them are waders including the lapwing, redshank and snipe, whilst in among grasses and reeds may be seen the reed warbler and reed bunting.

Wet tussocky meadows, such as found along many river valley flood-plains and around lakes, are particularly attractive areas for a number of breeding birds. Such areas often flood in winter, sometimes for several months but, as they dry out towards the end of the season, they begin to become suitable for nesting.

The first birds to arrive on the meadows are often redshanks, coming in as early as March. Redshanks are waders, and they have the distinctive long legs of that group which, in this case, are bright red, as their name suggests. At rest, they are an inconspicuous brownish-grey, but when they take flight they reveal a white rump and a broad white stripe extending up the back, while the wings are brown with a broad white bar on the trailing edges. This plumage pattern together with the red legs and the distinctive flute-like whistling call make identification easy. The birds return to their breeding grounds from the coast or other wintering areas, and noisily take up territories with much calling and displaying. The males call, making a trisyllabic whistling sound, from a fence post, or in flight, as they hover up and down like yo-yos. The redshank's nest is a grass-lined depression, usually under or close to a tussock of sedges or rushes, and the female usually lays a clutch of four speckled eggs. They are much more likely to breed in rough cattle-grazed pasture or very tussocky areas, rather than in mown meadows or evenly-grazed pastures, as they seem to need the tussocks for their nest-sites. The eggs may often be laid before March is out and this makes breeding a risky business since there may still be floods, frosts and even snow at this time of year. One brood is the rule but they will relay if something happens to the first clutch. Generally, redshanks have been declining as a breeding bird, partly because of the drainage of their habitat, though in many cases they have also decreased where the habitat has remained apparently the same. Apart from wet meadows and bogs, their prime breeding sites are on salt-marshes all round the coasts.

Two relatives of the redshank that breed regularly in wet meadows are the snipe and the lapwing, whilst two other waders that have made a welcome comeback as rare breeding birds of wetland are the ruff and the black-tailed godwit. Snipe advertise their presence during the breeding season by a loud call and by an extraordinary noise called drumming. This is produced by the male when he flies sharply downwards and is caused by the two outer tail feathers vibrating rhythmically in the wind, producing a bleating sound; it is a particularly evocative feature of wet meadow

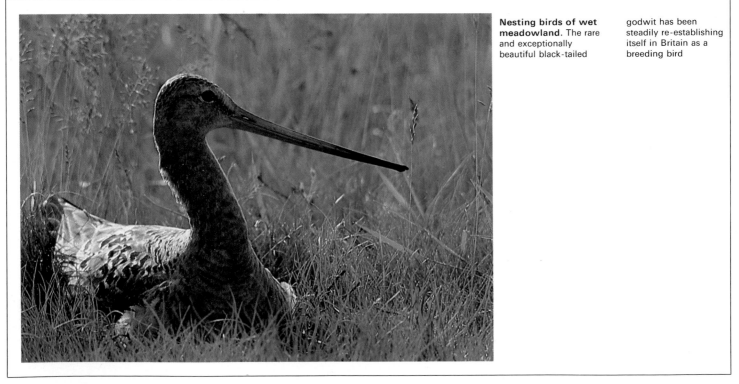

Nesting birds of wet meadowland. The rare and exceptionally beautiful black-tailed godwit has been steadily re-establishing itself in Britain as a breeding bird

areas in spring. It was over 150 years ago that the beautiful black-tailed godwit disappeared as a breeding bird in Britain, partly through loss of fenland habitat in eastern England and because so many were caught and sold as table delicacies. But, in 1952, they returned to breed in East Anglia, and have since become established on protected sites in Somerset and elsewhere – a success of the enlightened attitude towards birds and their conservation. The extraordinary-looking ruff and its female, the reeve, followed a similar pattern, becoming largely extinct as breeding birds over a century ago. Then, in 1963, a few pairs began to breed in the Ouse Washes in Cambridgeshire, and from there they have gradually extended their range to other parts of the country. They are still a very rare bird, but there is hope that this attractive wader, with its exaggerated courtship display, may become a frequent sight again in Britain.

All of the birds mentioned so far are waders but one, quite unrelated bird, which breeds primarily in wet meadows is the lovely yellow wagtail. They are wholly migratory birds, returning to Britain from Africa in April and May, announcing their return to the breeding ground with a series of distinctive high-pitched 'tseep' sounds. They are distinctly more yellow than their stream-dwelling cousins the grey wagtails, and are a most attractive sight as they cross the meadow in bounding flight or as the male perches on a post or bush to sing his feeble song.

The grey wagtail nests on rock ledges under cliffs or bridges. They prefer quick flowing brooks or upland streams but may be found alongside slow flowing lowland rivers.

Snipe probe for worms and other invertebrates in soft ground in marshes, with their long sensitive bills. They are most active at dusk in summer and usually are first noticed when they perform their territorial display flight in which they fan their tail feathers out and plunge at a steep angle with a distinctive 'bleating' or drumming sound. Normally when flushed they have an evasive zig-zag flight and make a *skaap* call. 27 cm.

The shoveler strains watery mud through its large spoon-shaped bill, sifting out small seeds and invertebrates. It breeds in the shallows of scattered lowland lakes, sometimes in small colonies. Our breeders migrate in autumn to be replaced by others from further north. 48 cm.

The sedge warbler is found throughout Britain in 'high marsh' where you might see its brief, fluttering song flights, rising steeply then dropping with wings outstretched. The song is more varied than the reed warbler's, often mimicking other birds. Note the distinct eye-stripe and streaked back. Summer visitor. Numbers have dropped noticeably in recent years following droughts in its wintering grounds south of the Sahara. 13 cm.

Like other waders, redshank will often be seen swimming when feeding. The pied wagtail below can be recognised from afar by its bouncing flight.

The breeding birds of wet meadowland are a beautiful group, and this picture shows the majority of them in their habitat

BIRDS OF FRESHWATER

Water is a veritable mecca for birds throughout the year. It provides abundant food, safety from predators and many nest-sites around the edges. The next few spreads look at the immense variety of birds that live on, around or over the water.

Almost all British birds visit water at some stage, whether for drinking, bathing or feeding, but there are a number of groups of birds specially adapted to water, which live most of their lives on or within its environs. The swans, ducks and geese come readily to mind, but the grebes, divers, heron, kingfisher and moorhen also depend on this habitat. We have already seen just how productive a place freshwater is, unless it is polluted or very cold or acid, and most water-birds take advantage of this by feeding at or close to the top of the food-chain. Some, such as the majestic osprey, the merganser and divers, and the grey heron, are fish-eaters, often taking large fish that are themselves carnivores; others such as the smaller grebes and certain ducks especially the pochard and tufted duck dive for small fish, crustacea, insects and other invertebrates. There are also birds that feed primarily on aquatic plant food, such as mallard or wigeon, while some ducks, like the teal, specialise in seeds of water plants when they are available.

Water-birds, therefore, utilise all aspects of water-life for feeding and they can often occur in large quantities because of the abundance of food available. It is also particularly noticeable that many birds congregate at water in winter because, unless it is so frozen that food is inaccessible to them, life in freshwater can continue

A family of mute swans the most numerous of our swans with eight cygnets, floating down a lowland chalk river

at a higher pace than in terrestrial areas. Generally, the temperature of water remains above that of the land during winter (although it may not feel like it, if you put your hand in) and there is not the same dead, dormant period as on the land.

A large body of water also makes a wonderful safe haven for birds at any time of year. Terrestrial predators, like foxes cannot easily catch them, and there are very few aquatic pred-

are particularly sensitive to disturbance, so they tend to seek out the larger lakes where they can remain in the middle. As a result water bodies are very good places for birdwatching and many large ponds and lakes have hides constructed by them, in the certain knowledge that there will be something for visitors to see.

Water-birds also play their part in the aquatic ecosystem, not just as predators and consumers, but in other

ways, too. Some plants have seeds that are dispersed by ducks and other plant-feeders; the pondweeds, for example, have seeds that germinate much better if they have passed through the gut of waterfowl. This means that they are also likely to be well distributed, since ducks will often have moved feeding sites between the time that they eat the seed and when they get rid of it again. Similarly, a small pond snail *Potamopyrgus*

ators that can tackle an adult bird. They are not wholly protected from the activities of man, however, but are generally much less subject to disturbance and the larger the water body is, the more birds can stay there unaffected. Some birds like shoveler

The illustration above shows some of the ducks which you are likely to see dabbling or diving on Britain's freshwaters

jenkinsii is believed to have been spread throughout Britain on the feet of waterfowl, and many other creatures are thought to be distributed by water-birds from one site to another, even crossing the sea when birds migrate.

BIRDS OF FRESHWATER

Some of our most fascinating and beautiful birds are those called divers. Most people have seen the great crested grebe on our reservoirs and lakes but few will be familiar with the rare divers found in Scotland.

One group of birds that is especially well adapted to life on the water is the divers. Two species of these magnificent birds breed regularly in Britain and a third species – the great northern diver – winters regularly, and very occasionally nests here. A fourth species, the white-billed diver, is seen very occasionally as a vagrant from North America. The great northern diver is a large and spectacular bird, and it is sad that it does not breed here regularly. Its call, which has given rise to the name loon in North America, is one of the strangest and wildest of all bird calls, like an eerie mad whooping laugh, which echoes over the wild hills where the bird occurs.

All the divers are ideally suited to aquatic life, with webbed feet and legs set well back on the body for efficient propulsion in water. They coast about on the surface of the water looking for prey, often ducking their head below the surface to get a better view. On sighting something interesting, they sink below the surface with barely a ripple, and can then swim submerged at great speed in pursuit of fish or other food such as crustaceans. They are known to regularly dive down to ten metres or more, and there are even records of them becoming entangled in fishing nets at depths of 70 metres, which must be the greatest depths reached by birds underwater. In contrast, when on land, they are ungainly and slow, looking rather unbalanced with their legs so far to the back of the body, though they are graceful and fast in flight.

The commonest of our divers is the red-throated diver. This species breeds in the north on a wide variety of freshwater bodies, including tiny lochans far from the sea, which has allowed it to become quite common on the offshore islands where larger lakes are virtually absent. The birds frequently fly quite long distances during the breeding season from their nesting pool to other aquatic feeding

A little grebe or dabchick brooding over her newly-hatched chicks on her nest on a flooded gravel pit in southern England

grounds, which may be larger lakes or the sea. There are estimated to be at least 1,000 pairs of red-throated divers in the country, all breeding in Scotland or Northern Ireland. The black-throated diver is rather more selective in its breeding habits and tends to choose larger lakes where more food is available; it, therefore, travels less far to feed during the breeding season. It is, as a result, a much rarer bird and there are probably only about 150 pairs, all to be found in Scotland.

The rather similar grebes are related to the divers, but are not so completely adapted for aquatic life their feet being only partially webbed. Six species have been recorded in Britain, though only two breed commonly. The beautiful great crested grebe almost became extinct in Britain 100 years ago, because its plumage, especially the feathers from the head, was in great demand to decorate ladies' hats. At one stage, there were estimated to be only 40 pairs of this formerly common bird in the country. Fortunately, fashions and attitudes towards birds changed, and it has steadily increased until now great crested grebes are to be seen on most suitable waters throughout the country. Their courtship is an attractive and remarkable feature of their life, notable for the series of elaborate postures and gestures by both birds and, because it takes place out on the open water, it may often be seen by the interested birdwatcher. The little grebe, or dabchick, is a common and widespread bird, though it is often overlooked. It tends to keep to cover more than its larger relative, betraying its presence by a loud distinctive call, consisting of a series of rapidly repeated notes, rising to a crescendo and then falling again. Even when it is visible out on the water, if often dives below the surface for remarkably long periods, coming up somewhere quite different with its prey in its beak. Two other species of grebe breed, though both are rare; the Slavonian grebe has spread slowly and steadily from the time of the first Scottish record in 1908, while the black-necked grebe has remained scattered and rare.

This picture shows all the native breeding species of grebes and divers found in Britain and the regular visitors

BIRDS OF FRESHWATER

Throughout the 1970s and early 1980s our rivers and lakes were becoming cleaner allowing our waterside dwelling birds to prosper. There are signs that this progress has now slowed putting these beautiful birds again at risk.

Two of the most fascinating and beautiful waterside birds are the dipper and the kingfisher, though very different in their own ways. The kingfisher is one of our most beautifully coloured and exotic looking species of birds, with its dramatic plumage of sapphire, brick-red and green. It is most often seen as a streak of colour flashing past as it flies upstream, though it is surprising how many people have never seen a kingfisher at all. Once you are familiar with its high-pitched repetitive call, often uttered in flight, this is a good clue to its presence. Kingfishers are primarily fish-eaters, though they will also take some large invertebrate prey such as dragonfly larvae or water beetles. Their nests are built at the end of long tunnels into a bank, excavated by both birds and often as much as a metre in length. The white, almost spherical eggs are laid on a bed of thin fishbones.

Kingfishers are widely spread throughout the lowlands, mainly on rivers and canals, though they are never common because they are limited by extent of their habitat and the need for fairly large territories along a river. Their numbers fluctuate considerably according to the severity of winters, and a high proportion will die if the weather is so cold that most waters freeze over. For example, one study showed that there was a pair of kingfishers every two to three kilometres along the Thames before the severe 1962/63 winter, but that the numbers were down to about one pair per 30 to 35 kilometres after the winter.

The dipper is another attractive, though very different, waterside bird. It, too, feeds almost exclusively in rivers and nests by them usually

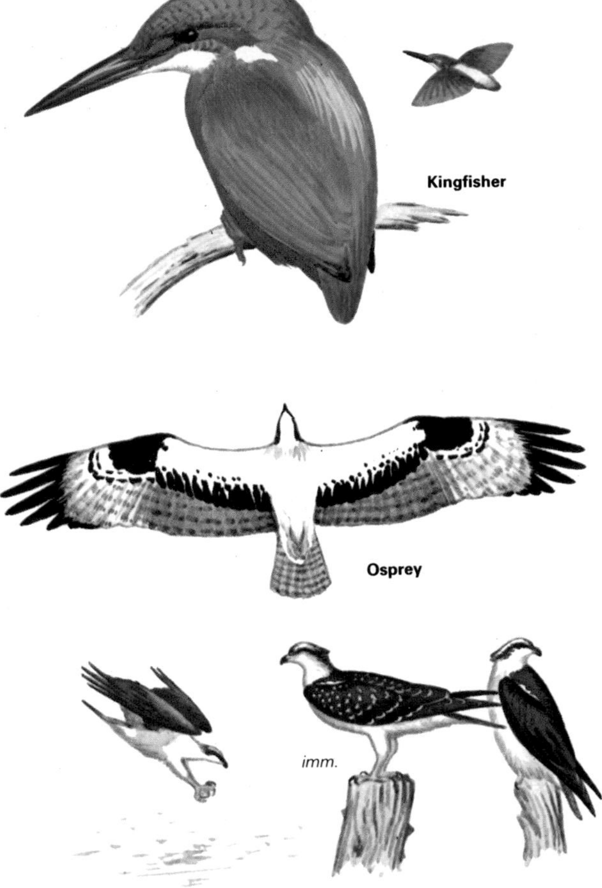

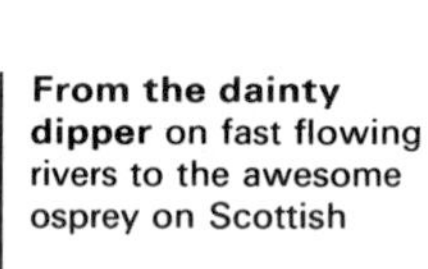

From the dainty dipper on fast flowing rivers to the awesome osprey on Scottish lakes, Britain's waters supply a livelihood to a great variety of birdlife

under an old bridge or behind a waterfall. They favour fast-flowing rivers, particularly in upland areas, and they are absent from most of the south and east. One fascinating feature about dippers is the way in which they search for food. From their perch on a midstream boulder, they will either hop, or gradually wade, into deep water but, rather than simply diving or swimming like other aquatic birds, they are known to actually walk along underwater looking for invertebrate food. The dipper's third eyelid – its nictating membrane – is particularly thick, and it is believed to protect the bird's eyes from grit and other particles whilst underwater. Although appearing white in the air, it becomes transparent underwater, allowing the bird to walk about and see what it is doing. When submerged, the dipper's strong legs and feet help to hold it down against its natural buoyancy, whilst its wings are used for maintaining balance and propulsion rather like the fins of a fish. Its main food is insect larvae, especially caddis flies, stoneflies and other inhabitants of these oxygen-rich upland streams.

There are many other birds that tend to nest near freshwater because of the plentiful supply of suitable food. The pretty grey wagtail, for example, nests on walls or bridges by streams, especially in western Britain, and it is expert at catching insects both in flight or on the ground, making use of the particularly large numbers that can be found in riverside habitats. At the opposite end of the scale is the magnificent osprey; this majestic and beautiful bird became extinct in Britain in about 1916, through persecution by gamekeepers and egg-collectors. Then, in the early 1950s, a pair returned to breed in Scotland, and they became a conservation success story. A traditional long-standing nest-site at Loch Garten is open to public viewing through the efforts of the owners, the Royal Society for the Protection of Birds, whilst elsewhere in Scotland 20 or more pairs of these beautiful birds breed. Ospreys are our only fish-eating hawks, and it is a marvellous spectacle watching them drop from 50 or 60 metres down onto a fish which is then carried off, head facing forwards, to be eaten elsewhere. If the osprey should tackle a larger fish than normal, it may make a number of attempts to rise from the water again, though it usually succeeds. We can only hope that their steady increase in numbers continues, as they are one of our most beautiful birds.

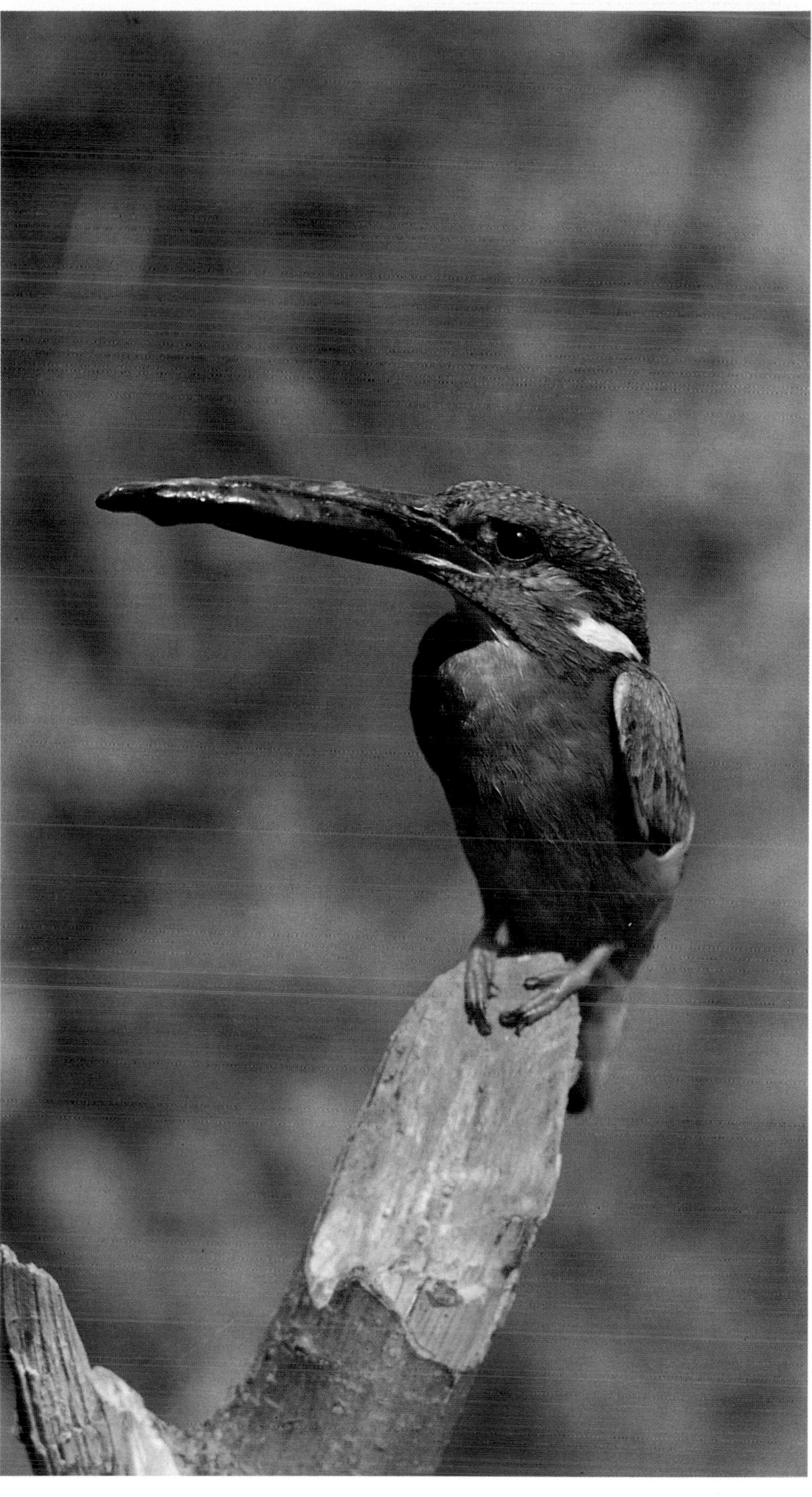

The colourful kingfisher shows all its power and grace when snapping up fish with its menacing dagger-like bill

BIRDS OF FRESHWATER, RAILS

Coots and moorhens those familiar denizens of our town canals, ponds and rivers are members of a group of birds called the 'rails'. The Sawbills also covered here have 'saw-edged' beaks and the heron, discussed on page 190, is here for comparison.

The rail family, which includes the water rail, moorhen and coot, is a particularly aquatic group, with two very familiar water-birds amongst them. The moorhen and the coot are both common and rather similar in general appearance, but are distinguished by the colour of the face and beak, which are white in the coot and red in the moorhen. Generally, the moorhen is the shyer of the two, skulking about in vegetation and only swimming around the edges of the pond rather than out into the middle. It feeds on almost anything, including invertebrates, seeds and other plant food, and may even be seen climbing up bushes in autumn to pick blackberries! Like many water-birds, moorhens fly poorly and reluctantly, skittering clumsily over the water and only really taking off when they have to. Their jerky swimming, bobbing head and flashing white tail-side feathers are very distinctive. Coots tend to be more conspicuous, though slightly less ubiquitous because they spend more time out on the open water and form large flocks. Although they are aggressive territorial birds, they are also very sociable and tend to nest in loose colonies as well as gathering in flocks on reservoirs and estuaries in the winter.

Here is a wide variety of aquatic birds including the ubiquitous coot and moorhen, familiar residents of town ponds, the heron and mergansers

The third member of the rail family, which is associated with water, is much less familiar and hardly ever seen. The water rail is not a rare bird, by any means, but it tends to spend most of its time hidden deep within reed-beds or other lake-fringing vegetation, and hardly ever shows itself. In fact, it is best detected by its eerie loud wailing call, which sounds rather like a startled pig! In winter, our native breeding population is enlarged by numbers of continental migrants but they are barely more conspicuous than the residents; it is difficult to imagine such an ungainly, skulking bird flying across the North Sea!

Most of the large duck family are aquatic at some time or other, as their webbed feet testify. Some species have been mentioned in connection with their habit of spending the winter on the coast (see page 182), but one interesting group within the ducks which has not been discussed is the sawbills. There are three species that regularly occur in Britain, two of which breed, and all three have distinctive saw-edged beaks (hence the group name) which are designed for catching and holding fish. The non-breeding bird is the smew, a very attractive white and black duck; small numbers visit lakes and reservoirs in south and east England in winter. Its main breeding ground is in Scandinavia, where it usually nests in holes in trees near to water.

The two resident species are the goosander and the red-breasted merganser, and both are attractive and impressive birds. The larger of the two, the goosander, is rather too efficient at catching fish for its own good, and it has been heavily persecuted by bailiffs in intensively fished areas. Despite this, the goosander has been spreading from its Scottish breeding stronghold southwards into lowland Scotland and northern England. It is one of the few ducks that habitually nests in holes in trees, or occasionally in holes in the bank, along the larger northern rivers. In winter, they gather on large lakes and reservoirs further south, including the area around London, where they can be easily mistaken for grebes. The rather similar red-breasted merganser is slightly smaller and has a chestnut breast and an untidy crest. It occurs in similar places, breeding along rivers and on lochs in the north, and is also spreading southwards. There are now small populations in northern England and north Wales, despite ill-informed persecution of this lovely bird. Unlike the goosander, they nest on the ground like most other ducks, and in winter they tend to head for the coast rather than inland waters. Both species have a marvellously attractive and elaborate courtship display in the breeding season which involves such posturing, standing up in the water and wing-stretching.

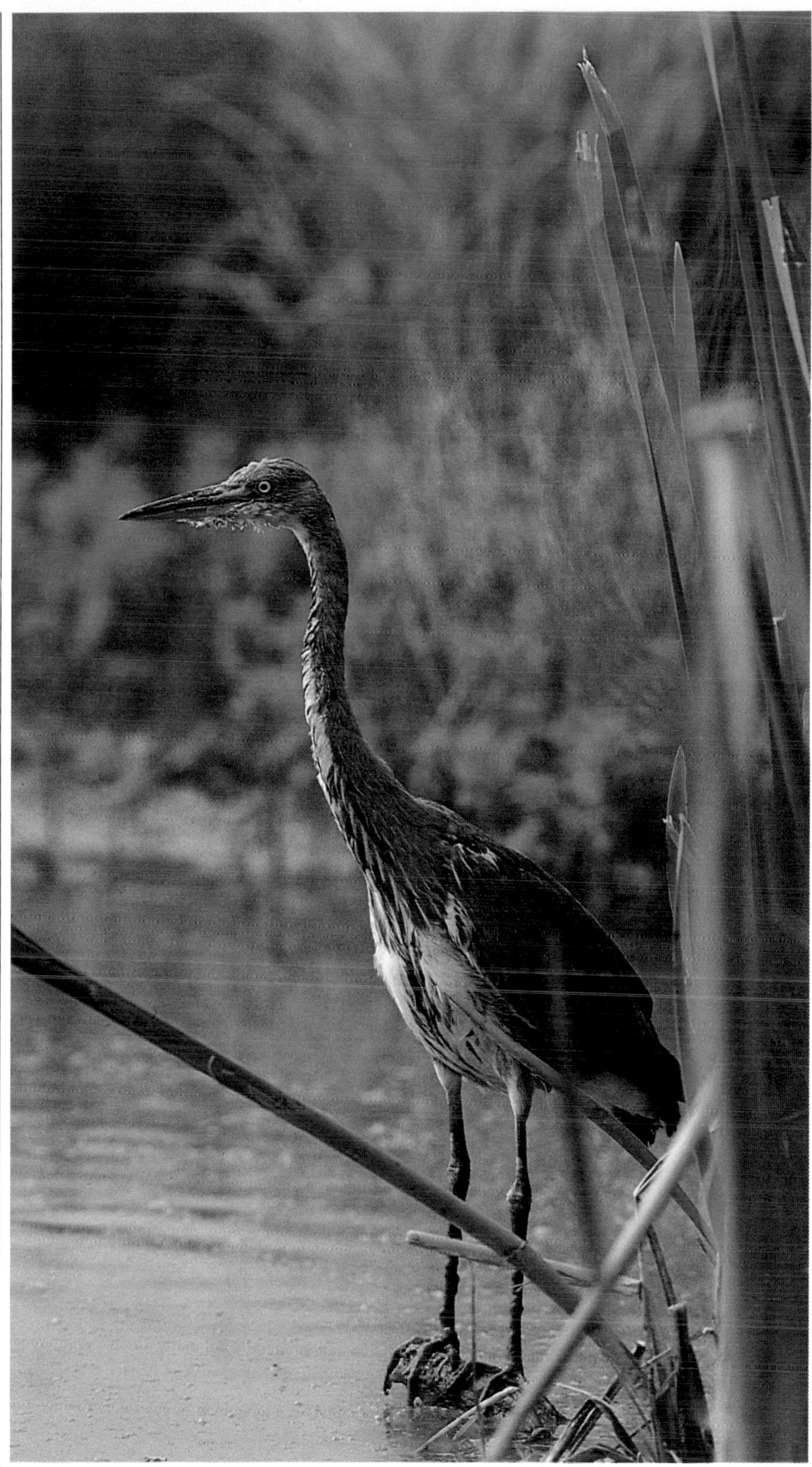

The heron is one of our largest birds and can be regularly seen throughout Britain

BIRDS OF TOWNS AND CITIES

The acres of concrete and pavements in towns and cities hardly seem to be ideal places for birds; yet, more and more birds are beginning to find the food and warmth of our cities to their liking, and there are even a number of birds that seldom occur anywhere else.

Even if you exclude those green, private havens – gardens – (see page 218), the birdlife of cities can be remarkably rich and varied. Although in some respects the city is inhospitable and sterile, in other ways it may be very welcoming as far as birds are concerned. Clearly, the inner parts of towns and cities are far from being natural places, yet they mimic natural situations in many respects. Tall buildings such as warehouses, office blocks and cathedrals are being increasingly used by cliff-nesting birds from kestrels to kittiwakes. The eaves of houses make perfect nesting sites for those former cliff-dwellers – house martins – whilst holes under the eaves are perfect for swifts which probably once nested in caves and trees, and the tree-hole dwelling starlings. Scattered amongst these man-made cliffs and caves are reservoirs, parks, street-trees, old canals, the edges of railway lines and many other places, all of which can support birds at some time of the year.

Besides the availability of all these man-made niches and semi-natural situations, towns and cities also offer more shelter and warmth than much of the countryside, larger variety of foods for those species which can exploit them and, possibly, even greater freedom from disturbance. De-

A sign of summer over, flocks of house martins gather on overhead wires waiting to start their migration south for the winter

spite the bustling life of a city, some places can be surprisingly inaccessible, either because they are not open to the public, or surrounded by private land, or because they are virtually impossible to get at, like the faces of many a high-rise building.

The black redstart provides a fascinating example of how cities can provide something that the countryside lacks. This beautiful little bird is primarily a southern European species, breeding in warm rocky areas, and Britain is at the extreme northern edge of its climatic range. However, the rubble left on London's second world war bomb-sites was discovered by the birds and adopted as a suitable nesting habitat, similar in character to the condition of these old bomb-sites has changed and most have been tidied and built on. The black redstart has largely moved to other habitats; it now finds that power stations and railway yards are to its taste and in power stations it is greatly aided by the warm effluent water from the cooling towers which supports high densities of midges on which it feeds! This epitomises some of the advantages that the town can provide for birds.

A bird that has now become so wholly dependent on houses for nesting that natural nesting sites are unknown is the swift. Swifts are quite extraordinary birds, totally adapted for aerial life, though once a year they come back to land to breed, and nowadays they are entirely dependent on the roof cavities of houses in the older parts of towns and cities for their nest-sites. One of the most famous nest sites is a colony inhabiting the University Museum Tower in Oxford.

When visiting or building the nest, the swifts approach the hole from the air, land briefly on the edge, then slither inside onto the nest; when leaving, they simply drop out, and are instantly in flight. They are quite unsuited to life on the land and, indeed, the newly-fledged youngsters may spend the first two years of their life without touching the ground or a perch at all! It is only when breeding

its natural home, and with the added warmth that a city offers. Within a few years, singing black redstarts could be heard all over the wastelands of London, and three-quarters of the breeding population of this rare bird occurred in London! Not suprisingly,

Swifts are a common sight careering around houses at dusk shrieking as they dip and dive. The collared dove has spread through Britain over the past 30 years. It is now common in most areas, right up to north Scotland

that they come to land and the rest of their life, including sleeping, is spent on the wing. Somebody once calculated that the oldest swifts, and they are known to have lived for at least 16 years, may have flown over four million miles in their lives!

BIRDS IN THE GARDEN

Most people first get to know birds through those they see in their garden, and we are fortunate in this country in having so many birds that do visit gardens, ranging from the common robins and blackbirds to the less frequent nuthatches and great spotted woodpeckers.

Gardens make very good habitats for many species of birds, especially those that like scrub or woodland edges, or have particular associations with man. Although the garden is an artificial environment, it is actually made up of a dense concentration of (usually) highly managed imitations of natural situations. No permanent pond the size of a garden pond would be likely to exist for long in the wild, yet those in gardens offer many of the same features. Intensively flowery herbaceous borders will attract a high density of insects, which will suit the insectivorous birds like spotted flycatchers; while such features as shrubberies, hedges and orchards provide safe breeding, feeding and roosting sites. If you add to this the extra dimension of food provided throughout the cold season, and the extra warmth and shelter that most gardens provide, you have a recipe for a potential bird paradise!

Of course, not all birds can adapt to the garden situation. Some, like ospreys or golden eagles, need more space and different food; others, like pied flycatchers, have specialised habitat requirements that normal gardens simply cannot fulfil. There are, too, the disadvantages of high densities of domestic cats which can catch a considerable number of birds, but those birds that can adapt to the garden environment may reach very high densities.

Garden birds fall roughly into three groups. There are those that are resident in and around the garden for much of the year, nesting and feeding there like robins, thrushes, blackbirds and the common tits; these are usually the most familiar and best-loved birds. Then, there are those birds that are summer visitors to this country and simply use the garden as a place to nest and possibly feed, during the breeding season only – this group includes birds like the spotted flycatcher, blackcap (though a small number do winter here) and house

A beautiful part-albino blackbird living in a garden where it has become accustomed to coming regularly for food

martin. Then, thirdly, there are birds which move into gardens in winter for the extra food supplies provided there; these may be birds that are resident in more natural habitats nearby, like nuthatches or great spotted woodpeckers, or they may be birds that have come to Britain for the winter and find some of their food in gardens. This group includes birds such as redwings (a lovely thrush

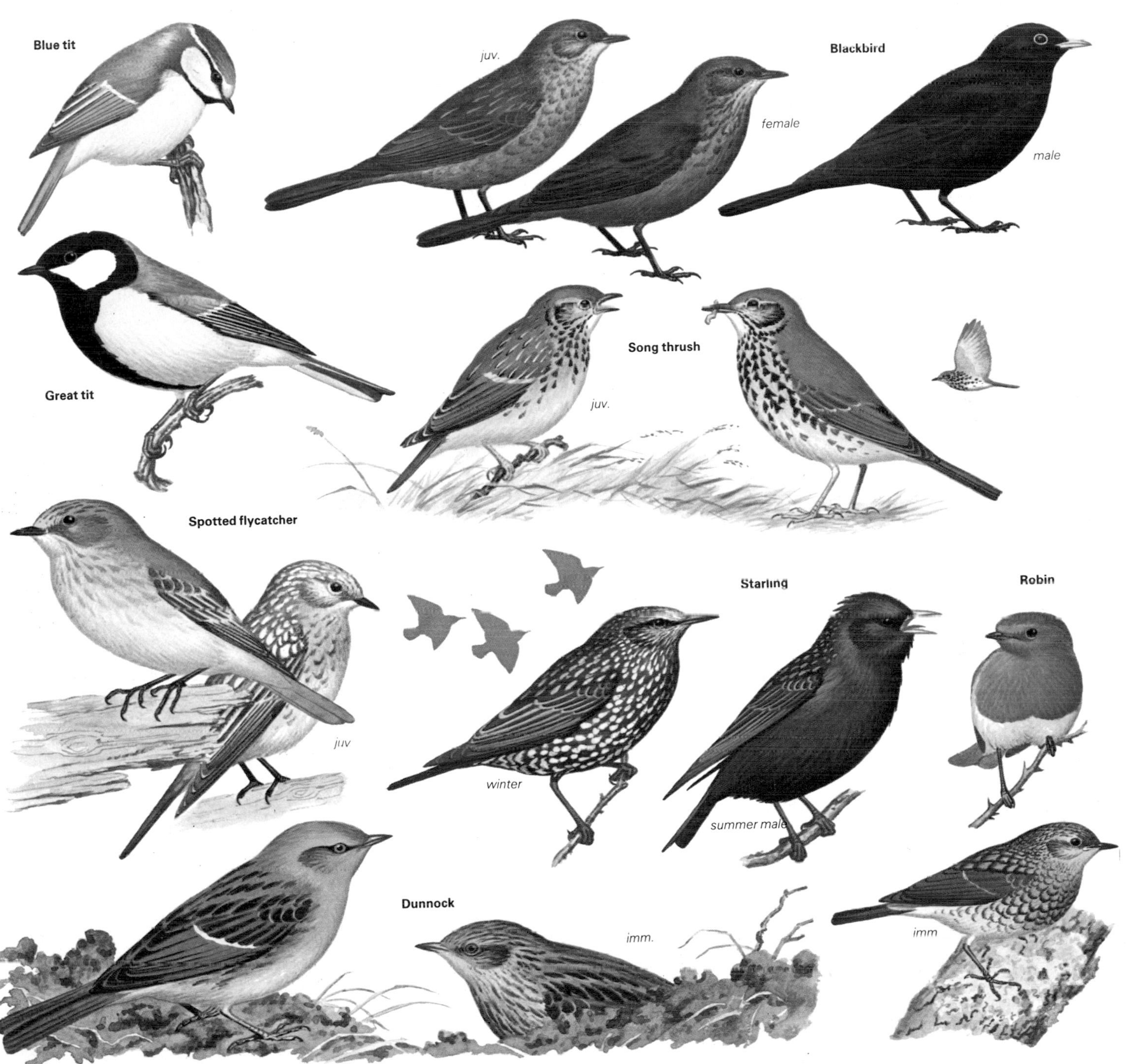

with red flanks and a pale eye-stripe), siskins, and even great rarities like the exotic waxwing.

Siskins are pretty finches looking something like a cross between a greenfinch and a canary. They do breed in Britain, especially in the north, but they also visit this country in winter as migrants from further east, and they have recently taken to visiting peanut dispensers in a big way. Their natural foods include conifer, birch or alder seeds, but they obviously find peanuts an acceptable substitute, and will spend ages on garden feeders, fighting off all comers and gorging themselves.

As long as the food put out is suitable – mainly items having a high fat and protein content – then it almost certainly helps birds to survive the cold weather in larger numbers, and raises the populations generally. For many birds, winter is the time of highest mortality that determines their population levels, so reducing deaths by feeding can only help. The frail little insectivorous warbler, the blackcap, now winters more and more in Britain, and this is partly due to its ability to transfer to bird-table feeding at this time when its normal insect food is not available. When spring comes, and the migrants return, the residents revert to their natural insect diet.

The illustration above shows most of the characteristic birds you are likely to find visiting an average town garden

THE TELL-TALE SIGNS OF BIRDS

At all times of year, many birds leave signs of their presence in the form of food remains and in the characteristic form of their droppings. With experience, these signs can be used to detect what birds are about and what they are eating.

Wherever you look there are valuable clues to tell you which birds are about, even though the birds themselves may not be visible. For they leave signs of their presence in the form of food remains, pellets and droppings.

When a bird consumes any food whole, much of it will be very indigestible. This particularly applies to predatory birds which may eat other birds, mammals or big insects whole, and they have to ingest large quantities of fur, feathers, bones and chitin (the material that makes up the skeletons of insects). Many birds get rid of this material by regurgitating pellets, which they bring up through their beaks. The indigestible parts of the food are collected in the gizzard, which lies in front of the stomach, formed into a hard lump, and eventually coughed up with a quantity of mucus to aid its passage through the throat. Pellets are produced by all sorts of birds, by no means only predatory birds, and those of many small birds are overlooked. The large, readily-visible pellets belonging to birds of prey are most often found, but others such as those from rooks or gulls are occasionally picked up. A selection is illustrated here, and it is often possible to identify the originator of a pellet by its size, shape and contents. Birds of prey, for example, make pellets that are long and thin, whilst those produced by gulls tend to be round.

It is an interesting exercise to collect pellets and dissect them, to find out what is being eaten. Soak the pellets in warm water in a shallow dish for about half-an-hour, then, using two darning or dissecting needles, tease them apart carefully. You can pick out any bones and obvious remains carefully, clean them up, and leave them to dry on absorbent paper. Now, you can attempt to identify the bones and other items. If you mount the best specimens on a white card, all together, with informa-

The gruesome remains of a pigeon, clinically killed, plucked and eaten by a sparrowhawk near a wood in Somerset

tion about the place where they were found, the date and a description of the pellet, when you have identified each item, they can be used for reference. If kept in a dry place, such collections will keep indefinitely.

Droppings are also very distinctive, and can often be used to discover which birds are present and what they are eating (see illustration). Nest-sites, especially of larger predators, the undigested remains of the woodpecker's ant food; blackbird droppings turn purple when they have been feeding on elderberries or reddish when they have been eating yew berries and so on.

Besides pellets and droppings, birds may often leave parts of the actual food as evidence of their presence. The 'kills' of peregrines or sparrowhawks, for example, each have a distinctive pattern of discarded feathers. Hazel nuts, which are eaten by quite a variety of birds and mammals (and insects!) are each opened in a different way, and with practice you can learn to identify the consumer (see illustration). Conifer cones, too, are attacked by many birds to obtain the seeds. Crossbills slice through each cone-scale before removing the seed, whilst woodpeckers

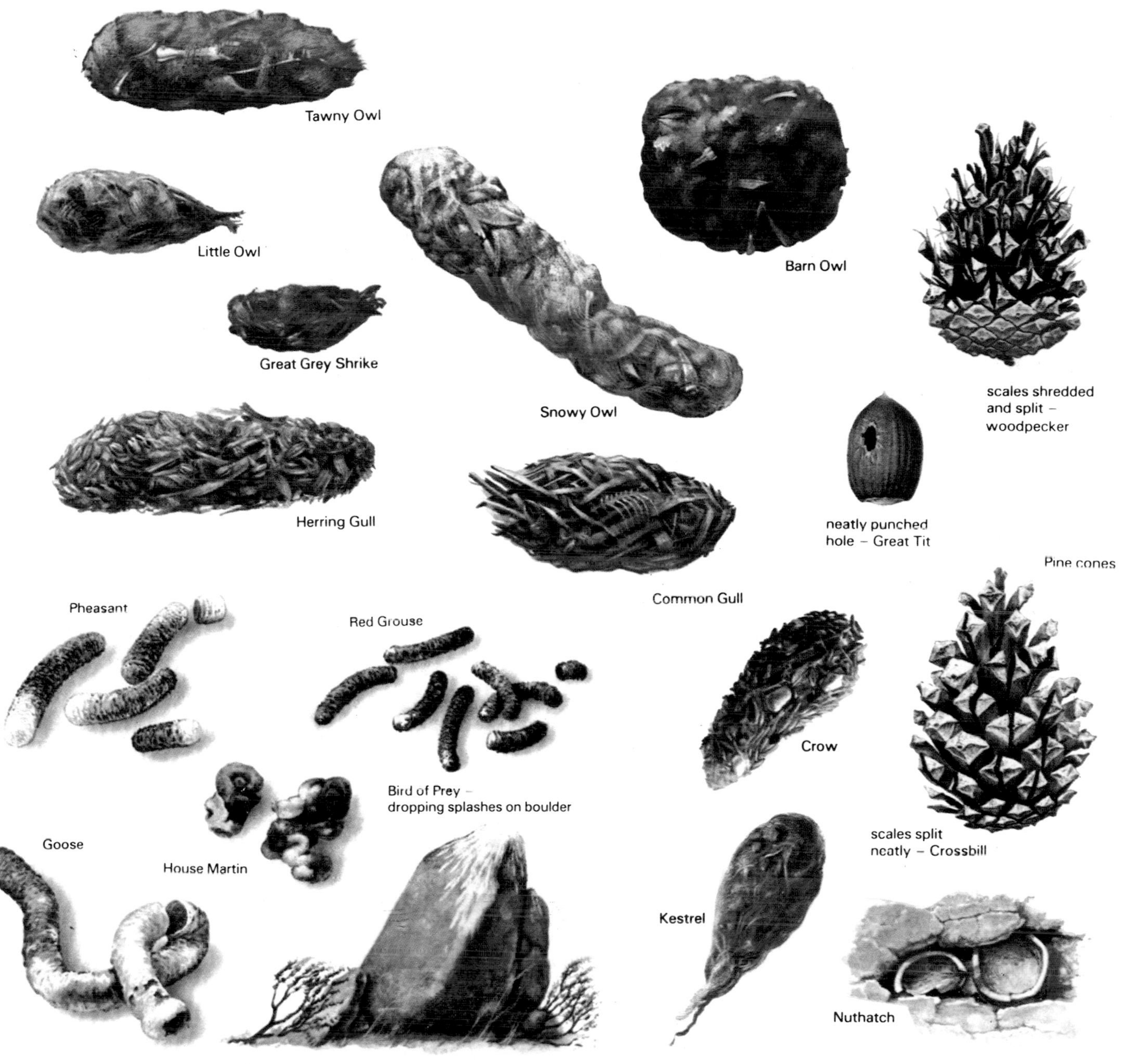

can often be seen at a distance by their external 'whitewash' of droppings or, on a smaller scale, it is often possible to find and identify individual droppings. For example, the green woodpecker leaves droppings that look like discarded cigar ash, and they contain

The dropping, pellets and feeding signs of birds will allow you to tell which birds are around even though they may not be in sight

– as befits their strength and habits – are rather less subtle and excavate the cones in a more damaging way.

The possibilities for finding signs of birds and their feeding habits are endless, and the closer you look, the better you will be rewarded.

HOW TO GO BIRDWATCHING

Birdwatching is one of the most fascinating and lasting of hobbies, and you can pursue it any level, with virtually no outlay of money. Like most pursuits, though, the more you put into it the more you get out, and here we give some brief guidance on how to start.

Birds are almost everywhere in the countryside, as the preceding pages have shown, and any outing will reveal several different species. Most people, however, will find it frustrating that the views they have of birds are inadequate; either they are too far away, the light is too poor to see well or, more often than not, the bird is seen against the light making it appear only as a silhouette. The best way around these difficulties is to use a pair of binoculars, which may not solve every viewing difficulty, but they do greatly increase your capabilities and enjoyment. If you have never tried watching birds through binoculars, do try it – it can be quite a revelation!

Binoculars come in an enormous variety of shapes and sizes. It can be tempting, when first looking for a pair, to go for the high magnification often advertised by such slogans as 'see across the channel'! For birdwatching such pairs are best avoided, as they are very difficult to handle and give poor colour definition and low-light viewing ability. Binocular capabilities are always quoted as a pair of numbers, such as '8 x 30', or '10 x 50'; the first number indicates the magnification, or strength, compared to the naked eye, whilst the second figure is the diameter of the objective lens – the

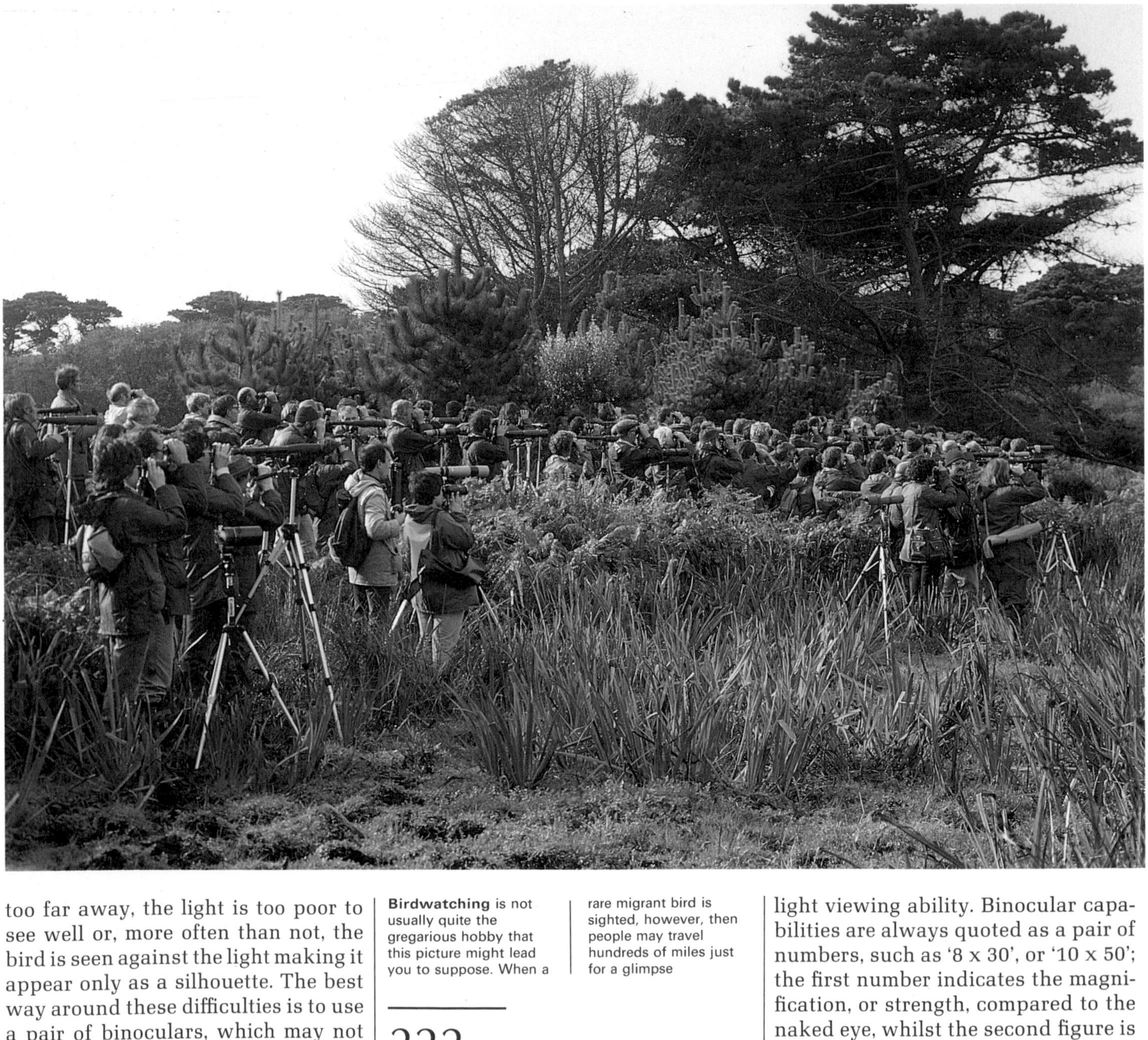

Birdwatching is not usually quite the gregarious hobby that this picture might lead you to suppose. When a rare migrant bird is sighted, however, then people may travel hundreds of miles just for a glimpse

large lens farthest from the eye. The relationship between these two figures is important as dividing the first into the second gives you an idea of the light-gathering power of the binoculars and the higher this figure is, the better. For example, a pair of 8 x 40 binoculars has a light-gathering power of 40 divided by eight which equals five, whilst a pair of 20 x 50 binoculars only has a light-gathering capability of two-and-a-half. For general purpose viewing, a figure of at least five for this characteristic should be looked for, whilst a magnification of between seven and ten is about right for most needs. Such binoculars will greatly enhance your pleasure, especially if they are of reasonably good quality. Carry them whenever you go out, take them in the car and keep them by the window into the garden when you are at home, and you will be well rewarded.

A second, very cheap, birdwatching accessory is a notebook and pencil. This should be pocket-sized and hardbacked, and a pencil is generally better than a pen, as it is unaffected by wet and you know exactly when it is going to run out. Use it to make notes for identification, sketches and general information on what you have seen and where. With an unfamiliar bird, there is often insufficient time to look it up in the book and check everything, so watch it carefully and note down any important features such as 'white eye-stripe', 'pale yellow rump' and so on, as well as size and where you saw it. This will prove invaluable when you do come to sort it out, and also makes you better at observing birds rather than just seeing them.

There are birds everywhere, but some places are undoubtedly better than others. The preceding pages have given some idea of where to look. A good starting point is the coast, especially in winter, or large inland freshwater lakes. If you join one of the bird protection or nature conservation societies (such as the Royal Society for the Protection of Birds or a local Nature Conservation Trust – see appendix), you will almost certainly be rewarded with some well placed hides to visit, which allow views of a range of birds at close quarters. Many reserves have wardens, too, who will assist with finding birds if they are not too busy. Wherever you go, a good field-guide is essential and the bibliography gives a few ideas for books.

Purpose built hides, such as this one at an RSPB reserve, allow birdwatchers to view the birds in comfort and without disturbing them

Finally, it is very rewarding to learn a range of bird calls and songs, especially those used in the breeding season. There are records available with the calls or you can go out with someone who knows them. This gives a new dimension to birdwatching.

An Introduction to

British Mammals

Mammals are warm-blooded vertebrate animals, which bear live young that they suckle with milk, and they usually have fur rather than feathers or scales. In Britain, we have about 60 species of mammal living in the wild, and they include the whales, seals, bats, rodents, the lagomorphs (rabbits and hares) and deer to name but a few.

With a few exceptions, mammals are really very little known as the great majority have adopted a nocturnal, or at the very least crepuscular (evening and early morning) lifestyle, avoiding contact with man wherever possible. The ones we most often see include the grey squirrel, which is an introduced species from North America, though totally at home here now; moles in the form of molchills and runs, hedgehogs, rabbits and, occasionally, deer if you are in an area where they are common. The remainder, though, are hardly ever seen casually, and you need to make a particular effort to see them.

Our mammal fauna is actually rather poor in species (though many people who would be surprised to learn that there were as many as 60 species), for there is a world total of over 5,000 species. This is partly because relatively few were able to colonise Britain from Europe before the land bridge was breached, and even fewer were able to recolonise Ireland as it was further away from mainland Europe. It is also the result of man's activities and his deliberate and accidental clashes with wild animals. Since the last Ice Age, without going too far back into the colder early days, we have lost species like the wolf, beaver, wild boar, elk and European lynx, largely as a result of habitat destruction and direct persecution by man. Even today, there is one bat species, the mouse-eared bat, which is just about to become extinct, so the record is a sorry one.

Nevertheless, there is still a surprising diversity and interest in the mammal fauna that we have left, as the following pages show.

A young fox-cub, playing in the grass

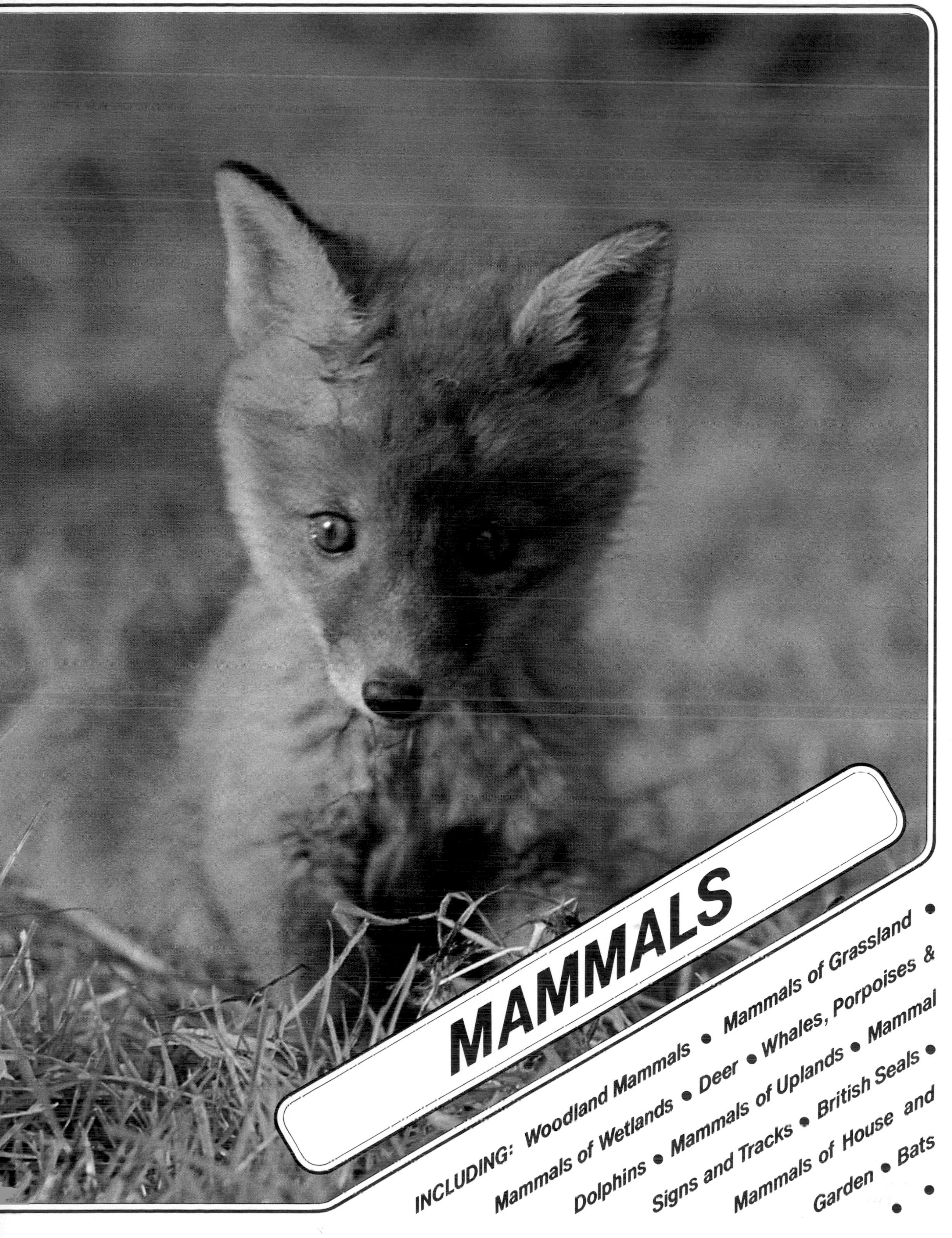

MAMMALS

INCLUDING: Woodland Mammals • Mammals of Grassland • Mammals of Wetlands • Deer • Whales, Porpoises & Dolphins • Mammals of Uplands • Mammal Signs and Tracks • British Seals • Mammals of House and Garden • Bats • •

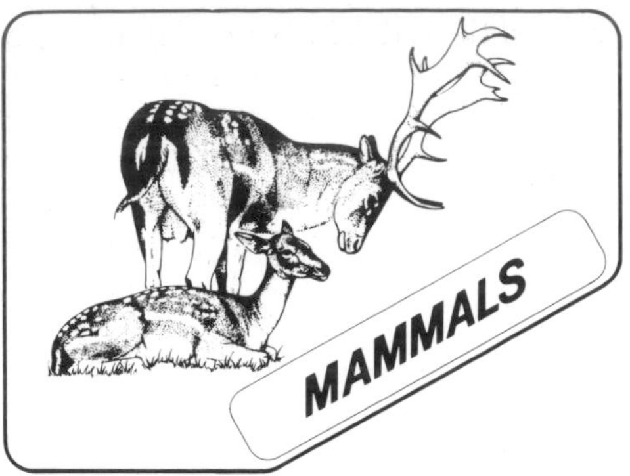

WOODLAND MAMMALS

Woodlands are undoubtedly the finest place for our mammals, the home to more species than any other situation. It is here that we can find foxes, badgers, deer, squirrels, dormice and innumerable others, living almost unnoticed deep in the trees.

Woodland makes an ideal habitat for mammals. There is an abundance of food in the form of grazing and browsing, fruit and nuts, and invertebrate prey, and plenty of dense cover for breeding, sleeping and feeding. As far as mammals are concerned, the species of herbs and shrubs in a wood are of less importance than its general structure, associated with particular trees or bushes. The red squirrel, for example, is most at home with conifers rather than deciduous trees, whilst the dormouse prefers the presence of hazel bushes. Apart from these exceptions, the structure is more important, and a well-managed ancient wood with a wide variety of trees and shrubs, plenty of glades, banks and wet areas will always have a rich fauna.

Badgers are typical common woodland animals. They will make their homes out in the open occasionally, but most frequently the entrances to their 'setts' are to be found in woods. These setts are extensive underground burrows, often built up by many generations of badgers, with conspicuous piles of earth at the entrances. There are often several holes, some of which will be obvious 'front doors', whilst others will be tucked away in the undergrowth, rarely seen and only infrequently used. Badgers spend the daylight hours below ground, emerging at dusk or later to forage for food, which they often find well away from their home bases. Although classified as carnivores, they have a very wide diet, which includes many vegetable items such as roots and nuts, as well as the staple diet of earthworms. They will often come to gardens or rubbish bins for bread, bones, and anything else edible. They are very partial to honey and bee and wasp larvae, and it is not uncommon to see nests dug out by them.

Foxes are frequent in woodland,

Pipistrelle bat
Pipistrellus pipistrellus

Long-eared bat
Plecotus auritus

Field vole
Microtus agrestis

Noctule bat
Nyctalus noctula

Dormouse
Muscardinus avellanarius

Field mouse
Apodemus sylvaticus

Pygmy shrew
Sorex minutus

Bank vole
Clethrionomys glareolus

too, sometimes living in old badger setts, though they are equally common in grassland (see page 230).

We have two species of squirrel in Britain, one native and one introduced. The commonest species over much of the county is the grey squirrel, introduced from North America, and now considered as something of a pest for the damage it does to woodland trees. It is simply too successful for its own good in some areas, though it is a popular visitor to parks where it may become very tame. The native red squirrel tends to live in areas where the grey is rare or absent, partly because the two require slightly different habitats, but also due to competition between them, though it would hardly be true to say that the grey has ousted the red. The beautiful little red squirrel still occurs widely in northern Britain and sporadically in strongholds further south, such as Norfolk, the Isle of Wight, and Brownsea Island in Poole harbour. Grey squirrels are rigorously excluded from the last two places, though they do occasionally turn up despite the barrier of water.

There are also two species of dormice, which are squirrel-like rodents of British woodlands. Again, there is one native and one introduced species, though in this case the introduced one has remained rare. The native dormouse is a lovely little animal, most often found in lowland broad-leaved woodland with plenty of hazel. They particularly like hazel coppice, where they breed and hibernate. The edible, or fat dormouse, looks like a small squirrel, with its bushy tail, and is considerably larger than the native species. It was introduced into the Chilterns in 1902, from southern Europe, but it has remained localised in this area, and has never become abundant like the grey squirrel.

Apart from several bats which are also common in woodlands there are many other small mammals that abound in the lower layers of a wood. These include wood mice, yellow-necked mice, bank voles, field voles and both species of insectivorous shrew. They are all predominantly nocturnal and the mice, in particular, may climb widely through bushes and trees in search of food.

Squirrels usually split nuts; voles and mice with smaller jaws chew a hole through the shell

drey

Red squirrel
Sciurus vulgaris

Grey squirrel
Sciurus carolinensis

This hazelnut has been cleanly split from top to bottom by a squirrel. Favourite eating places can be littered with the remains of split shells. Young squirrels, less adept than the adults, may chew the nut first

Most mammals can be found in woodlands at some time or other, as there is so much food and cover, but the illustration above left shows some of the more frequent residents or visitors, including two of the more typical woodland bats

A male badger (top) out foraging at night in woodland in the New Forest

Two squirrels (above) that occur in Britain; the native red squirrel occurs mainly in north and west Britain, while the introduced North American grey squirrel has been gradually spreading throughout the country, becoming a forestry pest in many areas

Cones are gnawed almost completely bald by squirrels. They leave the top intact since there are no seeds to be found at the tip

MAMMALS IN GRASSLAND

Grassland may not appear to be a very suitable habitat for mammals, yet a surprising number of species, often in very high numbers, can occur there, from mice and voles, through to the predators like foxes, weasels and stoats.

There are actually relatively few mammals that live permanently in grassland; mammals are quite mobile creatures and they will often use several habitats, perhaps breeding in one and feeding in another, or even ranging over a very wide range of different sorts of countryside, like foxes. Our native red foxes are common everywhere throughout the country, and they are one of the most adaptable 'all-purpose' mammals that we have. They live underground in 'earths', which are smaller and less complex than badger setts, and lack the massive earth pile outside. The earths may be in woodland, on railway banks or, as often as not, on grassland amongst a bit of cover. Foxes are largely nocturnal so you tend not to notice them, but in winter their calls are often heard at night – the bark of the dog fox and the strange screaming call of the vixen.

A much more specific grassland mammal is the brown hare. These attractive animals, which look rather like large rabbts with long black-tipped ears, are completely at home in

A young weasel (top) moving alertly through long grass, constantly looking out for prey. The stoat with which the weasel can be confused always has a black tip to its tail Although originally a woodland mammal foxes are becoming a common sight in towns where they scavenge from dustbins. In summer they bask during the day in quiet sunny corners venturing out at night

wide open grassy areas, and rarely stray into other habitats. They survive by being alert and fast, and using the open space to ensure that no predator ever approaches close to them without being seen. They never use burrows, and the tiny young (the leverets) are born furry and ready for action, unlike the helpless young produced by rabbits in underground burrows. Hares are well known for their habit of rushing about madly in spring and occasionally 'boxing' with a partner hence the expression 'Mad as a March hare'. Unfortunately, hares seem to have declined in recent years, partly due to loss of habitat and perhaps through build-up of chemical residues in their bodies, though they may still be common in favourable habitats which can include such places as the grassy outer parts of airfields.

Rabbits are important and familiar components of the grassland ecosystem. Numbers can be very large where they do occur, and their grazing has a considerable effect on the sward keeping it short and grassy and favouring certain flowers at the expense of others. Some butterflies, like the silver-spotted skipper, are particularly associated with rabbit-grazed turf, and others have only been able to survive the decline of sheep-grazing because the rabbits have kept the grass short. Rabbits can breed extremely rapidly in favourable conditions, and they often become a pest when adjacent to crops. The introduction of the virus disease, myxamatosis, decimated rabbit populations in the 1950s and since, and the disease still breaks out periodically, killing or maiming a proportion of the population. In fact, at the height of the disease, the effect on many downland sites was quite serious as rank grass and scrub became established, and in many cases the areas have never returned to grassland.

An animal that may be extremely abundant in grassland, and is in absolutely no danger of extinction, though it is very rarely seen, is the ubiquitous mole. Molehills are a familiar sight everywhere on the mainland, though these animals do not occur in Ireland nor on most of the smaller offshore islands. Moles spend virtually all their time below ground in extensive burrows, where they feed on earthworms and other invertebrate prey. They are active most of the time, but are unlikely to be seen at the surface except at night, particularly during wet weather. They lead a solitary existence, meeting other moles only for the purpose of mating, which takes place in February or March. They are extraordinarily powerful and rapid diggers, able to disappear from view in seconds if placed on the ground, and capable of moving about 200 grams of soil per minute!

Rabbits were brought to Britain from France in Plantagenet times. They were kept in walled warrens where they were bred for meat and fur by the Lord of the Manor. Until their escape into the wild in the 16th and 17th centuries rabbits were regarded as a luxury meat, but they soon became the staple of the peasants

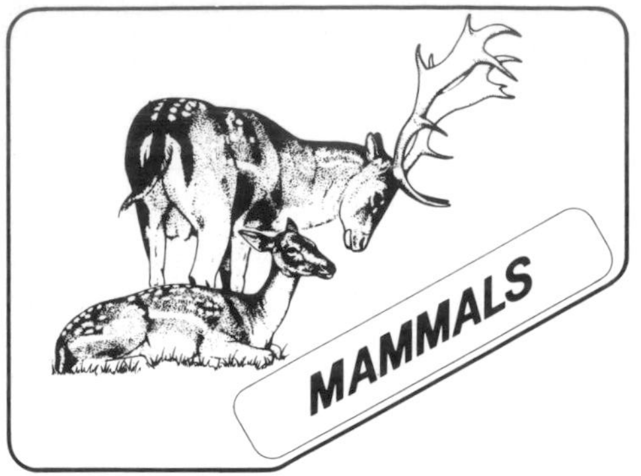

MAMMALS OF WETLANDS

Reedbeds and other wet places are the home of several mammals, including the beautiful but now rare otter, and some exotic and unusual animals like the coypu and the Chinese water deer.

Considering the amount of food available and the abundance of cover, it is surprising how few native mammals are found in and around water. In fact, of those that do occur, many are introduced species, from as far away as China, that have found and exploited a vacant niche in our countryside. Examples include coypu from South America, mink from North America or Chinese water deer from north-east China. The delightful little water vole, or water rat as it is sometimes known, is almost certainly the most often seen of our waterside mammals. It is reasonably common over most of the country, and is much more diurnal (daylight-loving) than most mammals so tends to be seen more frequently. Water voles are normally to be found in and around any clean water areas, which can be streams, rivers or lakes, where they make extensive burrow systems in the banks. These usually have entrances both above and below water, and the voles, which swim well, either enter the water directly from the burrows or from the bank with a soft 'plop'. They swim by using all four legs, both above and below water, but use the ability as a means of getting from one feeding site to another or away from predators, rather than for feeding itself. They live almost exclusively on bankside vegetation, such as sedges, which they grasp in their forepaws and eat selectively, discarding the stumps and tough pieces. Despite their alternative name of water rat, they are only distantly related to rats, and are one of our most attractive and appealing mammals.

Our smallest waterside mammal is the water shrew, with a body length of only about nine centimetres. Despite their name, they will live in habitats away from water but are most common there and are better adapted to a waterside existence than other shrews. They are voracious predators, and are active almost all the time, as they need to eat roughly their own weight in food each day to survive. Water shrews regularly take to the water to hunt, where they swim in search of anything they can catch including tadpoles, water beetles, small fishes and even young frogs. They have slightly poisonous saliva, which may help to subdue some of the larger animals that they attack, and when prey is caught in the water it is dragged ashore to be eaten. When they are swimming underwater, they have to paddle very rapidly to stay below the surface, because a trapped layer of air in their fur makes them

These four mammals may often be found in, or near, water. The otter and water vole are native species. The mink escaped from fur-farms in the early 1980s. The coypu is now only found wild in isolated areas of East Anglia

very buoyant. They live and breed in bankside burrows with entrances both above and below water, and when the young leave the nest at about a month old, they often travel in a procession behind their mother!

Our largest native freshwater mammal is the otter. These beautiful and graceful animals are highly adapted to a waterside existence, as powerful and agile swimmers with thick waterproof fur. Once, they were common and widespread, so much so that there were packs of otterhounds in many areas, specifically for hunting otters as foxhounds do with foxes. Now, though, they are a very rare animal in the lowlands, and are accorded full legal protection, though they are still relatively common in some northern and western areas of Britain. They live mainly along clean, well-vegetated streams with plenty of cover and little disturbance, and a good supply of their main food – fish. You are very unlikely to see an otter though it is not uncommon to find evidence of their presence in the form of droppings – spraints – or other marks. In north and west Scotland, quite high numbers of otters live on the coast and on sea-lochs, and here they are frequently active in the day, so they are more often seen. Their main prey is fish which they hunt underwater often coming into conflict with man as a result. Their ability to see well underwater helps them to locate and catch their food; fishes are normally seized from below and killed in the water, before being taken to the shore and consumed at leisure. Otters will also eat frogs, small birds and mammals if they have the opportunity. They may also take mussels and many other types of shellfish. They leave the remains on the bankside.

The water shrew is now not common, as they need clean water to live in and a large exclusive area of bank and river to forage in

An otter, now one of our rarest and most elusive mammals, swimming in a highland stream. They are at present being re-introduced into East Anglia

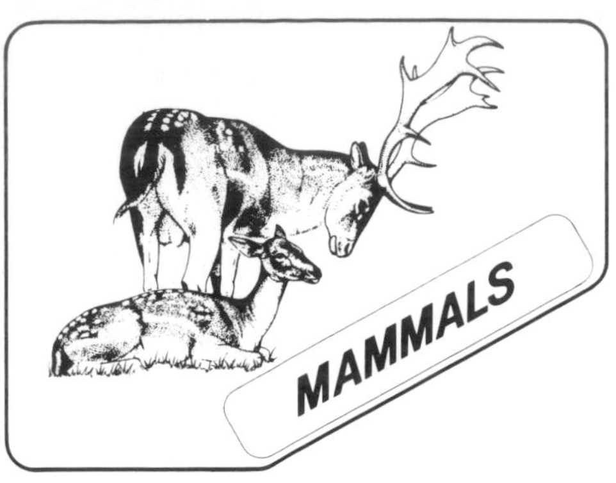

BRITISH BATS

Most people would be surprised to learn that there are 15 different species of British bats, and they make up over one-third of the species of land mammals in the country. They are to be found in almost every habitat, and have fascinating life-cycles, quite different from other mammals.

Bats are small, soft furry mammals, which have developed the ability to fly by means of wings formed from skin stretched over extended finger bones. Like other mammals, they are warm-blooded and bear live young which they suckle with milk but, in other respects, they are distinctly different largely as a result of their nocturnal, airborne way of life.

As is well known, bats detect prey and avoid obstacles in the dark by means of a sophisticated echo-sounding system, involving the emission of sounds and the reception and analysis of the echoes returned to them. The system is highly developed, and gives bats a very precise ability to locate and catch flying prey and even, in some species, to pick insect prey off leaves. In fact, the two families of bats represented in Britain have slightly different systems for producing and receiving sounds. The horseshoe bats emit sounds through the nostrils, which are focused into a narrow beam of sound by a cone-shaped trumpet of flesh on the snout, while moving its head from side to side to scan the air ahead. All the other 13 species send out sounds through the mouth, and they have a spike of flesh in their ears known as the tragus (which is absent in the horseshoe bats) to help receive the reflected echoes. All bats are active mainly in the warmer months of the year spending most of the winter hibernating in suitable sites. Different species have different preferred roosts, which may be roof spaces, caves, mines or hollow trees, though particularly favourable roosts may support half-a-dozen or more species. Bats will move roosts regularly, and the summer daytime ones are different from those used in the winter when temperature and environmental conditions are critical. All species roost by hanging upside down; the two horseshoe bats hang visibly from roofs and projecting objects, whilst

Pipistrelle
Pipistrellus pipistrellus

Noctule
Nyctalus noctula

Brown long-eared bat
Plecotus auritus

Leister's bat
Nyctalus leisleri

The pipistrelle bat is the smallest and commonest European bat. Noctules emerge early evening and may be mistaken for swifts. Leister's bats are sometimes seen even in central London

most other species creep into crevices and holes.

In general, bats have rather poorly defined habitat preferences, though some have an affinity with a particular type of place. Pipistrelles, for example, are strongly associated with man by virtue of their preference for using houses as roosts and breeding areas, and serotine bats are almost equally dependent on them. Other species will use houses, especially in summer, but are by no means confined to them. The noctule bat, Leisler's bat, Bechstein's bat and the barbastelle are often found in old woodland, though other species do occur there, and many use hollow trees as roosts at sometime or other. The problem with these sites is that it is extremely difficult to discover what bats, if any, are present in a hole in a tree. Much of our information comes from observation of bats emerging or chance records when trees are felled, because it is normally impossible to enter trees to look. The horseshoe bats are particularly associated with large caves and mines, especially for their winter roosts; in caves like those of Wookey Hole and Cheddar gorge in the Mendips, they were once so abundant that guides would use poles to knock quantities down from the roof to show visitors!

Sadly, all bats have declined dramatically during this century, and especially in recent decades. The reasons are complex and varied, though they certainly include loss of feeding habitat, and roosting and breeding sites, a reduction in the number of flying insects, and deaths and reduced breeding as a result of the absorption of insecticides, especially those used to combat woodworm in roof cavities. At least half of the British species of bats are uncommon and many of them very rare. Species such as the greater horseshoe bat have declined to the point where there is serious concern for their future in this country, whilst the mouse-eared bat seems certain to become extinct in the near future since no females are now known from this country. All species are protected rigorously by law, and public interest in bats is at an all time high, yet the decline seems likely to continue through factors that are difficult to control. It is up to everyone to encourage roosts wherever they are found.

How bats navigate

Most people have heard of the bat's legendary 'echo-location' system which they use to navigate in the dark and to find and catch food. Bats emit a series of very high pitched shrieks usually above the range of human hearing, although some young children can hear them. These sound waves bounce off anything around them and the echoes are picked up by the bat and translated into a sound picture of its surroundings. This radar system is very accurate and can locate an insect as small as a moth at some distance.

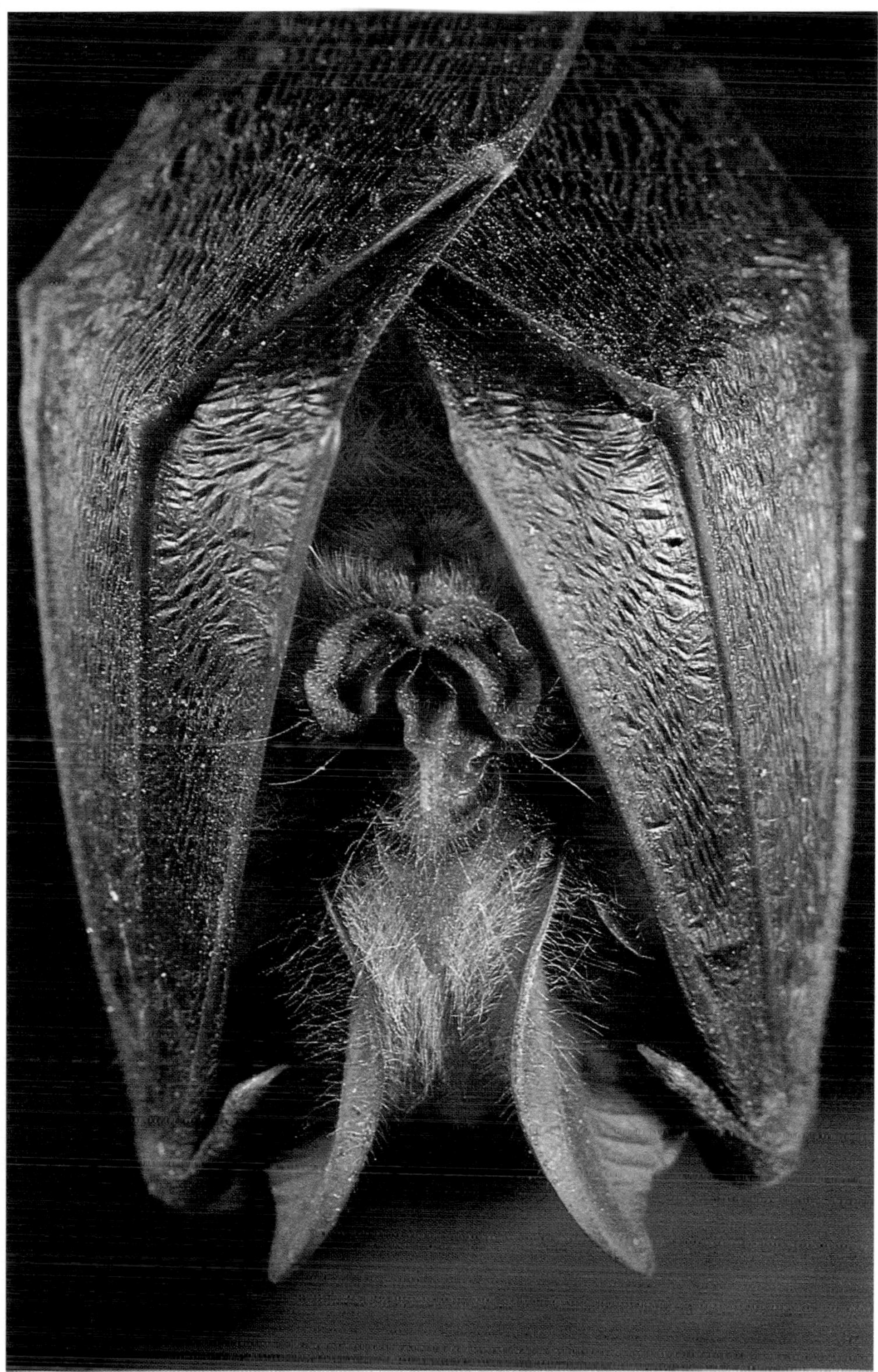

A lesser horseshoe bat hanging upside-down from the roof of a cave where it has its winter roost. These bats are now very rare but may be rarely seen in south and west England and parts of Wales

WHALES, PORPOISES & DOLPHINS

Our largest mammals live, not on the land, but in the sea around our coasts, and they look far more like fish than true mammals. At least ten species of these extraordinary creatures are found regularly around our shores.

The group known as the cetaceans includes the whales, dolphins and porpoises and are all closely-related species of aquatic mammals. Although looking something like large fish, such as the sharks, they differ in that they are warm-blooded, they breathe air with the use of lungs and they bear live young that are suckled on the mother's milk – all indisputable mammalian characteristics. Nevertheless, they are totally marine animals, spending their whole life at sea and are quite unable to cope with being stranded on land.

There are about 80 species of cetaceans worldwide, though we can only expect to see a small proportion in British waters. The majority of species belong to the toothed whales which, as their name suggests, have teeth and lead a predatory carnivorous existence, feeding on fish, squid or other animal food. A much smaller number of species belong to the group known as the baleen or whalebone whales; they have a distinctive set of horny plates in their mouth (the whalebone) with which they strain small planktonic organisms from the sea as food. Most of the baleen whales need not be very agile, and are particularly big; they include the world's largest mammal, the blue whale. Although six species of baleen whale have been recorded from British waters, only one – the lesser rorqual – is seen at all regularly; the larger common rorqual also visits occasionally.

The toothed whales are generally more likely to be encountered in coastal waters, and they often come quite close inshore. Seventeen species have been recorded from British waters, though only about eight are seen regularly, and these are mainly the smaller dolphins and porpoises. The most frequent visitor is probably the common porpoise, which is also the smallest of the whales at under two metres long. They occur all around the coasts and are particularly seen in late summer or early autumn – though

A dead pilot whale, grounded on the saltmarsh of the Wash. Note the very bulbous head and very long front flippers

no-one is quite sure where they are at other times. They are often found in estuaries, and may even swim some way up the larger rivers, following fish such as herring and whiting. They usually occur in small 'schools', though large groups are sometimes seen. Common dolphins are rather rarer since we are at the northern edge of their predominantly warm water range and, though they may spend the – a long projecting snout. Other species of dolphin occur, too, such as the pilot whale, Risso's dolphin and the killer whale. The killer whale is a large dolphin which can reach up to ten metres in length; it occurs fairly commonly in British waters. Though highly carnivorous it is a fish-feeder and its 'killer' epithet is unjustified as far as humans are concerned. Pilot whales are also large dolphins, and they are most often encountered when stranded on the coast. When one whale or dolphin becomes beached, it seems that its distress signals attract the remainder of the school which may also suffer a similar fate even if efforts are made by local people to prevent the remainder from coming ashore. It is still by no means clear quite why these mass-strandings take place, though plenty of theories exist.

Ten of the most frequently seen species of whales and porpoises, including those most often stranded on the shore.

winters here feeding, they always go further south to breed. They are most often seen off the south and west coasts, and are rare in the east. They are a little larger than the common porpoise, but are usually distinguishable by the noticeable dolphin 'beak',

At one time, all strandings of the whale family were supposed to be reported by law, since they were 'fish royal' and became the property of the crown. This has given historical information about the distribution of the group; though this law no longer applies.

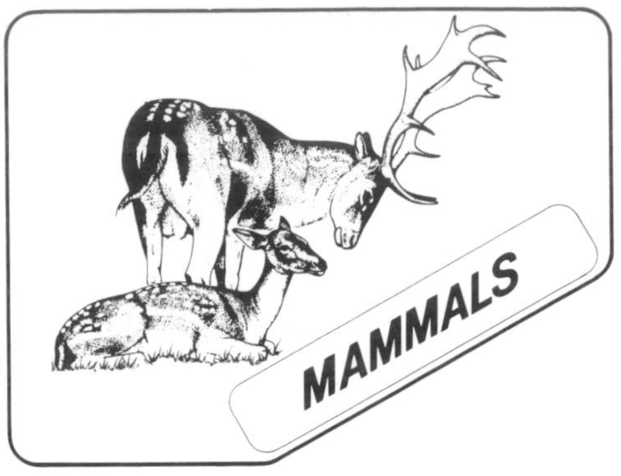

BRITISH SEALS

Around the quieter coasts of Britain, there are two species of seals to be found breeding and feeding. These are the grey seal, of which well over half the world population occur in British waters, and the common seal.

Seals are highly adapted marine mammals that spend most of their life at sea, but they differ from the whales in that they are tied to land for the breeding season. Each year, seals haul out on their different beaches to breed, but for the rest of the year the grey seal, in particular, may travel huge distances in search of fish, just coming ashore for occasional rests.

The grey seal was once feared to be in danger of extinction, with only an estimated 500 animals left (though this was probably an underestimate), yet now there are at least 75,000 breeding round the coasts of Britain. Once, they were hunted mercilessly for their oil and skin, but artificial substitutes, and changing attitudes and laws, have freed them from this pressure. The depopulation of Scottish islands has also provided more undisturbed breeding and loafing areas, so helping the recovery and expansion of the population.

Seals are difficult animals to study and follow, but it is known that they will travel huge distances in the non-breeding part of the year, often hundreds of miles. They are very fast, agile swimmers using their powerful back flippers and streamlined bodies, and they can remain submerged for very long periods of time considering they are air breathing mammals. Special adaptations permit them to remain alert and active underwater for up to half-an-hour, which gives them plenty of time to find and catch their prey,

A young grey seal peering out of the sea off Grassholm island, west Wales, in May. The pups are born in autumn, so this one is probably about six months old

even in deep water. They mainly feed on fish, though similar animals, such as squid and octopus, may be eaten, and they are voracious predators, eating at least four-and-a-half kilos per day.

Grey seals breed in autumn and, at about this time, they begin to congregate on selected rocky beaches and coves, individuals apparently returning to the same one each year. The males arrive first and take up favourable positions, followed a few days later by the females. Most of the females will be pregnant from the previous year's breeding season and, within a day or two of their arrival, they give birth to their pups, which are almost invariably single. They are suckled for about three weeks, during which time they gain an immense amount of weight on the diet of very fat-rich milk from the mother, reaching 35 to 40 kilos by the time they are weaned! The mother then loses interest in the pup, and mating with the males begins. The adults leave the site soon after, abandoning the young pup to look after itself, and it is not long before it, too, enters the sea. It is believed that females may live for 40 years or more, while males live for rather less, so, although only one pup is born, and they may not become pregnant every year, a female can produce quite a few young throughout her life.

The common seal, though more frequent throughout the world, is rarer than the grey seal in British waters. They have a preference for more sheltered waters than grey seals, and occur especially in estuaries and bays around the coasts. Most of them occur in Scotland, but there is a sizeable population of about 6,000 resident seals in eastern England, mainly around The Wash. They often travel well inland up rivers, and have been recorded at Teddington, on the Thames, as well as in many freshwater lochs. Although generally rather shy animals, preferring areas well away from people, they may occasionally become accustomed to human presence and remain where they are as boats pass by, sometimes taking an interest in the occupants!

Although the two seals are broadly similar in appearance, they can be distinguished with practice. The grey seal is larger and greyer, and has a distinctive straight-bridged, Roman nose, whilst the smaller, browner common seal has a more dog-like face, with a definite concave part between the nose and forehead. The coat of the common seal, though variable in colour and overlapping with the grey, is more likely to be distinctly spotted rather than blotchy, as with the grey seal. Seals on sandy and very sheltered areas are more likely to be common seals, as they prefer such sites.

Our two native species of seals: the larger grey seal has a distinct 'Roman Nose', while the smaller common seal has a much more dog-like face profile

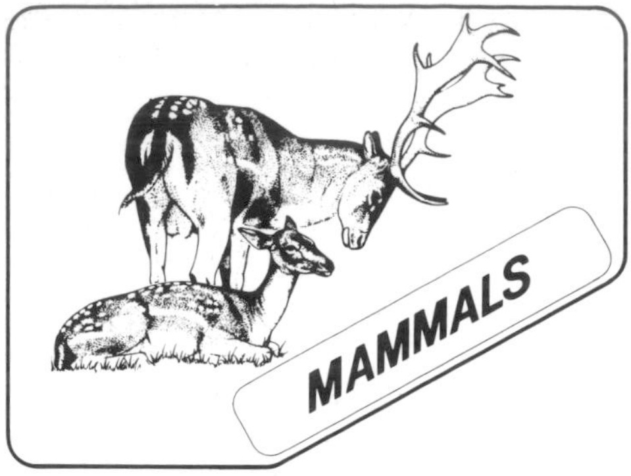

BRITISH DEER

Deer are probably the most conspicuous and easily seen of our larger mammals and most people have watched them at sometime or other. In fact, there are seven species to be found in the wild today, though only two are really native.

Deer are Britain's largest land mammals, with the red deer taking the honours for the biggest of all. Although our genuinely native fauna of deer is restricted to the red and roe deer, it is also possible to see five other species in the wild – the fallow, muntjac, sika, Chinese water deer and reindeer. Deer-watching is a very rewarding occupation, since they are animals that are often active in the day, and are large enough to see easily. With practice and care, you can quite soon begin to anticipate their habits and see them regularly.

The native red deer is one of our most magnificent mammals. Its main populations are in Scotland, though there are also sizeable populations in the uplands of Exmoor and the Quantock hills in Somerset, and wild lowland places like the New Forest, in Hampshire. They are, by preference, a forest animal, but the lack of forest and the amount of disturbance in many such areas has forced them onto the open hills, though they will return to lower, more wooded ground in winter. Many have taken to living in the increasing areas of conifer plantation in Scotland, and in Exmoor they spend most of their time in the wooded coombes or deep valleys. For most of the year, the majestic males, or stags, with their large forked antlers, live separately from the females and young. Each autumn, though, they come together for a noisy breeding period known as the rut. The stags, which should all be in prime condition after a summer of good feeding, move into the areas where the hinds live, and become noisy and conspicuous by virtue of their loud roaring and bellowing. Each stag attempts to col-

A group of fallow deer bucks (males) grazing in the early morning sunshine in the New Forest. These are wild deer as opposed to the semi-domesticated parkland deer

Red deer stags may measure up to 120cm to the shoulder, and with their magnificent antlers are a stunning sight. Roe deer are smaller at around 65cm to the shoulder and have only small, simple antlers. The Sika was first

lect together a harem of females with which to mate, and his success will depend upon his strength and skill. Generally males are in the prime of life at seven to eight years old, and these stags will be most successful and may gather as many as 15 to 20 hinds. Stags under about five years old rarely succeed in getting any hinds at all, and stags over 11 or 12 fare no better. The contests for females are generally settled by a great deal of displaying and showing of strength, the weaker animal giving way readily, though there are occasional real fights when two evenly-matched males clash. A good deal of time is spent as rivals size each other up, and if one decides his opponent looks too strong or roars too loudly, he will simply walk away. After the harems are sorted out, the stags mate with each hind as they become ready and the group gradually disperses. The stags, looked in such prime condition a month earlier, emerge from the rut thin and greatly weakened, though they have the rest of the autumn to build up reserves before the winter.

The other native deer, the roe deer, has remained primarily a woodland animal. It is genuinely native in northern areas, and most southern populations started with animals introduced from the Continent. It is a species that has done well as a result of the extensive conifer plantations all over the country, and it is most likely to be seen in such places. They provide cover and shelter, and some feeding, and act as a base for excursions into the countryside. Roe deer can be a problem in managed woods where they eat or damage the young trees, and many programmes of coppicing falter or fail because roe or fallow deer prevent regeneration. Roe are much more solitary than most deer and are usually seen just in ones and twos but, like the others, they come together for the rutting season which takes place in July and August.

Very different in both size and habitat is the lovely reindeer. It was once abundant in the post-glacial landscape of Britain, but at some stage it died out completely. Since 1952, a herd has been living semi-wild in the Cairngorms after an introduction from Lapland, surviving on a diet of lichens, mosses and other plants. In winter, they continue to forage successfully, scraping away snow with their feet or antlers to expose more food. They are an attractive and welcome addition to our upland countryside.

Amongst the other species, you are most likely to come across the beautiful and graceful fallow deer. They are probably the commonest species to be seen in parkland, especially in the south, and here you can often approach closely enough to see – and photograph – them clearly. The broad flattened antlers of the males, together with the beautifully dappled soft brown coat are very distinctive, making for easy identification for most of the year, though hinds and young animals can be a little more difficult. Watching deer in parks is an excellent way to begin to get to know them, before looking for their wilder cousins.

The sika deer was first introduced into this country in the 17th century and is now well established in Dorset and Hampshire, West Yorkshire and scattered localities throughout Scotland. It is a relative of the red deer with which it can interbreed and has the same shaped antlers although it is a smaller animal; 70–80 cm at the shoulder. It prefers mixed woodland with a dense groundcover in which it can rest during the day.

introduced into this country in the 17th century and is now established in Dorset, Hampshire, Yorkshire and parts of Scotland. The muntjac escaped from Woburn Abbey in Bedfordshire at the turn of the century

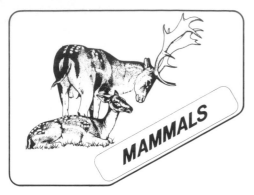

HOUSE & GARDEN MAMMALS

Although mammals are the shiest of creatures, a surprising number have discovered the advantages of living close to man and our houses and gardens support more mammals than you might think, from bats in the roof to hedgehogs under the garden shed.

Most mammals spend much of their time keeping away from man, becoming active only at night and living in secluded areas of deep cover. A few, though, live in close association with people in towns, gardens and even houses. Some are there incidentally, because the garden or house provides something akin to a wild situation, whilst others specifically live with man for the food and extra warmth.

One of the best known examples of an animal gradually discovering that man is a good provider of food is the fox. Once, foxes were almost entirely rural creatures, but over the last 30 or 40 years, they have entered towns and gardens in ever-increasing numbers, and are now well established in most English cities as far north as Nottingham, as well as the two major Scottish cities. Interestingly enough, intensive studies have shown that fox populations in the larger towns are often quite considerably higher than in the surrounding countryside, reaching a density of five fox families per square kilometre. Their diet in cities is enormously varied and has been shown to include food from rubbish bins, windfall fruit, food put out for them, or for other animals, as well as the more typical array of birds, young mammals and earthworms. Many foxes breed well within the towns, even in large gardens, rather than simply coming into the urban area to feed at night and leaving again by day.

A more typical and long established associate of man is the house mouse. It is probably our most successful and abundant mammal, and it thrives on this close relationship. In fact, like grey squirrels and rabbits, the house mouse is not a native of Britain, but came into the country with man, almost certainly in prehistoric times; its wild ancestors are central Asian in origin. Our homes and outbuildings provide an abun-

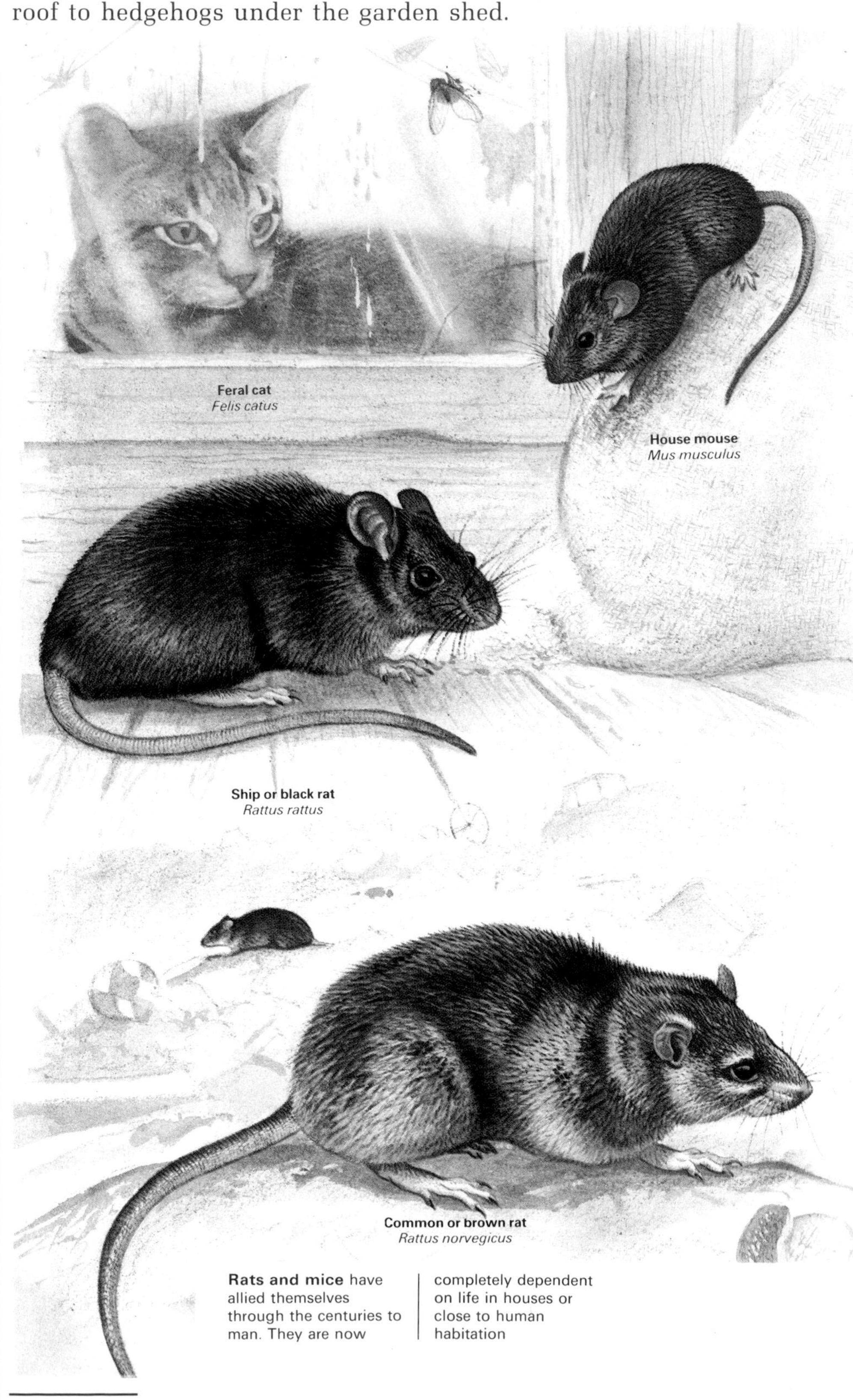

Rats and mice have allied themselves through the centuries to man. They are now completely dependent on life in houses or close to human habitation

dance of warm, well protected nest-sites for house mice in holes, behind skirting-boards and in cracks. There is also often an abundance of food in the form of scraps, rubbish, bird-food, dog-food and so on, though not all households provide as much as the mice need. Many house mice spend part of the year indoors, in houses or perhaps in farm buildings, but forage much more widely outside in the warm and productive summer months. Mice can, of course, be a considerable pest on farms where they eat and contaminate stored grain, though they are not as serious a problem as rats; also modern storage methods leave less possibilities for them. House mice can be incredibly prolific breeders which allows the population to expand rapidly when conditions are good, and in more stable populations vast numbers of young mice fall prey to a wide variety of predators. The female house mice can breed when they are as young as six weeks old, and may produce up to ten or twelve litters in a year, each containing up to a dozen young, though rather lower reproduction rates are more normal. Perhaps the most popular garden visitor and resident is the spiny hedgehog. Though most at home in woodland, they will readily take to gardens in semi-rural areas or towns where there is plenty of open space, and they are familiar nocturnal visitors for bread and milk. They often nest under garden sheds, along the bottoms of hedges or even behind compost heaps, and they are particularly welcome for the quantity of slugs that they consume, though the hedgehogs themselves may suffer if they eat slugs that have eaten slug-killer. Hedgehogs also eat beetles, earwigs, snails and earthworms.

A grey squirrel visiting a rural garden for food, where they compete vigorously with birds for titbits. In some parts they are becoming so numerous they are regarded as pests

MAMMALS OF THE UPLANDS

Even the wild, treeless uplands of Britain have their own special wildlife. There are species that stay high in the hills all year, changing the colour of their coat to match the snow and others, like the untameable wildcat which ranges widely over the upland habitat wherever food can be found.

The environment of the uplands is not one that is particularly conducive to mammals just as it is not especially good for invertebrates or birds. Mammals, however, are surprisingly mobile and many species will move into mountain areas in the warmer months of the year, leaving again when the cold sets in and food runs short.

Our most specifically montane mammal, at least as far as mainland Britain is concerned, is the mountain hare. This is a rather smaller version of the related brown hare, and is indigenous only in the Scottish highlands and parts of Ireland. They live on high, heathery moorlands, and spend most of the day in a hollow in the heather which they have eaten out for themselves. In autumn, their coat begins to change colour, as white gradually takes over from brown, with first the flanks going white followed by the rest of the body and finally the head. In winter, the hares stay quite high up on the hills, often higher than in summer, living in a scrape or hollow. Unusually, they also make burrows and keep them clear of snow, but they run away from them if disturbed, and do not use them for breeding, so their function is a little obscure.

They feed exclusively on plants, taking mainly heather, sedges, cotton grass and other upland species. Like the brown hare, they tend to keep to open areas, using their alertness and great speed to avoid predators. In

Reindeer were once common native animals in Britain, becoming extinct many centuries ago, though they now flourish as a re-introduced herd in the Cairngorms

winter, they continue to feed on anything protruding from the snow or located beneath it, but in very severe weather or if everything is ice-covered they may die of starvation. Their main enemies are the various montane or moorland predators, especially foxes wildcats and golden eagles. In Ireland, the common hare is absent, so the mountain hare has partly taken its niche and leads a more lowland existence without changing its colour in winter.

The wildcat is probably our fiercest and wildest mammal. Although there are populations of feral cats – domestic cats that have gone back to the wild all over the country, the true wild cat is an exclusively Scottish mountain species. Once, it extended country. More recently, though, its numbers and range have steadily expanded as persecution has decreased, and it seems to be spreading slowly southwards. Although wildcats do look very like a tabby cat, they are larger and stronger than the domestic version and have a markedly ring-striped tail, with a dark line of fur running down the spine. In keeping with their formerly extensive lowland range, wildcats tend to be found in the lower and more sheltered parts of the uplands, usually below about 500 metres. They are frequent in conifer plantations, and the extensive planting of these in the uplands has probably helped them to increase again, using them as bases from which to range more widely.

Many other predatory carnivores occur in the uplands. Some, like the fox, weasel and stoat, are widespread species elsewhere but two others are now confined to hilly, wilder areas. These are the polecat and the pine marten, both of which are members of the weasel family. The polecat is a most attractive mammal with a distinctive white face that has markings like a bandit's mask on it. Surprisingly, it is confined to hilly areas in Wales and the Welsh borderlands, where it mainly occurs in woods, especially conifer plantations. The pine marten is another very beautiful and rare animal, which has its stronghold in the Scottish highlands but is also found in hilly areas in northern England, Wales and Ireland. It was once

Four of our distinctive upland mammals, together with a useful guide to their prints in the snow – you are more likely to see their tracks than the mammals themselves

much more widely over Britain, but loss of habitat, persecution by gamekeepers and other factors, led to its range continually contracting until it became confined to Scotland. In fact, in the 1920s, when its population was probably at its lowest ebb, fears were expressed for its future in this hunted for its rich reddish thick fur as well as being persecuted by keepers, but now it leads a much safer existence and the spread of conifer plantations has, again, provided the cover and food to allow it to increase its numbers although it is still a very rare and elusive mammal.

MAMMAL SIGNS AND TRACKS

Even though mammals are so secretive and rarely seen, most of them leave evidence of some sort in the form of food remains, droppings, nests or tracks. Once you learn to look out for these, you discover a fascinating new field of interest, which can often tell you far more than looking for the animals themselves.

Most mammals are nocturnal in their habits, or at least mainly active in the early morning and in the evening, so they are rarely seen. There are some obvious exceptions to this like grey squirrels and rabbits but, other than for these species, one of the most rewarding ways of finding out about the presence of mammals is by looking for their signs. These may take all sorts of forms, including food remains, tracks in snow or in the mud, a tuft of hair on some barbed wire, droppings, pathways through the woods, or the nests or lairs of the animals; virtually all such signs can be identified down to the mammal that produced them.

Going out on a snowy day, preferably early in the morning is a good way to start. Although some species are hibernating and therefore leaving no evidence, winter is a good time to be looking out for mammals as those that do remain active tend to be much more conspicuous due to the lack of cover and the need to search constantly for food. On the day after a medium to heavy fall of snow, look in any area of open countryside and you should very quickly come across sets of tracks. These may be the distinctive asymmetrical prints of a rabbit, the dog-like track of a fox, or the 'slots' of a deer. If there are few tracks on the first morning, try going back a day later, because some mammals may have lain up for the worst of the weather, only emerging as it improves. If there has been an overnight frost, the prints will show up much better than in soft snow. Take a good field guide to tracks (see bibliography) with you, and start looking – it is a pity to miss the opportunity provided by snow, especially if you live in the parts of the country where it is a rarity.

Tracks of mammals can also be seen at other times of year, if you look in the right places, especially in wet mud, lake margins and even on wet sand if the adjacent habitats are appropriate. For the rest of the year, it is more reliable to look at other signs. You may, for example, notice clear-cut animal paths through grass or a wood; in the absence of tracks, you can try following these to their origin – perhaps a badger sett – or looking out for barbed wire where the animals

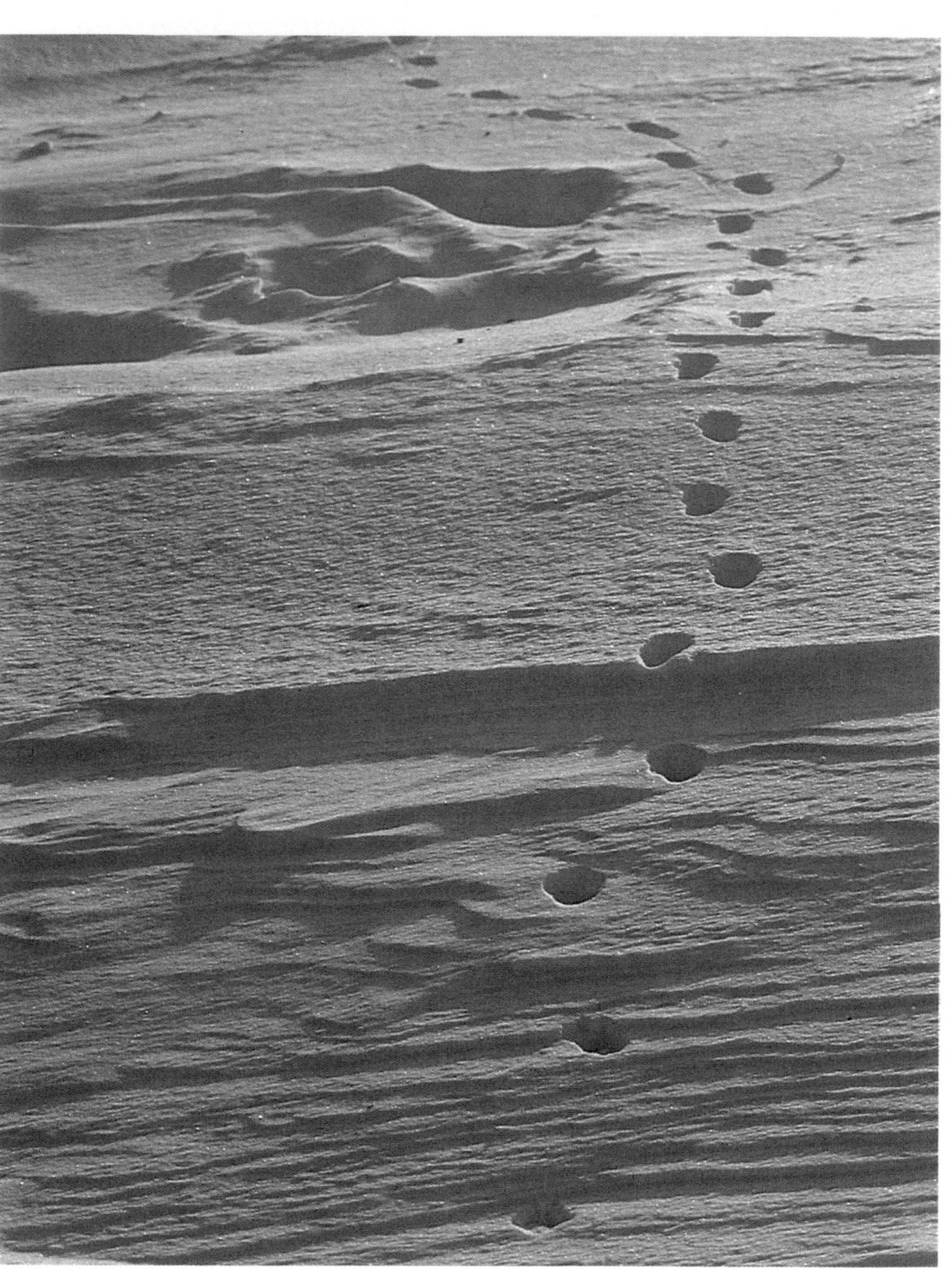

The tracks of a fox as it moves across a snowy pasture in south Wales. The period after a good snowfall is wonderful not only for seeing and recognising what animals are about, but also for finding out where they are going

may regularly lose tufts of hair. The hair can usually be identified quite easily, taking into account the habitat and the height of the wire, too. That of badgers, for instance, looks like the bristles of an old-fashioned shaving brush!

Discarded nut-shells are useful evidence, since each animal opens nuts in a different way. If you look below hazel bushes or cherry trees and collect up the nuts or 'pips' that you find, you should discover the evidence of several species. For example, squirrels split nuts lengthways into two halves, whilst mice and voles gnaw small holes in the shell; with a good illustration and a careful look, you can then go on to work out which mouse or vole species made the holes. Pine and other conifer cones tell a similar story, but you will have to consider the eating patterns of birds here.

The shape and appearance of the droppings of each mammal is distinctive, too, and you can usually work out the species straight away. As a general rule, those of herbivores are small, round and smooth, whilst those of carnivores tend to be large, cylindrical and lumpy, often with a point at one end, and they are produced in smaller numbers. With some rare species like the otter, the droppings are often the main clue to the animal's presence in an area, so they are well worth looking out for.

Besides all these smaller forms of evidence, there is the presence of the animals' homes; the untidy squirrel's drey in the fork of a tree, the huge mound of earth outside a badger's sett or a series of rabbit holes to name but a few. In some cases, again, the nests may be the easiest way to detect the presence of an animal in an area; for example, the summer nests of harvest mice last through to the following winter and can be found quite readily in tall vegetation. The possibilities for survey and discovery are endless if you keep your eyes and ears open!

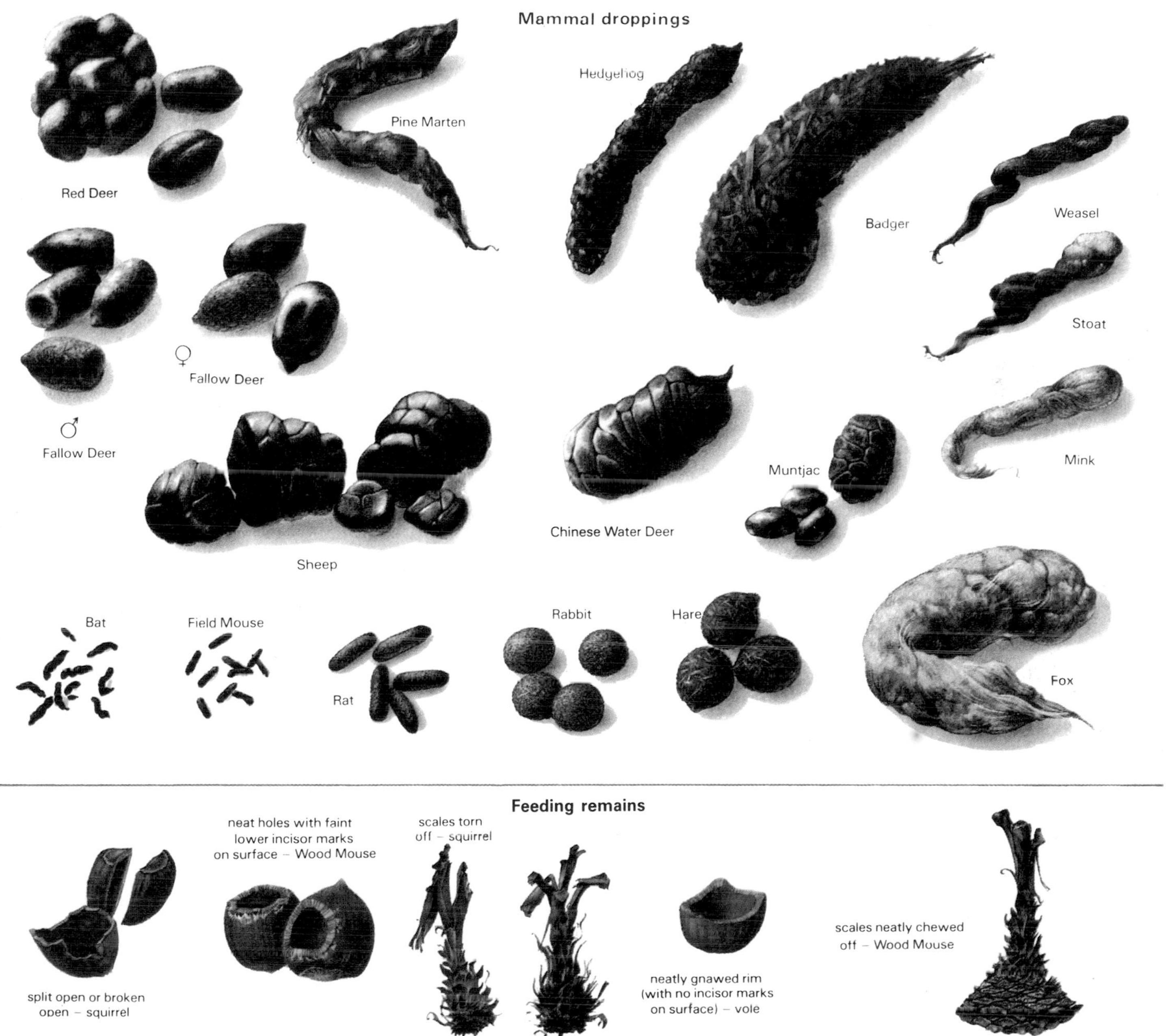

Most mammals leave characteristically shaped or coloured droppings which are one of the most positive and easily found field signs the tracker is likely to encounter. Look also for their feeding signs, some are shown above

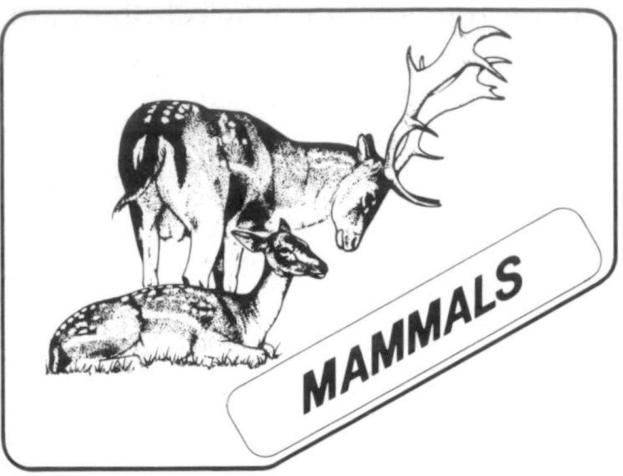

WATCHING MAMMALS

There is nothing more rewarding and exciting than getting close to a genuinely wild animal, without it knowing that you are there. This is never easy but a basic knowledge of fieldcraft will help you to get as close as possible.

Reading about mammals or seeing them in zoos and wildlife parks are both interesting occupations, but there is nothing quite like watching animals in the wild, for really learning about them. To be able to do this, you do need a little more thought and preparation than is necessary for the average country walk, and a small amount of equipment.

As with birdwatching, a pair of binoculars is an invaluable aid to give you a better view of mammals, especially if you cannot get as close as you wish. For mammal-watching, you can follow almost exactly the same requirements as for birdwatching in your choice of binoculars (see page 000), and obviously, many people will use the same pair for both activities. Clothing and footwear are also very important in mammal-watching; although mammals tend to have very little perception of colour, they do notice differences in tone, and are much more likely to spot an orange anorak than a dull green coat. You should be able to move quietly in whatever you do wear, without rustling or jangling, as almost all mammals have a good sense of hearing. Shoes should not squeak or tap on hard ground. If you plan to stay in one place for long, make sure you have enough clothing on to keep warm, as bursts of running on the spot will hardly attract any animals!

Mammals differ from birds in that they have an exceptionally good sense of smell, infinitely better than ours. Thus, when trying to approach any animal, you not only have to take into account vision and hearing, but also smell, which depends on the direction of the wind. In fact, many mammals rely most on their sense of smell, only using sight for confirmation. So, if looking generally for animals, it is best to walk upwind, other factors permitting, and if trying to approach some animals that have not yet seen you, then always make sure that you are moving into the wind. You can check wind direction unobtrusively by raising a wetted finger or releasing some dust or leaves. Whenever you are out stalking, it is better to avoid smoking, or wearing after-shave or perfume, or anything that may make you more likely to be detected.

An important skill to learn is to

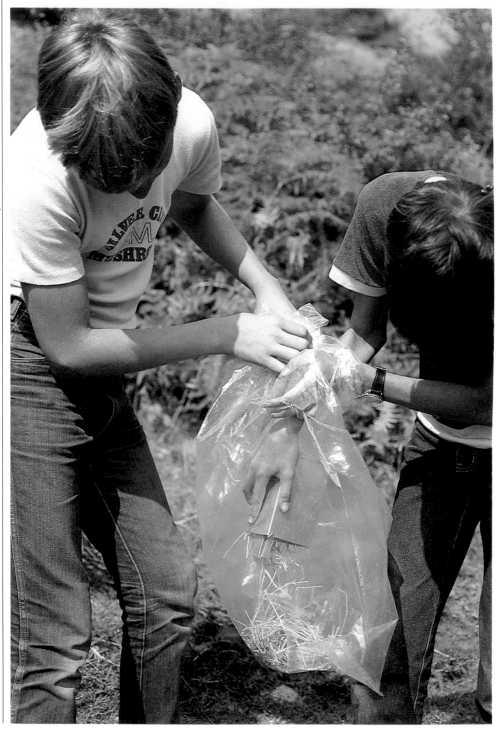

take your time. One suggestion is to move as slowly as you can, and then halve the speed! If you watch a cat stalking something, it will move incredibly slowly and patiently, often stopping still for several minutes if it thinks it needs to, and you need to do the same. Use any natural cover available, such as rocks, bushes, trees, but always go round corners or over brows very gently, in the hope of seeing something before it sees you. If approaching a likely site, like a glade or a pond, go very very slowly and carefully. Once some animals have spotted you, there is little point in continuing to stalk them assiduously; you will obtain reasonable views.

One good way to get close to mammals is by watching them at their nests or lairs. Badgers are particularly good examples as their setts are very obvious and long-established, and most people find one at sometime or other. The same general principles apply to rabbits, foxes and other animals with a home base. Unless you are on private land (with permission), it is better not to put a hide up, since this will almost certainly attract unwanted attention, and you leave your scent on it anyway which will unsettle your quarry. It is better to find natural cover to watch from, where the site and wind-direction dictates. Very few mammals look upwards into trees (as in Britain we do not have any true arboreal predators), and a position in a tree or in a specially-sited tower hide (such as exist in many plantations) will give a good view with very little likelihood of being seen. If you are high off the ground your scent will carry less, too.

Whichever way you attempt to approach mammals, be sure not to harrass them, or to do anything that may jeopardise their survival. Young animals and mothers with young are particularly vulnerable to disturbance, but even given these caveats,

Watching mammals
Left: Emptying out the bedding material from a 'Longworth' trap to see what has been caught. **Right**: A young fallow doe caught unawares by the photographer after careful stalking

they will almost certainly continue to watch you, and will be alarmed by your odd behaviour. It is better to behave as though you had not seen them, and walk diagonally, looking at the ground or away from them. You will never get very close this way, but there is a wonderful range of possibilities awaiting anyone with a little time and plenty of patience.

Conservation and Wildlife Organisations

Amateur Entomologists Society (AES)
c/o The Hawthorns, Frating Road,
Great Bromley, Colchester CO7 7JN.
Holds meetings, study groups and passes on information about entomology via a quarterly bulletin. It is particularly interested in the encouragement of young people and novices.

Association for the Protection of Rural Scotland
14a Napier Road, Edinburgh EH10 5AY.
031 229 1898
Concerned with the protection of Scottish rural scenery and amenities. Information service, meetings. An annual report is issued to all members.

Botanical Society of the British Isles
c/o Department of Botany, British Museum (Natural History), Cromwell Road, London SW7 5BD.
01 589 6323
This Society promotes all aspects of plant conservation but is particularly interested in British flowering plants and ferns. Organises surveys of British plants and communicates information via its regular journal, Newsletter and other publications. Members can be amateur or professional botanists.

British Association of Nature Conservationists (BANC)
Dept. of Landscape Architecture, Sheffield University, Sheffield S10 2TH.
0742 768555
Provides a forum for debate about all aspects of nature conservation. Through its quarterly journal 'ECOS' it reviews the conservation scene and disseminates information on a cross section of issues and views. It holds an annual conference and has regular meetings as well as commissioning special reports on important conservation issues.

British Bee Keepers Association
Royal Show Ground, Stoneleigh,
Warwickshire CV8 2LZ.
0203 552404
Through meetings, conferences and its monthly publication, 'Bee Craft', this association aims to 'further the craft of keeping bees'.

British Butterfly Conservation Society
Tudor House, Quorn, Leicestershire
LE12 8AD.
0509 41280
Encourages interest in butterflies through meetings and exhibitions, and via its members publication 'The News'. Its aims are to protect British butterflies both by field conservation and captive breeding and release.

British Deer Society
Church Farm, Lower Basildon, Reading.
Berkshire R68 9NH.
07357 4094
Its main objectives are to study deer in Britain and promote the spread of knowledge in all aspects of deer biology and management. It produces a magazine 'Deer' and organises conferences and meetings.

British Ecological Society
Burlington House, Piccadilly, London
W1V 0LQ.
01 434 2641
Promotes all aspects of ecology. It publishes a quarterly Bulletin and separate journals of, 'Ecology', 'Animal Ecology' and 'Applied Ecology'.

British Entomological and Natural History Society
c/o The Alpine Club, 74 South Audley Street, London W1.
Encourages the study of natural history with particular emphasis on entomology and insect conservation. Organises meetings, exhibitions and supplies information.

British Herpetological Society
20 Queensbury Place, London SW7.
01 581 2657
Involved with the conservation and captive breeding and release of European reptiles and amphibians. Through its publication 'British Journal of Herpetology' members are kept informed of research, meetings and exhibitions.

British Lichen Society
Dept. of Plant Sciences,
University of Bath
Bath
Avon BA2 7AY.
Aims to encourage interest in the study of lichens. It produces a magazine 'Lichenologist' three times a year and a bulletin twice a year.

British Naturalists Association
6 Chancery Place, The Green,
Writtle, Essex CM1 3DY
0245 420756
Concerned with preserving wildlife and the natural beauty of conservation areas and sanctuaries. It produces specialist publications and a magazine 'Country-Side' three times each year.

British Ornithologists Union
c/o Zoological Society of London,
Regent's Park, London NW1 4RY
01 586 4443
A rather learned body whose aim is to advance the science of ornithology. It produces a quarterly publication called 'Ibis'.

British Pteridological Society
Dept. of Botany, British Museum (Nat Hist),
Cromwell Road,
London SW7 5BD.
Is concerned with the study and conservation of ferns. It produces an annual magazine 'The Fern Gazette', and a Bulletin, as well as holding conferences and recording fern distribution.

British Trust for Conservation Volunteers (BCTV)
36 St Mary's Street, Wallingford, Oxon.
OX10 0EU.
0491 39766
Young people over 16, undertake practical conservation work on nature reserves and other wildlife sites. The Trust co-operates closely with the RSNC, local authorities and other wildlife organisations. It produces a quarterly magazine 'Conserver' and produces handbooks on conservation techniques.

British Trust for Ornithology (BTO)
Beech Grove, Station Road, Tring, Herts.
HP23 5NR.
044282 3461
Appealing especially to the serious ornithologist. Undertakes ambitious surveys and research programmes and is involved in the Bird Ringing Scheme with a team of professional biologists. The Trust produces a quarterly journal 'Bird Study' and a newsletter 'BTO News'.

Commons Open Spaces and Footpaths Preservation Society
25a Bell Street, Henley-on-Thames,
Oxfordshire RG9 2BA.
0491 573535
Concerned with the preservation for public

use of commons and village greens, bridleways and footpaths. It publishes a journal three times a year and pamphlets on preservation issues.

Council for Environmental Conservation (CoEnCo)
80 York Way,
London N1.
01 278 4736
Concerned with nature conservation in its widest sense: pollution, waste disposal, recreation and preservation of listed buildings. It has an information service which deals with queries on environmental matters from government, public and the media. Produces a monthly newsletter 'Habitat'.

Council for the Protection of Rural England (CPRE)
4 Hobart Place, London SW7W 0HY.
01 235 9481
Promotes the improvement, protection and preservation of the English countryside. Publishes a magazine 'Countryside Campaign' three times each year. Very lively!

Council for the Protection of Rural Wales, (Cymdeithas Diogelu Cymru Wledig) (CPRW)
31 High Street, Welshpool, Powys SY21 7JP.
0938 2525
Activities and aims similar to (CPRE). Produces a newsletter three times each year.

Countryside Commission
John Dower House, Crescent Place, Cheltenham, Glos. GL50 3RA.
0242 521381
(Welsh Office, Ladywell Houses, Newtown, Powys SY16 1RD. 0686 26799)
Countryside Commission for Scotland
Battleby, Redgorton, Perth PH1 3EW.
0738 2721
Designates National Parks, AONBs and proposes long distance footpaths and bridleways. Encourages setting up of country parks and picnic sites. They are the principal official bodies concerned with the countryside as an amenity.

Dry Stone Walling Association
National Federation of Young Farmers' Clubs, YFC Centre, National Agricultural Centre, Kenilworth, Warks CV8 2LG
0203 56131
Fosters the interest in dry stone walling and dyking. It produces a bulletin for members and operates a register of recommended craftsmen.

Farming and Wildlife Trust (FWT)
The Lodge, Sandy, Bedfordshire.
0767 80551
Aims to reconcile the interests of farming and conservation. There are 65 county groups which contain representatives of all the major conservation groups and National Farmers' Union. Produces a series of Information Leaflets on conservation and farming.

Fauna and Flora Preservation Society
8–12 Camden High Street
London NW1 0JH
01 387 9656
Takes a major interest in the flora and fauna of the British Isles.

Field Studies Council
62 Wilson Street, London EC2A 2BU.
01 247 4651
A charitable organisation which runs its own residential field centres in various parts of the country. Courses on aspects of wildlife and the countryside are run for all ages.

Forestry Commission
231 Corstorphine Road, Edinburgh EH12 7AT.
031 334 0303
Official government organisation concerned principally with producing timber commercially. From its establishment in 1919 up until quite recently, the Commission bought up and planted great tracts of land and planted them with hundreds of square miles of fast-growing exotic conifers. This regime almost totally destroys any indigenous wildlife and completely changes the landscape. Recent policy has been to encourage wildlife and to open its forests for recreation. In its consultative document 'Broadleaves in Britain', the Commission seems to have changed its outlook and is advocating wider planting and conservation of broadleaved trees. Some wildlife and conservation groups think the Forestry Commission could do more to protect semi-natural habitats.

Friends of the Earth (FOE)
377 City Road, London EC1V 1NA.
01 837 0731
Acts as a pressure group for rational use of natural resources and attacks environmental abuse by legal means. It is particularly active in fighting for habitat protection. A quarterly supporters bulletin is available.

Friends of the Lake District
Gowan Knott, Kendal Road, Staveley, Kendal, Cumbria LA8 9LP.
0539 821201
Campaigns to protect the landscape and beauty of the Lake District and Cumbria. Produces a quarterly bulletin and a monthly newsletter.

Greenpeace
36 Graham Square, London N1.
01 387 5370
Well known for its non-violent action in international wildlife issues such as whaling, sealing and dumping of radioactive waste.

The Institute of Terrestrial Ecology (ITE)
One of the several research units under the umbrella of the National Environment Research Council, on a par with such as the Medical Research Council. It undertakes fundamental research into aspects of the ecology of animals and plants at six research stations throughout Britain. It publishes summaries of research and other reports.

The Mammal Society
141 Newmarket Road, Cambridge CB5 8HA.
0223 351870
Concerned with the collection of data and study of mammals, their movements and distribution.

Marine Biological Association of the United Kingdom
The Laboratory, Citadel Hill, Plymouth, Devon PL1 2PB.
0752 221761
Advances the marine zoological and botanical knowledge and researches the life, conditions and habits of ocean life. Provides information and issues a journal.

Men of the Trees
Turner's Hill Road,
Crawley Down, Crawley, Sussex RH10 4HL.
0342 712536
Advocates the planting and protection of trees throughout the world. It produces a twice yearly magazine 'Trees'.

National Shire Horse Society
East of England Showground, Peterborough PE2 0XE.
0733 234451
Promotes the old English breeds of Shire horses. Every year it holds the National Heavy Horse Show.

National Trust
36 Queen Anne's Gate, London SW1H 9AS.
01 222 9251

National Trust for Scotland
5 Charlotte Square, Edinburgh, EH2 4OU.
031 226 5922

National Trust for Northern Ireland
Rowallane, St Field, Ballynahinch, Co Down BT24 7LH.
0238 510721
The oldest voluntary conservation body in Britain. It now owns about one per cent of our total land area and ten per cent of our coastline (400 miles). Apart from its historic buildings, monuments and so on, it safeguards considerable areas of our most beautiful countryside. The Trust is financed

by voluntary contributions and the subscriptions of members. It also runs a National Trust Junior Division.

Nature Conservancy Council (NCC) (England)
Northminster House, Northminster, Peterborough PE1 1UA.
0733 40345
NCC (Scotland), 12 Hope Terrace, Edinburgh EH9 2AS.
031 447 4784
NCC (Wales), Plas Penrhos, Penrhos Road, Bangor, Gwynedd LL57 2LQ.
0248 355141
The NCC was established by Act of Parliament in 1973 as the successor to the Nature Conservancy which was set up in 1949. It is a government funded organisation which is responsible for the National Nature Reserves and Sites of Special Scientific Interest (SSSIs). The NCC is governed by a Council whose members are appointed by the Secretary of State for the Environment.

The Otter Trust
Earsham, nr Bungay, Suffolk NR35 2AF.
0986 3470
Actively promotes the reintroduction of otters into areas of Britain where pesticides and other problems have removed them.' They own a 47 acre otter haven in Norfolk and a breeding facility at Earsham.

Ramblers' Association
1–5 Wandsworth Road, London SW8.
01 582 6826
Protects the public's rights of access to the 120,000 miles of public footpath through England and Wales. It also encourages the care and preservation of the countryside as a whole. It produces a members' magazine 'Rucksack' three times a year.

Royal Society for Nature Conservation (RSNC)
22, The Green, Nettleham, Lincoln LN2 2NR.
0522 752 326
This is the United Kingdom's largest voluntary organisation concerned with all aspects of wildlife conservation. It runs nature reserves (*see* Countryside Conservation and Protection Areas) and coordinates the activities of 46 local Nature Conservation Trusts (*see* below). It produces an illustrated quarterly magazine 'Natural World', free to members, which is a forum for all those interested or involved in the whole range of conservation work.
Watch: The Watch Trust for Environmental Education is sponsored by the RSNC and *The Sunday Times*. It is a national club for 8 to 18-year-olds, with more than 15,000 members and 250 area groups.

Royal Society for the Protection of Birds (RSPB)
The Lodge, Sandy, Bedfordshire SG19 2DL.
0767 80551
The largest organisation concerned with the conservation of birds and their habitats. It has over 360,000 members kept in touch through their magazine 'Birds'. It has been the major driving force in persuading Parliament to pass legislation to protect birds and is actively involved in enforcing these laws. The Society runs its own reserves (*see* Countryside Conservation and Protection Areas).

Royal Society for the Prevention of Cruelty to Animals (RSPCA)
Addresses and telephone numbers of local offices may be found in the telephone book.

Royal Entomological Society (RES)
41 Queen's Gate, London SW7 5HU.
01 584 8361
Society for amateur and professional entomologists which encourages the study of insects. It holds meetings and symposia and publishes a number of journals and a series of identification guides.

Royal Forestry Society (of England, Wales and Northern Ireland) (RFS)
102 High Street, Tring, Herts. HP23 4HH.
Concerned with the furthering of knowledge and practice of forestry and arboriculture. Publishes books, pamphlets and a quarterly 'Journal of Forestry'.

Royal Scottish Forestry Society (RSFS)
11 Atholl Crescent, Edinburgh EH3 8HE.
031 229 8180
Similar aims as RFS. Publishes a quarterly magazine 'Scottish Forestry'.

Rural Preservation Association (RPA)
The Old Police Station, Lark Lane, Liverpool 17.
051 728 7011
Primarily concerned with the enrichment of the urban environment. It also advocates the preservation of the countryside as a whole. Produces a twice yearly magazine 'Natterjack'.

The Scottish Field Studies Association (SFSA)
Kindrogan Field Centre, Enochdhu, Blairgowrie, Perthshire PH10 7PG.
025 081 286
Holds courses to study all aspects of natural sciences, natural history and conservation at its own residential field centre.

Scottish Ornithologists Club
Scottish Centre for Ornithology and Bird Protection, 21 Regent Terrace, Edinburgh EH7 5BT.
031 556 6042
Concerned with the study of Scottish ornithology and the protection of rare birds. It holds conferences and meetings and has an information service and library. It produces a quarterly journal 'Scottish Birds' and an annual 'Scottish Bird Report'.

Scottish Rights of Way Society Ltd
52 Plewlands Gardens, Edinburgh EH10 5JR.
031 447 9242
Preserves and defends Scottish public rights of way. It also undertakes the setting up and maintenance of guideposts. Produces maps and a booklet.

Scottish Wildlife Trust
25 Johnston Terrace, Edinburgh EH1 2NH.
031 226 4602
The national organisation of Scotland concerned with all aspects of wildlife conservation. It liaises with the government and landowners on wildlife issues and arranges lectures for public information. It runs over 40 nature reserves and produces a journal 'Scottish Wildlife' three times a year.

Tree Council
35 Belgrave Square, London SW1.
01 235 8854
Promotes the planting and cultivation of trees in Britain.

Ulster Society for the Preservation of the Countryside (USPC)
West Winds, Carney Hill, Hollywood, Co. Down BT18 OJR.
02317 2300
Concerned with a wide range of activities to do with conservation and improvements of the Northern Irish countryside. It holds lectures in association with Queens University, Belfast and New University of Ulster, Coleraine. A journal 'Countryside News' is produced twice yearly.

Wildfowl Trust
Slimbridge, Gloucester GL2 7BT.
045 389 333
Sir Peter Scott set up the Trust in 1946 to study and conserve wildfowl. It now runs seven reserves throughout the country and has the most comprehensive collection of wildfowl to be found anywhere in the world.

The Woodland Trust
Autumn Park, Grantham, Lincs NG31 6LL
0476 74297
A registered charity which buys up areas of broadleaved woodland to protect them.

World Wildlife Fund (WWF – UK)
Panda House, 11–13 Ockford Road, Godalming, Surrey GU7 1QU.
04868 20551
Is an international charitable organisation which, in the United Kingdom, concerns itself with the relationship between agricultural policy and habitat loss, badgers and bovine tuberculosis, and the problems of grey seals and fisheries amongst many others. It also works on international issues such as trade in endangered species and the exploitation of resources in Antarctica.

Selected Bibliography

Arnold, E.N. & Burton, J.A. 1978. *A Field Guide to Reptiles and Amphibians of Britain and Europe*. Collins.

Bruun, B. et al. 1986. *Country Life Guide to Birds of Britain and Europe*. Hamlyn.

Campbell, A.C. 1984. *Country Life Guide to the Seashore and Shallow Seas of Britain and Europe*. Hamlyn.

Chinery, M. 1986 *Collins Guide to Insects of Britain and Western Europe*. Collins.

Colebourn, P. & Gibbons, R. 1987. *Britain's Natural Heritage: Reading Our Countryside's Past*. Blandford Press.

Corbet, C. 1980. *The Mammals of Britain & Europe*. Collins.

Corbet, G. (ed.) 1977. *The Handbook of British Mammals* 2nd ed. Blackwell Scientific Publications.

Gibbons, R. 1986. *Country Life Guide to Dragonflies and Damselflies of Britain and N. Europe*. Hamlyn.

Gibbons, R. and Wilson, P. 1986. *The Wildlife Photographer: A Complete Guide*. Blandford Press.

Jones, Dick. 1983. *The Country Life Guide to Spiders of Britain and N. Europe*. Hamlyn.

Morris, P. (ed.) 1982. *The Country Life Guide to the Countryside of Britain and N. Europe*. Hamlyn.

Newdick, J. 1979. *The Complete Freshwater Fishes of the British Isles*. A. & C. Black.

Perring, F. 1984. *RSNC Guide to British Wild Flowers*. Hamlyn.

Readers' Digest Nature Lovers' Library: 1984. *Field Guide to the Animals of Britain*.

Readers' Digest Nature Lovers' Library: 1984. *Field Guide to the Waterlife of Britain*.

Rose, F. 1981. *The Wildflower Key*. Warne.

Skinner, B. 1984. *Guide to the Moths of the British Isles*. Viking Press.

Stebbings, R.E. 1986. *Which Bat Is It?* Mammal Society & Vincent Wildlife Trust.

Thomas, J.A. 1986. *RSNC Guide to Butterflies of the British Isles*. Hamlyn.

Whalley, P. 1980. *Butterfly Watching*. Severn House Naturalists Library.

Acknowledgements

Photographic Acknowledgements

Biofotos, Farnham: Heather Angel 20; Frank V. Blackburn, front jacket inset; D. W. H. Clark 103 bottom; John Glover 34; Hamlyn Publishing Group: Adrian Davies 8–9 top, 49, 75, Peter Loughran 17, 27, 31, 51, 57 left and right, 60, 76, 89, 113, 118 left and right, 121, 127, 133, 138, 144, 148, 174–5, 175, 208; Natural History Photographic Agency, Ardingly: G. I. Bernard 167, Jeff Goodman 164; Natural Image, Ringwood: Robin Fletcher title page, 10–11, 98–9, 134, 136, 160, 176–7, 194, 224–5, 227, 236, 238, 241, 247, Bob Gibbons 8–9 bottom, 13, 15, 19, 23, 25, 28, 33, 35, 36–7, 40, 42, 45, 47, 52, 55, 59, 64, 66, 68, 70, 72, 77, 79, 81, 82, 83, 85, 86, 87, 92, 94, 97, 106, 108, 111, 112, 114–15, 117 top, 122, 125, 142, 150, 152–3, 154, 158, 162, 171, 178, 181, 182, 186, 198, 218, 228, 231, 242, Peter Wilson endpapers, 56, 129, 131, 156–7, 168, 185, 188, 189, 193, 196, 200, 206, 210, 213, 233, 234, Michael J. Woods 216, 220, 244, 246; Nature Photographers, Basingstoke: Robin Bush 223, E. A. Janes 90, Chris and Jo Knights 205, Roger Tidman 222; Swift Picture Library, Ringwood: M. King 203, Mike Read 173, 215; J. A. Thomas 101 top; K. J. Willmott 101 centre and bottom, 103 top, 104 top and bottom, 117 bottom.

Artwork Acknowledgements

Copyright © Stan Morse, Midsummer Books: 4, 5 (except seahorse, fish and birds © The Hamlyn Publishing Group Limited), 12, 14, 18, 19, 22, 24, 26, 29, 30, 33, 38, 39, 41, 43, 44, 48, 49, 54, 67, 73 bottom, 78, 88, 91, 93, 95, 100 right, 110, 113, 114, 116, 117, 120, 123, 124 right, 126–127, 130, 132, 169, 230, 235, 237.

Copyright © The Hamlyn Publishing Group: 12, 14, 16, 46–47, 50, 51, 53, 55, 58, 61, 62, 63, 65, 69, 71, 73 top, 74, 80, 84, 96, 100 left, 102–103, 105, 106, 107, 109, 119, 124 left, 128, 135, 137, 139, 140–141, 143, 145, 146–147, 149, 151, 155, 159, 161, 163, 165, 166, 170, 172, 179, 180, 181, 183, 184, 187, 189, 190, 191, 192, 194, 195, 197, 199, 201, 202, 204, 207, 209, 211, 212, 214, 217, 219, 221, 226, 227, 228, 229, 231, 232, 238, 239, 240, 243, 245.

This artwork may be found in other books published by The Hamlyn Publishing Group Limited.

INDEX

I

J

K

L

M

N

O

P

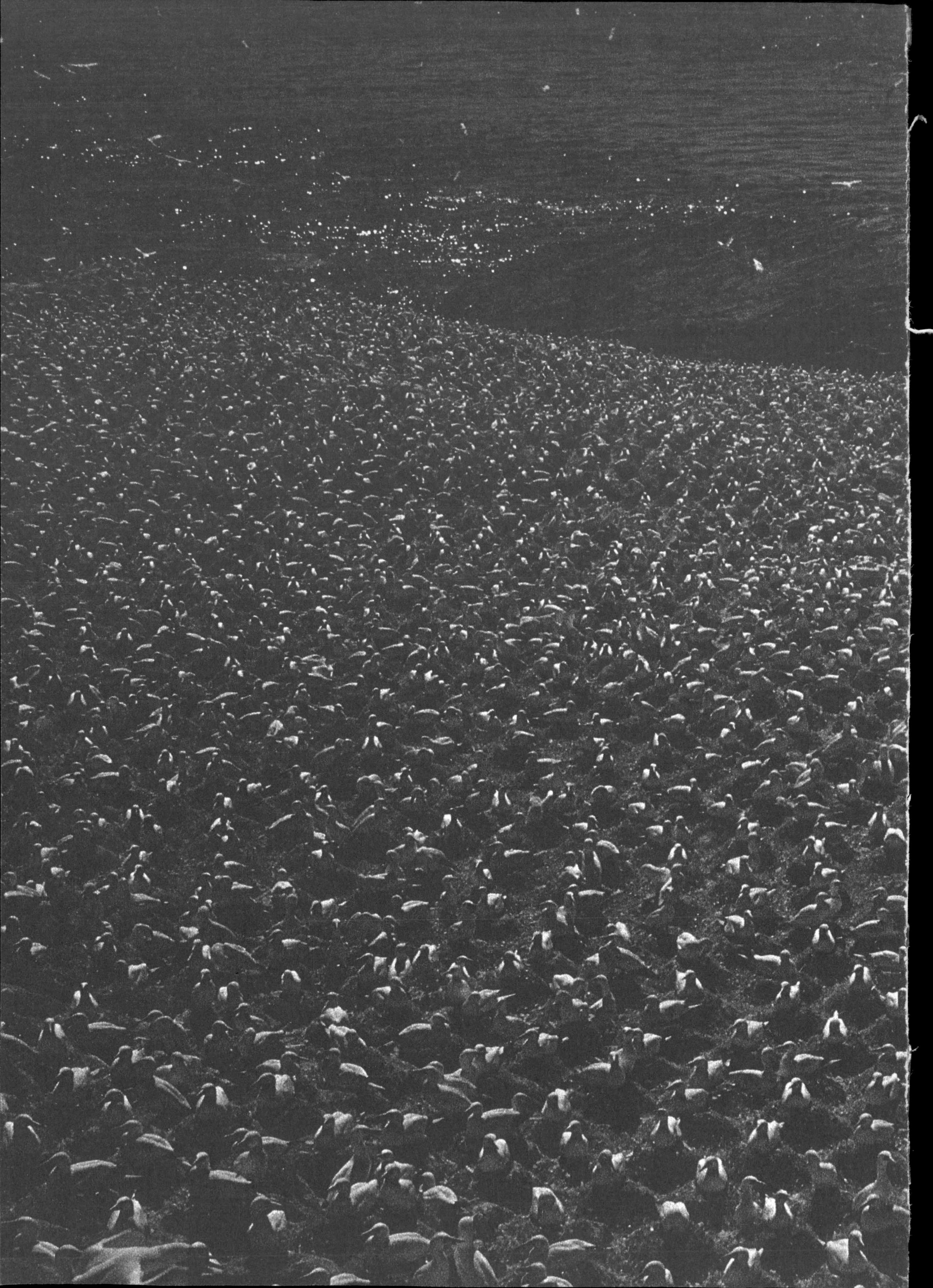